Banana Skins

Skins

The secrets of the slips and screw-ups that brought the famous down to earth

Published in 2006 by

Bene Factum Publishing Ltd
7, Thorney Crescent, Battersea, London SW11 3TR

ISBN (PB)   1-903071-07-0   (978-1-903071-07-6)
       (HB)   1-903071-13-5   (978-1-903071-13-7)

Printed in China on behalf of Compass Press Limited

Banana Skins

The secrets of the slips and screw-ups that brought the famous down to earth

Donough O'Brien

FOREWORD BY
Jonathan Aitken

Art Directors: *Tony Hannaford, Prue Fox, Rosemary Gooding and Donough O'Brien*
Additional contributors: *Edmond O'Brien, John Akeroyd, Murrough O'Brien, Barry Palin, John Blake, Roland Wells and Liz Cowley*
Editors: *Liz Cowley and Auriol Griffith-Jones*
BENE FACTUM PUBLISHING

Contents

Ghastly Gaffes & Blurted Blunders 141

Sloth & Inattention 171

Naivety & Gullibility 201

Lies & Treachery 237

Anger & Revenge   267

Miscalculation & Ill-judgement   291

Eccentricity, Addiction & Obsession   347

Index   382

Acknowledgements

Innumerable people and organisations have helped to make this book possible, to verify these stories and to fill the pages with photographs, paintings and illustrations. Let us try to thank you. Please forgive us if we have left anyone out.

Peter Ackroyd
Aeroplane magazine
After the Battle magazine
The Hon. Brian Alexander
Earl Alexander of Tunis
Lady Elizabeth Anson
Hugh Beevor
John Blake
Bletchley Park
Buck's Club
Michael Campbell-Bowling
Canterbury Cathedral
Cavalry and Guards Club
Tony and Sylvia Chesterman
Cliveden
Colonial National Historical Park
Major General Patrick Cordingley
The late Sir John Cowley
Tony Cowland
Civic Museum of Cremona
Bryan Coode
Daimler Chrysler
Dyson UK
Edison National Historic Site
Edwards Air Force Base
Elvis Presley Enterprises Inc
Eton College
Paul Fielding

Ford Motor Company
John d Green
Colonel Tom Hall
Hamburg Chamber of Commerce
Historic Pullman Foundation
Richard Holmes
Terry Howard
Imperial War Museum, Duxford
Indianapolis Motor Speedway
Irish Guards
The Jamestown Foundation
Sir John Keegan
The late Earl of Lichfield
Danny Litani
Frank Lowe
Louisiana State Museum
Joanna Lumley
Robert McAlpine Ltd
Sir William McAlpine Bt
Laurence McDonnell
David McDonough
Hugh Millais
Moët & Chandon
Lord Monteagle
Sir Stirling Moss
Museum of the Jewish Community of Venice
National Army Museum
National Civil Rights Museum
National Maritime Museum
New York Historical Society
Nome Tourist Information
O'Brien Trust
Ulick O'Connor
Marta Palfalvi

Sarah Palin
The Parachute Regiment
Henry Poole & Co
Portsmouth Historic Dockyard
Air Commodore HA Probert
The RAF Changi Association
Raffles Hotel
Gerald Ratner
David Rattray
Richmond Golf Club
Royal Aeronautical Society
Royal Air Force Club
Royal Botanic Gardens, Kew
Royal Military Academy, Sandhurst
Royal Observatory, Greenwich
Thomas Ryan
David Sheffield
Society of the Monument to the Children's Casualties of War
Chris Spring
Spring O'Brien Inc
The Hon. Michael Spring-Rice
Stowe School
Clare Sutton
Charles Thompson
J. Walter Thompson
Tolpuddle Martyrs Museum
US National Park Service: (Alcatraz Island)
Volkswagen
General Chuck Yeager Inc

Picture Credits

Where possible picture credits have been given on the appropriate page, next to the individual images. However, where this is impractical, additional credits are acknowledged below. Every effort has been made to acknowledge all sources. If any picture have, in error, not been credited, please contact the publisher.

Cover Design: Paul Fielding. Photograph Jupiter Images

Corbis: 4, 9, 11, 13, 16, 17, 18, 19, 22, 26, 30, 37, 43, 62, 64, 89, 99, 100, 122, 139, 143, 149, 175, 186, 200, 203, 218, 225, 239, 241, 247, 253, 257, 259, 268, 283, 296

Michael Grimsdale: all line drawings, paintings pages 38, 268

Cavalry & Guards Club: 108, 162

Chris Craymer: 10

Bryan Coode: 249, 250

Tony Cowland: 178

Richard Grenville: 91

The late Tony Eckersley: 16, 41, 59, 72, 93, 185, 283, 322

Clare Sutton: 63, 166, 305

Lichfield Studio: 71, (Bissett, Caine, Lumley) 155

John d. Green: 70, 71 (Rampling)

Raffles Hotel: 47

Sarners Ltd: 90

After the Battle: 105

David Shepherd: 65

Rhoda and Robert Burns: Map 205

Charles Thompson: 211, 313

Thomas Ryan: 188, 279

National Army Museum: 345

Imperial War Museum: 300, 344

Timken, Aerospace Smithsonian: 114

National Portrait Gallery: 155

Frank Wootton: 124

Stowe School: 367, 368

Donough O'Brien: 40, 73, 78, 83, 104, 116, 123, 128, 135, 136, 183, 255, 315, 318, 327, 350, 351, 361

www.hellfirepass.com: 288

Author's Note

LICHFIELD

My darling wife, Liz, who first thought up the idea of *Banana Skins,* has been forced to live with the consequences ever since. With a long career as a professional writer herself, she has been invaluable in guiding me, improving my English and editing these stories.

An advertising guru once said to her, 'If you try to write to everyone, you end up writing to no-one.'

Nevertheless, we have tried to make this book as broadly appealing as possible, by ranging from the fun and frivolous 'banana skins' so beloved by the tabloids to the serious and deadly slips that have changed the course of history.

I can only hope that this won't be my 'banana skin.'

The Author, pictured by his recreation of an American railroad in the Rockies, as it would have looked some 50 years ago.

A touch of eccentricity certainly helps with a concept like 'Banana Skins.'

Foreword

Banana Skinologists are rare birds. In their exotic aviary, my perch is all too well known – hence Donough O'Brien's invitation to write this foreword.

Icarus was the first head bird of this flock. His mistake in flying too close to the sun has been repeated over and over again in modern times as the anti-heroes and anti-heroines of these pages so well demonstrate. The quest for a place in the sun – whether that means power, wealth or celebrity – is often accompanied by high risk-taking. A common fault among the high rollers that take such risks is

that when they reach the top table, they can easily become arrogant authors of their own destruction.

The odds in the high rollers' casino have changed in the last two or three decades. Media deference is as extinct as the dinosaurs. Investigative journalism, in all its forms from tabloid stings to broadsheet editors condoning forgery, is the new zeitgeist.

Those of us who have experienced Icarian-like crashes to earth should not be too loud in our complaints about the new ground rules. 'Politicians who do not like the press are like sea captains who do not like the sea', said Enoch Powell. He was right. A lot of investigative journalism is unedifying but so are its targets. Those who slip on the proverbial banana skin have often peeled it and dropped it at their own feet.

Donough O'Brien has chronicled his stories of falls from grace with style and sensitivity. He strikes notes of humour, balance and even sympathy which were missing from the media reporting of these sagas in their heyday, but he pulls no punches.

Elegantly written and illustrated, *Banana Skins* is a colourful period piece which deserves to become a collector's item. It is full of insightful angles and inside information which take the reader behind the headlines of the original stories. Embarrassing for a few but enjoyable for many, *Banana Skins* is a riveting read.

Jonathan Aitken

lust&love

'The pleasure is
momentary, the
position ridiculous
and the expense
damnable.'
Lord Chesterfield

'How in hell can
you handle love
without turning
your life upside
down?'
Lauren Bacall

Boris Becker & the Nobu restaurant

The flame-haired golden child of tennis, Boris Becker, rocketed to fame at age seventeen when he became the youngest ever Wimbledon Champion in 1985. The sporting legend went on to win the coveted Wimbledon title twice more, and amassed a remarkable total of 49 tennis titles, including two Australian Opens and one US Open. His formidable talent and admirable application secured him a sizeable personal fortune, and a reputation as one of the heroes of the sport.

Becker was obsessive, and often hysterical when faced with the prospect of defeat. He was also somewhat unworldly about women, as if surprised by his sexual appeal, 'No idea. I'm not especially rich or pretty. I'm no Adonis and my manhood isn't over-enormous.'

When he fell for his wife, Barbara Felthus, his German female fans were outraged. He even received racist death threats because he was with a 'black witch.'

At Wimbledon in 1999, Becker was beaten in the final by Pat Rafter, and very upset, he immediately announced

Angela Ermakova

his retirement. But what should have been the respectable end to a prosperous and glittering career turned quickly into the first faltering steps of Becker's downfall.

That evening, a seven months' pregnant Barbara begged him to stay at home in a two-hour argument, but instead he went out drinking. He exchanged several sultry glances across the bar of celeb-strewn London sushi restaurant, Nobu, with Algerian–Russian model Angela Ermakova. Her looks said 'she wants something from you' as Becker wrote in his memoir. Quite so. They

went upstairs for five minutes.

Becker's rocky marriage was not helped by his next problem. In February 2000 he received a fax from Angela Ermakova, informing him that his Nobu baby was now due: *'Dear Herr Becker. We met at Nobu in London. The result of the meeting is now 8 months old.'*

Becker was horrified and confused. 'Of course, I remembered that meeting but, damn it, it was impossible. I will refrain from describing how we did it or rather how we did not do it.'

We too shall refrain, but confine ourselves to mentioning that Becker was convinced he was a victim of a Russian mafia plot to implant his sperm and to blackmail him out of money. He and his lawyers apparently backed off from what became a physically dangerous line of enquiry.

The child was subsequently proved to be Becker's through DNA testing, although she carried such strikingly similar features to the former Wimbledon champion that this appeared to be a somewhat redundant formality. In his paternity case, Boris ended up giving the Russian model between £3.1 million and £4.6 million for what he acidly describes as 'the most expensive five seconds of my life'.

His payment to Angela was dwarfed by the $20 million that his broken marriage cost him. Then a tax-evasion charge caused him fresh troubles and certain business ventures were unsuccessful.

These have been tough years for Germany's former pride and joy. However, Boris Becker remains philosophical about his life. And, to be fair, despite his trials, he has somehow remained popular with a large percentage of his countrymen, and managed to rise out of the crucible still relatively wealthy.

'I got thrown into the sea at seventeen and it was a case of sink or swim. I somehow made it to land, but I swallowed a lot of water on the way.'

> *'The most expensive five seconds of my life'*

Fergie and her toes

It is hard to imagine the sheer horror of breakfast at Balmoral Castle in August 1992. The newspapers had just arrived, and there could be no doubt that Fergie's mother-in-law, the Queen, was hardly going to be amused by the *Daily Mirror*.

Sarah Ferguson first met the Queen's second son, Prince Andrew as a little girl, while her father, Major Ronnie Ferguson,

Happier times. Fergie with Andrew and the Queen

Fergie had grown into a bubbling, fun-loving redhead, sharing with Andrew a penchant for 'idiot jokes' of the 'whoopee cushion' variety. They fell for each other and were married in July 1986, amid the usual British hysterical adulation for royalty, already fuelled by the glamour of the Charles and Diana wedding.

Andrew, a stickler for duty, immediately returned to the Navy. In their first year of marriage, he only saw his new wife for 40 days.

Understandably, she begged him to come home more often, and after the birth of his first daughter Beatrice, he asked Prince Philip if he could leave the Royal Navy. Philip, who had himself been forced to give up a promising naval career for his own royal marriage to the Queen, now laid down the law fatally for the second time. Thus Andrew was trapped between his marriage, his royal family and his career.

Adding to her problems, Fergie was now turned on by the media, and criticised for her rather frivolous behaviour, her profligate spending, and her fluctuating weight and poor dress sense (so unlike the media's darling, Diana.) Pressed for money, during one of Andrew's rare visits the couple raised £250,000 by allowing *Hello* magazine

was playing polo at Windsor. But it was not until years later that her friend Princess Diana organised another meeting at Royal Ascot. By now, Andrew was a national hero, having faced real danger as a naval helicopter pilot in the Falklands War, first acting as a decoy for deadly Argentinian Exocet missiles, and, then filmed saving survivors from the blazing *Atlantic Conveyor* when it was hit by one of them.

Good-looking, he soon justified his nickname 'Randy Andy', sometimes arriving at a girlfriend's house already in pyjamas. His relationship with his first love, actress Koo Stark, had been halted by his father Prince Philip after her role in a mildly erotic film was revealed. If they had only known of the banana skins to come, the Royal Family might well have welcomed her.

into their home. Many thought that it brought the Royal Family down to a 'Footballers' Wives' level, especially a furious Queen Mother. Fergie was carpeted by the Palace. Andrew buried himself in the Navy.

Fergie, like many young 'naval widows', then began to look around, but typically, without too much discretion. A Texas oil millionaire, Steve Wyatt, met Fergie at a country house party in December 1989. Andrew was later to be shocked by public photographs of his daughters Beatrice and Eugenie with Wyatt's arms round them. However, this was only a foretaste of the appalling photographs that lay in store for him.

In 1992, the author was with a friend of Fergie, when the telephone rang. It was another friend, asking where the Duchess should go on holiday. My friend said, 'Tell her somewhere really quiet.' (The author interjected, 'Damp and disappointing.') 'Above all, try to keep her away from that odious, bald 'financial advisor' fellow, who seems to be hanging around.'

Johnny Bryan, the 'financial advisor', could, said a pal, 'corrupt anyone.' Jerry Hall had once insisted he was even 'a bad influence on Mick Jagger!' While Bryan appeared to be rich, shouting finance into two mobile phones, he owned next to nothing and confided that what he really sought was celebrity. 'I want to go into restaurants and have people recognise me.' His wish was about to come true.

The Duchess, her children, security men and Bryan all went to a secluded villa outside San Tropez. Not secluded enough. Hundreds of yards away in the bushes. a photographer snapped away. Through his long lens, he not only caught a topless Fergie in intimate poses with Bryan, and with her daughters nearby. The final banana skin in the bunch was her feet being kissed, or her 'toes sucked', as the media would prefer it.

One week later, when Fergie was actually at Balmoral with the Royal Family, the *Daily Mirror* broke the story, with the pictures spread across ten pages. The Queen literally and understandably asked her to pack her bags and leave.

In spite of everything, Andrew and Fergie have remained close. After commanding HMS *Cottesmore,* Andrew finally quit the naval career that had wrecked his marriage.

As many of Andrew's friends have observed, 'all he really wants is the woman he lost.'

'It is hard to imagine the sheer horror of breakfast at Balmoral Castle that August morning.'

Charles Parnell & Kitty O'Shea's missing inheritance

Many people patiently await legacies from elderly relatives. They frequently fail to materialize, which is usually little more than disappointing. However, for an Irish politician with his career threatened by an adulterous love affair, failure to benefit from a legacy sealed his political fate. It also set back Ireland's nationhood for a generation.

Charles Stewart Parnell, MP for County Meath, dominated British and Irish parliamentary life for 15 years of his short life, and his name still resounds in Ireland. In spite of being of Anglo-Irish Protestant Establishment stock, with a fine house set in 5000 acres in County Wicklow, Parnell strongly espoused the nationalist Irish cause – from his 'maiden speech' in the House of Commons in 1876. 'Why should Ireland be treated as a geographical fragment? Ireland is not a geographical fragment but a nation.' This constant theme would shake the British political establishment.

Parnell's life was never going to be conventional or straightforward. An elusive, enigmatic figure, as a child he had been the only boy in a girls' boarding school, enough to set off all manner of eccentricity or rebellion. A tempestuous man, he failed to get his degree at Cambridge, 'sent down' after a fist fight with a manure merchant. At Westminster, Parnell became leader of the Irish Nationalist MPs, and, from 1879, President of the Land League, a radical organization agitating for land reform for Irish tenant farmers impoverished by poor potato crops and cheap imported food. Consummate politician that he was, Parnell ambiguously retained links with all sorts of revolutionary organizations such as the Irish Republican Brotherhood.

Parnell tried to work with Prime Minister William Gladstone towards a Home Rule Bill for Ireland, but Gladstone became exasperated by Parnell's nationalist agenda. Indeed, Parnell spent the winter of 1881-82, a time of great unrest in the Irish countryside, in Dublin's Kilmainham Jail, famous as a prison for Irish patriots. But the 1880s were otherwise Parnell's heyday. He returned to work with Gladstone for an Irish Home Rule Bill

(sadly lost by just 30 votes in 1886.)

With a huge party of 86 behind him, Parnell was dubbed 'the uncrowned King of Ireland'. One more effort might have made Ireland free. But he seemed strangely absent from some of his duties, because by then he had already sown the seeds of his downfall. In 1880 Parnell fell in love with Katharine ('Kitty') O'Shea, the separated wife of Captain William O'Shea, a sometime dashing cavalryman turned workaday MP for County Clare. Wishing to bathe in the reflected glory of Parnell, and anyway pursuing his own affair with his wife's sister, O'Shea made little attempt to see off his rival. Above all, he was keen to benefit from the estate of Kitty's rich aged aunt before upsetting the applecart by initiating divorce proceedings.

Meanwhile, Parnell frequently stayed with Kitty in Eltham, Essex, and under assumed names at various addresses in southern England. He was a devoted lover, addressing her in his letters as his *'own Wifie'* and *'dearest Queen.'* But disaster struck. When the aunt died in 1889, the will cut out Captain O'Shea, who joined the rest of the family to contest it. When Kitty refused his demand for £20,000, he sued for divorce. The affair went very public in court and the gutter press had a field day. A sincere, campaigning politician, Parnell was portrayed as a character in a bad French farce. His reputation was in tatters, not just among the strong non-conformist element in the Liberal party but also among Irish Catholics, egged on by vindictive priests who discouraged congregations from voting for 'adultery'.

In December 1890, Irish Nationalist MPs met to decide Parnell's fate, voting by 45 to 29 to depose a once unassailable leader. The party split into Parnellite and anti-Parnellite factions. His career ruined, Parnell married Kitty. But his health had broken, as was his political power. Only months later he died near Brighton, and was buried in Glasnevin cemetery in Dublin, the traditional resting place of Irish patriots.

The tragic result of his love affair was that it would be another 30 years before Home Rule at last came to Ireland, and then only after the violence of the Easter Rising of 1916, and then a savage War of Independence, and a Civil War in 1922–23 when Irishmen tragically fought each other over the Treaty with Britain. Had he not been brought down, Parnell might have made it happen much earlier and considerably more peacefully.

Last
Will
And
Testament
of
Maria Wood

His love affair cost Ireland thirty years of tragedy and bloodshed.

The Prince of Wales, Lady Furness and Mrs Simpson

'You look after him while I am away. See that he doesn't get into any mischief.'

The Californian naval base of San Diego was agog with anticipation. In 1920, Britain's heir to the throne, the Prince of Wales, was to be the guest of honour at a grand ball when the battleship HMS *Renown* put into port.

At the ball was a young naval Lieutenant, Winfield Spencer, and his wife Wallis. Like millions of girls of her age she had fantasized for years about the Prince as the most handsome, most royal and most eligible bachelor in the world. In her diary she even kept a photograph of him in his Grenadier Guards uniform fighting in France. After the evening was over, she was not to see him again for ten years, and it was to be in vastly different circumstances.

Now divorced and married to an Anglo-American businessman, Ernest Simpson, Wallis had moved to London. There, she fell in with fellow Americans; the famous and beautiful Morgan sisters – Consuelo, Thelma, and thirdly, Gloria, who was already married to the fabulously rich Vanderbilt.

Thelma had married the shipping magnate Viscount Furness in 1926, but three years later her marriage had faltered and she met and charmed the Prince of Wales. Indeed, she joined him on a safari in Kenya and they made love under the stars – the *'most romantic time of my life.'*

Thelma Furness's sensuality enabled her to supplant his former lover, the more intellectual Freda Dudley Ward, and for five years she was the unofficial hostess at the Prince's country home, Fort Belvedere. She was also kind enough to introduce the Simpsons to the Prince, and even ask him to intercede to bend the rules so that her friend, divorcée Wallis Simpson, could be presented at Court.

However, in 1934, Thelma decided to visit her twin sister Gloria Vanderbilt in the United States, a trip that would take six weeks with the slow liner crossings.

When Wallis mentioned that the Prince would be 'so lonely', Thelma kindly and guilessly replied, 'You look after him while I am away. See that he doesn't get into any mischief.'

The Duke and Duchess of Windsor, on their wedding day, betraying anxiety for the future

This was a banana skin with huge implications. Wallis and the Prince duly fell for each other, and Thelma returned to find the Prince sharing private jokes with Wallis, even witnessing, at a dinner party at Fort Belvedere, Wallis playfully smacking the Prince's hand. Amazed by such an intimate gesture, Thelma met the eyes of her friend. 'That one cold, defiant glance told me everything.' Next morning, Thelma packed her bags and left forever.

The new affair quickly became an open secret in 'society', while the general public was oblivious. However, when King George V died in 1936, the Prince became Edward VIII, and a major crisis developed. He was determined to marry Wallis, now divorced from Edward Simpson, but Prime Minister Stanley Baldwin, the cabinet and the Church could not contemplate the King marrying a twice-divorced woman.

Under huge pressure, he was to abdicate on 11 December 1936, declaring on the radio, 'I have found it impossible to discharge my duties as King, as I would wish to do, without the help and support of the woman I love.' The couple went off to live a lifetime of rootless exile. For the most part, the elegantly slim Wallis had to content herself as a fashion icon, while her theory that a woman 'could never be too thin or too rich' perhaps summed up her attitude.

As for Thelma, she spent the next thirty-five years wondering what would have happened to her, to her Prince and to Britain if she had not decided to visit her sister.

Louis Réard and his little bathing suit

Louis Réard had a problem. A car engineer by training, he had agreed to help his mother with her swimwear business, and in 1946 he discovered that their rival Jacques Heim was planning a tiny two-piece bathing suit, '*L'Atome*', and was going to advertise it as 'the smallest bathing suit in the world'.

In fact, two-piece bathing suits were nothing new. Ancient Sicilian mosaics depicted them, and during the recent Second World War, the American Government had patriotically encouraged them as a 10% reduction in fabric.

Réard, the saleman, realised he needed something extra – or at least extra small, 30 square inches, and he planned to launch his miniature sensation on July 5 1946. However, he needed a name and he needed a model. The name came to him just four days before the launch. In the Pacific, the Americans had tested two atomic bombs against ships, from tiny submarines right up to the massive and historic *Prinz Eugen*, *Saratoga* and *Nevada*. The place was called Bikini Atoll.

As for a model, that presented a problem. Not one of the usual Paris models would contemplate wearing the tiny garment, so Réard hired Micheline Bernadini. She was quite relaxed, because she was normally a nude dancer at the Casino de Paris.

The 'Bikini' was a brief sensation and Micheline received 50,000 fan letters. But as a product it began to look like a banana skin, because there was a wave of conservative reaction. Three Catholic countries banned it outright; Italy, Portugal and Spain. This was hardly surprising. After all, Louis Réard had forbidden his own wife to wear it. Beauty contests like 'Miss World' banned it and Silvana Pampanini lost her 'Miss Italy' title. Hollywood decided not to allow it on cinema screens. Esther Williams, America's swimming film star vowed never to wear something that was only for 'disgusting old voyeurs'. America's beaches and pools remained 'Bikini-free' for years, with women plainly following the advice of *Modern Girl* magazine, '*It is hardly necessary to waste words over the so-called Bikini since it is inconceivable that any girl of tact and decency would ever wear such a thing.*'

So that seemed to be that. The Bikini

seemed to be on the way to becoming a product banana skin like the Ford Edsel and the Strand cigarette.

It was not for eleven years that rescue arrived in the lovely shape of Brigitte Bardot in the French film *'And God Created Woman'*. That was the sensation the Bikini needed. More established and courageous stars like Marilyn Monroe and Jayne Mansfield quickly followed, and in 1960 Brian Hylands finally persuaded America's teenagers with his hit *'Itsy Bitsy Teenie Weenie Yellow Polka Bikini'*. Then, three years later Annette Funicello and Frankie Avalon started a series of seven *'Beach Party'* films, the last called *'How to stuff a Bikini'*. Raquel Welch was propelled to stardom by her fur bikini in *'One million Years BC'*, and Ursula Andress set the tone for all Bond girls as she emerged from the sea in *'Dr No'*.

Nowadays we have our beaches full of Bikinis (or often almost nude), and our television screens full of *Baywatch* or its equivalents, so it's hard to remember that the skimpy, sexy garment named after an atomic explosion was for nearly a decade a commercial banana skin.

Brigitte Bardot, who at last made the bikini popular

David Blunkett & Kimberley Quinn

When a British tourist on the island of Corfu recognised David Blunkett, Britain's Home Secretary, he simply assumed that the younger woman with him was his daughter, and the little boy his grandson. He did not realise that Kimberley Quinn was, in fact, Blunkett's lover, and the boy was his son. And David Blunkett did not know that Kimberley was pregnant again and that disaster was about to engulf them all.

David Blunkett hardly appeared to be the womanising type. Blind since birth, he had courageously fought his way up through the Labour Party, from a left-winger in Sheffield to a somewhat right-wing Home Secretary. But in reality, he is an emotional, sensitive and passionate man. Indeed it was his passion for poetry that first introduced him to the lively and glamorous American, Kimberley Fortier. Hearing her on the radio, he was intrigued, and agreed to be interviewed by her for *The Spectator*. Soon, they were firm friends, and by February 2002 also lovers. William was born nine months later, with Blunkett at her bedside for the five nights of the difficult birth. Despite the fact that she was married, and that she and Blunkett were often seen openly together, at home and abroad, Blunkett's stolid image,amazingly, seems to have stopped anyone questioning the relationship.

All this ended in August 2004, when the *News of the World* broke the story, but with uncharacteristic restraint, not mentioning Kimberley's name. But only two days later, the whole story, in other newspapers, unravelled. Kimberley began to panic and tried to distance herself, now changing her name to Quinn, that of her surprisingly supportive husband Stephen, a magazine director. However, Blunkett did not simply fade away. As he had once said in an interview, 'I've just got to keep going. It's tenacity. What I do relish is not being defeated.' He made every attempt to establish the paternity of both children. DNA had already proved William was his son. Now Blunkett doggedly insisted that the unborn baby should be tested. All of this was damaging for the Government and embarrassing enough for Blunkett, but not yet politically fatal.

However, Kimberley's love turned to something closer to hatred. She and her friends started to 'spin' the media. But, one revelation went too far. This was that, at Kimberley's request, Blunkett had used her Filipina nanny, Leoncia Casalme, as an example to his department of how slowly visas were being granted. Not surprisingly, his civil servants quickly obliged by 'fast-tracking' the nanny. It was a real banana skin, soon compounded by a robust denial by Blunkett, (so similar to John Profumo, forty years earlier). As Sir John Grieve, Permanent Secretary at the Home Office, observed, 'It's often the case with ministerial resignations. It's the change of

Before the party was over. Kimberley Quinn and David Blunkett

story or the initial rebuttal that doesn't stand up that becomes the point.'

David Blunkett was finally forced to resign on Thursday, 15 December 2004, a man brought down by his own complex passions.

The real irony is that when Kimberley's baby was born, he was found not to be Blunkett's after all. It emerged that his lover, for whom he had risked everything, had been spreading her favours rather more widely than anyone could have imagined.

'In ministerial resignation, it's the change of story that becomes the point.'

The 'It Girl' & the secretary's revenge

When we hear the words 'It Girl', we think of British upper class minor celebrities. But the first 'It Girl' was Clara Bow after she starred in the film 'It.' However, it was even more appropriate that *Mantrap* was the 1926 film that made Clara Bow famous. For once, a screen presence truly reflected a star's real personality.

Clara was labelled the first 'It Girl' by the movie fan magazines, and her scarlet bow-shaped lips and flaming hair were copied by millions of American women. She used to drive down Hollywood's Sunset Boulevard in a red open sports car, with her dogs and monkey, all dyed red to match her hair. Her freewheeling attitude was confirmed by her revelation that she never wore underwear.

Rescued from the slums of Brooklyn by winning a *Motion Picture* beauty contest, Clara Bow never looked back. As well as her sensuous looks, she had genuine acting talent and stunning screen presence and quickly became the most popular female star in America, receiving an incredible 45,000 fan letters a month. But her sexual

There were few Hollywood men who escaped a hectic night with the insatiable star.

enthusiasm also became a legend in the movie business. There were few actors and directors who escaped a hectic night or an exhausting longer affair with this beautiful but insatiable star. Indeed, her engagements to leading men like Roland Gilbert and Gary Cooper were described by one paper as being *'as frequent and enduring as the average girl's headaches'.* Guilelessly, she did little to hide her scandalous behaviour. As *Photoplay* wrote, *'She disregards all laws of convention and hopes to get away with it.'* The coach of the football team of the University of California is even said to have posted a locker-room notice banning his young players from their habit of visiting her *en masse.*

None of this really mattered as long as the gossip was confined to the rarefied world of Hollywood. But a banana skin was lurking. In 1931, her close friend, manager and secretary, Daisy DeVoe, was suspected of stealing from her, and Clara was persuaded by her cowboy actor lover, Rex Bell, to have her arrested. Revenge was sweet and devastating. Daisy sold her memoirs to *The Coast Reporter,* a tabloid newspaper, and all Clara's secrets, especially about men and sex, were revealed.

Times had changed. What might have been acceptable in the flapper freedom of the 'Roaring Twenties' was no longer funny in 1931, with America gripped by the misery of the Depression. Her latest film *No Limit* opened to empty theatres. Paramount, which had suffered enough from scandal, starting with Fatty Arbuckle and the infamous bathroom scandal, stopped her studio contract, and her career was effectively ruined. Only Rex Bell, later Governor of Nevada, stood by her and later married her.

But Clara Bow had slipped so badly that she never made it back to stardom.

John Profumo & Christine Keeler

One day in 1961, a worried Conservative MP friend had phoned the author's father Toby O'Brien, once the Tory Party's PR Director, and asked;

'Who among our MP friends would you call the most keen on the girls?'

'Jack Profumo, of course'.

'And among our friends in the Upper House?'

'Bill Astor, I suppose'.

'A right and left, Toby. There's going to

be a terrible stink'.

On the face of it, the story looks simple, a cabinet minister brought down by a few days of lust. But things were more complicated. Christine Keeler was a strikingly beautiful and sensual girl who had run away from home and, still only 16, danced half-naked at Murray's cabaret club, where she was discovered by Stephen Ward, a society osteopath and artist with amazing social connections. She lived with him platonically at his Wimpole Mews flat, 'like brother and sister'. Ward was, however, just about the only man with whom she and her new friend Mandy Rice-Davies *did* have platonic relationships.

It was at Lord Astor's magnificent estate of Cliveden that Christine and Jack Profumo met. Ward rented the cottage by the swimming pool, and one evening Christine was surprised, when swimming naked, by the guests of Astor's house party, including Ayub Khan, the ruler of Pakistan, and John Profumo, Secretary of State for War, and his wife, former film star Valerie Hobson. Later, Profumo and Keeler had an affair. It was very passionate but very brief and might have been forgotten by history but for the rest of Christine's tangled sex life. This not only included sleeping with Eugene Ivanov, the Soviet Naval Attaché (and a spy), but also with two West Indians, 'Lucky' Gordon and Johnnie Edgecombe, who quarrelled over her. Things started to get out of control when 'Lucky' was slashed with a razor and Johnnie pulled a pistol outside Ward's flat and started shooting at the door to get in, before escaping in a minicab.

With the police and media attention, Christine became famous as a 'sexual scalp', even for visitors like the 'Rat-Pack's' Peter Lawford. But storm clouds were gathering. Christine began talking to powerful people who were out to get both Ward and Profumo. Short of money, she agreed to sell her story to the media, handing over a note that Profumo had written. When Edgecombe's trial came up, Christine fled to Spain. The headlines talked of THE MISSING MODEL, and then parliamentary pressure built up on Profumo, led by Labour's George Wigg and Barbara Castle. Profumo

'There was no impropriety whatsoever in my acquaintance-ship with Miss Keeler.'

Christine Keeler

'Well, he would, wouldn't he?'

then planted his own banana skin in the form of a personal statement to the House of Commons, 'Miss Keeler and I were on friendly terms. There was no impropriety whatsoever in my acquaintanceship with Miss Keeler'. (At least he did not say 'that woman', like Bill Clinton.) The urbane Prime Minister, Harold Macmillan, unable to believe that a former fellow officer would solemnly lie, naively took the statement at face value.

But everything quickly unravelled. Ward was charged with 'living on immoral earnings', which was, in fact, one of the things he had not been doing. Profumo was forced to retract his statement, and resigned. The media had a field day, helped by Mandy's classic line when told that Lord Astor had denied sleeping with her. 'Well, he would, wouldn't he?' People focused not just on the salacious details, but on the security threat posed by Christine's simultaneous affair with Profumo and Ivanov, who had been recalled to Moscow, never to be seen again. Dramatically and tragically, Ward took an overdose on the last day of the trial and died. Macmillan's government was tarnished with 'sleaze', enabling Harold

Wilson to step into power two years later.

The story is complicated enough and has banana skins to hand out in bunches – Ward, Keeler, Astor, Profumo, Macmillan. But in her book, *The Truth at Last,* Christine Keeler claims something much more significant, revealed both to the police and to Lord Denning. But they ignored one half of the story, preferring the spurious 'living off immoral earnings'. She claims that at frequent meetings in Ward's flat were the extraordinary combination of Anthony Blunt (later exposed as the 'fourth man' in the Soviet spy ring of Philby, Burgess and Maclean), Ivanov, and Roger Hollis, the head of MI5, who was later examined and cleared several times as a possible Soviet master spy.

Here is the final banana skin for British security. If people had listened alertly to Christine about those deeply suspicious meetings, Blunt would have been questioned at once, Ivanov arrested, Hollis grilled in a new light and Philby just prevented from escaping from Beirut to Russia (Page 244).

But with withering American attitudes to Britain's leaky security, it seems that it was much easier for everybody to label Keeler as a tart, Ward as a pimp and Profumo as a philanderer.

The videos of Pamela Anderson & Paris Hilton

Modern communications have huge advantages over the letters and telegrams of yesteryear. Now everything is instant– television, radio, financial data, email, texting and the internet.

But this speed and accessibility can have serious draw-backs. Inattention often means that emails are sent or copied to the wrong people – never to be withdrawn. Many of us will remember the poor girl who sent her banker boyfriend a lascivious email describing their night of passion. Gentleman that he was, he then saw fit to boast by copying it to all his friends, who felt that they, in turn, should send it on to their chums. It spread like a virus until literally millions ended up sharing their little secrets, and the unfortunate girl lost her job as well as her reputation.

Two of the most famous and glamorous women in the world have managed to create their own electronic banana skins – Pamela Anderson and Paris Hilton. They come from very different financial backgrounds.

Pamela Anderson was born in Canada, the daughter of a furnace repairman and a waitress. At school she was known as 'Rubber Band' because of her amazingly flexible body, one soon to

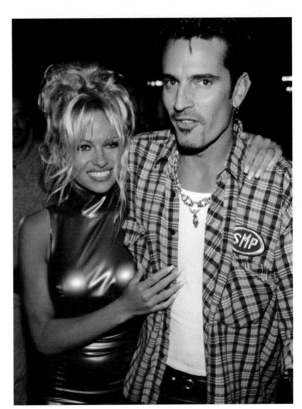

Pamela Anderson and Tommy Lee

be worth a fortune.

At a Vancouver football game, Pamela was photographed in a Labatt T-shirt and, projected on to the big screen, the arena erupted. Labatt Breweries made her a model, and her voluptuous shape soon

Paris Hilton, suitably dressed for a Playboy anniversary party.

Perhaps her first banana skin was meeting wild man Tommy Lee of the pop group 'Motley Crue' and marrying him on a beach. But her next one was far worse; the sex-video she and Tommy made on their honeymoon. This was stolen and was soon to become the most watched footage on the Internet. As a piece of film action, it was watched by many more viewers than *Barb Wire,* her awful film that won the 1997 Razzie Awards for 'worst new star', 'worst actress', 'worst picture', and 'worst screen couple.'

Paris Hilton came from a very different background, an heiress and great-granddaughter of Conrad Hilton of Hilton Hotels, and, along with her sister, Nicky, leading figures in the shallow celebrity scene of America. Paris managed two video banana skins, one making love to boyfriend, Rick Solomon, which duly leaked on to the Internet, dubbed 'One night in Paris'. This was soon followed by another – this time involving *Playboy* playmate Licole Lenz and Scary Movie 3 star Simone Rex. Once again she had to apologise to her family.

Most celebrities complain of being hounded by people invading their privacy. Pamela and Paris manage to bring it on.

adorned the walls of bars, pubs, and the October 1989 issue of *Playboy.* Her big break was *Baywatch,* where as 'C J Parker', she starred as a pneumatic and skimpily-clad lifeguard, becoming a household name.

Bill Clinton & Monica Lewinsky

Most of us have great difficulty in comprehending the extraordinary predatory sexual behaviour of some US Presidents. We didn't know it at the time, but John Kennedy's sexual appetite was virtually insatiable and the risks he successfully and brazenly took in engaging in extramarital activity behind Jackie's back, and within the White House itself, were scarcely believable. But not one word leaked out to the electorate.

Alas, no such tactful secrecy surrounded the Lewinsky scandal. The bare facts were stated by Bill Clinton in his memoir. *'During the government shutdown in late 1995, when very few people were allowed to come to work in the White House, and those who were there were working late, I'd had an inappropriate encounter with Monica Lewinsky and would do so again on other occasions between November and April, when she left the White House for the Pentagon.'* But this was written long after the secret affair had blown over and blown up. At the time, he vigorously and repeatedly denied having had such a relationship. And that was what landed him in such seriously deep water.

Clinton's problems began a few months later when Monica, after leaving her highly exciting internship at the White House, was moved to the Pentagon. Vivacious, attractive and chatty by nature, she soon became friendly with Linda Tripp, a career government worker, and in the summer of 1996, boasted graphically of her alleged relationship with the President. Tripp began secretly taping Monica as she gushed about her affair with the world's most powerful man.

The rumours spread, and events began to unravel. In December 1997,

The picture that Ken Starr used to prove there had been an affair

Monica was subpoenaed by the lawyers of Paula Jones, who was suing the President for sexual harassment. The lawyers thought that, if they could prove that the President was a serial adulterer, it would make Paula's case more plausible. Monica Lewinsky was summoned to the White House privately by a worried Clinton, where he urged her to be 'evasive' in her answers in the Paula Jones lawsuit.

Thus, in January 1998, Monica Lewinsky dutifully filed an affidavit in the Paula Jones case in which she denied ever having a sexual relationship with the President. Linda Tripp, whose motives are questionable, then contacted Ken Starr, the Independent Counsel, who was looking into some rather shady Arkansas land dealings that the Clintons had been involved in many years before his Presidency – the so-called Whitewater Investigation. Tripp told Starr about the Monica Lewinsky tapes and implied that Clinton had told Monica to lie under oath about the affair.

Starr, who appears to have been politically motivated and was determined to nail the President for something, then contacted the Attorney General to get permission to expand his Whitewater probe, and to investigate formally the possibility of 'subornation of perjury' and 'obstruction of justice' in the Paula Jones case. To Clinton's consternation, his Attorney General agreed.

On January 17 1998 Clinton gave his deposition in the Jones lawsuit, in which he denied ever having had a relationship with Monica. 'I did not have sexual relations with that woman.' His wife Hillary, locked into a political marriage, gritted her teeth. But several news organisations were on to the story, and the relationship was now out in the open, although Clinton continued to deny both its existence and that he had urged Monica to lie about it.

Six days later, William Ginsburg, who had agreed to act as Monica's attorney, announced that Monica would 'tell all' in exchange for immunity from prosecution for lying in the Paula Jones case. Over the next months the case filled the world's headlines, with all its shaming, grubby details (not least, the infamous 'soiled blue dress'). Meetings with foreign leaders must have been a trial, at the very least. Curiously, however, the American public was by now showing signs of becoming bored with the whole sorry saga. Although the majority believed that he did have an affair with Monica, they did not think it warranted impeachment. How times have changed. Just a few years before, such a sordid affair, falsely denied, would have rightly brought down a leader or forced him to resign, as it did Jack Profumo in Britain (page 14) Now it was largely shrugged off as a sporting dalliance of little moral or political note.

Eventually, however, it did lead to Clinton's impeachment by the House of Representatives in December 1998, only the second President in US history to be impeached. Even so, he was acquitted after a trial in the Senate in February 1999. In a statement, he said afterwards, 'I tried to walk a fine line between acting lawfully and testifying falsely, but I realise that I did not fully accomplish that goal and that certain of my responses to questions about Ms Lewinsky were false.'

While Clinton's popularity was not, apparently, too badly dented and the patient, steely Hillary has since built her own career, the principal long-term effect was to give a moral edge to the Republicans over the tainted Democrats and, in 2000, to donate to George W. Bush a narrow Presidential victory over Al Gore.

Star-struck Monica became something of a star herself. But she, unwittingly, may have helped to give us the Bush administrations and then the war in Iraq. It is hard to think of a more serious slip than that.

Mussolini & his change of mistresses

Nobody could accuse Benito Mussolini of being inhuman. Indeed, in many ways he was all too human. He had considerable charm and a hypnotic personality. An excellent writer and journalist, the Italians flocked to hear him speak. He brought many practical and social improvements to Italian life ('the trains ran on time'). But he could be weak, lacking in judgement, bombastic and only too able to fool himself.

Mussolini was also passionate, over-sexed and very attractive to women, which helped to lead to his downfall. In 1910, he had married Rachele Guidi, a domestic servant who was to remain a faithful and supportive wife in spite of his many affairs. But two other women were to dominate Mussolini's life. One was beneficial, and the other a disaster. In 1915, Mussolini became Editor of

Exmoor, walking a female Great Dane called 'Rinka', loaned to him 'for protection.' He was confronted by Andrew Newton, a former airline pilot, who shot Rinka dead and then pointed the gun at Scott. It failed to fire, either in error, or perhaps on purpose. Newton was jailed, and when he was released in April 1977, he claimed that he had been hired to kill Scott. Jeremy Thorpe was implicated with three others for conspiracy to murder. At his trial, his barrister, the up-and-coming George Carman, QC , kept Thorpe out of the witness box. The judge called Scott 'a crook, liar, whiner, parasite, fraud.'

Thorpe and the others were acquitted, but his political career was finished by the revelations.

He lost his seat a week before the trial at an election, with the writer Auberon Waugh famously standing for the 'Dog Lovers' Party, after which Thorpe contracted Parkinson's disease and retired from public life.

Hughes, Oaten & an old Liberal problem

As a political party, the Liberals have always adopted a rather superior stance, the high moral ground, compared with their 'power-hungry' Labour and Tory opponents.

So the turmoil in early 2006 came as something of a surprise. After the demise of Charles Kennedy as leader, due to alcohol problems, two of his potential successors were destroyed as soon as the media spotlight shone upon them.

The hardworking married MP for Winchester, Mark Oaten, had been portrayed as the Lib Dem's answer to David Cameron. Instead, the *News of the World* suddenly revealed 'unspeakable acts with one or more rent boys' (He has since revealed one excuse as being that he was going prematurely bald!) A few days later,

Simon Hughes was forced to admit to *The Sun* that he, too, had had homosexual relationships. His leadership bid was scuppered, and the party decided on the worthy Menzies Campbell. Its poll-ratings devastated, its sponsors horrified, its supporters shell-shocked, the party had been well and truly wrecked by sex.

In fact, sexual problems have been one of the Liberal's great banana skins. William Gladstone had the habit of bringing 'fallen women' home, feeding them and trying to persuade them to change their ways, then flagellating himself for his evil thoughts. David Lloyd George was known as the 'Old Goat', keeping two households and six mistresses at once. When one complained that she was playing second fiddle, he retorted, 'be grateful that you are at least in the orchestra.' Luckily, both politicians lived in an era of media restraint.

In more modern times, Paddy Ashdown became known as 'Paddy Pantsdown' after his affair with his secretary was revealed. Surprisingly, he retained his popularity. But Mark Oaten and Simon Hughes have shared the same fate as Jeremy Thorpe. Secrets of a homosexual past have come back to haunt them. That's the point, of course. They were *secrets* and the British do not like being fooled.

Mind you, the British are a bit strange about sex generally. A few years ago, a young couple made love quite openly in a crowded railway carriage from Brighton to London. Nobody said a word. But when they had a satisfying post-coital cigarette, they were immediately arrested.

The British do not like being fooled

Britney Spears and her virginity

All through the history of film and popular music, certain song and dance numbers have become icons for a whole generation. Earlier audiences might have voted for Fred Astaire and Ginger Rogers in *Top Hat*, Gene Kelly in *Singing in the Rain* or maybe Donald O'Connor with *Make them Laugh*. In the more recent age of video, many of us would opt for Queen with *Bohemian Rhapsody*, Michael Jackson with *Thriller*, or perhaps the Spice Girls with *If you wanna be my lover* and Kylie Minogue with *Can't get you out of my head*.

Aged only 11, the precocious Britney Spears presented Disney's TV series *The Mickey Mouse Club* along with future boyfriend Justin Timberlake and Christina Aguilera. Then she burst on to the pop scene, singing *Baby, one more*

Justin Timberlake and Britney Spears

time. The fact that she was still a young schoolgirl – and was dressed up as an even younger one – added to the prurient appeal, and it certainly grabbed the world's attention. Britney has been a star ever since.

However, she has become famous for several other things. For a young girl from a small town in Louisiana, she appears – perhaps understandably – somewhat geographically challenged. 'I've never really wanted to go to Japan, simply because I don't like eating fish, and I know that's very popular out there in Africa'. 'Where the hell is Australia anyway'. 'I love seeing all my Mexican fans from the north.'

She also appears to treat marriage somewhat casually. With the unfortunate Jason Alexander, in Las Vegas, it lasted just 55 hours. 'That thing was a total ugh. I was not in love at all.' One hopes that Kevin Federline will last a little longer, but it looks unlikely.

But what made Britney really famous was her announcement that she was a virgin, and would remain one until she was married. This made her a role model round the world, and a heroine for the American 'True Love Waits' pro-chastity movement. Indeed, her virginity was trumpeted like a marketing tool. According to her agent, a 'businessmen offered $7.5 million for her first night and her virginity'. To which Britney replied, 'It's a disgusting offer. He should take a cold shower and leave me alone.' (Fine, but why did her agent reveal the offer?)

There was always something suspicious about her three-day apparently chaste getaway in a hotel in Rio de Janiero with childhood friend, Justin Timberlake.

Indeed it was he who finally slipped up Britney, 'She lost her virginity a while ago – and I should know.'

Overnight, she was forced to drop the air of innocence, attempting to cash in on a raunchier image ever since – even, notoriously, kissing Madonna on stage.

A difficult balancing act, the pop music world.

Where the hell is Australia, anyway?

Princess Diana & her men

Most of us would recognise the problem: friends or relations who have the unfortunate habit of consistently and unerringly ending up with the wrong people as their partners. The Spencer family from Althorp in Sussex had just such a daughter. Diana was shy and pleasant but not exactly an intellectual (not achieving a single 'O' level). She would, however, grow up to be a great beauty with stunning fashion sense, although her choice of men would prove disastrous.

First of all, there was a rather older man, who was almost equally shy and diffident, but regarded as the world's 'best catch' for any girl. He was rich enough but without a real job – because, unusually, the post in the family firm for which he was destined was firmly occupied by his mother, who was not about to give it up easily. Much more serious, he also showed every sign of still being in love with an old girlfriend called Camilla. Nevertheless, Diana persuaded herself (or was persuaded) that she was in love and went ahead and married Charles, the Prince of Wales, at the most 'romantic' and most televised wedding in history, with a billion avid viewers across the world.

Alas, we now know that however much the world wanted the union to work, the two of them were incompatible. Diana came to think of Charles as cold and unfeeling, while he felt she was neurotic and hysterical. Even with the birth of two sons, they were sadly to drift acrimoniously apart, with both camps trying to get their views across in the media– in the so-called 'War of the Waleses'. Separated and then divorced, Charles eventually went back to his old flame, Camilla.

One might have thought that Diana, as one of the most popular and ultra glamorous icons of the age, would now have no trouble finding a suitable replacement for her Prince. Far from it. Diana went into the arms of a series of men who were to prove hopeless choices. First, there were two cavalry officers, the right class perhaps, but not the right type. James Gilbey became famous for his embarrassing and intercepted (and perhaps leaked) telephone calls known as 'Squidgygate,' while James Hewitt proved an even less suitable companion, and is regarded by many as the 'cad of the century'. He eventually sold his story and even attempted to sell her love letters for £10 million. Diana then, unwisely sought solace and love with the likes of bodyguards, actors and pop stars, even enjoying a much-publicised relationship with England's rugby captain, Will Carling. This did Carling no good at all. His wife, Julia, promptly left him.

In spite of these revelations, Diana's position as the media's darling was hardly dented, because her picture in any paper or magazine ensured many more copies sold. She was to have a fateful love-hate relationship with the media as the most famous and most photographed woman on earth, a one-woman international business that the media dared not leave alone.

There seems to have been a rather desperate element in Diana's almost predatory approach to those she wanted, some reportedly smuggled into Kensington Palace in the boot of her car. The Pakistani surgeon, Hasnat Khan, was often pursued by mobile telephone right into the operating theatre.

The same happened with the art dealer Oliver Hoare, who received so many calls at all times of day or night that his wife called in the police, who traced the calls back to Diana who was asked to desist. It is not often that a Princess has the equivalent of an Anti Social Behaviour Order brought against her.

Finally, amidst the usual blaze of media frenzy that always pursued Diana, there was Dodi Al Fayed, the playboy son of Mohammed Al Fayed, the contro-versial Egyptian owner of Harrods, who has had a consistent mutual quarrel with the Establishment over his refused British citizenship. Of all of them, Dodi would have been the 'least preferred' stepfather for the two Princes that the Royal Family could ever have imagined. Whether or not she would ever have settled down with Dodi, we will never know, because of the tragedy of that car crash in Paris, fatal to both of them.

What we do know is that, on reflection, poor Diana might have been much happier marrying a nice,

The body language says it all. Diana presents a polo cup to James Hewitt

supportive, tweedy Sussex landowner – perhaps only distinguishable from his friends' wives because of her looks and the stylish cut of her jodhpurs or Barbour jackets.

For Prince Charles it has proved a happier ending, now married to his first love, Camilla, a woman who so plainly suits him. It will take years for the international glamour of Diana to fade, but most people in Britain are beginning to feel that Charles, at least, has now made the right choice.

Attila the Hun and his new bride

Attila the Hun emerges from the mists of history as a very unpleasant character, a brutal conqueror with few saving graces. To this day, his name is synonymous with appalling savagery; however, it was not to be that flaw that brought him down. Like many great men, he was felled by a woman.

The once invincible Roman Empire was split in two and in decline. But, however much trouble the Romans were having with barbarians like the Goths and Vandals, they were as nothing compared with the Huns, nomadic steppe tribes who emerged from the east. Disciplined horse warriors, they had, curiously, been the first to invent the stirrup, enabling them to fire arrows in all directions at full speed, swamping their enemies.

Having ruthlessly pushed tribes like the Goths against, and into, the Roman Empire, the Huns themselves moved into Europe when Attila was a young man. At twenty-nine, Attila inherited the Hun leadership from his uncle in 433, at first ruling jointly with his brother Bleda, whom he murdered. Then, taking an even more aggressive stance, he raided far into both the Eastern and Western Roman Empires, extracting both money and hostages. The savage cruelty of the conquests shook even the most hardened observers. When Roman ambassadors were on their way to meet Attila, they were forced to camp outside the recently ravaged city of Naissus, because the river banks were covered with human bones, and the stench of death was so great that nobody could enter the city.

Edward Gibbon, in his *Rise and Fall of the Roman Empire*, painted a vivid portrait of this 'Scourge of God', a man who inspired so much fear and loathing that he has passed into folk-memory, *'genuine deformity'* … *'large head, a swarthy complexion, small, deep-set eyes, a flat nose, a few hairs in place of a beard, broad shoulders, and a short square body'*. He added that Attila rolled his eyes horribly; indeed, it is said that no other leader could look him in the eye without flinching. This was, at first glance, not a man who would seem very attractive to the opposite sex. Yet, he was always surrounded by women, with many wives and concubines.

In fact, it was a woman who gave Attila his excuse for his greatest invasion. Honoria, the sister of the previous Emperor Valentinian, had a scandalous affair with her steward. Imprisoned, she smuggled out her ring and a letter to Attila asking him to be her 'champion'. He promptly treated this as a marriage proposal and demanded half the Western Empire as his dowry! Then, pretending he was merely collecting his just rewards, he stormed with his colossal army of half a million across the Rhine, and proceeded to sack many of Europe's great cities. He was only checked at the 'Battle of the Catalaunian Fields', near Chalons in the Champagne country of northern France. Tens of thousands perished on both sides.

Undeterred, Attila invaded Italy the following spring, and laid waste her countryside and cities, with the usual bloodshed and cruelty. The prosperous city of Aquileia was one of those razed completely, leaving no trace. Indeed, Venice was specially built in a lagoon to give protection against Attila. Pope Leo I persuaded him to turn back from Rome, although Attila took away a huge hoard of gold and, more important, the promise of Honoria, still hoping to add her to his collection of wives – with her substantial dowry. He then returned to

Venice was built on mud flats to escape the Huns.

Hungary, having issued a stern warning of the severe consequences of reneging on the deal.

Unfortunately for the long-term prospects of the Huns, he failed to wait for his up-market Roman lady, but in the meantime selected yet another bride, the beautiful young Gothic Ildico. It was a serious slip. Attila probably suffered from high blood pressure – Gibbon noted how he never ate his greens ('flesh was his only food'). In any event, after a particularly drunken wedding feast, he retired to bed with his bride and failed to appear in the morning. His officers burst into his quarters to find Ildico distraught (an obvious suspect) and Attila dead, his lungs flooded with blood. Overcome by excitement and excess, he had apparently burst a blood-vessel.

His stricken men gashed themselves with their swords, so that 'the greatest of all warriors should be mourned with no feminine lamentations and with no tears, but with the blood of men'. They were, no doubt, none too pleased with the female influence on his passing.

Attila's empire immediately fell apart, as sons and generals fought over the spoils. We can be thankful that one night of middle-aged lust saved Europe from being a Hunnish kingdom.

Sadly for the Huns, Attila failed to wait for his up-market Roman bride

John Major and his 'family values'

For most of his career, not many people would claim that John Major was very exciting, either as a politician or as a man.

The son of a trapeze artist, Major grew up in one of London's less elegant suburbs, Brixton, and tried a career as a bus conductor, and then was unemployed for months, until landing a banking job. Tall and quite good-looking, he then did rather well in the Conservative Party, becoming M.P. for Huntingdon in 1979, Foreign Secretary, then Chancellor of the Exchequer, until finally, in 1990, he was propelled into being Prime Minister when Margaret Thatcher fell victim to a coup. However, in spite of some notable successes, he was always regarded as a little bit dull. Television's *Spitting Image* portrayed him as a grey man, who ate dinner with his wife, Norma, only breaking his silence to intone, 'Nice peas, dear.'

There was also something rather hesitant and sanctimonious in his attitude to the myriad sex scandals that

'I am a little surprised, not at Mrs Currie's revelations, but at the temporary lapse in John Major's taste.'

bedevilled the Tory Party; Cecil Parkinson and his pregnant assistant Sarah Keays; David Mellor and his Chelsea strip with Antonia de Sancha; Lord Archer with his law case over Monica Coghlan; and the incorrigible Alan Clark with his coven of women. Indeed, when two magazines accused Major of having an affair with a Downing Street caterer, Clare Latimer, he sued 'to protect his good name'. He won, destroying *Skallywag* and crippling the *New Stateman*.

Now cloaked in this whiter-than-white (or greyer-than-grey) image, he made his 'back to basics' plea for Britain to return to 'family values'. He even went so far in 1993 as to paint a bizarre and scarcely recognisable image of the country he loved. 'What does this England mean to me? I shall tell you. It means lukewarm beer, the sound of cricket ball against willow, old dears cycling to church, rosy-faced bobbies patrolling every suburban high street – and, once a week or so, really getting stuck into a curry.'

Most people thought he meant Britain's favourite dish. Not so. In 2002, Edwina Currie revealed that she and John Major had started a 'passionate' four-year affair in 1984 when he was Chief Whip. Up until then, the vivacious and pushy Edwina Currie had been famous for two things. One was her steamy political novels. Suddenly, everybody remembered her first effort, *A Parliamentary Affair*, which featured an outspoken female M.P. and a party Whip getting very close. '*Then he came at her again, more urgently and hungrily, pushing his tongue down far into her mouth, reaching for her, clutching her body. There was no stopping now. He groaned and whispered her name.*'

The other was her sudden assertion as Minister for Food that most of Britain's eggs were riddled with dangerous *salmonella* bacteria. This was her political banana skin. Sales dropped 60%, with 5,000 producers bankrupted and the egg industry brought to its knees. Margaret

Thatcher forced her to resign.

When her belated revelations came out, reactions about John Major were mixed. Tony Parsons of the *Daily Mirror* focused on the hypocrisy. 'LIAR, LIAR, GREY MARKS & SPENCER'S Y-FRONTS ON FIRE'. He went on to muse, *'What a pity this scandal did not break when it would have had most impact – sometime late in 1992. It would have stuffed the last Tory government overnight. Major would have had to resign and John Smith would almost certainly have been elected Prime Minister of a sensible Labour government. We would have been spared the unspeakable sham of Tony Blair.'* Clare Latimer in *The Times*, claimed she had always been a decoy 'to distract from the real affair'. The Tory-supporting *Daily Telegraph* pointed out how Major's administration had been hobbled by his fear of exposure, *'It explains why he was always so nervous of the press and obsessed by it, why he dealt so badly with the sex scandals that plagued his term of office'.*

Some of the media reflected the public's new and grudging admiration. *The Guardian* likened him to an even more famous philanderer. *'Now he is revealed as a flesh and blood chancer – almost in the Bill Clinton class'.*

Edwina Currie denied she was out for revenge for not being given political promotion, even a Cabinet post. In an interview with *The Times*, she insisted, amidst bursts of tears, 'I don't want to do any damage. I don't want to hurt anybody'. She seems not to have thought too much about John Major, Norma Major or, for that matter, her own husband. She seemed to cloak herself in the mantle of a woman scorned, 'The most hurtful thing is to look at John's autobiography and find I wasn't even in the index. Well, it is time to put that picture straight'.

She has rebuilt her career as an author and broadcaster, and was even used to promote the *Perfect Omelette* cookbook with Delia Smith and Gordon Ramsay to support the egg industry – now, hopefully, salmonella-free.

However, she must look back and wonder if describing her affair with Major was such a good thing. Her book did not sell very well, she lost a lot of friends and she had to endure the barbs of others. The most damning came from Lady Archer, no stranger to the tribulations of extra-marital sex. 'I am a little surprised, not at Mrs Currie's revelations, but at the temporary lapse in John Major's taste'.

Samson & Delilah

'A strong and angry man, far too easily seduced and cheated by pretty women.'

Most of us remember the rather satisfying story of the final moments of Samson's life, when he uses his last strength to bring down the temple and kill his tormentors, the Philistines. But unless we are avid Bible readers, we tend to forget how he found himself in such a fix in the first place. Sadly, his is the classic story of a strong man brought down by a weakness for women.

Manoah and his infertile wife were visited by the Angel of the Lord and told they would have a son, provided 'they ate only clean food and drank no alcohol.' Above all, they must never cut the child's hair.

Samson grew up extremely strong. But his parents faced a problem when he wanted to marry a girl from the Philistines, effectively the Israelites' rulers and occupiers. On the way to visit her in Timnah, Samson was attacked by a lion, which he killed easily with his bare hands – telling nobody. On the way back, he saw that a swarm of bees had settled in the lion's carcass. Thoughtfully, he took some honey and gave it to his parents.

At the week-long feast to celebrate his marriage, he set a riddle for his new wife's thirty companions, betting thirty sets of clothing, 'Out of the eater came forth food, out of the strong came forth weakness.' Unable to work it out, they bullied his wife, and told her to extract the secret somehow. For seven nights, she cried and nagged him so badly that he relented. She told her friends the answer, 'What is sweeter than honey? What is stronger than a lion?' A furious Samson was duly forced to go and beat up some men in Ashkelon to obtain the clothes. He was even angrier when he returned to discover that his wife had been given to another. He quickly exacted revenge by destroying the Philistines' crops with 300 foxes trailing blazing firebrands. But his own people, now fearful of reprisals, bound him and handed him over. But Samson easily snapped the ropes and took immediate and violent action. He apparently 'smote a thousand Philistines with the jawbone of an ass.'

We already have the picture of a very strong and angry man, but who was easily seduced and cheated by pretty women. And after another twenty years as a 'Judge' or leader, he seemed to have learned nothing when he fell for Delilah. She was liberally bribed with silver by the Philistines to discover the secret of the strength that had been such a problem for them. After constant pestering, he at first said it was 'seven fresh bowstrings', with which, when asleep, she bound him. When the Philistines arrived, he easily broke free. Most men would have been pretty suspicious even at this stage. The next night it was 'new ropes.' Same result. Then, it was 'seven locks of his hair braided.' Result: more running Philistines. By now, anyone but a complete idiot might have suspected, especially as Delilah kept up the pressure. But, as with the Timnah woman, he seemed to be either so infatuated or unresistant to nagging that he cracked and blurted out the secret. So when he was asleep, Delilah shaved his head. His strength was gone. A gang of Philistines overpowered and blinded him. The poor fellow was put to work grinding corn.

The triumphant Philistines then slipped on their own banana skins. First, foolishly and forgetfully, they let his hair grow, and then they brought him out to mock him at a great feast. He positioned himself between two of the key pillars holding up the temple, prayed to the Lord for strength and brought down the lot, killing thousands, hopefully including Delilah.

It is a fine revenge story. But, much more important, it should be a warning never to reveal too much to anyone you love. Unless you are very, very sure of them.

Queen Maria Luisa & her foolish favourite

Illicit passion has played its role in shaping the destinies of many nations, but seldom as disastrously as with Queen Maria Luisa of Spain, wife of Carlos IV, an amiable, weak King who preferred hunting to either ruling or controlling his wife. She herself was not particularly attractive, with a beaky nose, pinched mouth and beady eyes. Although this did not seem to stop her from bedding a procession of nobility, politicians and even lusty soldiers.

Eventually, her eyes alighted on Manuel de Godoy, a well-built,

'Promoting
the Queen's
young lover
was
nothing
short of a
catastrophe
for Spain.'

handsome and rather vacant impoverished aristocrat, sixteen years her junior, who was serving in the Royal Bodyguard. Soon this unlikely object of her affections was made rich and was created, by her pliant husband the King, first a general and then the Duke of Alcudia at the tender age of twenty-four. No real harm, so far.

The real slip was that Marie Luisa then persuaded her foolish husband to appoint Godoy Prime Minister, a post he was to hold for sixteen years. This was nothing short of a catastrophe for Spain. Completely out of his depth, Godoy managed to get embroiled unsuccessfully in the French Revolution, to cede Spain's precious Louisiana Territory to the French (and thence to the United States); to wreck Spain's economy by declaring war on England thus cutting the country off from its rich South American colonies; to have his fleet destroyed at Trafalgar; his country invaded by Napoleon in 1808; and to see his overindulgent King and love-besotted Queen deposed and sent into exile, where he eventually joined them

Poor Godoy was to live on in France in poverty and disgrace for another fifty-eight years – plenty of time to regret his slippery slope of foolishness.

Among the results of Godoy's promotion was the French invasion of Spain, with its attendant horrors.

GOYA

Alderman Story & his District

America's history of prostitution has always been a battle between licence and prudery. New York and Chicago had plenty of 'sporting houses', and women had flooded into booming ports like San Francisco and mining towns like Cripple Creek, Colorado and Butte, Montana, where the 'light-ladies' were a full ten per cent of the 10,000 population. What is more, many of the legendary names of the West had a very close relationship with bordellos. Calamity Jane was the daughter of a prostitute; 'Butch Cassidy' and 'The Sundance Kid' worked out of a brothel in Fort Worth; and Doc Holiday was a friend of 'Big Nose' Kate and 'Squirrel Tooth' Alice in Tombstone.

But New Orleans had established its real leadership in vice decades before. By the middle of the eighteenth century its reputation was made in this area, not least because of the women shipped in from France by Louis XIV and Louis XV. Puritan morality elsewhere in America only served to boost the city's attraction.

In 1867, the 'madams' of New Orleans were required to purchase licenses, and soon 30 blocks were filled with brothels, ranging upwards in style from Clip Joints, Cribs, Whorehouses,

Bordellos, Houses of Assignation, Sporting Houses and Mansions. Enthusiastic visitors from all over the country had only to walk off the trains and into Basin Street.

It was in 1898 that Alderman Sidney Story stepped into history. He hated prostitution, but failed to stop it. So his theory was: 'if you can't eliminate prostitution, at least you can isolate it'. He therefore persuaded the city's Board of Aldermen to define a 'District' that legalised brothels, and outside of which prostitution became illegal.

At a stroke he succeeded in creating the world's ultimate 'red light' district. Unfortunately, this was a real banana skin for poor Sidney Story, because the obscure politician's name would forever be known for 'Storyville', as the District was immediately and cynically dubbed.

Even more infuriating was that he had another pet hate, jazz. The brothels and dance halls of Storyville became the perfect places for jazz musicians. Even the tunes sounded like a street map, with *Burgundy Street Blues, Dauphin Street*

Blues, Bourbon Street Parade, Basin Street Blues, Canal Street Blues, St Phillips Street Breakdown, Perdido Street Blues.

Mahogany Hall Stomp salutes the very finest brothel in the whole country, at 235 Basin Street. Mahogany Hall was listed in the *Blue Book*, the 'Guide for Gentlemen', and, like many of the elegant and relaxing Storyville establishments, boasted sumptuous décor, delicious food, the finest wines and spirits, and, of course, the most beautiful girls. Ragtime was played by piano players like 'Jelly Roll' Morton (you should be able to guess what a jelly roll was). Indeed, jazz itself was used as a word for sex. Musically, jazz was an amalgam of black work songs (the Blues), New Orleans marching music and Creole sophistication. The names of those who learned their trade in Storyville echo with us 80 years later: Kid Ory, Bunk Johnson, Sidney Bechet, 'King' Oliver and, of course, a little kid on a cart delivering coal to the brothels called Louis Armstrong.

We might never have heard of these giants at all if America had not entered the Great War in 1917. The Navy, fearful of Storyville's potential health or crime effects on its young recruits, persuaded the city to close the 'District' down. The musicians, the madams and the girls all headed north.

Demolished and made into a housing estate, Storyville disappeared. But, at least it saved the good Alderman any more embarrassment and a further slide in his reputation.

> ## Storyville was the world's ultimate red light district.

Louis Armstrong, the kid who delivered coal to the brothels

GRIMSDALE

avarice & greed

'Greed, for lack of a better word, is good. Greed is right. Greed works.'

Michael Douglas in 'Wall Street'

'To what do you not drive human hearts, cursed craving for gold!'

Virgil

Imelda Marcos & her shopping basket

'*There wasn't one pie, one cash register, one scam that this pair didn't have their sticky fingers in.*'

Imelda Marcos yawned in court, 'I get so tired of hearing 'one million dollars here, one million dollars there. It's so petty.'

But then, this was typical of one of the most selfish and greedy woman of all time. Imelda took great pains to hide her poor origins, when she slept on milk crates and sang for American GIs in return for candy. However, in 1954 she won the 'Miss Manila' beauty contest and was introduced to Ferdinand Marcos with whom she was to make history. In 1966 Marcos became President of the Philippines, ironically on an anti-corruption platform. For the next twenty years, Ferdinand and Imelda would regard their poor country as a personal fiefdom, looting it of an estimated ten billion dollars.

Other rulers have ruthlessly robbed their people. But Imelda, the 'Steel Butterfly', was to finesse the whole process to grotesque proportions. Most of us remember her collection of shoes – three thousand pairs of Gucci, Dior and Lagerfeld – but this was just part of the picture. She thought nothing of splashing $500,000 a week on shopping, and in 1983 spent $6 million on a seven day buying frenzy in New York. Once, in Switzerland, she spent a staggering $12 million in a single day. US defence aid dollars plus some of the proceeds of dozens of corporations went straight to the Marcoses. '*There wasn't one pie, one cash register, one scam going that this pair didn't have their sticky fingers in.*' There was also a much darker side. To suppress opposition, thousands of political enemies in the Philippines were jailed, tortured and murdered.

Eventually, their arrogance was to be their downfall. Senator Begnigno Aquino, who had been imprisoned and exiled by Marcos, was mysteriously shot dead on his return to Manila airport in 1983. That was the beginning of the end for Imelda and

Ferdinand Marcos. Three years later Aquino's widow, Cory, with the help of the Army, finally toppled Marcos who fled with his family. Gradually, the colossal extent of their thievery was revealed. Ferdinand died in exile and shame, and Imelda faced the doubtful honour of being the only wife of a head of state to stand trial in the United States, for fraud, grand larceny and racketeering. Amazingly, she was found not guilty.

The Filipinos must be very forgiving. Imelda returned to the islands, was indicted for embezzlement, with over 100 cases pending, and actually had the nerve to run for President in 1992. Unrepentant, in 2001 she even opened a museum featuring her famous shoes, saying outrageously, 'Filipinos don't wallow in what is miserable and ugly. They recycle the bad things into beauty.'

The British & India's salt

India was the 'Jewel in the Crown' of the British Empire, her richest and most populous country and the largest market for English products. It is extraordinary to think that the banana skin which helped England to lose this 'jewel' was salt.

Salt, sodium chloride, is now so easily available and cheap that we never think about it. We even call it 'Common Salt'. But it was not always so. We all need salt - it plays a vital role in our physical health. Our bodies store only six ounces of it. If we sweat, we lose it. In hot climates and with physical effort, 2 to 3 ounces can be lost in just a day. If not replaced, the results are serious or even catastrophic. Blood pressure falls, the brain is starved of blood; lassitude, apathy, muscular weakness and then unconsciousness follow. Before the saline drip was invented, it was impossible to feed unconscious people, so they simply died.

Nowhere was salt more critical than in India, hot and with a mainly vegetarian populace unable to replace salt by eating meat. So it comes as a shock to find that from the earliest days of the East India Company, the British decided to tax salt, and, indeed, to make it the largest source of revenue for the Company. It is even more startling to find that the British

'A monstrous system, almost impossible to find in any civilized country'

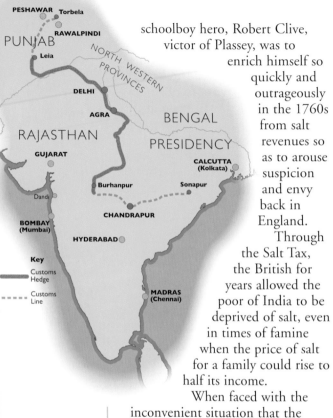

schoolboy hero, Robert Clive, victor of Plassey, was to enrich himself so quickly and outrageously in the 1760s from salt revenues so as to arouse suspicion and envy back in England.

Through the Salt Tax, the British for years allowed the poor of India to be deprived of salt, even in times of famine when the price of salt for a family could rise to half its income.

When faced with the inconvenient situation that the Indian rulers who were beyond British territorial control refused to tax the salt for their own people, the British then did something at once technically brilliant and morally appalling. Outraged, Sir John Strachey (Lytton's uncle) wrote :
'There grew up gradually a monstrous system of which it would be almost impossible to find a parallel in any tolerably civilised country.'

He was referring to the Imperial Customs Line, and more particularly, to the 'Great Hedge of India', which began in 1854 as a dry hedge, annually involving 150,000 tons of thorny material. A live hedge proved cheaper and more effective. No less than 14 feet high and 12 feet deep, it was made of Babool, Indian Plum, Carounda and Prickly Pear, locked in with Thorny Creeper. As part of the 2,500 mile Custom Line, the hedge was soon a colossal 1500 miles long, making it the second largest man-made structure on earth, only surpassed by China's Great Wall. It took 14,000 armed men to maintain and to patrol the Line, with a customs gate nearly every mile – all to stop salt smuggling.

The Line and the Hedge were abandoned in 1879, but only because the tax-free Indian states had now been seized and the tax differences removed. But the inhumane Salt Tax remained to plague India for decades, part of a hated policy. Because, in addition to the Tax, India's own salt works were forcibly closed down to protect the price of the Cheshire salt being shipped thousands of miles from Liverpool. Hard-nosed business was allowed to wreck humane social thinking and sensible politics. Lack of salt in the great famines of 1866 and 1879 meant that more Indians died through the Salt Tax than Jews died in the Holocaust.

Surely, someone in government should have remembered that a century earlier ill-judged taxes had lost Britain her American colonies. And in France, the savage *gabelle* salt tax had helped the rulers literally to lose their heads.

The hatred caused by the Salt Tax was exactly why Gandhi chose salt as a symbol for 'passive resistance', culminating in his peaceful and hugely popular 200-mile march in 1930. He led thousands of his followers to pick salt from the beach at Dandi, where they were brutally attacked by the authorities, leaving two dead and 320 injured. Just seventeen years later, centuries of British rule ended. Britain's greedy attitude towards salt had more than played its part.

Salt taxes lost some rulers their empires, and others their heads.

Martha Stewart & her silly share deal

In the 1980s and 90s Martha Stewart was an icon - America's arbiter of good taste and idealised lifestyle. She built up a company, Martha Stewart Living Omnimedia Inc, which she took public in 1999, becoming one of the richest people in the US, and appeared in *Forbes* magazine's list of the 400 wealthiest Americans in 2000 and 2001. Her company produced the *Martha Stewart Living* and *Martha Stewart Weddings* magazines, a newspaper column, a TV show and a popular line of home products, 'Martha Stewart Everyday.' All of which makes it pretty silly and very curious indeed that she

should have jeopardised her reputation and her huge public business for the sake of a very small personal share deal, designed to prevent her losing money rather than gaining it.

The shares were in a company called ImClone, a New York based biotechnology company, run by a friend of Martha's called Sam Waksal. The company had invented an anti-cancer drug, Erbitux, that would have made the company – and the shareholders – a lot of money if it achieved

recognition by the Food and Drug Administration. The application was duly lodged, but on December 28 2001, the FDA rejected it, sending ImClone shares tumbling. Curiously enough, Martha had sold her 4000 shares the day before, thus avoiding a loss of $45,673, which must have been, to her, a truly trifling sum.

Needless to say, this convenient share sale aroused immediate suspicion of insider dealing, but it wasn't until a year and a half later that she was indicted - and even then it was not for insider trading, but for 'making false statements', and 'securities fraud.' These indictments related to propping up the share price of her own company, which was falling, due to the adverse publicity about its figurehead.'

Assistant US Attorney General, James Comey announced, 'This criminal case is about lying. Lying to the FBI; lying to the Stock Exchange Commission, and lying to investors. That is conduct that will not be tolerated. Martha Stewart is being prosecuted not because of who she is, but what she did.' Many people might question why he felt the need to add the last sentence. Was it a determination to make an example of a public figure to deter 'white collar' crime? Or were the

'*A small personal matter has been blown up out of all proportion.*'

authorities fed up with the hubris displayed by such people?

Martha pleaded not guilty to the charges, but had to resign as CEO of her company in June 2003. She intoned rather piously, 'My decision reflects the enormous sense of responsibility I feel to our shareholders and to all those who have worked so hard to make Martha Stewart Living Omnimedia a success.'

When the case eventually came to trial in July 2004, Martha was sentenced to five months in prison and five months in home confinement, for 'obstructing a federal securities investigation.' She then made a defiant public declaration that 'a small personal matter' had been blown up out of all proportion and urged supporters to stick with her company's products. On this news, shares in Martha Stewart Omnimedia Inc leapt by 37%, but still remained well below their price when the investigation was first announced.

On March 3 2005, Martha was released from her minimum security, women-only West Virginia prison, known as 'Camp Cupcake'. She then started to serve the home detention portion of her sentence in the comfort of her 153-acre estate, which she had bought in 2000 for $16 million and had been renovating.

Being very good at manipulating the media, she had cleverly decided to go to prison, rather than waiting for the results of her still-pending appeal. This meant that she managed to turn herself from villain to victim. By 2005, stock in her company had more than quadrupled since the day she was sentenced. Although the problems are not yet over - after her house arrest, she'll still be on probation for two years – there are signs of recovery.

Martha Stewart Living Omnimedia has announced plans for Martha to write a column for their flagship magazine, and she is scheduled to star in two TV shows. There is also talk of plans to launch a clothing line. Although she faces a Securities and Exchange Commission insider trading case, rumour has it that she will be allowed to return to the helm of her company.

All in all, although Martha is a banana skin case, she is one of the few who have proved that it is possible, after a slip, to recover your equilibrium if you can keep your balance.

Barings & its 'rogue trader'

Barings' Nick Leeson was the hottest trader in Singapore. He was earning £200,000 a year, lived in a smart apartment with his pretty wife, Lisa, and he was about to collect a $450,000 bonus. The day after tomorrow would be his 28th birthday. To many, a dream come true. But on Thursday, 23 February 1995, Leeson was sitting on a secret so terrible that he and Lisa had to escape from Singapore that very night.

Barings Bank was founded in 1763, the world's first 'merchant bank.' It had financed mining in the Congo, the wool trade in Australia, the building of the Panama Canal. It had become banker for the Royal Family, its directors receiving peerages for their efforts. It was this venerable institution that Nick Leeson, a Watford plasterer's son, joined aged twenty-two. He soon learned that administrative efficiency was not Barings' strong card; indeed it gave him his big opportunity. For ten months in Jakarta he slaved to make sense of a hundred million pounds worth of

chaotic share certificates, steadily organising them and selling them off, reducing Barings' dangerous exposure to its balance sheet. In the vault, he found a fellow employee, blonde Lisa Sims, staring at the piles of certificates. The two were soon in love and married.

Leeson's success in Indonesia led to his appointment as General Manager of a futures and options trading seat on SIMEX, the Singapore International Monetary Exchange. The future looked rosy indeed. However, apart from being somewhat inefficient, Barings was also mean. It paid low wages to the junior staff and, to save money, it refused to appoint a separate settlements and accounting manager. Thus Leeson was both in charge of the 'back and front offices', and not subject to any local scrutiny. This broke a fundamental rule of banking. It was to prove fatal.

In frantic trading conditions, small mistakes often occur, so 'error accounts' exist, and Nick created one with the lucky Chinese number eight, 88888. Not long afterwards, an inexperienced female trader made a mistake of £20,000. To protect her, Leeson hid the loss in 88888. Market changes soon pushed it to £60,000. In 1992, he shoved no less than 30 losses into 88888. It became a very bad habit.

Then SIMEX sent Philippe Bonnefoy to Barings. This was the good news. He became its largest customer, and soon Barings was easily the biggest trader on SIMEX and Leeson was becoming a star. But another colleague's mistake meant more losses had to be hidden in 88888. Leeson often managed to trade out of losses into profit, feeding his gambler's instincts. Barings in London was sending millions daily to support Leeson's trading – some of the money secretly showing up in 88888. In 1994, the hidden losses had hit £50 million. Leeson received a £135,000 bonus in February, but was then terrified by the news that Ash Lewis, was to audit his operations. She arrived, a cool, competent Barings Director, who would have seen through 88888 in a moment. But she was suddenly recalled to London, the next banana skin for Barings.And before the audit in July, Leeson simply invented a fictitious £50 million transfer from Citibank.

By now, Leeson appeared to be delivering enough 'profits' to fund bonuses all over the world, and no doubt blinded by their own greed, nobody at Barings seemed to notice. As Leeson wrote, *'The only good thing about hiding losses from these people was*

'The Barings people were always too busy and self-important. They had the attention span of a gnat.'

it was so easy. They were always too busy and too self-important, and were always on the telephone. They had the attention span of a gnat.'

By the end of 1994, 88888 showed losses of £160 million, and at Christmas in London, Nick desperately tried to tell his wife that he did not want to return. Of course, she did not understand. A few weeks later, distraught, she called Nick at SIMEX. She had just had a miscarriage. Staring at a £200 million loss, he dared not even leave the trading booth.

Things began to close in. SIMEX was complaining, London was getting worried about the cash calls and then the Kobe earthquake knocked the market. To cover up a fictitious trade of $78 million, Leeson ended up forging and faxing letters of authorisation to himself. 'Once I forged those documents I knew I was damned.'

Interestingly, at no time did Leeson try to make money for himself. He was simply trying to trade himself out of a chaotic black hole of his own creation. For a few more days in February, he traded frantically and recklessly, but the market would not rescue him. Now his bosses at last wanted real explanations. Meetings were being scheduled. Even the financial press were calling with questions. On Thursday night, he left a note,'I'm sorry' He and a confused, stricken Lisa flew to Kuala Lumpur and disappeared.

Raffles Hotel, symbol of the trading reputation of Singapore, threatened by the Barings' collapse

At a remote resort they saw the first newspaper headlines, BRITISH MERCHANT BANK COLLAPSE. So huge had been the losses, now £830 million, that, after 233 years, Barings had simply gone bust. Everyone was looking for a 'rogue trader' called Leeson. His face filled the front pages and the television screens. Nick and Lisa were duly caught in Frankfurt trying to get back to London. He eventually surrendered to Singapore and spent four years in jail, let out early for good behaviour, and to fight, successfully, cancer. Lisa, sadly, divorced him for another trader.

Barings, castigated by the authorities for its laxness, was sold to the Dutch bank ING for just one pound.

Pope Leo X & his sale of indulgences

'When the coin in the coffer sings, the soul from Purgatory springs!'

The cause of the trouble: over spending on St Peter's

In 1517, Leo X, Pope of Rome, 'servant of the servants of God', and, as a Medici, the richest potentate in Europe, still needed money. His extravagance, patronage of the arts and the ruinous cost of building St Peter's Basilica had drained the Papal coffers. So he hit upon a scheme for raising the cash. All might have gone well but for the meddling of an unknown Augustinian monk in Germany. Martin Luther's reaction to the Pope's plans was not only to change the spiritual agenda of the West, but the map of Europe and the world.

For years, the church had wrestled with the problem of what happens to the soul after death. The Roman Catholic Church accordingly devised, over the centuries, the notion of 'Purgatory', a region, or state, in which souls were purified before their ascent to Heaven. This ostensibly charitable notion had profound implications for Christian theology. Hell was diminished,

Heaven arguably diluted. But, above all, simple believers were offered a means to help themselves and their loved ones, and heavenly bureaucracy could be circumvented. Where primitive Christianity emphasized the importance of charity in the salvation of one's own soul, early Renaissance Christianity told the faithful that they could intervene in the cause of the dead.

Leo X now took this one stage further. Wandering 'pardoners' offered 'indulgences' (effectively, parole cards), in return for contributions to the restoration of St Peter's. In rough translation, the rhyme ran, 'When the coin in the coffer sings, the soul from Purgatory springs! 'Perhaps the most energetic such preacher was the Dominican John Tetzel, who roamed Germany, encouraging the peasants to pay up. He claimed to grant indulgences not only for sins committed, but even for sins anticipated. The policy, alas, failed him, when a knight who had requested an indulgence from Tetzel for a robbery he intended to commit then cheerfully robbed him of the money

given for his Indulgence.

However, one earnest young theologian from Eisleben was not amused by such anecdotes. Martin Luther had shown himself to be a prodigy and an eccentric. At the age of just 23 he was the University of Wittenberg's most esteemed scholar. But, like many great thinkers, he was a martyr to melancholy, endlessly obsessing over the Last Judgement and the terrible power of guilt. Curiously, the physical manifestation of this paranoia was acute constipation. His 'Damascus Road', as all reliable authorities attest, happened in his privy. Musing on *St Paul's letter to the Romans*, he felt that he had finally solved the problem of man's relation to God: 'the Righteous shall live by faith.' It was the equivalent of saying, 'There is nothing you can do to earn salvation, you can only believe. If you don't believe, your good actions are as damned as your bad ones.'

What remains fascinating is his initial conviction that this in no way undermined the doctrine of the Roman church. However, Rome, and its representatives, thought differently. After Luther nailed to the door of the Wittenberg church his objections to what he called 'the Babylonian captivity of the Church', he was asked, in 1518, to explain himself. Cajetan, the papal legate, refused even to consider Luther's arguments, demanding only that he retract.

Predictably, this attitude only served to radicalise Luther. He questioned the authority of Pope over scripture and reason, and even that of the ecumenical councils. Provisionally excommunicated by the Pope on 15 June 1520, he went on to declare, before Emperor Charles V at the Diet of Worms, 'Here I stand, I can do no other. God help me. Amen.'

Leo X must bear a great deal of the blame for the religious cataclysm which ensued. He need not have antagonised a serious seeker after truth, and, above all, he should never have given licence to those who proclaimed that salvation could be bought.

The results of his greed caused a complete split in the Christian faith, endless religious wars, the destruction of the monasteries in England, the defeat of the Armada, the English Civil War, the exodus of the Huguenots from France, the settling of North America by Protestants and the violent division of Ireland that haunts us today. Quite a toll for a little money-raising.

'Here I stand, I can do no other. God help me. Amen.'

The perfect crime: make Portugal forge millions of notes, and give them to him

On Saturday 9 November 1929, Sir William Waterlow, Bt. became the six hundred and second Lord Mayor of London. Thousands lined the route of the traditional Lord Mayor's Show, with its clattering cavalry and shiny coaches. He would serve for one year, and during that time a furious Portuguese Government would have to wait to decide the fate of a man in a Lisbon jail. For Sir William had been the unwitting dupe of the most spectacular swindle in history.

Waterlow and Son was one of the great security printers. They printed Britain's postage stamps and her one pound and ten shilling notes, as well as notes for foreign governments. On the morning of 4 December 1924, as Chairman, Sir William received a Dutch visitor, Karel Marang van Ysselveere, who explained that he was a member of a Dutch syndicate 'coming to the aid of Portugal's colony of Angola.' They were to advance Angola $5 million, and the Bank of Portugal would permit them to print banknotes,

Alves Reis

later to be overprinted 'ANGOLA'. Marang handed over an impressive contract. What Sir William did not know, and neither did Marang, was that they were looking at a complete forgery, the creation of the mastermind of the swindle, Alves Reis.

Artur Alves Reis was a young, balding, penniless businessman of twenty eight. Back in 1916 he had arrived in backward, poor Angola with a bride and an impressive diploma from 'The Polytechnic School of Engineering at Oxford University.' Only his wife was real. After some success as an engineer, he returned to Portugal and planned to create a perfect crime. He would make Portugal forge millions of her bank notes and give them to him.

Marang and Sir William agreed that the Vasco de Gama 500 Escudo note was the most suitable, because Waterlow's already had the plates. But, of course, Sir William insisted on confirmation from the Bank of Portugal in writing. Reis quickly went to work on a modified contract, together with a letter from the bank's

Governor, Camacho Rodriquez, confirming an initial order of 200,000 notes and stating that for political reasons all arrangements and correspondence should be through Marang. (Reis typed the letter on what he imagined the Governor's letterhead might look like, and simply copied his signature from a banknote.)

So keen was Sir William to gain the order over his competitor that he ignored warnings from Waterlow's representative in Lisbon. He did, however, do some checking of his own. He investigated Marang, who seemed respectable, and he thought it prudent to break the agreement and send a letter of confirmation direct to Governor Camacho. But by one of the great financial banana skins of history, the letter was lost in the mail. Reis' luck was holding.

Soon the notes were printed, collected by taxi, and sent by train to Portugal. They never went near Angola, nor were they overprinted 'ANGOLA'. An elaborate system of 'money-laundering' swung into action, mainly by black market currency dealers in the foreign exchange city of Oporto. So much money was soon in circulation that the Bank of Portugal itself was forced to quell rumours of forgery. Reis even created the Bank of Angola & Metropole, and through it, made huge investments in Angola, where he became a hero. He then conceived a bold idea to eliminate the risk of the Bank of Portugal discovering his ruse. He tried to buy it. As the share price began to rise, a suspicious newspaper, *O Seculo*, began to investigate. 'WHAT'S GOING ON?' was the first in a series of startling headlines.

Reis was on the ship *Adolf Woerman* returning from an acquisition spree in Angola when things really started to unravel. In Oporto, a currency dealer, Manoel de Sousa, had *almost* jumped to the right conclusion and went to the local Bank of Portugal office claiming that the notes were counterfeit. Police surrounded the Bank of Angola & Metropole and its manager was thrown in jail. But when the Bank of Portugal's counterfeit expert arrived from Lisbon, he was forced to declare the notes genuine – which, in a sense, they were.

Red faces and recriminations all round. But not for long. The next day an alert official noticed a bank note number was the same as one on another note. Then many more. Alves Reis' luck had run out. On 6 December 1925, he was arrested on the ship's gangplank.

Reis would stay in jail for nineteen years, Marang was acquitted, Sir William was ousted by his jealous cousin Edgar and died in 1931 tainted by the scandal. Waterlow's was crippled by one of the longest trials in legal history, and eventually was taken over by rival De la Rue. But the most serious consequence of this colossal, multiple banana skin was that Antonio Salazar, after clearing up the mess as Portugal's Minister of Finance, became the longest ruling dictator in Europe.

George Pullman and his company town

At first, George Pullman was an American hero. He brought long-awaited and inexpensive comfort to America's railways. In 1864, he launched his *Pioneer* sleeping car with its ingenious system of upper berths – let down at night and folded away during the day.

Four years later his first dining car, *Delmonico*, appeared, named after the famed New York gourmet restaurant. Pullman was soon leasing his cars to railroads all over the country, fully staffed and equipped by his Pullman Palace Car Company. His dining cars set culinary standards as superb as the finest big city restaurants, with even twelve course meals not unusual. Another innovation, paternalistic but self-serving, was his almost exclusive hiring of black staff whose smiling helpfulness became a legend for a century.

In 1880, George Pullman also became famous for his ultimate 'company town'. He purchased 4,000 acres in open prairie near Chicago, put up a new factory and surrounded it with houses, all with indoor plumbing, gas and electricity, and built by company workshops and Pullman employees. The broad, tree-lined streets and parks of Pullman, Illinois, were pleasantly landscaped and there was a gasworks, a hotel, library, theatre, post office, schools, parks and tree nursery.

However, there were drawbacks to this claustrophobic existence. Designed to keep his workers from the evils of Chicago, he allowed no drinking in

Pullman. All residents were employees, their pay cheques drawn from the Pullman Bank, and their rent – set by the Pullman Company agent – was required to be paid at the same time. George Pullman plainly regarded the town as another money-making enterprise: 'We are landlord and employers. That is all there is of it.'

However, the town was to be a trap for both his workers, and for Pullman, his downfall. An economic depression in 1893 meant that orders for Pullman cars fell. George Pullman laid off 2,200 of his 5,500 workforce and cut wages for the rest by 25 per cent. At the same time, he did not reduce the rents in his town, and they were deducted as usual. Infuriated and desperate, the Pullman workers went on strike. The American Railway Union supported them, and its members refused to work trains that had Pullman cars, disrupting the whole network, including the US mail. Violence broke out in the railyards of Chicago, 12,000 troops were called out, two men were killed, and Eugene V. Debs, the American Railway Union President, was jailed.

In just weeks, George Pullman slid from being one of the respected men in America to being one of the most hated.

NO WONDER IT'S POPULAR..

THE PULLMAN
Single Occupancy Section

SO MUCH EXTRA CONVENIENCE
AT SO LITTLE ADDITIONAL COST

9 ways to travel in comfort by PULLMAN

YOU'RE SAFE AND SURE
WHEN YOU TRAVEL BY

Pullman

...COSTS LESS THAN YOU THINK!

The style, comfort, cuisine and service in Pullman's magnificent cars, dominated Americas railroads for decades

The town's pastor, the Rev William Cawardine, went as far as to say that he 'was destined to be regarded as stubborn, ungenerous, autocratic and a prime example of all that is worst about capitalism'.

Pullman, when he died four years later, had to be buried under tons of steel and concrete lest his grave be desecrated.

Lord Elgin & his marbles

In the late eighteenth century, a quiet revolution was occurring in England. Far less dramatic than its French counterpart, it was to have consequences for the world every bit as profound. The Humanist 'Enlightenment' had begun, and the educated classes were largely putting away their bibles and turning to art instead for spiritual instruction. Culture was curative; the soul as well as the senses, it was believed, could benefit from art. And, for the children of the Enlightenment, led by the Society of the Dilettanti, the icon of great art was the elegant statuary of ancient Greece.

But how could one see such art at first hand? Whoever wished to travel in the eastern Mediterranean could certainly expect to face great discomfort on the notoriously violent Aegean; there were illnesses still abroad there which had been conquered elsewhere in Europe, and above all, such a traveller would have to contend with the ruling Ottoman Turks, who had become, however unfairly, a byword in the West for deceit, idleness and wayward cruelty.

However, the seventh Earl of Elgin, a noble Scottish landowner who believed passionately in the creed of art as spiritual illumination, was not to be deterred in his quest. His mission was to result in a priceless cultural treasure for the nation, but for himself nothing but heartbreak, illness, obloquy and financial ruin.

It all began with a hint from his friend, the architect Thomas Harrison, who, like Elgin, was convinced of the need for British artists to emulate ancient Greek standards of statuary. Four Italian artists were engaged to visit the hill-top Acropolis in Athens and make detailed drawings and plaster casts of the Parthenon, the temple to the goddess Athena, built by Pericles in the 5th century BC, and the finest Doric temple in the world. At this stage, there was no talk of removing anything, although excavation was mooted. The Turkish authorities, then ruling Greece, were initially amused by what they saw as a rather Quixotic venture, and were sporadically compliant. Then a seismic shift in international relations radically changed their attitude and gave Elgin an opportunity he had never dreamed of. In 1801, Nelson and the British drove Napoleon from Egypt, a Turkish province. Turkey was now Britain's grateful debtor. Moreover, Elgin was by then British Ambassador to the Turkish capital, Constantinople.

Elgin's enthusiastic chaplain, Philip Hunt, who had previously tried to remove the Lion's Gate of the Palace of Mycenae and the Athens Erechthium to Britain, began to hint to the Voevod, or Military Governor of Athens, that perhaps some of the statuary round the Parthenon could be removed. Elgin, initially reluctant, suddenly saw the advantages of his influence at Constantinople, and gave his consent. *A firman*, an imperial document, was duly issued which appeared to give Elgin unlimited rights of excavation. Soon, scaffolding was sprouting all around the magnificent ancient monument, and the superb statues or metopes, which adorned the frieze around the Parthenon, were removed bit by bit.

And in no gentle fashion either. Heads fell off as the 300 workers struggled to remove the great slabs of marble, and great damage was done to the stone which remained. But the Turks neither protested nor cared. It seemed that Elgin had secured a prize beyond avarice with nothing to stand in his way. However, it soon became apparent that the Parthenon lay under an ancient curse every bit as pernicious as that myth ascribed to the tomb of Tutenkhamen.

Elgin was becoming obsessed. More and more, he was heard to speak of 'my marbles', and it was (rightly) feared that he intended to use them as exterior

The Parthenon

decoration for his Scottish seat, Broom Hall. A whole series of catastrophes now ensued. HMS *Mentor*, his flagship, was wrecked, carrying tons of statuary with it. He then made a disastrous detour to France that resulted in his imprisonment, and then in 1806, when he finally returned home almost ruined, he discovered that his wife had been having an affair, after which she abruptly left him. Next came his downfall in reputation, when in 1809, he fell victim to the jealous spite of the intellectual Dilettanti Society. More damaging still was the ire of the poet Lord Byron, who, having visited Athens, declared Elgin's supposed act of 'conservation' to be an act of mutilation. *'Quod non fecerunt Gothi, fecerunt Scoti'.* (What the Goths spared, the Scots destroyed.)

A commission was set up in 1816 to investigate Elgin, and the questions were not friendly. Did the firman expressly give Elgin the right to remove the stones? Had Elgin not abused his position as Ambassador for private gain? Did Elgin in fact have any title to the statues at all? Surprisingly perhaps, the commission exonerated him, but his great passion had broken him. Sick from syphilis and unable to recoup from the British Government more than half the money he had spent on his grand project, he died in terrible debt.

The argument over both the morality - and indeed legality - of his actions rages now as then. For the Greeks, the Elgin marbles represent a rape of their national soul, while for the British, they have become an adopted symbol of their country. How appropriate, one might think, that a building raised on the spoils of pillage should itself be pillaged; that, built to commemorate a mighty empire, it should become the legacy of another.

Elgin made many disastrous slips, and his motives remain unclear to this day – though personal gain was clearly a late development. What is certain is that all of the disasters of his later life can be ascribed to his hubristic decision to appropriate the stones, rather than have them drawn and copied. Many say he dared the Gods, forgetting – great classicist though he was – how those of Ancient Greece knew how to punish greed and arrogance all too well.

> **'What the Goths spared, the Scots destroyed.'**

General Motors & America's streetcars

When he was being considered as U.S. Secretary of Defense in 1953, Charles Wilson spoke about his former employer General Motors. 'For years I thought that what was good for our country was good for General Motors and vice versa.' His words are belied by a sorry tale that haunts the American nation to this day.

By 1930, the United States had the finest public transport system in the world. On 14,000 miles of rail, and in most major cities, the people travelled in electric streetcars, or out into the countryside in fast 'inter-urbans.' These not only connected but actually created suburban communities, whether along the wind-swept shores near Chicago or in the sunshine near Los Angeles. There, everyone rode Pacific Electric's 'Big Red Cars'.

You might think that a quiet, cheap, efficient and non-polluting transit system would suit everyone. Not quite. Above all, it did not suit General Motors who were, of course, in the business of selling buses and automobiles.

However, for a while the electric transit companies were safe, because in most cases they were owned by local electricity companies, who were happy to sustain them because of the base load of electricity the streetcars used, especially when so many other customers had been eliminated by the ravages of the Depression. But in 1935, a suspiciously useful 'Public Utility Holding Company Act' was passed which forced the electricity companies to sell their transit companies. And guess who bought them? The answer was National City Lines, a consortium of General Motors, Firestone Tire and Phillips Petroleum or Pacific City Lines (General Motors, Standard Oil, Mack Truck) or various other similar groupings. And guess what they did? They tore up the lines and scrapped the cars, replacing them with buses. Streetcars began to disappear from most American cities.

One hero tried to warn both the American people and the officers who ran their cities. In 1946, E. Jay Quinby sent out his own 36 page leaflet which began: *'This is an urgent warning that there is a careful, planned campaign to swindle you out of your most important and valuable public utilities - your*

'The streetcar named Desire', the most famous one in the world, now thankfully returned to New Orleans

Electric Railway System.'

Belatedly, Quinby's charges stirred the Federal Government, which eventually charged GM – not for the socially devastating act of ripping out the streetcar lines, but for creating a monopoly. Each company was fined a mere $5,000 (the cost of one bus) and the senior executives a ridiculous one dollar each.

It was too little and much too late because the damage was already done, brutally and cynically. It was also a real banana skin for the American people. Many think that the huge, polluting freeway-covered sprawl of Los Angeles might never have developed as it did, if the 'Big Red Cars' had stayed. Nor perhaps the ghettos and racial divisions that led to the Watts Riots.

> *'There is a planned campaign to swindle you out of your most valuable public utilities.'*

Quinby's words were truly prophetic: *'You will realize too late that the electric railway is more comfortable, more reliable, safer and cheaper to use than the bus system. But what can you do about it once you have permitted the tracks to be torn up? Who do you find to finance another de-luxe transit system for your city?'*

Sixty years later we know the answer - the taxpayer has had to pay. Whether in San Francisco, San José, Sacramento, Los Angeles, Washington, Baltimore, Denver, Portland, (or for that matter Dublin), billions are being spent to replace something which should never have gone.

In this case, what was good for General Motors was certainly not good for the country.

Lloyd's of London & the new 'names'

For three hundred years, to be a member of Lloyd's of London was a mark of wealth, social standing and British exclusivity. Then, quite suddenly, everything went terribly wrong.

By 1650, the coffee houses of London had become a vital part of Britain's trade, and a primary source of reliable maritime information. Indeed, the famous diarist, Samuel Pepys, thought the news he received about shipping in his coffee house was much more valuable to him than that he gleaned as Secretary to the Admiralty. Edward Lloyd's first coffee house in Tower Street near the river Thames became so popular with tradesmen and ship owners that in 1691 he had to move to bigger quarters on Lombard Street. Lloyd realised the immense value of the information that was changing hands on his premises, and five years later launched *Lloyd's List*, full of shipping news that was provided by correspondents around the world.

Insuring ships and their cargoes had always been vital, and brokers would visit 'risk takers' in the coffee houses, who would sign the deal by writing their names under the contract. Nowhere was more popular with these marine 'underwriters' than Lloyd's, confirming its dominant position in mercantile shipping. In 1771, seventy-nine underwriters subscribed £100 each to form the Society of Lloyd's. Later, the members became known as 'Names', committing their personal wealth to cover their customers' potential losses.

The obvious personal risk that the 'Names' were gambling their total wealth, 'down to the last shirt stud,' was no real danger while Lloyd's stuck to maritime underwriting. This was because the outcome of a ship's voyage was known within one year, and all claims settled within three. But when Lloyd's branched out into other forms of insurance, it required a long 'tail' of re-insurance liability, sometimes going

back fifty years. And much of this was in fast-growing America, a country which takes her law even more seriously than her business.

For most of its arcane but successful existence, the 'Names' at Lloyd's were a small and intimate coterie of rich, upper-class and honourable people who would never have dreamed of cheating their friends and peers. Thus, it all worked impeccably for three centuries.

However, in the 1970s, the built-in

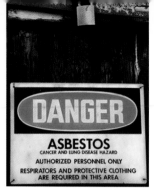

The new Names were not told of the tsunami of claims over the horizon.

danger of those long 'tails' of risk became apparent to an alert group of insiders. Pollution and health hazards, and especially asbestos, were about to come to court in the United States, and the resulting flood of unlimited claims would hit Lloyd's and its syndicates and potentially wipe them out. As a result, some members' agents at Lloyd's hit on the simple idea of quickly recruiting thousands of new 'Names' to cover the risk. The minimum capital required was dropped, and huge numbers of new 'Names' were recruited, increasing from 6,000 in 1975 to 32,000 in 1988. Apparently, this was called the 'recruit to dilute' campaign. There was a favourable tax regime at the time, so the task was not that difficult, and financial advisers, brokers and even banks on commission advised their clients and friends in good faith to join. These new members now tended to be middle-class men and women from the UK, but also from the United States, Canada, Australia and South Africa, countries in which Lloyd's had rightly earned a great reputation. These were about to face a banana skin that would ruin many of them. Most were not very rich,

more likely to be professional people or retired officers with substantial gratuities and pensions, and they could ill-afford the losses that were about to engulf them. While all were properly warned of the general risks, they were not told about the approaching tsunami of claims just over the horizon, and many found themselves in the syndicates most at risk. At the same time, unnoticed, 4,000 old 'Names' had quietly resigned or had moved to safe syndicates.

By 1980, the first American asbestos law suits had hit home, and the floodgates opened. For a while, a complex 'spiral' of re-insurance hid the true position, but from 1991 the cash calls became horrific as reserves dwindled, also hit by the bad luck of a number of 'normal' disasters, like the *Amoco Cadiz* rig explosion and the *Exxon Valdez* oil tanker spill in Alaska.

As had been secretly planned, the new 'Names' inevitably took the brunt, and many found their lives ruined. There were thirty suicides.

Lloyd's has now recovered its poise and much of its image as the world's centre for insurance. There are still plenty of 'Names', but there are also a great many people who will never forget that fateful period in Lloyds' history.

envy & jealousy

'*Jealousy is all the fun you think they had.*'
Erica Jong

'*We can always sympathise with our friends' tragedies but never with their triumphs.*'
Oscar Wilde

Pisa & its bell tower

Twelth century Pisa was one of the great trading cities of Italy, its wealth based upon its mercantile strength and its fate locked in continuous trading and jealous military rivalry with other cities, particularly Florence. Envious of her rivals, in the image race Pisa was determined not to be outdone.

Knowing that Florence was planning its magnificent domed cathedral, Pisa's architects designed a bell tower as a dramatic competitive gesture, part of a group of buildings called the Piazza de Miracolo, comprising the cathedral, baptistry and cemetery. Just how dramatic, but how unmiraculous it was, emerged soon after construction began in 1173, when a pronounced lean appeared in the structure. Builders tried to compensate, and the lean then reversed the other way. The tower took a very long time to complete, no less than two hundred years, because of interruptions caused by wars with Florence and Genoa, and the bells were installed in 1392. By then, the lean was 2.5 degrees from the vertical. This was a classic case of envious competition leading to rushed inattention and poor surveying, because it emerged

Jealousy of Florence made them rush the construction.

that the tower had been built on an ancient riverbed of soft, sandy soil, and the foundation was much too shallow for a structure of 14,000 tons.

However, the earlier banana skin of embarrassment and wounded pride for the citizens of Pisa was ameliorated in more modern times by a new breed of visitor. Starting with young gentlemen on the 'Grand Tour', so-called tourists began to flock to Pisa to look at its curious leaning tower. For all its treasures, the Uffizi, the Pitti Palace and Brunelleschi's magnificent cathedral dome, Florence, bizarrely, had been outdone by Pisa's blunder.

However, this unexpected bounty could not last forever. During 1989, when the lean was 5.5 degrees, a million visitors climbed the tower's 294 steps, but experts suddenly warned that the landmark was now dangerous. For twelve years it was closed, while methods were worked out to stop the lean and even to straighten it, just enough to preserve the building, but not enough to ruin its tourist appeal.

It was to be a British engineering team that came up with the complex solution, involving 870 tons of weights on one side and the careful, slow drilling out of the soil. Gradually, the tower settled back on to the reducing soil, its lean eventually stopping at five degrees.

In June 2001, to a great fanfare, the tower was re-opened to the public on the Feast of San Ranieri, Pisa's patron saint. Now guaranteed for three hundred years, 'The Leaning Tower of Pisa' has kept its unique drawing power to those who lean towards the Christian faith, or simply as a building that should never have survived such inattention at its birth.

Even Florence could not compete with Pisa's strange phenomenon.

Monty & his 'Bridge too far'

One of the most dramatic and tragic failures of World War II was fuelled by envy.

It was always likely to be a risky business, a bold, narrow thrust into Germany to 'win the war in forty four'. For months the Allied commanders had debated, often heatedly, about the best way to beat the Germans in the west. Britain's difficult and opinionated Field Marshal Bernard Montgomery advocated a dagger-like thrust through Holland into the industrial Ruhr. The Americans favoured a broad push on all fronts. Indeed, if there were to be any thrusts, they would far prefer Montgomery's

bitter rival, American General George Patton, to attack from the south.

After the D-Day landings, the Allies were bogged down for weeks, but now Paris and Brussels were liberated and the Germans seemed disorganised and close to defeat. Montgomery's idea, Operation *'Market Garden'*, was audacious. Thirty thousand British, American and Polish airborne troops were to be flown behind enemy lines to capture the eight bridges that spanned the network of canals and rivers on the Dutch/German border. An armoured corps would follow up, cross the captured bridges and pour into Germany. Montgomery was reluctantly given his head by the American Supreme Commander Eisenhower, won over by the political argument that V2 rockets launched from Holland were now landing in London.

The attack had to be planned in just six days, a rush contrasting with Montgomery's normal meticulous style. Success depended on the British assessment of the Germans being ' weak, disorderly and dispirited'. However, the Dutch Resistance suddenly reported that SS troops were near Arnhem. They were

Monty became ever more jealous of the Americans.

right. Two crack SS panzer divisions, had arrived there to rest and regroup. A low-level Spitfire then photographed their camouflaged tanks. The operation should have been cancelled at once. But the banana skin of over-confidence struck. The Intelligence Officer who was trying to warn everyone was sent on sick leave to keep him quiet – perhaps because so many attacks had been cancelled and the airborne troops were thirsting to get on with it, *'restless, frustrated and ready for anything',* as one officer later wrote.

Almost at once, things started to go wrong. After successful landings by American paratroopers on the first two bridges, the spearhead of the armoured corps, the tanks of the Irish Guards, were advancing to 'The Island', the exposed, narrow road raised above the fields between Nijmegen and Arnhem, the danger of which the Dutch again had tried to warn the British planners,. *'Suddenly, there was a clang, and a Sherman tank's sprocket wheel came flying lazily over the trees.I knew we were in big trouble',* recalled a young officer as eight more tanks exploded. And, it was not just the Irish Guards that were in trouble. So was the whole plan. Soon, rows of burning vehicles blocked the road for hours, victims of the lethal

German anti-tank guns, and even of infantry with *Panzerfaust* rockets. The 'cavalry to the rescue' were already running badly late.

At Arnhem, 'the bridge too far', it was even worse. The British airborne forces had landed seven miles away to avoid the town's anti-aircraft *flak* – the one thing that never materialised. To reach Arnhem quickly, they needed speed and communications. But their reconaissance jeeps did not arrive, and incredibly, none of their radios worked. So they could neither coordinate with each other or with Allied commanders. It was a catastrophe. The lightly armed airborne forces fought against German heavy tanks for eight days with incredible bravery. But, short of ammunition and supplies, they were either, killed, wounded, forced to surrender or to escape by night back across the Rhine. Out of 10,000 men, only 2,163 made it to safety.

Why did this multiple banana skin happen? Almost certainly everyone was blindly following the overconfidence of Montgomery, an egotistical and complex man. After the war, Montgomery was asked to list the three greatest commanders in history. Without hesitation, he named Alexander the Great, Napoleon and then – himself.

DAVID SHEPHERD/THE PARACHUTE REGIMENT

And he was not joking. Years later at Wellington School, he read the lesson. 'And God said unto the Israelites, and I have to say, I agree with him.' Believing absolutely in his high opinion of himself, he was jealous of the growing dominance of the Americans and envious of their masses of equipment. Thus he was determined to spite them and to pull off his own 'British victory', abandoning the cautious attention to detail that usually served him so well.

The banana skin of Arnhem was a great tragedy, because 'Monty' was, in retrospect, probably right to opt for a single powerful push into Germany. If only he had been less difficult and less jealous of his own side, he might just have pulled it off and won the war in 1944. The Russians might not have reached Berlin first, and there might have been no Iron Curtain and no Cold War.

The airborne troops defend one end of the bridge.

The Hunt Brothers & the world's silver

It was late at night at La Guardia airport. Three Boeing 707s with taped-over identification landed from Texas. Apart from the crews, there were a dozen armed cowboys from the Circle K Ranch, especially chosen for their marksmanship. A convoy of armoured trucks arrived from New York City, and the cowboys helped load in the cargo – 40 million ounces of silver. The cowboys settled into their seats and the planes took off for Switzerland. Sounds like a 'J.R.'Ewing plot in the *Dallas* TV series? No, this was real life and part of one of the greatest speculations of all time.

By the spring of 1974, the word was spreading in the world's silver-trading floors that a mysterious Texan had taken delivery of more silver than anyone in history. From New York to London to Tokyo, everyone was asking, 'Who is Nelson Bunker Hunt?' Who indeed.

Bunker Hunt was a bespectacled,

'Who is Nelson Bunker Hunt?'

overweight figure in cheap suits, with a passion for ice cream, and the curious habit of looking for loose change that had fallen down the sides of sofas, despite being one of the richest people on earth. He was the second son of a Texan legend, H.L. Hunt, who was one of the first of the oil independents; a man who had 15 children by three wives and who really could be a prototype for J.R. Ewing. When his oldest and favourite son Hassie was struck down by mental illness, H.L. Hunt bullied and belittled the next-in-line, Bunker, who was always desperate to prove his worth to his eccentric and irascible father. After $250 million dollars worth of unsuccessful oil exploration and dry holes, Bunker eventually found the Sarir Field in Libya. His share was worth seven billion dollars, twice his father's assets. Combined with his stake in the huge family business, he was then at 35 the richest individual in the world. He had made his point.

However, in 1970, Bunker and his brother Herbert started to do something rather strange. They began to buy silver, first as a hedge against inflation, and at first in 'penny packets' of 10,000 ounces. As the world became tougher (not least by Colonel Gaddafi's nationalisation of Bunker's Libyan oilfield), they began to go deeper into silver. By 1974 they had 55 million ounces – nine per cent of the world's supply. Hence the strange Circle K flight to Zurich, which was to avoid paying taxes in Texas on the huge horde.

Bunker then embarked on a quest for partners in his silver deals: first the Shah of Iran, then King Faisal of Saudi Arabia, then President Marcos of the Philippines. Finally, in 1978, Texan Governor, John Connolly introduced him to Saudi Sheik Khaled Ben Mahfouz. The result was a Bermudan company with Bunker and Herbert and two Saudis appointed as directors, which proceeded to buy 90 million ounces of silver. The price of silver doubled to $8 an ounce.

Soon the Hunts and their partners held 200 million ounces, half the world's deliverable supply of silver, and the price went on rocketing, peaking at $50. The Hunts had made a theoretical profit of $3.5 billion. But the commodity exchanges panicked and began to tighten the rules. With such huge prices, coins and silverware were now worth selling and flooded on to the market. On January 22, 1980, the price fell $10 in a single day. The price continued to drift downwards. On March 25, the Hunts' broker made a $135 million margin call. 'We can't make it', said Herbert to his stunned caller. 'Shut it down,' decided Bunker. On March 27 the price of silver collapsed and Wall Street followed suit, the Dow Jones index dropping to its worst level for five years. Even the Federal Reserve Chairman, Paul Volker, had to get involved in the bail out which followed and which mortgaged the Hunt family assets. Bunker's oldest sister Margaret finally asked him what on earth had he been trying to achieve. He sheepishly replied, 'I was just trying to make some money.'

When you are jealous of your father and try to outdo him, it can be a distinctly slippery slope.

'I was just trying to make some money.'

IOS, Bernie Cornfeld & Robert Vesco

There is no doubt that Bernie Cornfeld was a man with a vision. He said he would make his creation, Investors Overseas Services, the most important economic force in the Free World. And this small, tubby, bearded former social worker nearly succeeded – before the bubble burst.

His basic idea was quite simple. It was to persuade a huge number of people to put their savings into mutual funds, controlled from 'offshore' locations where it was possible to avoid taxation and regulation. To do this he employed a super-motivated sales-force, which soon numbered 10,000. A brilliant salesman, his opening gambit with potential recruits was 'Do you sincerely want to be rich?' While appealing directly to their envy and greed, it was also a subtle question, because many people would rather be happy than lead a life of high-pressure salesmanship.

'Do you sincerely want to be rich?'

There was nothing particularly unusual, even in the 60s, about people investing in offshore mutual funds. What was unusual about IOS was its success in getting great numbers of ordinary people to entrust it with their savings. This was achieved by salesmanship on a previously unheard of scale. Bernie became the 'prophet of people's capitalism' and some members of his team, who 'sincerely wanted to be rich,' indeed became very rich. Well over a hundred of them became millionaires led by Bernie himself, who, flaunting a glamorous and lavish lifestyle, had amassed over $150 million (a billion dollars today.)

Building on the foundation of its mutual offshore funds, IOS, safely based in Geneva out of reach of the US authorities, also created a complex web of banks, insurance companies and real estate promotions. The slogan was 'Total Financial Service' – and millions of people fell for it, believing that their savings were in safe, but dynamic hands. By 1968, IOS had a million shareholders and had raised $2.5 billion.

However, in reality, and under the noses of the Swiss authorities, financial malpractice on a colossal scale was taking place within the complicated structure of IOS. This included illegal currency transactions; customers' money held on trust being used to finance deals for the company and its directors' benefit; consistent misrepresentation of the investment performance of its largest fund, and disguising the basic nature of the best known fund – the so-called

'Fund of Funds.' Supposed to offer investors a diversity of investment advice, it merely charged them a double fee on the pretence of doing so. IOS also sold $100 million worth of its own shares to the public on the basis of grossly misleading prospectuses – and the money was then used for the benefit of the directors.

These were just some ways in which people were misled into believing that IOS was all about creating wealth for the many, when in fact it was about making shedloads of money for the few, most of all Bernie. At the peak of IOS's activities, he owned two castles and townhouses and apartments in several capital cities. He also had racehorses, boats, planes, fast cars and even fashion houses and model agencies, showing off his 'harem' of 20 beautiful girlfriends. No wonder his envious followers wanted to emulate him.

But by 1970, the stock market had dived, and the IOS edifice started to crumble as the real state of affairs began to leak out. It could no longer be concealed that the profits were nowhere near expectations, that the sales operation was making a loss, and that the money raised from the public issue of shares had all been spent. The stock collapsed from $18 to $2. Bernie, having just been forced to sell his shares and sever his links with the company he had created, left for Beverly Hills, eventually to marry Heidi Fleiss, the 'Hollywood Madam.'

Bernie Cornfeld and friends

The 'white knight' who had invited himself in to rescue IOS was a taciturn businessman called Robert Vesco. With his spartan lifestyle, IOS investors and shareholders heaved a sigh of relief as Vesco appeared to have clawed back some of the money. Their optimism was shortlived as another banana skin loomed. Vesco, too, looted the company, but was caught by the Watergate investigation bribing the Nixon election campaign with $200,000 in used bills. Vesco vanished with most of the rest of the IOS money. He then wandered from country to country in Central America, even featuring in *Forbes* magazine's famous 'rich list' with the job title of 'felon', until he behaved badly enough for even the Cubans to slam him into jail.

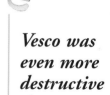

Vesco was even more destructive than Cornfeld.

Cleverly seduced by envy and greed, most of those IOS hopefuls who had so 'sincerely wanted to be rich,' ended up a great deal poorer and wiser.

Sibylla's & the reserve guest list

Sibylla's founders, Terry Howard and George Harrison

For three brief years a discotheque in London became the very centre of Britain's 'Swinging Sixties,' and it happened quite casually.

Up until then there had only been two stylish establishments to replace the fading, upper class dinner-jacketed nightclubs of London. These were Mark Birley's 'Annabel's', still going strong all these years later, and the first genuine, lively sixties-style discotheque, the 'Ad Lib', in Leicester Square.

One night in 1965 at the 'Ad Lib', Beatle George Harrison turned to his friend, Terry Howard and said, 'You know, we are spending too much money in this club. Why don't we start our own?'

So a new club was born, with George Harrison as a shareholder, and named after Terry Howard's girlfriend Sibylla Edmonstone, a beautiful Marshall Field heiress. Designed by the leading new interior designer David Mlinaric, it was not only an elegant club but had the major advantage that the cleverly designed sound system was loud when you were on the dance floor and much quieter three feet away with the speakers pointed vertically downwards and carefully controlled so you could talk when you were sitting down. This sensible concept seems to have been lost for modern clubbers.

Word spread about the new club and its opening. Anybody who was anybody wanted to go. Not surprisingly. Guests invited included all the Beatles and all the Rolling Stones, rising actors and actresses like Michael Caine, Julie Christie, Charlotte Rampling, Sue Lloyd, Edina Ronay, Lesley Caron, Jacqui Bissett and Anita Harris, plus TV personalities like Lance Percival and pop-music gurus, such as Cathy McGowan and Alan Freeman. The new wave of photographers were represented by David Bailey, Terry

Donovan, John d. Green and Patrick Lichfield, while models Celia Hammond, Joanna Lumley and Annagret wore clothes designed by fellow-guests Mary Quant and Sue Locke.

The dangers of envy resulted in one major media banana skin. A month earlier, the writer Anthony Haden-Guest, who was planning a feature for *Queen* magazine (now *Harpers Bazaar*) dropped in and asked who was coming to the opening party. Terry Howard casually gave him a typed draft list that was lying on the table, forgetting that this was a working list and included cryptic notes about the people invited. More dangerously there was a reserve list of 100 'less interesting people' to be invited only if any of the first 200 could not turn up.

Unfortunately, the whole list was typeset word for word and reproduced in *Queen*, which caused sensational offence to the reserve list.

And as the reserve list included some quite important people (or certainly those who thought they were important), it was hardly surprising that they never became members.

Terry Howard still wonders if that is why the club only lasted three years.

*Some of those who **were** invited: Sue Lloyd, Jacqui Bissett, Michael Caine, Charlotte Rampling and Joanna Lumley*

Wall Street & its Crash

The 'Wall Street Crash', history's greatest financial cataclysm, was above all created by envy and greed. Wall Street, named after the wall erected by the Dutch across Manhattan to keep out 'bears, Indians and the British', had, by 1929, become the symbol of a whole country gripped by a frenzy of speculation as the 'Roaring Twenties' ended.

While much of America was still poor, bizarrely the country was awash with money for speculation. Diverted from traditional uses like land and commodities, money had to go into stocks and bonds. A banana skin that fuelled the fever was the rule that people could buy shares 'on margin', putting down just 10% and often with money borrowed from their brokers. This was fine, of course, if stocks went up, but ruinous if they fell. As one stockbroker put it, 'A puff of wind – and they and their stocks bought on margin could be blown away for ever.' Two million Americans 'played the market', but dangerously 600,000 of these were 'minnows' – on margin. Many were women, with 5,000 establishments provided for the 'Ladybulls'. Every cocktail party and dinner was dominated by market talk. All over the country, people crouched over the 'tickers'; thousands of little machines that steadily spewed out a ticker tape with stock prices.

Unworldly and unwary speculators were also pushed further in their folly by the 'pools.' Heavyweight groups of Wall Street insiders, backed by pools of money, would ramp up chosen stocks, then quietly unload them on to the eager 'minnows', while they themselves pulled out with fat profits. Journalists would have been bribed to praise such stocks. Responsible trading gave way to fairground huckstering and buying AOT, 'Any Old Thing', was now the rage.

Above all, the banana skin of envy was laid by rumours of someone else getting rich quick, not just the big boys, but the little, ordinary folk: the broker's valet who had made $250,000; the nurse with $30,000 following the tips of grateful patients; secretaries with mink coats and flashy cars; the waiter at the Stock Exchange Luncheon Club who had resigned $90,000 richer, as a result

'A puff of wind and they could be blown away for ever'.

of tips from his customers. The frenzy created ridiculous situations, like the Fifth Avenue hostess whose cook flounced out when she was refused her own ticker in her kitchen, or the chauffeur who would not work until the market had closed. Jockeys were lobbying for shorter races so 'they should not be too long away from the ticker.' Cinemas and even synagogues placed tickers in their entrances. The Cunard liner *Berengaria* was the first to provide a complete brokerage office. The rich could go on speculating in mid-Atlantic.

The terrible temptation to get rich even led to real fraud. In Flint, Michigan, the staff of the town's bank, owned by Charles Mott of General Motors, were secretly gambling their customers' money.

There were a few who began to scent danger. Joe Kennedy, the father of JFK, decided to keep his cash out of the market when his favourite bootblack, Pat Bologna, 'started giving *him* tips.' Others thought that when that regal bank, the House of Morgan, entered the game and started a secret list of favoured customers, insider trading was going too far.

The crisis for Wall Street started far away in London when Clarence Hatry's steel empire, itself a speculation, collapsed. A tremor of worry crossed the Atlantic. On Wednesday, October 23,

Edward Simmonds, the President of the New York Stock Exchange was on honeymoon in Honolulu while his overbearing deputy, Richard Whitney, himself heavily in debt, decided to go to the races. Jack Morgan, the bank's senior partner, was in Scotland shooting grouse. All seemed calm. But, just after noon, the market broke and shares plummeted.

The next day uneasy crowds gathered in Wall Street. Even the police arrived, 'in case of trouble.' After just 25 minutes of trading, the market started to crash and panic enveloped the trading floor. Brokers who were normally '*not allowed to run, curse, push or go coatless*' became a screaming, roaring rabble. Almost unnoticed, up in the visitor's gallery Winston Churchill staring with amazement. Far out to sea on the *Berengaria*, Helena Rubinstein, the cosmetics queen, calmly sold 50,000 Westinghouse shares and walked away a million dollars poorer.

At 12.20, Charles Mitchell, President of National City Bank, the largest in the country, was seen elbowing his way coatless through the crowds and entering, 23 Wall Street, the hallowed House of Morgan. There he met Thomas Lamont

Winston Churchill stared, amazed, at the scenes in the Exchange.

of Morgans and four other bankers, 'representing $6 billion in banking resources.' The market steadied, remembering how in the panic of 1907 the towering figure of J. Pierpoint Morgan, with his friends, had saved the day. At 1.30 Richard Whitney, the broker for Morgan and the other bankers, strode on to the floor and, moved from post to post, ostentatiously buying shares. Prices steadied, some gained a little. By the close of 'Black Thursday' investors had *only* lost $3 billion. But thousands of small 'minnows' had been wiped out.

On Friday, President Hoover intoned, 'The fundamental business of the country, that is production and distri-bution of commodities, is on a sound and prosperous basis.' Secretly he had been dreading a catastrophe for months.

The market closed slightly up. Over the weekend sightseers came to gawp at the scene of 'Black Thursday.' On the Monday prices steadied a little, but just at the close they fell sharply and ominously. Everyone held their breath.

On Tuesday, October 29, all hell broke loose, as stocks plummeted amidst scenes of pandemonium. 'Men roared like a lot of lions and tigers', recalled William Crawford, the Superintendent, *'They hollered, they screamed, they clawed at one another's collars. It was like a bunch of crazy men.'* One even dropped to the floor, 'spluttering incoherencies.' In fact, he was not mad; he had only dropped his dentures. Another, 'resembling a Bowery bum', staggered from the meleé, moaning 'I'm sold out, out, out!' Two billion dollars were lost in thirty minutes. It went on and on, with the ticker hopelessly behind the tragedy unfolding. Men wept openly, while others prayed on their knees. Messengers and taxis were steadily delivering thousands of doom-laden margin calls. At 5.32 the ticker signed off, TOTAL SALES TODAY 16,383,700 GOOD NIGHT. Hardly the right words. New York's losses were $10 billion, twice the currency in circulation. The total loss came to a devastating $50 billion, and the first suicide reports came in.

At least one million Americans were wiped out by the crash of 'Tragic Tuesday', but many more were affected who had borrowed to buy houses and cars, to be paid off by stock winnings that never came. The market bottomed out at a tenth of its 1929 peak. Then the Government created two banana skins of its own. First, President Hoover, against

'It was like a bunch of crazy men.'

all advice, imposed tariffs on imports. 22 countries retaliated. Foreign trade duly stopped in its tracks. Second, the money supply was shrunk. In America and all over the world business slowed, workers were laid off and unemployment soared. Thousands of banks failed. The tragic 'Depression' with its soup kitchens, hoboes and 'Hooverville' shanty towns had arrived. Nowhere was it worse than in Germany, with no more loans from America and millions jobless. Now, Adolf Hitler stepped into the social economic and political vacuum.

Sadly, the banana skin of the 'Wall Street Crash', created by frivolous envy and greed, would directly lead to the real horrors of World War II.

Crassus & his Parthian shot

By all historic accounts, Marcus Licinius Crassus was not a very pleasant man. Known as *Dives*, 'The Rich', by 70BC he had become the wealthiest man in Rome, through silver mines and slaves. He was also a huge property owner, his portfolio augmented by his ownership of Rome's fire service and his cruel habit of turning up with his fire crews and negotiating very slowly while houses were burning, with the owners then forced to sell at knock-down prices.

If Jesus had not been born seventy years later, we might have more readily associated the awful punishment of crucifixion and its symbolism of the cross with Crassus – because it was Crassus who crushed the slave revolt of Spartacus and then lined a hundred miles of the Appian Way into Rome with crucified men, while setting up 10,000 banqueting tables in the Forum and feeding Rome for days. Could that be why we use the word 'crass'?

In 60 BC, Crassus found himself the political bridge between two great military rivals – Julius Caesar and Pompey – in the First Triumvirate which governed the Roman Empire.

However, human envy intervened. Simply ruling and making money were not enough for him; Crassus wanted to emulate the military exploits of his two colleagues. Thus, without authority and at his own expense, he sought glory by invading Parthia.

It was his banana skin, because, with his inexperience, the campaign was a disaster. In 52 BC he lost the battle of Carrhae and his nerve broke. Both Crassus and his son, together with

He should have stuck to making money.

20,000 unfortunate and badly led Romans died, many victims of the 'Parthian Shot' – arrows fired backwards across the horses' backs, which we now record as a 'parting shot' in a conversation.

The effect on Rome of Crassus's foolhardy adventure was immediate. Without his presence, Pompey and Caesar were soon bitter enemies and Caesar crossed the Rubicon to begin a bloody civil war that would affect the known world for decades.

Crassus should perhaps have stuck to making money.

The Parthian Shot

'The' Mrs Astor & the Vanderbilt's Ball

'Society' was just 400 people.

There has probably never been anyone else who so completely dominated her social scene. Caroline Schermerhorn had come from wealthy mercantile Dutch stock, and, in spite of her rather bulbous nose and heavy jaw, had managed to marry a real prize, William B. Astor Jr, from the fabulously rich Astor family. Her husband, after giving her four daughters and a son, ordered himself a huge yacht and sailed off to be one of the original millionaire playboys.

Caroline, on her own and with the marriage prospects of her daughters in mind, turned to a 'social expert', a Southern gentleman called Ward McAllister. Under his Svengali-type influence, 'The' Mrs Astor, as she called herself, started to dictate how the rich in New York should behave. Indeed, it was the capacity of her ballroom at 350 Fifth Avenue that precisely determined how large 'Society' could be – just 400 people! Soon 'Society' and members of McAllister's 'Social Register' were involved in a rigid ritual of Patriarchs' Balls, soirées, dancing classes and dinners. Caroline's weekly 'Mystic Rose' dinners were the most exclusive, elaborate feasts of ten courses served on gold plate.

In addition to the obvious targets to be excluded from 'Society', like Catholics and Jews, it became vital for Mrs Astor to keep out some real competitors. Top of the list were the Vanderbilts, the even more *nouveau* and more *riche* railroad millionaires. For years she succeeded. But there was a new kid on the block, Alva Vanderbilt. She was not only just as rich as the Astors, but had built the smartest house in town at 660 Fifth Avenue and was now preparing to welcome 1,000 guests to the city's finest and most expensive ball ever. The mutual envy between the families had the city agog. It looked as if power was shifting to a new Queen Bee. Then, Alva prepared her knock-out blow.

In one of the planned Star Quadrilles of 'approved young ladies' was Carrie Astor. After the girls had been practising for weeks, Alva suddenly told Carrie she was no longer invited 'because your mother has never called on me.' Desperate not to miss the Ball, Carrie bullied her reluctant mother into paying the requisite formal visit to Alva. The Vanderbilts had made it into 'Society', and Caroline Astor's unique and exclusive power had slipped for ever.

Mrs Caroline Astor

Bertillon & the identical prisoners

From the dawn of history, we have searched for some sure way of identifying one person from another. Of the systems to emerge, two stand out – fingerprinting and anthropometry, the technique of measuring the body.

Fingerprinting is much older. In ancient Babylon, fingerprints were used on clay tablets for business transactions. In the 2nd century BC in China, thumbprints were found on clay seals used on documents. In 14th century Persia, official government papers had fingerprints – and one government official, a doctor, observed that no two fingerprints were exactly alike.

In 1686, Marcello Malpighi, Professor of Anatomy at the University of Bologna, noted the existence of ridges, spirals and loops in fingerprints. In 1823, John Evangelist Purkinji of the University of Breslau, revealed nine fingerprint patterns, but, like Malpighi, he made no mention of their value for identification.

Sir William Herschel, Chief Magistrate in Jungipoor, India, first used fingerprints in 1858 on native contracts.

On a whim, Herschel asked a local businessman to impress his handprint on the back of a contract. The idea was merely to frighten him out of repudiating his signature. Herschel then made a habit of requiring palm prints, and later, the prints of the right index and middle fingers on every contract. Personal contact with the document, the locals believed, made the contract more binding than if they simply signed it. Thus, the first wide-scale, modern-day use of fingerprints was started not upon scientific evidence, but upon superstitious beliefs.

A Scotsman, Dr Henry Faulds, working in Tokyo, sent his own studies to Charles Darwin, who was by then old and ill – but he passed them to his cousin Sir Francis Galton in 1880.

Twelve years later Galton published his book *Fingerprints*, complete with a classification system. He also calculated the odds against two individuals having the same fingerprints as 1 in 64 billion. Galton's work inspired Juan Vucetich in Argentina, who was to perfect an excellent fingerprinting system, soon adopted in all of South America.

A rival system, however, had been created by a Frenchman, Alphonse Bertillon, a police clerk in Paris. The son of an anthropologist, his theory was that key measurements of the body do not change after the age of twenty. From this he set up an elaborate system of 'anthropometry', involving eleven precise measurements: Body height, outstretched reach of both arms, trunk height, width of the head, length of the head, length of the right ear, width of the right ear, length of the left foot, length of the left middle finger, length of the left little finger and length of the left forearm.

These were noted on cards with photographs, skin and hair colour and other details. 'Bertillonage' seemed a great step forward. It was adopted not only in France but also swept Europe

and the United States. Galton and advocates of fingerprinting were sceptical and expressed their doubts about the statistical odds. In addition, anthropometrics relied upon the recorder being perfectly exact in his measurements. If tired or inattentive, the measurements could be faulty, and fail to identify an individual. If suspects were drunk, ill, or uncooperative, this would also result in inaccuracy. Moreover, the system was very slow, the equipment cumbersome and expensive, and furthermore, it depended on a massive filing system. Above all, unlike fingerprints, anthropometry did not connect a suspect with a weapon or a crime scene.

Nevertheless, Alphonse Bertillon was heaped with praise and honours, and even arrogantly put himself forward as a handwriting expert, repeatedly and disgracefully contributing in 1899 to the false accusations in the Dreyfus Case, which wracked France (page 262.)

However, a banana skin was lying in wait which vindicated all the doubters. In 1903, prisoner Will West was delivered to Leavenworth Prison, Kansas. He was duly processed using the Bertillon System and denied having been there before. The records clerk did not believe him, and in triumph, retrieved a Bertillon card. The trouble was that it belonged to another prisoner of the same name, William West, who had been in the prison for two years and who even looked identical. Their fingerprints were, of course, completely different.

The 'West' incident wrecked everything for Bertillon, as the disturbing news swept the police forces of the world. However, instead of acknowledging the superiority of fingerprinting, he would obstinately and jealously cling to his system. His envy even made him snub Vucetich rudely when he came to Paris. It did no good. Fingerprinting triumphed, and Bertillon died an embittered man.

Alphonse Bertillon

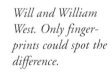

Will and William West. Only fingerprints could spot the difference.

Mark Clark & the capture of Rome

For those of us who were lucky enough to know him, Field Marshal Alexander was one of the nicest people you could meet. Winston Churchill regarded him as 'the personification of the British officer and gentleman'. But there would be times when 'Alex' was probably too nice.

The younger son of an Earl, Harold Alexander joined the Irish Guards in 1911, and in the slaughter of the trenches of the Western Front, aged just 24, rose to command their Second Battalion, soon to be a Brigadier at 27. Two decades later, commanding the rearguard at Dunkirk, he was famously the last man off the beach. He was once again to taste the bitterness

'Alex'

of retreat in the face of superior odds in Burma against the Japanese in 1942. But only months later, he was Commander in Chief of the Middle East, and as Montgomery's supportive superior, masterminded victory over Rommel in North Africa. There are many who knew, or served with Alexander, who felt strongly that he was overshadowed in the media by his egotistic, publicity-seeking deputy, Montgomery, probably because of Alex's legendary modest and gentlemanly charm. King George VI once visited Alexander and Monty in their desert headquarters. After an hour of declaiming how exactly he was going to use 'his' troops, Monty was briefly called away. Alex quietly apologised to his Monarch that neither had been able to get a word in, commenting ruefully, 'I'm afraid he may be after my job.' 'Thank God for that', replied his Majesty, 'I thought he was after mine.'

In many ways, 'Alex' and the Allies' Supreme Commander, Eisenhower, shared the same crucial skill of leading vast armies from different nations while containing, with great diplomacy, the ambitions and rivalries of prima donnas like 'Monty' and George Patton. When Alex was appointed to invade the so-called 'soft underbelly of Europe', Italy, he had also to face a new reality. The Americans in the alliance were becoming ever more dominant, and he would be lumbered with subordinates who were far from ideal. Major General Mark Clark was one of them. Although very brave and a first class planner and organiser, Clark's character was flawed with conceit, ambition, vanity and envy. His obsessions and disobedience were to cost the Allies dear.

When Mussolini was deposed by the Italian King, the Germans had reacted decisively, invading Italy and blocking the Allies with their Gustav Line, especially at the pivotal point of Monte Cassino. Alexander decided to outflank them with a bold amphibious landing further north at Anzio. However, its commander, General Lucas, was not only a feeble and indecisive officer, he had been told privately by Mark Clark 'not to stick his neck out'. Thus the Allies, having landed unopposed, simply sat in their crowded beachhead and were furiously counter-attacked by the Germans. There, they were trapped for three long months. Churchill bitterly complained that he had hoped to 'land a wildcat' and all he got was 'a beached whale.'

Alexander then planned a breakout designed to trap the German forces and to end the war in Italy. 'Operation DIADEM' caught out the Germans, and did indeed smash at last through the Gustav Line, also allowing the Anzio forces to break out. After two weeks, just as Alexander had planned, US General Truscott was approaching Valmontone and was poised to close the escape route for the whole German 10th and 14th Armies. Suddenly, he received a strange order from Mark Clark. Truscott was to abandon his course and head north-west for Rome. Knowing the implications, Truscott was dumbfounded and appalled, and he challenged the order. But his demand to speak personally to Mark Clark by radio was refused. He was obliged to obey. Alan Whicker, as a war correspondent the only British officer in Rome, still recalls his contempt at watching Mark Clark preening himself for photographers, while the Germans were escaping north to fight another day – or, rather, what turned out to be 330 bloody and bitter days.

Driven by envy, Mark Clark had become obsessed with upstaging his colleagues both in Italy and in England, and had decided to reap the 'glory' of taking Rome – just before the D-Day landings in Normandy would make Italy a publicity backwater – and especially before the British, who had actually no

Alan Whicker watched with contempt as Mark Clark preened himself

intention of going near Rome.

The result of his disobedience in pursuit of personal glory was disastrous. It condemned the Italians to a year of brutal occupation and the Allies to a year of warfare. It prevented them from reaching Austria months before the Soviets, and perhaps ending the war much earlier, with huge human and political benefits. A seething Churchill confined himself to calling the event 'unfortunate'. He also commented that 'the one thing that was worse than having allies is not having them'.

In some armies, German, Japanese and Russian, Mark Clark would have been dismissed, or even shot, for such an act of fatal disobedience. As it was, he was promoted and went on to a distinguished military career, his picture on the cover of *Time* magazine three times.

Louis XIV & the Huguenots

Civil wars are the most tragic and divisive, and the so-called 'Wars of Religion' in France between 1562 and 1598 actually amounted to no less than nine civil wars marked with devastation and atrocity, the most famous being the 'St Bartholomew's Day Massacre', when 3,000 Protestants or Huguenots were slaughtered. Catholic France had nearly allowed the growth of Protestantism to destroy the country.

Thus it was a welcome relief for France when a Huguenot, Henry of Navarre, finally prevailed, becoming Henry IV and beginning to re-unite the nation. Although he converted to Catholicism, ('Paris is worth a Mass') his historic Edict of Nantes of 1598 granted religious freedom to all. It also allowed the Huguenots control of 200 cities and towns, and their own protective armed forces. Huguenots became an important power in the land, providing most of the skilled workers, the merchants and manufacturers, the military and even the nobility. However, the Edict was a fragile compromise, with the real danger of insidious envy from the Catholic majority, jealous of Huguenot success (echoes of the persecution of the Jews in Hitler's Germany, the Asians in Idi Amin's Uganda and the Ibos in Nigeria). It also relied on the continuing support of the monarchy for its success.

This was not to be. Decades later Louis XIV came to power, a ruler who had made a boyhood vow to eliminate 'heresy'. Moreover, his principal advisor was the Catholic Cardinal, Mazarin, who, following in the footsteps of his mentor Cardinal Richelieu, preached the doctrine of absolute monarchy, and was hardly likely to encourage a successful Protestant 'state-within-a-state.'

From 1660 the pressure mounted. Huguenot churches were closed, conversion to Protestantism banned and known Huguenots were bullied by *dragonnades*, the billeting in their houses of soldiers or dragoons who had been instructed to behave badly. The King was pushed further by the enormous influence of a woman, Madame de Maintenon, whom he married in 1674. Her father had been a Huguenot, but she had become a Catholic, and like many converts to a cause, had also become a fanatic. However good she may have been for the King over the next thirty years, her religious influence was to prove disastrous. The result of their persecution was that many Huguenots simply pretended to be 'returnees' to the Catholic faith. This gave the King and his advisers an entirely false impression that the persecution had worked and that the Huguenots had been reduced to an unimportant, tiny handful.

So, when in 1685 Louis confidently revoked the Edict of Nantes at Fontainebleau, the results were an unpleasant, immediate and catastrophic surprise. The simple, jealous peasants rejoiced, and the fawning Court approved, echoing Madame de Sévigné, 'No King has ever done, or will ever do, a deed more memorable.' However, the writer Voltaire was far more accurate, calling the Revocation *'one of the greatest disasters that ever afflicted France.'*

He was right. Within months, nearly 500,000 Huguenots fled the country. They were the most industrious, best educated, richest and most influential. They arrived in England, Holland and the states of Germany to transform their economies, while crippling that of France. Merchant banking moved from Paris, and the 'City of London' was born. The rise of Britain and Prussia at the expense of France can be directly attributed to Louis' fatal miscalculation.

It affected military decisions too. The problems with Northern Ireland are still with us today because Catholic King James was defeated at the Battle of the Boyne in 1690 by an army of the Dutch King William, immeasurably strengthened by a thousand French Huguenot officers, commanded by a

The luxury of Versailles was to contrast with the wrecked economy of France.

'One of the greatest disasters that ever afflicted France'

Huguenot, Marshal Schomberg. Worse was to follow for France herself. Louis accepted the throne of Spain on behalf of his grandson. In the war that followed, his once victorious armies were to suffer defeat after defeat, culminating in the battle of Blenheim. By the end of that war, France actually faced starvation. The strange thing was, that just fifty years before, Philip II of Spain had made an identical error in expelling his 'Moriscos', and with just the same ruinous result.

Louis XIV was the longest ruler in Europe. Known as the 'Sun King', he created the magnificence of Versailles and had once taken France to a summit of splendour. But the extravagance of the monarchy was combined with economic and military weakness created by the flight of the Huguenots, and would ultimately doom France to decline, and eventually to revolution; a high price for being jealous of your neighbour and removing 'heresy.'

Goering & the stolen heads

Hermann Goering could have died in many ways. Perhaps in air combat during the First World War, leading Richtofen's fighter squadron. Maybe in the failed beer hall putsch in Munich in 1923 alongside Hitler, when seriously wounded by police gunfire. Or, when hugely fat, of overindulgence in food, drink and drugs. Perhaps in an Allied air raid. Or even, as it finally happened, in a Nuremberg cell awaiting trial for war crimes, killed by his own suicide pill in 1945.

But who could have imagined that he might have been assassinated by an English eccentric, furious with the Reichsmarschall for stealing some big game trophies? And, surprisingly how

that would have been a dreadful banana skin for his enemies.

To a casual outsider, Goering appeared the most attractive of the Nazis. Handsome and dashing, he had indeed been a fighter ace with 22 victories, winning Germany's equivalent of the Victoria Cross, the *Pour le Mérite* or 'Blue Max.' As a war hero, he had been a wonderful recruit for Adolf Hitler's tiny Nazi party, and had faithfully followed Hitler into the ill-fated Munich putsch, his bullet wound causing his later drug addiction and his obesity. When the Nazis came closer to power, he appeared to be the respectable, bluff and jovial one, but, in fact, was just as ruthless. It was he that exploited or, some say, organised the Reichstag fire that gave Hitler dictatorial power and consolidated it with both the Gestapo, Germany's feared secret police, and the first concentration camps.

But the seeds of his decline had been sown. As Hitler's right-hand man, he built up Germany's air force from nothing, but it had disorganised leadership and weak technical support. In his ever more grandiose uniforms, which he changed five times a day, he gradually became a faintly ridiculous and out of touch figure, ignoring the work on the details required for modern airpower. Indulging his hobbies, he also made himself Reichsminister for Hunting. A passionate hunter himself, he decorated Karinhall and Emmyhall, his East Prussian homes, with stags' heads and big game trophies.

And that is where John Guille Millais comes in. The son of the great Pre-Raphaelite artist, he himself was an intrepid explorer, a leading naturalist and well-known big game hunter. At the International Big Game Exhibition in Berlin, his heads and trophies had won twelve Gold Medals. But Goering had purloined six of them for himself, a bizarre act of envy and greed. So, in a fury, Millais packed his favourite Mannlicher-Schönauer .275, and set off to shoot the greedy and bulky Nazi, an easy enough target for such an excellent shot with a classic Austrian hunting rifle. Unluckily for him, but luckily for the world, Millais suddenly died of peritonitis on the train.

The world was indeed lucky, because Goering was to prove the most incompetent leader of his airforce. If he had been replaced by someone more intelligent and efficient, history might have been very different.

He was not only vainglorious, but arrogantly ran the Luftwaffe as his personal fiefdom, constantly ignoring bad news or good advice. His errors of judgement were catastrophic. In 1937 he cancelled the advanced plans for the 'Uralbomber', a fast long distance strategic bomber that could have ravaged all of Britain and much of Russia. Then, in 1939, he slowed the development of vital experimental aircraft. Germany's lead in jets and rockets was fatally postponed. At Dunkirk, he insisted, 'This is a special job for the

'The Few' began to outnumber Goering's fighters.

'If a bomb ever falls on Germany, you can call me Meyer!'

Luftwaffe'. So the panzers were halted for three days, and his planes tried to do their worst. But 338,000 trapped British and French troops duly escaped to fight another day. During the Battle of Britain, he under-estimated the British radar stations, and then cut his aircraft production so that the fighters of 'The Few' of the RAF actually began to outnumber his Luftwaffe's fighters. He even allowed Hitler, in a fit of pique, to turn at the critical moment from the battered RAF stations to bomb London. The battle was lost for Germany. His frivolous, overconfident words, 'If a bomb ever falls on Germany, you can call me Meyer', were to haunt him, as Germany was soon battered day and night from the air.

His mistakes continued as he tried to regain his lost prestige and Hitler's favour. He boasted that his weakened Luftwaffe could supply the 270,000 encircled, starving, freezing troops at Stalingrad. It was bound to fail. And even as Stalingrad's pathetic survivors were being marched East by the Russians, Goering was out hunting as usual, and receiving, on his birthday, a 2,400 piece Sevres china dinner set , enough for 150 close friends.

When finally given a winner, the superb Me 262 jet, the world's fastest interceptor fighter, he allowed his Führer to make it into a useless bomber. For all his bombast, he was a weak man. 'I always make up my mind to tell Hitler things, but the minute I enter his office my courage deserts me.'

Once the 'Iron Knight' of Nazi Germany, he retreated to Karinhall, dressed in bizarre, effeminate clothing and playing with his model railway, while his faithful Luftwaffe, short of planes, pilots and fuel, fought to the death. When the Russians approached Karinhall, trainloads of looted paintings and priceless treasures were sent south. Goering was captured and condemned at Nuremberg for war crimes, but died by his own hand two hours before he could face the gallows.

All in all, he had done a splendid job, in a succession of banana skins, to destroy his own country. Thank goodness Millais never reached him.

pride & overconfidence

‘ *Pride goeth before destruction, and an haughty spirit before a fall.* ’
Proverb

‘ *Pride, the never ending vice of fools* ’
Alexander Pope

Marie Antoinette & the people's cake

'Empty headed, she thinks only of having fun.'

'The people have no bread? Why, let them eat cake!' This insensitive remark about a starving populace seems at first glance to be the ultimate banana skin from a rich, spoiled, pretty young Queen living in the magnificent royal palace at Versailles. However, there is no evidence that Marie Antoinette ever uttered the words. Indeed, they have been attributed to others years before she was born. In fact, before she even arrived in Paris, Jean-Jacques Rousseau had quoted another princess using the words back in 1740. The problem for Marie Antoinette was that, by 1789, she had created so many other banana skins for herself that the French people expected her to say cruel and stupid things, and it was easy for radical agitators to pin the fatal words on to her.

Marie Antoinette was bound to be out of touch with the realities of ordinary French life. She was the daughter of the Holy Roman Emperor Francis I and the Empress Marie Theresa, who made the ruthless political decision to send her, aged just fourteen, to be married to the French heir to the throne, the Dauphin, binding together the two nations of Austria and France.

At Versailles she was shocked by what she found, and her first slip was to quarrel with Madame du Barry, King Louis XV's official mistress, whom she described as 'the stupidest and most impertinent of creatures'. But Madame du Barry effectively ran the huge and lavish Versailles Court with its 10,000 courtiers, so Marie Antoinette had to back down. But the damage was done. Casually spurning most conventions and codes, she also laughed at many of the elderly, further alienating whole sections of the Court ('why should I care for embittered, vindictive old maids?')

Nor was her marriage a great success, in that the future King Louis XVI was sexually awkward and did not even consummate the marriage for seven years. Thus it was hardly surprising that the maturing but flighty girl would create 'favourites' of attractive young nobles at court – the Comte d'Artois, the Duc de Lauzon and, above all, the handsome Swedish Count Axel Fersen. So scandal was never far away.

When her husband became Louis XVI, things did not improve. He devoted most of his time to work or to hunting, and Marie Antoinette surrounded herself with a dissolute clique of women devoted to flirting and gambling, who not only demanded privileges for their friends and families but encouraged huge extravagance – with lavish hairstyles by the hairdresser Léonard, topped with the luxuriant hats of Mme. Bertin.

The young Queen was convinced she was popular, but her mother in Vienna was more realistic and constantly worried. 'My daughter's fate can only be completely great or very unhappy. I count her halcyon days as over.'

Her brother, Emperor Joseph II, came to Paris to see for himself, and he then visited and saw more of the city in weeks than Louis and Marie Antoinette were to do in a lifetime. He was caustic about his sister, writing to their anxious mother, *'She is empty headed and driven to run all day from dissipation to dissipation. She thinks only of having fun.'* He was equally scathing to his sister's face and in his admonishing letters.

When at last the King's fumblings led to motherhood, Marie Antoinette's popularity briefly rose. But it was always to be fragile. Although she never normally bothered to interfere with politics, a brief war between Prussia and Austria led to her trying to get France to intercede. Suddenly the scatterbrained spendthrift had become *'L'Autrichienne'* ('The Austrian woman'), with a hint of

Marie Antoinette on her arrival at Versailles

treason towards France.

The French people, faced by poverty, and sometimes, actual starvation, were viewing the Court of Versailles and its ridiculous extravagance and privileges with increasingly grim emotions. It did not matter that the Queen was innocent in such scandals as the notorious 'Diamond Necklace Affair'. Such was her reputation, she was blamed in any case.

When France was wracked by financial crises, and the King was indecisive, she interfered in the choice of ministers and thus was blamed again when things went wrong. 'Madame Deficit' became her new nickname. New bread riots led to the 'cake' rumour, which the people fully believed.

With France descending into turmoil, Marie Antoinette helped to make the situation worse, encouraging the King to bring in troops, which resulted in the people seeking arms and the fall of the Bastille. Even when the King accepted the

Revolution, wearing the blue, red and white cockade, his wife did not understand the need for change and Versailles continued as before.

Finally, the country lost patience and removed the Royal Family to the Tuileries inside Paris, whence they then belatedly planned to escape, however not in the two fast carriages that the ever faithful Axel Fersen had recommended but, at Marie Antoinette's insistence, in a big lumbering 'Berlin'. And when they did escape undetected, they dawdled along and were promptly recaptured and brought back to Paris by a now enraged mob. Negotiations with the Assembly continued, but foreign armies, including that of Austria, threatened France. Marie Antoinette, *L'Autrichienne,* increasingly

Impossible to list the follies of this frivolous Princess, or to detect a sensible decision

appeared in a treasonous and counter-revolutionary light. Once again, she made a fatal mistake, refusing General Lafayette's protection in another chance to escape.

And so it was that first Louis and then Marie Antoinette faced with dignity their trials for treason, and then the horror of death by the guillotine.

It is almost impossible to list the innumerable slips and acts of folly committed by this frivolous princess, who was so completely and tragically unprepared for her life and fate.

It is equally difficult to detect a single, sensible decision. However, among all the banana skins, there were no cakes.

Nelson & the French sniper

If you visit the beautifully restored HMS *Victory* in Portsmouth, you will see a plaque set into the deck marking the exact spot where Nelson was struck down, mortally wounded. His was an unnecessary death and, for that matter, as historians point out, Trafalgar was an unnecessary battle.

It is true that of all the foreign invasion threats, including that of the Spanish Armada, (beaten by Drake and

the weather in 1588), and of Hitler, (beaten by the Battle of Britain in 1940), the planned invasion by Napoleon was probably the most dangerous and likely to succeed, although the French Emperor was always to be hampered by his lack of knowledge about the realities of sea power. 'The Channel is a mere ditch, and will be crossed as soon as someone has the courage to attempt it.'

His French Admiral, Villeneuve, had

RICHARD GRENVILLE

received the stern order, *'Come to the Channel. Bring our united fleet and England is ours. If you are only here for 24 hours, all will be over and six centuries of shame and insult will be avenged.'* British Admiral Jervis confidently and drily commented 'I do not say they cannot come, I only say they cannot come by sea.'

As a feint, Napoleon ordered Villeneuve to sail to the West Indies, to where he was pursued by Nelson. At a skirmish off Finisterre, Villeneuve lost his nerve and turned south, thus failing to fulfill his Emperor's orders to join the French navy at Brest. Instead, he joined a Spanish navy even more ramshackle and ill-trained than his own. He also knew that he was about to be replaced by Admiral Rosily. What is more, a frustrated Napoleon had already struck camp to march across Europe to conduct the brilliant Austerlitz campaign against the Russians and Austrians. The whole logic for a battle was therefore removed, but Napoleon petulantly ordered a now humiliated Villeneuve to attack anyway. The scene was now set for one of the

HMS Victory bravely enters her own trap.

most decisive events in history.

Villeneuve's formidable adversary, Admiral Horatio Nelson, was already a legend. In a long and brilliant naval career, he had lost an eye before his victory at Cape St Vincent and later his right arm. Off Copenhagen, he had ignored his vacillating superior's signals by famously holding his telescope to his missing eye. He had conducted an open and scandalous affair with Emma, the wife of Sir William Hamilton (albeit with her husband's acquiescence) and had a daughter by her, Horatia. Nobody would ever accuse Nelson of lack of courage, but perhaps of rashness.

The problem for Napoleon's 2,000 ships was that they had been blockaded in their ports for years by the Royal Navy which constantly patrolled, with nothing to do but watch and endlessly polish its superiority in seamanship and gunnery. However, the most efficient French Captain, the tiny Jean Jacques Etienne, Lucas was determined that his ship, the *Redoubtable*, would at least be superlatively trained in the one skill they *could* practice – musketry. His 40 selected marksmen were also taught the age-old maxim of any sniper. It is much more effective to kill an officer, and preferably a senior one, rather than an ordinary soldier or seaman.

In a light breeze, on 20 October 1805 the two great fleets approached each other at walking pace, so there was plenty of time, six hours, to prepare – and to worry. On the *Victory*, Nelson stood with his staff, including Dr William Beatty, the surgeon, who quietly expressed his unease that the four shiny stars embroidered on the Admiral's uniform would mark him as an obvious target when they were within range of rifle fire, and that he should change into a plain coat. 'Take care, Doctor, what you are about,' warned the Admiral's secretary. 'I would not be the man to mention such a matter to him.' Beatty tried but failed to do so, hovering near the Admiral, awaiting a chance to bring the subject up.

Eventually, it was the *Victory's* Captain, Thomas Hardy, who raised the question of the coat, suggesting that the decorations might catch the eye of a sniper. Nelson replied, 'I am aware it may be seen, but it is now too late to be shifting a coat.'

It was to be a brave, foolish and fatal slip. In fact, at 11 o'clock, Nelson did take the time to go below. He prayed and wrote letters and his diary for an hour. There, he could easily have changed his coat in seconds.

'It is now too late to be shifting a coat.'

An hour later, the *Victory* cut straight into the French line and was soon locked by collapsed spars and lines in a murderous embrace with Villeneuve's own flagship, the *Redoubtable*, whose crew was about to board her. This is when Captain Lucas's training came into its own. As he later reported: *'Then a heavy fire of musketry opened, in which Admiral Nelson fought at the head of his crew. Our firing, though, became so rapid, and was so much superior to his, that in less than a quarter of an hour we had silenced that of the* Victory *altogether. More than two hundred grenades were flung on board her, with the utmost success, her decks were strewn with the dead and wounded. Admiral Nelson was killed by the firing of our musketry. Immediately after this, the upper deck of the* Victory *became deserted, and she again ceased firing, but it proved difficult to board her because of the motion of the two vessels.'*

The *Victory* was saved by the sudden and welcome appearance of the British *Temeraire*, but Nelson, shot from high in the rigging by one of Lucas's well-trained snipers, was doomed. He was rushed below decks to the surgeon. 'Ah, Mr Beatty you can do nothing for me. I have a short time to live; my back is shot through.' After hours of long agony, Nelson was visited by Captain Hardy,

'We have got twelve or fourteen of the enemy's ships in our possession.' 'I hope none of our ships have struck?' asked Nelson. 'No, my Lord, there is no fear of that.' Later Hardy returned to report. After his last orders, Nelson said, 'Kiss me Hardy.' After the Captain had kissed his cheek, Nelson sighed, 'Now I am satisfied. Thank God I have done my duty.' Two hours later he was dead, one of Britain's great and tragic heroes.

Lucas had finally struck his colours and surrendered, and British and French sailors then struggled manfully together to save the brave *Redoubtable*, but she finally sank, shot to pieces and having sustained the worst casualties of the battle, with no less than 490 killed and 81 wounded out of 634 men.

Contrary to myth, Trafalgar did not stop an invasion of Britain, because Napoleon was already 800 miles away, winning his finest victory at Austerlitz. But it did give Britain complete command of the sea. She could now land her troops with impunity in Portugal and Spain, led by Napoleon's eventual nemesis on land, the Duke of Wellington. Indeed, Nelson's heroic but unnecessary death led directly to Waterloo. Even more important, the battle led to a century of naval dominance and the growth of the British Empire.

Nelson died a heroic but pointless death.

Jonathan Aitken & the Ritz bill

'Pride was the root cause of my evils' admitted Jonathan Aitken after years of crisis, disgrace and despair.

There was a time when he appeared to have everything. He was charming and good looking, the son of a Battle of Britain Spitfire pilot and Conservative MP, and the great nephew of the newspaper baron, Lord Beaverbrook. Educated at Eton and Oxford, he had written a book called *The Young Meteors*, which somewhat optimistically included the author among the young people predicted for greatness, and which certainly was meant to include Jonathan. When he became a Tory MP, the media described him as 'debonair' and 'swashbuckling.'

Such a 'tall poppy' was bound to make enemies as his career advanced. One, for a while, was Margaret Thatcher, after the young Aitken had turned down her daughter; 'he made Carol cry.' This helped to ensure he stayed for eighteen years on the back benches. But with John Major as Prime Minister, Jonathan became Minister of State for Defence in 1992 and two years later joined the Cabinet as Chief Secretary to the Treasury, controlling £300 billion of government expenditure and joining the Privy Council.

One of his undoubted advantages to both the Government and to Britain was his friendly relations with the Arab world. This resulted in two valuable interventions. One saved a huge contract with Kuwait for Warrior armoured personnel carriers and involved forceful persuasion by ex-Premier Margaret Thatcher, now friendly again with Jonathan. The second was to use John Major to fly to Saudi Arabia and to negotiate patiently for hours with King Fahd, thus rescuing a £4 billion sale of Tornado aircraft and saving 100,000 British jobs.

The Labour MP, Roy Hattersley, writing in the *Mail on Sunday*, predicted that Aitken was the most likely to succeed John Major, labelling him *'as the only Cabinet Minister who hasn't a single enemy.'* Not quite true. First, Michael Heseltine, the man who had brought down Thatcher, and a pretender for the throne, became an instant enemy. Much more serious, that very day a plot was being secretly hatched to 'bring Aitken down.' David Leigh, working for *Granada* and later *The Guardian*, wrote his Editor a memo accusing Aitken of *'pimping for the Saudis, taking commission on arms deals, and having stayed at the Ritz Paris, to take instructions from his paymaster, the Saudi heir, Prince Mohammed bin Fahd.'* In fact, a rather strange alliance had been forged between *The Guardian* and Mohammed al Fayed, the controversial owner of Harrods. When Fayed's application for British citizenship had been turned down, he had threatened John Major that he would bring down four Tory ministers, including Aitken. He asserted that Aitken 'owned two brothels for the use of Arabs,' had 'split millions of arms deals commissions with Mark Thatcher in the Ritz Paris and taken it away in cash', and 'had allowed his bill to be paid by another notorious arms dealer.' John Major regarded all this as blackmail and even informed the Crown Prosecution Service. Fayed's attitude was that the Government 'have shat on me' and was about to return the compliment.

The Guardian, who had in the past lambasted Fayed for his lies, now had its own reasons to attack Aitken. At a Commonwealth Press Association lunch he castigated *The Guardian* for its article TORIES FACE SAUDI'S CASH CLAIM, which accused Prince Bandar of having given £7 million to the Conservative Party in 1992. Unfortunately, the Chairman of *The Guardian* was hosting a large table and his group was humiliated by Jonathan's scathing attack and shocked to hear in public that Prince Bandar's writ was waiting for them back at their offices. (The paper later published an apology for its false report, and paid money to a charity named by the Prince.)

However, *The Guardian* now decided to go for Aitken, and with the help of Fayed. The results of this deadly alliance burst on to *The Guardian's* front page on April 10 1995 when Jonathan was in Switzerland. AITKEN TRIED TO ARRANGE GIRLS FOR SAUDI FRIENDS Inside was a further shock: AITKEN CONNECTIONS TO SECOND ARMS DEALER.

That night *Granada* aired 'Jonathan of Arabia' with Aitken portrayed ridiculously riding a camel in Bedouin robes covering a Savile Row suit, but with the serious accusations of repeating the brothel story and implying that he was the paid servant of Prince Mohammed

Left: the scene of Jonathan Aitken's downfall, the Ritz Hotel in Paris

'who had made Aitken extremely rich.' Aitken ('my blood boiling') then went way too far. He flew into London and decided to sue *The Guardian* and later *Granada* for libel, and did so very theatricall, with a famous, or infamous, speech which ended:

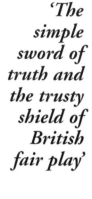

'The simple sword of truth and the trusty shield of British fair play'

'… If it falls to me to start a fight to cut out the cancer of bent and twisted journalism in our country with the simple sword of truth and the trusty shield of British fair play, so be it. I am ready for the fight. The fight against falsehood and those who pedal it.'

This speech made him, of course, no extra friends in the media, especially on the left. One *Daily Mirror* reporter tried to get information, saying 'We are out to bring Aitken down. If you give me a story, we'll give you £30,000.'

Jonathan Aitken faces a media frenzy

The legal and media pressure grew, and Aitken decided to resign from the Cabinet, realising he was 'damaged goods.' John Major was very kind, saying that among resignations 'None was so sad or unfair as yours.'

As preparations for the trial gathered pace, Aitken was certain that he would win on the serious charges of 'pimping, arms dealing and being in the pocket of Prince Mohammed.' But he had a small problem. The reason he had gone to the Ritz was because Prince Mohammed, on holiday in Paris, was according to Said Ayas his aide, 'keen to see his friend.' So Aitken checked into the Ritz (owned by Al Fayed). He was then rather put out to be told that the Prince had been called to a family event, so after killing time for 24 hours he left for Geneva. Said Ayas, perhaps rather embarrassed by Jonathan's wasted trip, offered, 'I'll take care of your bill.'

'Thanks', was Jonathan's unthinking and fatal response. Ayas, in line with Arab hospitality, had often paid his bills, but that was *before* Aitken was a Minister.

The Guardian was now on its implacable course. Tipped off by Fayed that Aitken had been in his hotel, *The Guardian* now forged a fax 'from Aitken's office' asking for a copy of the bill, which had a tell-tale note attached. 'Debiture a/c Mr Ayas.' They wrote asking Aitken about the bill. He now made his biggest mistake. Encouraged by Ayas (who had Saudi reasons for not wanting to have appeared to have paid the bill). Aitken, 'in a act of consummate folly' claimed that his wife Lolicia had paid it. He even got his daughter to sign a supporting statement.

When the trial started, Aitken appeared to be winning on all fronts. *The Guardian* legal team began to retract steadily from the main and serious allegations against Aitken. But just as things were going really well, a startling new piece of evidence arrived. British Airways ticket records unearthed by *The Guardian* proved that Lolicia had never been to Paris. On the comparatively tiny matter of who paid the bill, the whole serious and winnable libel case collapsed and all hell broke lose. Faced by paying the costs of *both* sides, Jonathan, in reality far from rich, went bankrupt.

To add to his downfall and disgrace, he was later to plead guilty to 'perjury and perverting the course of justice,' and was sentenced to 18 months in prison, serving seven. Most of his fellow prisoners were bemused by his sentence. Not only would they themselves expect to commit perjury routinely when pleading 'not guilty' but also one blurted out, 'they'd have to build gaols from here to Newcastle for all the coppers who should be banged up for perjury!'

Jonathan has rebuilt his life, taking a renewed interest in spirituality. But he has always regretted not paying that hotel bill himself.

Al Capone & his income tax

Al Capone was probably the most brutal and notorious gangster of all time. The young Alphonse had grown up as a vicious thief and enforcer in New York's dreadful Five Points district, earning the nickname 'Scarface'. In 1919, he moved to Chicago to join his mentor, the dapper and clever Johnny Torrio, to help him run the sprawling prostitution and gambling empire of 'Big Jim' Colisimo, Torrio's uncle.

Forced through Congress by a powerful temperance lobby, the Volstead Act had just been passed, prohibiting 'the sale or distribution of alchoholic drink'. Torrio saw the opportunity created by Prohibition, but Colisimo expressed himself reluctant to benefit from bootlegging. So Torrio used Al Capone to murder 'Big Jim', and then to help him to build up the vicious gangs that soon dominated the huge illegal liquor business. Thus Capone began the career that would make him notorious, openly fighting rival gangs for control, and often using hundreds of 'Chicago pianos' – devastating war surplus Thompson sub-machine guns.

'Have you gotten rid of that fellow Capone yet?'

In hindsight, it was unfortunate for the citizens of Chicago that he survived the 'Bootleg Battle of the Marne', when an amazing cavalcade of cars full of rival O'Bannion/Weiss gang members drove slowly past his Hawthorne Inn headquarters, riddling it with 5,000 bullets.

In spite of the general unpopularity of Prohibition, such blatant public shootings became a national scandal, culminating in the famous 'St Valentine's Day Massacre' when Capone, from his holiday home in Florida, organised the brutal shooting of seven men working for his rival, 'Bugs' Moran.

Enough was enough. President Herbert Hoover began to pester his colleagues: 'Have you gotten rid of that fellow Capone yet?' Secretary to the Treasury Andrew Mellon took on the task. However, in the end it was financial slip-ups that brought down Capone.

Living a blatantly opulent lifestyle and earning millions a year, an overconfident Capone had neglected to pay any income tax at all. It was to be a fatal slip. While Eliot Ness and his 'Untouchables' began to smash Capone's breweries and destroy his distribution, IRS agent Elmer Irey patiently built up the tax-evasion evidence. At first, Capone did not take this seriously. Then, too late, he offered to pay $400,000.

Even when faced with court, he was extremely confident, but then he had bribed every single member of the jury to acquit him. However, Judge Wilkerson quickly took the smile off his face when he started the trial by announcing, 'Judge Edwards has another trial commencing today. Go to his courtroom and bring me the entire panel of jurors. Take my panel to him'. An ashen-faced Capone was finally floored.

Alcatraz, Capone's involuntary home for seven years

Capone was sentenced to eleven years, much of it served in the famous prison on the Rock of Alcatraz. There, after seven years, he fell over in the canteen – a result of syphilis, contracted from prostitutes years before. Released, he lived out his final years in Florida, barking out meaningless orders to his patient companions. 'Nutty as a fruitcake' commented his long-term accountant, Jake 'Greasy Thumb' Guzik, famous for his pay-offs and corruption.

Perhaps Guzic should have done some more conventional accounting for his boss.

Lord Mountbatten & Dieppe

He was young and glamorous with the looks of a film star, a rich and royal cousin of the King, and as a dashing destroyer Captain, a hero. Just what Winston Churchill needed after a string of military reverses. He therefore promoted Lord Louis Mountbatten three grades, and made him 'Chief of Combined Operations.'

'Dickie' Mountbatten was very ambitious and keen to prove himself. He was, after all, the son of the First Sea Lord who had been forced in 1914 by public opinion to step down and to change his name from the German-sounding Battenberg. Initial combined operations successes like the successful raid on Bruneval to capture Germany's radar secrets were not enough for him. Mountbatten needed something bigger. So in 1942 'Operation Rutter', the raid on Dieppe, was conceived. It had three

The handsome
Lord Louis
Mountbatten

theoretical goals: to see if a port could be held for a short period, to obtain intelligence, and to gauge German reaction. Unofficial aims, however, were to bolster Churchill's weak position, to draw up the Luftwaffe and hit it hard, and to give the highly trained and bored Canadians something useful to do.

In May 1942, the Chiefs of Staff approved 'Rutter', although the Army and the Navy chiefs remained uneasy. On 7th July, because of bad weather, the raid was cancelled and the seasick troops returned to southern England. Everyone was convinced that Dieppe was off, forever. There was, from top to bottom, a sigh of relief.

According to a masterful book, *Military Intelligence Blunders,* by Colonel John Hughes Williams, Mountbatten then did something very strange. With a small staff, he furtively reinstated the Dieppe operation under the new code-name 'Jubilee', and kept its planning secret from the Chiefs of Staff. As he said on television in 1972, 'I made the unusual and, I suggest, rather bold

decision that we would remount the operation against Dieppe.' It was unusual to say the least. At two meetings, the Chiefs had turned down the idea. But the plans proceeded in secret, which meant that the normal up-to-date intelligence information could not be requested, nor was the raid cleared with the Inter Service Security Board.

Thus, on 19 August 1942, the raid went in, only to turn into a murderous fiasco. The allied ships blundered into a German coastal convoy, and the resulting 'firework display' fully alerted the defenders of Dieppe. The Canadians were shot to pieces by the hidden guns and machine-guns on their flanks, while 27 Churchill tanks scrabbled helplessly on the huge pebbles of the beach. Only 15 reached the esplanade, and then became stuck in front of the prepared tank traps – all of which intelligence would have revealed.

The French-Canadian reserve arrived to enter a 'blizzard of firing.' Of 600 of them, only 125 made it back to England. Even the Royal Air Force failed in its objectives, losing 112 fighters to the Luftwaffe's 44, its single worst defeat.

Field Marshal Sir Alan Brooke was away in Moscow with Churchill. General Nye, his deputy, and as the Vice Chief of the Imperial General Staff, the most senior officer in Britain, was furious that he knew absolutely nothing of the attack until the signals started streaming in on that very morning.

Mountbatten's raid had involved almost exclusively Canadian troops. It lasted just a few hours and left 2,700 killed, wounded or captured. As 4,000 landed, this meant a casualty rate higher than the Battle of the Somme.

There was an immediate cover-up, but Churchill's explanation in the House of Commons did not ring true. 'Dieppe was a reconnaissance in force – to which I gave my sanction'. Indeed, most would have been more likely to agree with the German defenders' battle report, *'This affair mocked all rules of military strategy and logic.'* Canadian opinion was, understandably, rather more bitter and personal.

Mountbatten got away with it, but many would never trust him again. The words 'Tricky Dickie' were applied to him years before anyone had heard of Richard Nixon.

He was always very defensive about his Dieppe banana skin, but nevertheless went on to be a 'British hero', a mentor to his great-nephew Prince Charles, and in spite of his flaws, considered a great man. And he certainly did not deserve to be murdered in old age by the IRA.

> *'This affair mocked all rules of miltary logic.'*

Volkswagen & the British car industry

With a great fanfare, Adolf Hitler launched his 'people's car,' or Volkswagen, in 1936. Designed by Ferdinand Porsche, it had an unusual rounded shape that soon earned it the affectionate name *Käfer* or Beetle, and was simple, cheap and practical with a rear-mounted, flat-four engine.

Soon 336,000 Germans eagerly paid for stamps in a *Kraft durch Freude* (Strength through joy) savings scheme for the cars to be produced at a new town called KdFStadt. However, only a handful of German civilians ever received their promised cars. War intervened and the giant factory was needed for its military version, the *Kübelwagen*, Germany's Jeep, and the amphibious *Schwimmwagen*.

With Germany beaten, in 1945 the Allies pondered what to do with the huge Volkswagenwerk, now in the British Zone of occupation. One Allied plan envisaged that only 20,000 cars should be produced each year in Germany, and all by Ford in Cologne. So initially

Hirst painted one VW green, and sold 20,000 to the British Army.

> **'If you think you are going to build cars in this place, you're a bloody fool, young man.'**

Volkswagen was destined to be broken up and its machine tools sold off for reparations. But many experts argued for the plant to be taken over by the British motor industry. The trouble was that with 3.5 million square feet, it was three times larger than any British factory. But that did not deter the voices who pushed for Volkswagen to become British-owned,

'…the Volkswagen is the most advanced and the most interesting car for quantity production. Both the car and the factory in which it is produced are wonderful achievements in their respective spheres.'

An organisational genius, Major Ivan Hirst, was put in charge of the factory, now renamed Wolfsburg after a nearby castle. By painting one car in military green, he cleverly persuaded the British

Army to start buying Volkswagens, and soon they ordered 20,000. However, Sir William Rootes, Chairman of Britain's Society of Manufacturers and Traders (SMMT), was initially very disparaging. 'It's quite unattractive to the average motor car buyer,' adding to Hirst, 'If you think you are going to build cars in this place, you're a bloody fool, young man.'

Nevertheless, the Control Commission sent three rather well-used vehicles, with engines, parts and drawings to Britain for evaluation and with the strong recommendation: *'The Volkswagen would appear to offer, with perhaps a few modifications, a possible solution of the cheap utility vehicle which would be acceptable to Britain and in overseas markets.'*

However, banana skins were lurking. Some members of the assessment team recognised it favourably, 'as an extremely cheap car, exceptionally good and very popular with military personnel.' They were right. In barter agreements in Germany, one Volkswagen could be swapped for 150 tons of cement or 200,000 bricks. But a disastrous form of British engineering snobbery and arrogance intervened. Ford of Britain was very negative and assessed the car as 'noisy' and 'uncomfortable.' The team from Humber, in spite of their own Chairman Sir William Rootes having a slight change of heart, was even more sniffy: *'The engine was, in certain details, most inefficient. It is very doubtful whether it was even capable of giving reliable service had it produced a performance commensurate with its size. We do not consider that the design represents any special brilliance, apart from certain of the detail points, and it is not to be regarded as an example of first class modern design to be copied by the British industry.'*

Faced by such lack of enthusiasm, it was in vain that the Control Commission's Colonel Boas spoke passionately to a meeting of the S.M.M.T., 'I have an intimate knowledge of this car and factory, and came to the conclusion that it was a first-class car and a novel piece of engineering. Its simple design lends itself to mass production and a small number of machine operations. The pre-war plan for the saloon car was 130-man hours. This figure has never been approached by any English car manufacturers. I consider that the acquisition of the complete plant for this country would be a splendid investment and would not only satisfy a low price demand of the domestic motor car, but be an extremely attractive proposition for overseas markets. Lastly,

it would form the nucleus of a national or semi-national motor industry in England.'

The answer to this excellent piece of perspicacity was very sad. *'British designers have nothing to learn in this branch of the industry.'* A disastrous slip of judgement indeed.

Other countries were interested, France, the United States, Australia and Brazil (which would one day have a huge Volkswagen plant.) As one onlooker remarked, 'Everyone seems interested in Volkswagen except the British.'

While the British decided not to acquire Volkswagen, with the limited objective of stopping rival countries obtaining it, they then ran it as a going concern. And, with its novel design and cheapness, the Beetle spread its wings. By 1948, Volkswagen workers earned 17% more than other German manufacturing workers. Exports were climbing and plants to assemble part-built cars were set up in Ireland and Brazil.

For a while, complacency reigned. The Board of Trade calmly reported, 'It is doubtful if German production and marketing would be such as seriously to challenge our strong position in most markets.' And the Control Commission in February 1949 went as far as to state:

'German exporters can never be expected to compete seriously with the United Kingdom.'

'In certain manufacturing industries, including motor vehicles, German exporters can never be expected to compete seriously with the United Kingdom. In this connection, motor vehicles (except possibly some special types) should be mentioned.'

Only when it was too late did the British car industry wake up to the danger, complaining that its best markets 'were being unfairly attacked by our former enemy now operating under British and American approval.' It had only itself to blame.

Volkswagen was handed over in 1949 to a trust controlled by the German government. Just five years later, the millionth Beetle (or *Bug, Coccinelle, Käfer, Fusca* etc) rolled off the line. And by 1972, it overtook the Ford Model T when it hit 16 million sales. Finally, it achieved over 21 million in 2000. Today its shape has been revived and sales are booming again.

In stark contrast, Britain's car industry has shrunk beyond recognition, with most firms gone or taken over by foreigners (including Rootes, now part of Daimler Chrysler).

Almost unbelievably, Volkswagen, the little car and the big factory spurned by the British, now owns Audi, NSU, SEAT, Skoda, Bugatti, Lamborghini and even quintessentially British Bentley.

This must be the greatest missed opportunity in automotive history.

What the British missed. Volkswagen owns these brands.

Leona Helmsley & the 'Little People'

Donald Trump, the billionaire property tycoon, was more than blunt in his opinion: 'She is a horrible, horrible human being'. He was referring to Leona Helmsley. And thousands, maybe millions, of people agree with him.

Lena Rosenthal was born to very poor Polish parents in New York in 1920 and after toying with several names, she settled on Leona. A striking and attractive woman, after two marriages she found herself aged 42 with no job, no money, no college education and a grown son to feed. She turned to real estate for which her brand of brash salesmanship excelled. At a property ball, she engineered that she should meet the fabulously rich Harry Helmsley, the 'King of real estate'. Within minutes, 'he

'We don't
pay taxes.
Only the
little
people
pay
taxes.'

was leading Leona smoothly and gracefully across the dance floor in a perfect waltz'. Within weeks she was a Senior Vice-President and Harry's lover. Soon they were married, Leona having gone literally from 'rags to riches' in just ten years.

It was Harry's dream hotel, the Helmsley Palace, which propelled Leona to fame or notoriety. Having been put in charge by her doting husband, Leona dominated the hotel and appeared in nationwide advertisements trumpeting headlines like *'The only Palace where the Queen stands guard.'* But the dark side of her personality emerged. A fanatic for detail, she treated the staff of the Helmsley Palace and their other hotels appallingly. She fired people, screamed obscenities and reduced grown men and

women to jelly. Soon dubbed 'The Queen of Mean', she did not even seem to care.

But her behaviour finally brought her down. She treated the contractors on their magnificent new house, Dunnellen Hall, just as badly, who, exasperated, mailed a parcel of invoices to the *New York Post*. This revealed that, by pretending the work was on Helmsley commercial properties, the Helmsleys had been avoiding income tax. 'We don't pay taxes. Only the little people pay taxes.' It was a remark which did not endear her to the eventual judge and jury, who sentenced her to 18 months in jail – Harry being now too ill to stand trial.

As banana skins go, Leona's story is imperfect. Harry having died in 1997, she is still one of the richest women in the world. But after unpleasant fights with family and employees, and rivals like Donald Trump, Leona does not have the longest list of great friends. A lonely old woman, she only has her dog for company, appropriately called 'Trouble.' Perhaps he has not noticed her personality flaws.

9 ♣

Helmsley Palace

♣ 6

Michael Collins & the 'Pass of the Flowers'

Michael Collins is one of the most attractive, charismatic and tragic figures in Irish history, a complex character, and a mixture of infectious, warm enthusiasm and ice-cold calculation. He knew Britain and the British, working at financial institutions in London in 1912. And it was there that he joined the Irish Republican Brotherhood.

In May 1914, after 900 years, Ireland was at last about to be free from Great Britain. After years of negotiation, the Home Rule Bill for Ireland had passed the House of Commons. But, within weeks, the outbreak of the Great War would fatally ensure its postponement.

In January 1916, under threat of conscription into the British Army, Collins set sail for Dublin in time to join the doomed Easter Rising. Collins was one of the survivors of the battle at the General Post Office and was captured. Luckily, the British did not recognise him. He escaped the firing squads that killed, to mounting horror in Ireland, many of the leaders of the Rising. So he survived to become a most formidable enemy. Released from prison in England, he returned to Ireland to start his war.

It was the threat of extending conscription to Ireland that once again was hardening resistance against Britain, coupled with restrictions on Irish language and sports. When the Great War ended, Sinn Fein MPs, those not in English jails, set up their own Parliament, Dail Eireann. On the day of its first sitting, the first shots of the Anglo-Irish War were being fired, far away in County Tipperary.

Collins masterminded the brilliant escape of his colleague Eamon de Valera from Lincoln Jail, who decided to go to America to raise support. In his absence, Collins then began a sophisticated intelligence war, with spies in Dublin Castle, where he even had the nerve to spend the night himself sifting through the British files. He also recruited the 'Squad', hand-picked trained assassins, who began killing informers and the more brutal policemen.

1920 was a year of terror, with killings and counter-killings, and the introduction of volunteers to fight in

Ireland, dubbed the 'Black and Tans', and the more effective ex-officer 'Auxiliaries'. Murder and atrocity escalated. By the end of the year, 50,000 troops and 15,000 policemen were in conflict with 15,000 Volunteers. Michael Collins, still an unknown and invisible figure to the British, coolly cycled round Dublin and plotted his next moves. The bleakest moment of the war was 'Bloody Sunday', when Collins' 'Squad' tracked down and wiped out the newly arrived 'Cairo Gang' of British intelligence officers. The furious authorities reacted by shooting 14 dead at a football match at Croke Park stadium, with many more wounded.

De Valera returned from America, in time for the first British peace feelers and a truce. He was plainly jealous of Collins, snarling as he arrived, 'We'll see who's the Big Fella'. But when de Valera first went to London, he pointedly excluded Collins from his group of negotiators. When the real negotiations began, however, de Valera refused to go and sent Collins, trapping him into signing a Treaty that, with furious resistance from Ulster Protestant 'loyalists, was forced to partition Ireland.

Britain's Lord Birkenhead said to Collins, 'I may have signed my political death warrant tonight.' Michael Collins replied, prophetically, 'I may have signed my actual death warrant.'

De Valera duly rejected the Treaty, the Irish split and a Civil War erupted. To avoid the return of the British, Collins was even forced ask them for field guns to shell his anti-Treaty former comrades holed up in Dublin's Four Courts. The tragic Civil War lasted eleven months, and killed more Irish than the war with Britain ever had.

And so it was that as the Irish Free State's Commander in Chief, Michael Collins, was touring the fighting. He felt confident enough and at home in his native West Cork, but was ambushed by a group of IRA men at Beal na Blath, the 'pass of flowers'. Perhaps it was pure bravery. Perhaps it was overconfidence after years of outwitting danger and the British. But instinct took over and he behaved more like a Sergeant than a General, a Minister, or perhaps, a future Head of State. He grabbed a rifle and shouted 'Let's fight, boys'. And rashly standing up, away from the cover of his armoured car, he was hit, in the failing light, by a last parting shot by a former British Army marksman,

'I may have signed my actual death warrant.'

Sonny O'Neil.

His tragic and unnecessary death caused an outpouring of grief which has never been equalled in Ireland. The sense of loss was shared by friends and foes alike, Irish and British.

Had he lived, Ireland might have been a very different place than under the colder, fanatic Eamon de Valera, and her history might have been very different.

Scott of the Antarctic & his dogs

Like most Englishmen, 'Scott of the Antarctic' was fond of animals, and especially dogs. Unlike most, his kindly sentimentality for the canine breed would kill him.

At the turn of the last century, being first to reach the North and South Poles had become an obsession for explorers. Two men emerged as rivals, Scott and Amundsen, with markedly different national backgrounds and attitudes.

Robert Scott had left his English home of Devonport to join the Royal Navy aged just thirteen, having enjoyed a country childhood among pets, and notably dogs, which gave him a lifelong aversion to the suffering of animals. Eventually he was promoted to Lieutenant and a torpedo specialist. He was encouraged by Sir Clements Markham, President of the Royal Geographical Society, to explore the Antarctic, and with Ernest Shackleton, Scott duly reached 'furthest South' in

'A moral cowardice, of which I am heartily ashamed'

December 1902. During this expedition, Scott was appalled by the way that they were forced to treat their weak dogs, killing them and feeding the meat to the survivors, 'a moral cowardice of which I am heartily ashamed.'

In contrast, his future rival, Roald Amundsen had very different views. He had decided from earliest boyhood to be a polar explorer, devouring every scrap of literature on the subject. He trained physically, with constant cross-country skiing, and even slept with the windows open in the freezing Norwegian winter to get used to the cold. To please his parents, he studied medicine, but when they died, he abandoned his books, turning to become an expert ship's master and navigator. Amundsen took three years conquering the ice-filled North West Passage between Canada and the North Pole, carefully noting how the Eskimos dressed to keep warm, what they ate to keep healthy, and above all, how they drove their sleds and dog teams expertly and swiftly across the frozen wastes.

In 1909, the pace of exploration speeded up. Shackleton had only just failed to reach the South Pole, so Amundsen set his own sights on the North Pole, only to be thwarted by the news that it had apparently been reached by the American, Robert Peary (using, incidentally, 133 dogs). So, '*just as quickly as the news had sped through the cables*', Amundsen, in some secrecy, switched objectives to the South Pole, for which Scott was well advanced in his own plans. The race was on.

However, the different attitudes of the two contenders was to determine the outcome. Amundsen planned to use light sleds, pulled by carefully selected sled dogs and with the ruthless and unsentimental plan to shoot some of the dogs to feed their meat to the others. Scott

would have nothing to do with such a practice, which to him amounted to premeditated and barbaric behaviour. And, as he also wrote, '*In my mind, no journey ever made with dogs can approach the height of that fine conception which is realised when a party of men go forth to face hardships, dangers and difficulties with their own unaided efforts. Surely, in this case the conquest is more nobly and splendidly won.*' Thus, after a few miles using tractors and ponies, he would use the 'morally superior' method of making his party haul their 200lb sleds hundreds of miles by human power; the equivalent of dragging 'heavy bathtubs across the Sahara.'

The results were sadly predictable. Amundsen's five light sleds, each pulled by 13 dogs, made rapid progress, reaching the South Pole in seven weeks and returning safely with the five men and eleven remaining dogs 'hale and hearty'.

By contrast, Scott led his team to tragic failure. The laborious pull to the Pole took much longer, and ended with all the disappointment of finding Amundsen's markers planted a month earlier. Scott wrote, '*Great God, this an awful place.*' The return leg was worse. Petty Officer, Edgar Evans was the first

Scott, a dog-loving gentlemen

'Great God, this is an awful place.'

a huge food and fuel dump. Scott's journal ended, *'Had we lived, I should have had a tale to tell of the hardihood, endurance and courage of my companions which would have stirred the heart of every Englishman. R.Scott. For God's sake, look after our people.'*

'A Gallant Gentleman' by J G Dollman (Courtesy of The Cavalry and Guards Club)

to die, suffering from a fall and then a physical and mental breakdown. The remaining four struggled on, with their sleds made heavier with rock specimens, because they were 'on a scientific expedition.' Then a snowstorm struck, and that 'very gallant gentleman', Captain Lawrence Oates – now suffering now from an old war wound and feeling that he would doom the others – made a heroic gesture. He walked out into the freezing blizzard. His calm last words resonate to this day. 'I'm just going outside. I may be some time.' His bravery sadly, did not help his companions. They died only 13 days later and were later found frozen to death in their little tent, just eleven miles from

For decades Britain, which sometimes celebrates tragic failures more than successes, has revelled in the story of 'Scott of the Antarctic.' Amundsen, who succeeded brilliantly, is ignored or reviled as 'a foreign cad who somehow beat our brave British amateur boys by unsporting, professional means.' However, today's generation has begun to question the attitudes that made courageous people like Scott do things 'for King and Country', the hard way and with a stiff upper lip. It also wonders whether Scott's expedition could have been better clothed, better fed and better led.

Above all, it now questions if Robert Scott should have been a touch less British in his attitude to dogs.

Bugsy Siegel & his desert dream

Ben Siegel's attractiveness and boyish charm hid a dark history. His criminal career started as a boy in New York – in protection – setting fire to pushcarts if the owners did not pay. Then he befriended a skinny kid called Meyer Lansky, and together they created the 'Bug and Meyer Mob', involved in illegal gambling and the stealing of cars. Ben Siegel was already called 'Bugsy' for his unpredictable violence, and he had always hated the name. However, it suited him well. Lansky hired him out as a contract killer, and his mob reputation was further enhanced in April 1931 when he played a key role in the Coney Island shooting of Joe 'The Boss' Masseria, in the distinguished company of Vito Genovese, Joe Adonis, Albert Anastasia and Lucky Luciano. He then created 'Murder Inc.', a team of Jewish assassins which enforced the crime syndicate's demands, while his charm was used to win over politicians and celebrities.

By 1937, Siegel had become a bit too 'hot' for New York, and was moved to Los Angeles, successfully taking over for Lansky the Dragna brothers' wire service that linked betting shops and gambling dens, netting six million dollars a year for the Mob.

Handsome and charismatic, he had by now teamed up with an old pal, the 'gangster actor ' George Raft, himself a former bootlegger. The local social leader, Countess Dorothy di Frasso, besotted with Siegel, introduced him to the cream of Hollywood society; Clark Gable, Jean Harlow, Norma Shearer and Gary Cooper. Siegel had made his own friends too, mostly pretty actresses, in spite of a wife and two daughters.

A beautiful, green-eyed redhead then came into his life, Virginia Hill. Herself a syndicate courier and blackmailer, she became his partner – both sexual and commercial – and helped Siegel to start the heroin and opium traffic coming up from Mexico.

In 1945, Bugsy Siegel also conceived his own grand dream, 'The Flamingo', a lavish casino and hotel outside Las Vegas. This tiny town in the barren heat of the Nevada desert had the twin attractions of being two hours from Los Angeles, and one could gamble there quite legally.

Siegel obtained rather reluctant backing from Lansky and Luciano, but he was inexperienced, distracted and overworked – and the costs soared. Materials were expensive, plans were changed and trees were sold to him many times over. After one bout of frustrated fury, he reassured the contractor, 'Don't worry, Del, we only kill each other'. He was close to the truth. At a conference in Havana, a furious Lucky Luciano discovered that not only had the construction costs rocketed from one to six million dollars, but also that Virginia Hill had been flying to Switzerland to deposit huge sums. Luciano, Genovese, Adonis and Frank Costello were all for contracting Charlie Fischetti to 'hit' Siegel at once. But his old boyhood friend and mentor, Meyer Lansky, convinced that Siegel was more an incompetent dreamer than a thief, begged them to hold off and await results until after the casino's opening, the day after Christmas 1946.

Unfortunately, the opening was dogged by bad luck. Two plane-loads of Hollywood stars and celebrities were grounded by Los Angeles fog. It poured with rain at Las Vegas, and for weeks gamblers' interest was tepid. Losses mounted. With suspicions not allayed that some of the money was sitting in Swiss banks, Luciano called Siegel and demanded that $5 million be returned. A fatally overconfident Siegel told him to 'go to hell,' and added that he would pay 'in his own good time.'

Arrogance usually has its own reward. On 30 June 1947, sitting in Virginia Hill's mansion while she was conveniently away, Benny Siegel was hit through the window by three bullets from a rifle.

'The Flamingo' was taken over by Siegel's underworld colleagues, and curiously, the notoriety of his death contributed to its success. Without him Las Vegas might still be a little village in the desert, and none of us would ever have heard of it.

Yamamoto & his broken codes

America's excellence in the ancient art of breaking an enemy's code was to be the nemesis of Japan's hero, Admiral Isoroku Yamamoto. In many ways, Yamamoto of all people should have been alert to the technical skills of his foes. Well-travelled and highly intelligent, his stint as Assistant Military Attaché in Washington had taught him both to like the Americans and to admire what they could achieve – especially under pressure.

But in 1941, he found himself the reluctant architect of the surprise attack on Pearl Harbor, but with mixed feelings and severe foreboding; *'In the first six to twelve months, I will win victory after victory. But if the war continues after that, I have no expectations of success.'*

He would have been even more anxious had he realised that America's code-breakers had been able to read the final instructions to Japan's embassies even before their own embassy staffs. It was only by catastrophic collective incompetence that the garrisons of Pearl Harbor and the Philippines were not ready and waiting to ambush the Japanese.

Even after success, Yamamoto's anxiety increased, 'I fear that all we have done is to awaken a sleeping giant and fill it with a desire for vengeance.' He was right. While Japan's forces rampaged through the East, their euphoric mood was suddenly shaken by the daring raid on Tokyo in April 1942 by Jimmy Doolittle's carrier-borne bombers. Feeling vulnerable, Japan decided to extend her safety zone by invading the island of Midway. Again code-breaking intervened.

Japan's unexpectedly rapid expansion had created a crucial problem. Her new naval codebook could not be distributed fast enough to far-flung ships and bases, and its planned introduction was fatally delayed – twice. The old code had been broken by the Allies, so the Americans detected that the Japanese were to feint at the Aleutians, with the main attack at 'AF', which was probably Midway. They tricked the

His experience working there should have taught him to fear America's technical skills.

'SBD Dauntless over the Akagi' by R.G. Smith (courtesy of Timken Aerospace/ Smithsonian)

Japanese by broadcasting that Midway's water distillation plant was broken. Sure enough, two days later, intercepts heard that *'AF is short of water'*. Thus, Admiral Chester Nimitz could confidently send his three carriers to Midway to set an ambush for an unsuspecting Yamamoto.

The Battle of Midway in June 1942 was a disaster for Yamamoto, losing him not only four carriers but hundreds of his experienced aviators. Indeed, it was a turning point of the war. There were to be no more Japanese victories, and soon there was another major defeat. After a bitter five-month struggle, Japan lost Guadalcanal in February 1943.

Yamamoto decided that a morale-boosting tour of Japan's outposts was required, but seemed to have learned nothing from the mysterious trap at Midway. His detailed schedule was sent out in code, which, as the Americans had broken it once again, told them that he would land at nine o'clock on the morning of 18 April at Bougainville. This was 375 miles from Guadalcanal, just close enough for America's twin-engined P-38 Lightning fighters. In a hectic four days, 18 of them were fitted with long-range fuel tanks and their crews selected and briefed. In complete radio silence, they flew off across the featureless Pacific at less than 100 feet. Exactly on time, they spotted and intercepted two bombers and their escorting Zero fighters. Both bombers were shot down. The revered Yamamoto was dead, a terrible blow for Japan.

In the area of code-breaking, the enemies of the Americans and the British should have learned the dangers of overconfidence.

In Yamamoto's case, the consequences proved both personal and terminal.

William Smith O'Brien & the widow's cabbage garden

He was a very unlikely candidate for an Irish revolutionary. William Smith O'Brien, Member of Parliament for Limerick, was a Baronet's brother, and educated at Harrow and Cambridge. But even he could not bear what was happening in Ireland.

The recent disasters had started with reliance on the potato, brought to Ireland by Sir Walter Raleigh. By 1845, Ireland's population had grown to a massive eight million, compared with England, Wales and Scotland totalling sixteen million. Such a huge number of people could only be sustained by the potato, 'the lazy crop', which could be left in the ground while the men went to work at other jobs, and could be grown on tiny plots of land. No less than three million people had become dependent on this one source of food.

Then a devastating disaster struck, *Phytophthora infestans,* the potato blight, which overnight could turn healthy potatoes into black, evil-smelling, rotting mush. It reduced the 1845 crop by one third; next year it was even worse, with three quarters lost. The removal of a staple food, rich in vitamins, caused immediate starvation, and worse, diseases like typhus, scurvy and dysentery.

Millions died. These disasters were quickly followed by mass immigration to escape; to England, the United States, Canada and Australia. Hundreds of 'Famine Ships' lay in North American harbours with their hapless passengers dying on board, or in quarantine stations in sight of freedom. Soon they were re-named 'Coffin Ships'.

By 1847, Ireland had lost over one quarter of its people. Weakened by deprivation and disease, her people were in despair. So, with three colleagues, William Smith O'Brien hatched the ill-fated 'Young Ireland Revolt' against British rule, to be fought under the French Revolution-inspired tricolor of green, white and orange, now Ireland's flag.

The British government, as usual fully informed by spies, was able to swamp Dublin with troops. Moreover, the conspirators were lulled into overconfidence by the optimistic promises, from all over Ireland, of 5,000 'fully armed men'.

But the clergy vigorously opposed the rising, and when a few poorly armed peasants did assemble, they quickly dispersed once they discovered that there was no free food and they were not

Unlikely rebel, William Smith O'Brien

allowed by the leaders to confiscate private property.

Having retreated south into the countryside, the almost farcical and humiliating reality was that the rebels mustered only 32 'fully armed men' and another 20 'prepared to throw stones'. On July 29 1848, this trusty band managed to intercept a troop of mounted constabulary who retreated into a stone cottage near the village of Ballingarry, owned by a widow. 'The Battle of Widow McCormick's Cabbage Garden' was interrupted by the furious lady returning home to find her house under fire and her children trapped inside. Fiercely, she ordered all the combatants to cease fire and go home, and this they did, rather shamefacedly. To add to his embarrassment, O'Brien was arrested by a suspicious guard at Thurles railway station – surely the only time that railway staff have arrested a man for High Treason.

He and the other three ringleaders were found guilty, and were among the last people to be sentenced to 'hanging, drawing and quartering.' The young Queen Victoria was horrified to find out what this entailed, and insisted that the

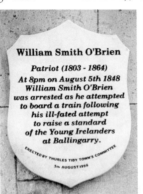

William Smith O'Brien

Patriot (1803 - 1864)

At 8pm on August 5th 1848 William Smith O'Brien was arrested as he attempted to board a train following his ill-fated attempt to raise a standard of the Young Irelanders at Ballingarry.

ERECTED BY THURLES TIDY TOWN'S COMMITTEE

5th AUGUST 1998

sentence be reduced to transportation to Australia. Smith O'Brien refused this clemency, demanding death or a Royal Pardon. A special Act, *'Transportation for Treason Act'* of 1849, was passed – just to be rid of him and his companions.

In the event, his exile had a far greater political effect than the abortive revolt. In Van Diemen's Land (now Tasmania), O'Brien, as an MP and probably the best-connected felon ever to be transported, became the natural focus of the anti-transportation movement. Curiously, this was Australian-led. Previously transported folk, now respectable with families, wanted to prevent the arrival every few weeks of ships carrying 'disrep-utable people.'

Smith O'Brien was eventually pardoned and his three companions escaped to America where one of them, Thomas Meagher, became famous as a Union General in the Civil War, leading the Irish Brigade. It would take over six decades before Ireland would achieve her freedom, either by political or military means. By then, her patriots had learned to plan further than a scrap in a cabbage patch.

The Catalpa & the Fenian escape

In Ireland's long struggle for freedom from Great Britain, the 'Fenians' were one of the great 'what ifs'. For providing a false dawn for Ireland, they rank with the gallant farce of the 'Young Ireland' revolt in 1848 (previous story) or Parnell's affair with Kitty O'Shea (page 6) Delay and betrayal would doom the Fenians to failure, but they did produce one of history's great escapes.

James Stephens, a veteran of the 1848 Rising, created in 1858 a new secret society both in Ireland and in New York, the Irish Republican Brotherhood, or 'The Fenians.' He had learned the lesson that success required arms and military skill. With Irishmen providing half of all Britain's troops, Stephens hit on the idea of recruiting soldiers in the regiments stationed in Ireland. By 1865, one third of the regular army and half the militia had been secretly sworn in as Fenians, ready to act on his orders and to rise in armed revolt, stiffened by hundreds of Irish-American officers experienced in the recent Civil War. But James Stephens then made a fatal slip. He hesitated and delayed. As John Devoy, the leader who had done most of the Fenian recruiting, wrote bitterly, *'All the risks and sacrifices were thrown away by incompetent and nerveless leadership.'*

Informers, the bane of Irish rebellions, then got wind of the plot and the British pounced. Hundreds of soldiers were court-martialled and imprisoned. For fear of a political backlash, the death penalty for treason was not used, replaced with imprisonment. And so in October 1867, a small group of 'military Fenians' found themselves on the *Hougoumont,* the last ship ever to take convicts to Australia. Bound for Fremantle prison 10,000 miles away, they included ex-trooper John Boyle O'Reilly, a handsome writer and poet. Contrary to the myth that the people transported to Australia were innocents who had merely stolen a crust of bread for their starving families, the *Hougoumont* was crowded with men sentenced for murder, manslaughter, armed robbery, rape and even incest.

John Boyle O'Reilly

After ten tedious weeks afloat, they were paraded in Fremantle, and told the prison rules. Many of these included the word 'death' in the routine punishments. They were reminded confidently that 'escape was impossible, through the cruel desert landscape or the shark-infested sea.'

The British were to prove far too overconfident. Within a year, O'Reilly had escaped. He had broken away from a work party, hidden in the bush and was rowed out by sympathisers twice to sea in a tiny boat and finally picked up by a whaler. It took months for him to reach the US, but O'Reilly, in Boston, became a successful writer and newspaper editor. However, he had not forgotten his comrades languishing in Fremantle. He met John Devoy and they hatched an amazing plan – to buy a ship, sail it to Fremantle and rescue the six remaining Fenians. They recruited Captain George Anthony who found the 200 ton whaler *Catalpa*. A touch of genius was to send out in advance two Irishmen to plot the operation on land. John Devlin would pose as 'Mr Collins', a wealthy American investor who charmed the little town of Fremantle, and the Governor, who even showed him round the prison. Word was passed to the prisoners, who were amazed that, after eight long years, escape might now be a possibility.

The *Catalpa* arrived after many months of difficulties, not least a near mutiny by the crew who could not understand why the ship was catching so few whales. All seemed ready. The Fenians were now 'trusties', working outside the prison. The local steam gunboat HMS *Conflict* had luckily just left. Horses and wagons stood by.

Very early on Easter Monday 1870, the plan swung into action. The men leapt into the wagons and galloped south to the beach at Rockingham. There was the *Catalpa's* longboat waiting. Desperately they rowed out into the surf, and only just in time. Police could be seen pouring on to the beach.

In Fremantle, the news broke. The great prison bell tolled the alarm. But the wires had been cut, and the *Conflict* could not be recalled. So the Government mail steamboat, the *Georgette,* was frantically commandeered and set off after the *Catalpa.* She had to turn back for lack of coal but returned the next day, now with a field gun lashed to her deck and crowded with police and soldiers. The two ships ran parallel, with Police Superintendent Stone furiously threatening Captain Anthony with attack. However, eventually the political dangers of firing on an American ship asserted themselves and the *Georgette* reluctantly turned back.

To the fury of the British, the men became heroes in America and the daring escape gave fresh heart to the Irish, but it would take five more decades before a well-organised military force would make Ireland became a nation again.

An amazing plan to 'spring' prisoners from a prison 10,000 miles away

Truman, MacArthur & the Chinese

The British troops in Korea were worried by the Americans. They never covered their flanks by moving into the hills, instead keeping to the roads while firing off unlimited amounts of ammunition at targets they could not see. Above all, they never seemed to dig trenches to protect themselves. On Thanksgiving Day, November 25, the British and other allies were both amazed and envious, as American troops in the front line were treated to flown-in turkeys and 'all the trimmings'. Sadly, it was to be the last day they would be envious of the Americans.

The Korean War had started five months earlier, when on a quiet Sunday, 25 June 1950, tanks and infantry of Kim Il-Sung's Communist North Korea poured across the border of the 38th Parallel. South Korea's inexperienced forces reeled back. The intervention of her ally, the United States, was hardly more propitious. The American army in Korea and Japan was a half-trained garrison – many had simply enlisted for the educational opportunities. It found itself fleeing from the Soviet and Chinese-trained North Koreans just as fast, as far and as ignominiously as its South Korean allies. Its few feeble anti-tank weapons bounced off the vintage T-34s spearheading the North Koreans' advance. Only American airpower saved a desperate situation and stabilised a final defensive line at the southern tip of Korea. United Nations forces also began to arrive including the British.

Appointed as Supreme Commander was General Douglas MacArthur, a truly extraordinary figure. A daring officer in the First World War, he had been an innovative Superintendent of West Point and then had been forced to abandon the Philippines to the Japanese, vowing 'I shall return.' He had indeed returned with large amphibious forces and three years of Pacific 'island-hopping.' He was brilliant, handsome, brave, self-publicising, arrogant and aloof. Even his wife called him 'General.'

It was MacArthur who had accepted the surrender of the Japanese in 1945 and was now their ruler, a regal and revered *shogun*, working with their Emperor. Now, despite being 70 years old, he rose to the Korean challenge. Against advice from all sides, he staged a daring landing at Inchon, halfway up the country. The North Koreans were soon in full retreat back up the peninsular, trying to escape his trap.

General Douglas MacArthur, flawed genius

After this unexpected triumph, it was not surprising that even President Harry Truman was in awe of MacArthur. Everybody else was. For his military superiors and for politicians, he was as difficult to control as some proud and distant Roman general. When Truman wanted to discuss the situation, he had to travel almost cap in hand to Wake Island. There he was assured that 'the Chinese were no problem.'

MacArthur's forces now planned to sweep north, across the 38th parallel, up into North Korea and on towards the Yalu River, the border with China. Thoroughly alarmed, the Chinese tried to warn the United States. On 30 September, Premier Zhou Enlai declared, *'The Chinese people absolutely will not tolerate foreign aggression, nor will they supinely tolerate seeing their neighbours being savagely invaded by the imperialists.'* Three days later, the Indian Ambassador was asked to brief the Allies urgently that China would definitely intervene if UN forces continued their advance. The Chinese Foreign Ministry repeated the warning. Suspecting bluff, neither MacArthur or Truman took heed. For MacArthur it was hubris, and for Truman domestic politics. Exasperated, the Chinese now infiltrated 130,000 troops across the Yalu. On November 1

they struck, chopping up several South Korean regiments. Six days later they broke off their action and disappeared into the snow. What more warnings could they give? But, amazingly on November 24, MacArthur started his 'win the war by Christmas' offensive and the GIs confidently tucked into their turkeys. The very next day the Chinese, now with 300,000 men, attacked with devastating force from where they had carefully hidden in the snowy mountains.

Briefly, there was contemptuous and ridiculous talk of *'not being afraid of Chinese laundrymen',* ignoring the fact that most Chinese troops had been fighting all their lives. In the West, the allied armies collapsed, constantly outflanked by Chinese from the hills, and, in panic, 'bug-out fever' took hold. One American Colonel said to his Executive Officer, 'Look around here. This is a sight that hasn't been seen for hundreds of years: the men of the whole United States Army fleeing from the battlefield, abandoning their wounded, running for

'The Chinese are no problem.'

Prisoners, very obviously Chinese. How many more warnings were required?

their lives.' Repairing US military honour in the East, the Marines, with British Royal Marines fighting with them, conducted an orderly, if murderous and freezing retreat.

But the harsh fact was that they were all back to the 38th parallel once more, and all this had happened in less than six months. The ill-judged decision to ignore the Chinese anxieties and warnings and not to conclude a negotiated truce proved catastrophic for all concerned. MacArthur, effectively, panicked and then publicly advocated either abandoning Korea, or the invasion of China or even the use of atomic bombs. He was finally dismissed for multiple insubordination by Truman in April 1951. Truman, who did not stand

for the Presidency, saw the Republican Eisenhower win on the pledge of 'ending the war'. The Chinese created their own banana skin when, flushed with success, they tried to turn their own limited intervention into a crushing symbolic victory– only to be mangled in turn by the firepower of a revitalised Allied army

Even more important, as the war dragged on in bloody stalemate for three more years, Korean casualties climbed to two million military and two million civilians. North and South Korea were shattered, and North Korea has never recovered.

This was also to be the first war that America did not win.

Lord North & the American Colonies

By nine o'clock on the night of 16 December 1773, Boston Harbour was littered with tea chests and the surface of the water was covered in tea. Britain was on its way to losing America.

Two men can be blamed for the historic break between Britain and the colonists. It was Chancellor of the Exchequer Charles Townsend who first set the scene in 1767 when he thought he had devised a good way of raising

money in the colonies; taxing *small and unimportant things* like lead, glass, paper and tea.

Three years later, Lord North, a Prime Minister acidly described by the famous writer and critic, Dr Johnson, as *'filling a chair with a mind as narrow as a neck of a vinegar cruet'*, then compounded Townsend's error. All his duties were repealed, except the Tea Tax, now useless as a money-raiser,

because it cost more to collect than the revenue it would raise. Despite this and the fears of more sensible Members of Parliament that there would be trouble, Lord North stubbornly kept the tax, 'as a mark of the supremacy of Parliament and as a declaration of its right to govern the colonies.'

'I can't but consider it an epoch in history.'

Keeping the tax on tea was also an attempt to help the East India Company, then in financial trouble, in spite of its growing but secret involvement with the Chinese opium trade. The British, in addition to sending tea direct to America, also decided to control smuggling – which annoyed most of the merchants, especially in Boston, who were themselves actively engaged in it.

So, opposition to the Tea Act grew rapidly, and finally exploded in Boston where three British ships laden with East Indian tea were anchored – the *Dartmouth, Eleanor* and the *Beaver*. After a mass meeting earlier in the day, the Captain of one of the ships, Francis Rotch, rode off to ask Governor Hutchison for exemption from the tax. When he returned to report that this had been refused, a thousand men, many disguised as Indians, burst from the meeting, ran down to the harbour, boarded the ships and hurled the offending 298 tea chests into the water.

John Adams, normally a moderate, was right when he said 'The people should never rise without doing something to be remembered, something notable and striking. This destruction of the tea is so bold, so firm, intrepid and inflexible, and it must have so important consequences, and so lasting, that I can't but consider it an epoch in history.'

Six years later, America declared its independence, and six years after that had won that independence by force of arms. The attempts by Charles Townsend and Lord North to raise a bit of cash from tea in the American colonies must rank in political stupidity with the Salt Tax in India. In the west and then the east, both resulted in the unnecessary loss of the two most important parts of a hard-won empire.

The Germans & the secrets of Bletchley Park

With their Enigma, the Germans could be forgiven for thinking that they had created an unbreakable code. It was a simple machine, developed for commercial purposes from a toy. It had movable rotors and a plugboard, the settings of which were all changed every 24 hours. Before they were overwhelmed by the Germans, the Poles had been able to recreate an actual Enigma machine, which they passed to the British. But without the codebook which decided each day's settings, the odds of breaking the code were an incredible *150 million, million, million to one*. No wonder the Germans were confident. But they had not allowed for Bletchley Park.

In August 1938, a motley group arrived at a large Victorian mansion in Buckinghamshire, under the guise of 'Captain Ridley's shooting party', the first of 9,000 who were to work at Bletchley Park on what was to be one of the most significant and secret efforts in British history. For the site was now 'Station X,' the Foreign Office's home for its 'Department of Communications' and MI6's most important centre for code-breaking.

At Bletchley Park, they did succeed in cracking the Enigma system. The fertile

brains of an extraordinary group of boffins and intellectuals, and the use of rows of Alan Turing's 'Bombes', electro-mechanical machines first envisaged by the Poles, so reduced the time to decipher the Enigma traffic that Britain's leaders and armed forces could react quickly enough to make a difference. The time came down from weeks, to days, to minutes. To break *Lorenz*, Hitler's own code, *Colossus*, the first programmable electronic computer was also built.

Bletchley Park was typically British and eccentric. The teams, working in crowded wooden huts, comprised linguists, mathematicians, chess players, crossword champions and technologists – anyone with the lateral thinking to break codes – backed by

furnished with Germany's complete order of battle.

Information was freely shared with the Americans who had liaison officers at Bletchley Park and who were able to concentrate their own brilliant effort, 'Magic', to break the Japanese 'Purple' code.

The banana skin for the Germans was that their own excellent code experts never imagined that Enigma was remotely compromised – and took no steps to protect themselves. The British also made great efforts to hide the success of Ultra, and trick the enemy into thinking that the intelligence had come from other sources.

At the end of a war which Bletchley Park may have shortened by two years, everything there was destroyed on Churchill's orders – the ' bombes', Colossus, and all the paperwork. Since everyone who had ever worked at Bletchley Park was sworn to secrecy, it took 20 years before even the British knew what went on there – so perhaps the Germans can be forgiven for their overconfidence.

'Ultra' discovered that hitherto unknown Peenemünde was asking for extra petrol rations. The resulting bombing raid set back the VI and V2 rockets by many months. (Courtesy of Frank Wootton)

an army of support staff. The overwhelming majority were women. They lived with nearby families or in hotels and pubs, often cycling many miles to work and they operated in 3 shifts, covering 24 hours a day.

Churchill used the codename 'Ultra' for the increasingly vital intelligence coming from Bletchley Park, which by 1941 was playing a crucial role in the battles of the Western Desert, and the Royal Navy was acting upon the U-boats' communications to win the war in the Atlantic. Before D-Day, the Allies were

Joseph McCarthy & the army

At Wheeling, West Virginia, the Junior Senator for Wisconsin electrified his audience when he held up a piece of paper 'listing 205 men who are active Communists and members of a spy ring and who are still working and shaping policy at the State Department.' February 1950 was the first time that most Americans had heard of Joe McCarthy. But within four years 'McCarthyism' had passed into the language to mean uncontrolled anti-red witch-hunting.

It was, admittedly, a nervous period for the United States. The Korean War was raging and the U.S. nuclear lead had been destroyed by genuine spies: David and Ruth Greenglass, Whittaker Chambers, Alger Hiss, Harry Gold, Morton Sobell and the Rosenbergs. But most public services no longer had any Communists and there was no 'list.' Indeed, McCarthy was never a serious investigator, more a politician making a name for himself, for example accusing the Truman government of 'being soft on Communism' and the Democrats of 'twenty years of treason'. But, however phoney and hysterical the charges may have been, actors and writers in Hollywood were hounded for being Left Wing by the 'House of Representatives Un-American Activities Committee.' This was followed by attacks on the broadcast industry, schools and colleges and many public companies. Hundreds of innocent people had their careers blighted and their lives ruined by this witch-hunt.

In 1952, the Republicans won power and McCarthy made himself Chairman of the obscure 'Investigation Sub-Committee of the Senate Committee on Government Operations', the new forum for his increasingly bizarre claims. Outraging the Army, he even accused its most senior officer, the revered General George Marshall *'of a conspiracy on a scale so immense as to dwarf any such venture in the history of man'*. A furious President Eisenhower, unlike Truman, carefully decided to wait to let McCarthy over-reach himself: 'I refuse to get into the gutter with that guy.'

McCarthy had been joined by his principal supporter and eventual nemesis, a fresh-faced and unscrupulous 25-year-old lawyer, Roy Cohn. It was he who would bring down his boss through a strange and unwinnable struggle with the Army.

Roy Cohn, later one of the best-

'I refuse to get into the gutter with that guy.'

Joe McCarthy with his sidekick and nemesis, Roy Cohn

'Have you no sense of decency, sir, at long last?'

known, if not notorious, homosexuals in America, had a handsome, rich young friend called David Schine who joined McCarthy's team. When the time came for Schine's military service, Cohn embarked on a crazed campaign first to try to defer Schine's enlistment, then to obtain him a commission, and when that failed, to obtain for him privileges not extended to his fellow private soldiers. Any lack of cooperation, from Secretary of the Army Robert Stevens downwards, resulted in Cohn threatening to 'wreck the Army' in the loyalty investigations. Eisenhower was described as *'mad and getting fed-up. It is his Army and he doesn't like McCarthy's tactics at all.'*

With its officers being pilloried, the Army retaliated, making public a *'Chronology of Events'* listing the innumerable improper interventions for Schine by Cohn and McCarthy, whose

case was not helped by Cohn, who quickly and clumsily created falsified and backdated memoranda.

McCarthy had been fatally damaged, and drinking heavily, had begun to slide, with his unpleasant, bullying tactics vividly exposed on live television to 80 million startled viewers. During 1954, his whining 'Point of order, Mr Chairman, Point of order', became the butt of comedians, and the two-month Army-McCarthy Hearings were soon dominated by the wily Army Counsel, Joe Welch. His crushing line is still remembered by those glued to their televisions, 'Senator, you have done enough. Have you no sense of decency, sir, at long last?' The gallery erupted in applause and an uncomprehending McCarthy, at long last wrecked by live TV, stammered to Cohn, 'What happened?'

It was the beginning of the end for Joe McCarthy, who died of alcoholism four years later. Roy Cohn slithered out from the mess to become one of America's most crooked lawyers and fixers, and died of AIDS in 1986.

The word 'McCarthyism' lives on, decades after the death of the bullying Senator. Even the dictionary puts it, *'The use of unfair investigatory or accusatory methods in order to suppress opposition.'*

Reinhard Heydrich & his open car

Until his death, few British or Americans would have heard of him, but of all the Nazi leaders, the icy, blond and slit-eyed Reinhard Heydrich was arguably the most evil and dangerous.

Heydrich was born into a comfortable and highly musical family; indeed his (violently anti-Semitic) father, Bruno, founded the Hallé Orchestra. However, a musical career was not for the young Heydrich. When his family's wealth was ruined by inflation, he joined the Navy and – a serial seducer – slept with the daughter of the shipyard director. Spurning her when he fell for his future wife, Linda von Osten, he was then cashiered out of the Navy.

Linda persuaded him to approach the fledgling Nazi party and her husband soon became the right arm of Heinrich Himmler. Hitler and Himmler used the inaccurate rumour that Heydrich had a Jewish grandmother to keep this dangerous character under control. Most people were simply terrified of him, seeing him as ' a young, evil god of death'. They had good reasons. It was the brilliant, ruthless Heydrich who helped to destroy Rohm and the SA in 'the night of the long knives'. He also unleashed *Kristallnacht*, the first public attack on the Jews, and engineered the fictitious assault on Gleiwitz radio station – the excuse to attack Poland – which started World War II. Even more significant, it was Heydrich who chaired the notorious lakeside Wannsee Conference which planned the 'Final Solution' for no less than 11 million Jews, and who directly commanded the Gestapo's 'Jewish expert' Adolph Eichmann, who succeeded in killing six million.

By 1942, Heydrich had created an unique power base: second in command of the SS, Head of the *Sicherheitsdienst* (SD) and of the *Reichssicherheitshauptamt* (RSHA), the overall security umbrella of the Reich. This coldly complex man also had a reckless streak. As a Captain on the Luftwaffe reserve, he flew combat missions in the Polish, French and Russian campaigns, and was once forced down behind Russian lines. Hitler quickly forbade any more such dangerous escapades.

When Heydrich was sent to Prague as

Heydrich, the 'Hangman of Prague'

Czechoslovakia's brutal master, he cleverly started to use his 'sugar and whip' method – combining harshness with rewards – and vital Czech production actually started to rise. In response, the British backed a Free Czech attempt on Heydrich's life.

Heydrich's contempt for the Czechs, coupled with his arrogance and over-confidence were to spell his doom. Being driven as usual in his open green sports Mercedes, he foolishly ordered his driver to stop when he saw a figure trying to shoot at him. Then a grenade was thrown and drove debris deep into his body. He managed to chase his assassin but collapsed after a few yards. His wounds were to turn septic and kill him in agony.

While publicly praising 'the man with an Iron Heart', in private Hitler was devastated and furious that his possible successor had died through his own fault and a self-inflicted banana skin, writing: *'Such heroic gestures as driving in an open, unarmoured vehicle are just damned stupidity, which serves the country not one whit. That a man as irreplaceable as Heydrich should expose himself to unnecessary danger, I can only condemn as stupid and idiotic'.*

The Nazis took a terrible revenge for the death of a favourite son. In an innocent Czech village called Lidice, all 173 men and boys were shot, 196 women and children sent to concen-tration camps, the houses dynamited and the rubble shipped away on a specially-built light railway. Finally, the place was ploughed flat. All this, the Germans gloatingly photographed and filmed, thus ensuring that Lidice and Heydrich's overconfidence would become famous forever.

'Children of Lidice', sculpture by Marie Uchytilova

The medical profession, Harvey, Jenner & Lister

You would think that, by its very nature, medicine would be peopled by those who genuinely wish to help others. However, this has not precluded the same kind of resistance to change that we see in other fields. Why have important new discoveries been greeted with anything other than immediate and respectful attention – let alone ridicule?

William Harvey was in a better position than most physicians to resist such ridicule. His wife Elizabeth was the daughter of the Court Physician to Queen Elizabeth I, and he himself went on to fill that role for James I and Charles I. But even he had to be very careful when he discovered the secrets of the way the heart pumped blood round the body. Because this was a direct contradiction to the theories of the great Galen. It did not matter that Galen had

Galen

died in Greece in 203 AD. All serious anatomical and physiological research had stopped then and there. Now, to refute Galen's inaccurate theories about the heart and lungs was to invite the end of your medical career. So Harvey prudently waited from 1615 to 1628, thirteen years, to publish his findings. Even then, controversy broke out and raged for twenty years. With the realisation that the body only had eight pints of blood, the practice of lancing,

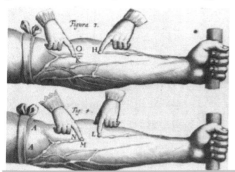

bleeding and the application of leeches, all 'to let out bad blood,' should have stopped at once. But we find that even 55 years later Charles II was being bled on his deathbed several times, which no doubt finished him off. If Harvey, as the Court Physician, could not get his ideas accepted, the problems for provincial medical pioneers were to prove even worse. Resistance to change would now be joined by good old British snobbery.

Smallpox was one of the most deadly and unpleasant diseases in the world. It kills a third of those it infects, and the survivors can be horribly 'pockmarked'. The body of Pharaoh Rameses V mummified in 1157 BC, bore the first disfiguring evidence of the disease which spread from Egypt to India and China and then came back into Europe with the Crusaders. As it was carried to the New World, it was to destroy whole civilisations and tribes in the Americas and devastate the aboriginals in Australia. In the last century alone, it killed 300 million people.

Edward Jenner was a country doctor in Gloucestershire who had studied nature since childhood. He had always been fascinated by the rural 'old wives' tale that milkmaids could not get smallpox. With unusually clear skin, they

William Harvey, luckily, did not follow the teaching of the great Galen (left)

Edward Jenner

were called 'pretty maids'. He noticed that milkmaids only contracted a weak version of smallpox – the non life-threatening cowpox. The pus in the blisters on their hands, Jenner concluded, must be somehow protect them. Jenner decided to try out his theory in 1796. A young boy called James Phipps would be his guinea pig. He took some pus from cowpox blisters on the hands of a milkmaid called Sarah, and 'injected' some of it into James, a process he repeated over a number of days, gradually increasing the amounts. He then deliberately injected the boy with smallpox. James became ill, but after a few days made a full recovery with no side effects. Jenner repeated his experiment, which worked every time, calling it vaccination, after 'vacca', the Latin for cow.

It seemed that he had made a brilliant discovery, vital for the health of the world. He then encountered the prejudices and conservatism of the medical world that dominated London. It could not accept that a 'country doctor' had made such an important

Ridiculous cartoons, with cows emerging from bodies

discovery, and Jenner was publicly humiliated when he brought his findings to London. Cartoons appeared showing people sprouting cows' heads. How many people died or were disfigured in the years that it took for doctors to accept vaccination? In 1801 he wrote, '*It has now become too manifest to admit of controversy, that the annihilation of the Small Pox, the most dreadful scourge of the human species, must be the final result of this practice.*' So successful was Jenner's discovery, which he never patented in order to keep the cost down, that in 1840 the government banned any other treatment for smallpox other than Jenner's.

In hospitals and on the operating table, the cure was often much worse than the problem. Surgery was a horrible ordeal before the invention of anaesthetics. What is more, the after-effects of surgery could and did kill in huge numbers. James Simpson was appalled that the mortality rate in British hospitals was 40%, and in France it was 60%. He pointed out that '*A man laid on an operating table in one of our surgical hospitals is exposed to more chances at death than was an English soldier on the battlefield of Waterloo.*'

Simpson also noticed that surgery in hospital attracted the 40% death rate, but at home only 11%. Semmelweis in Austria and Louis Pasteur in France were coming to the same conclusion – that the hospitals and the surgeons themselves *were inadvertently doing the killing*. Indeed they were. Surgeons would arrive from the morgue or other operations in their contaminated day clothes without washing their hands, 'to save time.' Indeed, surgeons often wore the same coats for months with no regard for sanitation, let alone sterilization or disinfection. A surgeon's frock coat was his insignia of office, and as stated by Fox; '*worn year in and year out until it acquired a crust of dirt and dried blood of which its owner was fiercely proud.*' Patients were lucky if the surgical instruments had even been washed in soapy water.

Joseph Lister, house surgeon at Edinburgh Royal Infirmary, was convinced by Pasteur's ideas that tiny living organisms floating in the air could cause contamination and infection. Lister decided to try out carbolic acid, a German invention being used in Carlisle to treat sewage. In 1865, a patient with a compound fracture of the thigh was admitted. Instead of dooming him by amputating or allowing the usual infection to develop on the broken skin, Lister treated the wound with cotton

soaked in carbolic acid. The man soon left, fully recovered, as did a young boy a few weeks later. Lister published the results in *The Lancet*. Amputation mortality rates in his ward now dropped from the usual 50% to 15%.

But once again the British medical fraternity took years to accept his methods. While foreign hospitals benefited, London still regarded him (like Jenner) as a 'provincial'. And this was even after he had saved Queen Victoria's life when she was threatened by an abscess. He helpfully produced a pamphlet for the French in their war against Prussia. Either it did not reach them or they ignored it, because losses were horrendous. The mortality rate after amputations performed by French military surgeons hovered at 75% or more. The official and appalling tally was 10,006 deaths among 13,173 soldiers who had minor amputations, such as fingers and toes.

Joseph Lister

The world has now accepted Lister's teachings on trying to protect patients from infection. But have we really? Britain now has the worst record of infection by the 'super-bug', MSRA. Infections have increased 600% in the last decade, and 5,000 people a year are dying. Are our hospitals becoming death traps once more?

Are our hospitals becoming death traps once more?

On 16 January, 1917, Arthur Zimmermann, Germany's bluff and good-humoured Foreign Minister, sent a coded telegram to his Embassy in Mexico City. It was to be the most stupid and momentous such message in history.

Zimmermann, a career diplomat, was Germany's first non-aristocratic Foreign Minister. Throughout his career, a certain naïveté was apparent. He was to be equally naïve over America's attitudes, and in his under-estimation of Britain's ability to break German codes.

In reality, London's brilliant and top secret Room 40 was to crack 15,000 key German messages during World War 1. It was there that the rather unlikely grey-haired figure of the Reverend William Montgomery studied Zimmermann's telegram. He immediately realised that, even partly decoded, it was crucially important and took it to his chief, the legendary Captain William Hall, RN, whom America's London Ambassador Walter Page described to President Woodrow Wilson, as *'a clear case of genius. All other secret service men are amateurs by comparison.'*

One glance at the decoded fragments of the telegram told Hall that here were words hinting at

Arthur Zimmerman

something cataclysmic. Phrases jumped out, like *'unrestricted submarine warfare'*, *'war with the USA'*, *'propose an alliance.'*

At that stage, both Britain and Germany were weak and exhausted from three years of bloody trench warfare. A reluctant Zimmermann had been persuaded by the generals that an all-out U-boat war was Germany's only chance. Bizarrely, he seemed to persuade himself that Mexico might actually side with Germany against the United States, her powerful neighbour to the north.

Room 40 struggled to recreate a perfectly complete telegram, because, while it had to convince the Americans, it must not reveal that the British had decyphered it. An advantage was that, ever since Germany's trans-Atlantic cables had been cut by the British, all her telegrams went indirectly. One route, curiously with permission from America, went through Washington. Two Zimmermann cables arrived at Room 40. Moreover, a British agent also got hold of a copy of the Western Union cable that reached Mexico via the German Embassy in Washington, (*see left*), complete with its different headings and serial number. Now the leak would look as if it had come from Mexico, not London.

Soon Hall's decoding was complete, and revealed these words:

WE INTEND TO BEGIN ON THE FIRST OF FEBRUARY UNRESTRICTED SUBMARINE WARFARE. WE SHALL ENDEAVOUR IN SPITE OF THIS TO KEEP THE UNITED STATES OF AMERICA NEUTRAL. IN THE EVENT OF THIS NOT SUCCEEDING, WE MAKE MEXICO A PROPOSAL OF ALLIANCE ON THE FOLLOWING BASIS:

MAKE WAR TOGETHER, MAKE PEACE TOGETHER, GENEROUS FINANCIAL SUPPORT, AND AN UNDERSTANDING ON OUR PART THAT MEXICO IS TO RE-CONQUER THE LOST TERRITORY IN TEXAS, NEW MEXICO AND ARIZONA. THE SETTLEMENT IN DETAIL IS LEFT TO YOU.

YOU WILL INFORM THE PRESIDENT [OF MEXICO] OF THE ABOVE MOST SECRETLY, AS SOON AS THE OUTBREAK OF WAR WITH THE UNITED STATES OF AMERICA IS CERTAIN AND ADD THE SUGGESTION THAT HE SHOULD, ON HIS OWN INITIATIVE, INVITE JAPAN TO IMMEDIATE ADHERENCE AND AT THE SAME TIME MEDIATE BETWEEN JAPAN AND OURSELVES.

PLEASE CALL THE PRESIDENT'S ATTENTION TO THE FACT THAT THE RUTHLESS EMPLOYMENT OF OUR SUBMARINES NOW OFFERS THE PROSPECT OF COMPELLING ENGLAND IN A FEW MONTHS TO MAKE PEACE.   ZIMMERMANN

The British knew that they held a huge propaganda coup. But would they have to use it? The Americans had broken diplomatic links with Germany, but had gone no further. After all, a reluctant President Wilson had been re-elected on the slogan: 'He kept us out of the war'. Finally, after many anxious days, on 22 February the British considered that they could wait no longer. Arthur Balfour, Secretary of State for Foreign Affairs, handed the telegram to the astounded Ambassador Walter Page in 'as a dramatic a moment as I remember'.

President Wilson, despite his reluctance to get involved in a European war, now decided to act. The Press Association was secretly given the story and, on 1 March, it broke in every US newspaper. A few suggested a 'British forgery', and the Mexicans, Japanese and Germans quickly denied it all. But then Zimmerman stepped on his own second banana skin by admitting: 'I cannot deny it. It is all true.' Now, American public opinion swung. Texans imagined German and Mexican troops marching in to take away their state. The West Coast envisaged a Japanese invasion.

On 2 April, President Wilson went to Congress to ask for war, citing the now infamous cable. Soon, American fresh troops would pour into Europe to tip the scale against Germany and the US became a world power.

Before he resigned (because of the telegram) in August, Zimmermann slipped again, helping to cook up the idea of sending Lenin to St Petersburg in a sealed train, thus launching the blight of Communism on the world.

Poor Arthur Zimmermann, who died in his bed in 1940, always seemed a little too confident in his ill thought out actions.

'As dramatic a moment as I remember'

The projectile & the battlefield

It is amazing how slowly some lessons sink in, however painful those lessons may be.

Mankind decided quite early that it was safer to attack things at long range, whether it be food or fellow human beings. Spears and catapults were all very well, but the bow and arrow emerged as the optimum weapon for hunter and soldier alike. It was the English who brought this weapon system to devastating military perfection, and their enemies really had no excuse for being repeatedly surprised. Three times did France, with five times the population, suffer defeat at the hands of the English during the Hundred Years War, a conflict which lasted from 1337 to 1443, covering the reigns of no less than five English and five French kings.

It may have been snobbery, with the French knights in their expensive armour only willing to test their 'chivalry' against their social equals on the English side. To them, nobody else mattered, least of all the archers, an ancillary force of social inferiors. Tragically, they had entirely missed the point.

The English or Welsh longbow was a formidable weapon, carefully created from a stave of yew, its heartwood compressing and its sapwood tensing. An experienced archer could fire fifteen steel-tipped arrows a minute, capable of penetrating armour at 350 yards. The repeated 110 lb draw required great strength, and yeoman archers were required to train regularly (golf and football were even banned for a while as a distraction from archery practice). A disciplined body of English archers could fill the sky with lethal arrows. The French chronicler Froissart recorded the deadly effect at Crécy in 1346: '*And ever still, the Englishmen shot where they saw the thickest press. The sharp arrows pierced the knights and the horses, and many fell, both horse and man. And when they were down they could not rise again, the press was so thick that one overthrew another.*'

In the eight hours of the battle, the French charged 16 times but were destroyed by the half million arrows that rained down on them.

The political and social effects on France were devastating. Among their 12,000 casualties were 1,200 knights and eleven princes, including 'Blind' King John of Bohemia, who had quixotically insisted on going into battle tied to two other knights. His wounded son, Charles, luckily survived to become Bohemia's favourite King, still revered in the Czech Republic.

Only ten years later, the pattern was repeated at Poitiers. Nobody seemed to be learning the lesson that the projectile was now dominant. You would think that if many of your ancestors had been killed by a weapon, you would pay real attention. But no. Decades later Henry V of England with 6,000 men faced more than 25,000 Frenchmen near the little village of Agincourt near Calais. No less

than 5,000 of the English were archers. The battle was a deadly replay. Once again, a whole French generation was crippled. Killed were the French commander, Charles D'Albert, and 500 members of France's noble elite, along with 5,000 other knights. The English lost less than 200 men.

When firearms arrived, English commanders were so frustrated by the short range and slow rate of fire of the musket, that they tried to bring back the longbow – but there were now not the men strong enough to work them.

Three centuries later, the technique well known to archers of imparting a spin to a projectile transformed the firearm into the rifle. The Americans taught the British the deadly lesson of the rifle's long range in the War of Independence. And it was the Americans in their Civil War who were to feel its effect on a mass scale. They had been warned; *'Put a man in a hole, with a good battery behind him and he will beat off three times his number, even if he is not a good soldier.'*

Several American Civil War battles had casualties to rival that of Waterloo. At Fredericksburg and Gettysburg, thousands of men were slaughtered by rifle fire in minutes. Did the many foreign military observers really notice?

And did they notice Plevna in 1877, where 15,000 Turks armed with long-range American Peabody-Martinis and short-range Winchester repeaters beat off 150,000 Russians? Or the Boers repeatedly pinning down the British in South Africa in 1900 with their deadly, hidden Mausers? Or the 60,000 Japanese who died in their 1905 assault on Port Arthur – with machine-guns now augmenting the rifles of the Russian

The English wanted longbows back, but now there were not men strong enough to work them.

defenders?

It was but a foretaste of a decade later. The generals had been given an accurate prophecy by a banker, I.S. Bloch in 1897. *'There will be increased slaughter on so terrible a scale as to render it impossible to get troops to push the battle to decisive issue … It will be a great war of entrenchments, the spade will be as indispensable as a rifle …'*

The obvious answer was to use the new petrol engine to power some form of armoured protection from the bullet – ie the tank, for which the technology was already created. But all the Generals entered the First World War under the false illusion that one only had to feed in enough men and bravery to create a breakthrough.

Of the deadly instrument of the slaughter to follow, General Haig even said, 'The machine-gun is a very over-rated weapon.' It was a remark many of our grandparents had cause to regret. There was even resistance when they were given the answer. Haig's A.D.C. said, with contempt, of the new tanks, 'The idea that cavalry will be replaced by these iron coaches is absurd, it is little short of treasonous.'

The results, too late, spoke for themselves. In Haig's most famous battle, the Somme, 680,000 Germans were

> *'The machine-gun is a very over-rated weapon.'*

killed and wounded, and 200,000 French and 420,000 British, with no less than 60,000 on the very first day. To gain one square mile at the Somme cost 5,277 casualties. At Passchendaele, it was 8,222. When tanks were used in 1918, the figure dropped to just 86.

The results of this second underesti-mation of the power of the projectile was a bloody four year stalemate. Stupidity in the face of self-evident change created not only the death of many millions of soldiers, but the impoverishment of Europe and the destruction of the flower of Britain, France, Germany, Italy and Russia.

Furthermore, the results of that were Communism, Fascism, Nazism and the Second World War.

Japan & a century of underestimation

It is not unfair to say that the Japanese have been underestimated since Commander Mathew Perry appeared in Tokyo Bay in 1852 and forced Japan to trade with the world – and thus also forced Japan to work out how to succeed in that world. The strange thing is that so many people and so many industries have woken up so late, so often.

Japan's combination of willpower and resourcefulness first shook a European power to its foundations when Russia lost an army at Port Arthur in 1905, together with two navies; one in the harbour, and then another which had sailed round the world, at the classic battle of Tsushima. The East began to realise that the West was not invincible – nor even always technically superior.

Three decades later, outsiders doubted stories of a nimble fighter-plane called the Zero, seen in Japan's war with China – and even thought that its skilful pilots must be foreign mercenaries. An overconfident racialism was leading to disaster. So the world appeared dumbstruck when Japan overwhelmed the East, destroyed the American fleet at Pearl Harbor, and took the Great British outposts of Hong Kong and Singapore,

rolling up Malaya and the Philippines and lapping up to the borders of India and Australia. Japan had the best trained armies, the finest naval airforce in the world, and the best ships, aircraft and torpedoes. Only three years of the application of the overwhelming strength of America, Britain, China and Australia were able to bring a country, with virtually no raw materials to its knees. And only the atomic bomb would give the Japanese the excuse to surrender.

Out of the ruins sprung an industrial giant. It was not just the *zaibatsu*, the huge traditional family trusts like Mitsui, Mitsubishi and Sumitomo. Japan soon recovered to dominate heavy industry, including shipbuilding. But it was also small entrepreneurs like Soichiro Honda, who in 1948 started attaching surplus generator engines to bicycles. *'Rather than use money, use your wisdom'* he said, and then showing the ambitious attitude of foregoing immediate reward for long-term benefits, 'If you're not Number One in the world, you can't be Number One in Japan.' Honda's motorcycles were superbly built; they did not cover the rider with oil and they had self-starters – a luxury (or essential) which took them

way beyond the 'bikers market'. But in Britain, the Marketing Director of Triumph complacently stated, 'We have nothing to fear from the Japanese; they will just open up the market for our bigger bikes'. Wrong. A few years later – along with its famous names like Triumph, Norton, Vincent, BSA – the British motorcycle industry was dead.

Among consumer products, it was the transistor radio which demonstrated the Japanese ability to enter a market and soon dominate it through low price and high quality. Engineers at Bell in 1947 perfected the transistor, replacing the bulky vacuum tube and making miniature radio sets feasible. Within seven years, the giants of radio, RCA, Zenith, General Electric, Raytheon in the US; Bush, Murphy in Britain; Thomson in France; and Telefunken in Germany all had their transistor radios blown away by Sony.

It was to be the same with black and white and then colour televisions. Later, it would be cameras, VCRs and computer games. The Japanese did not have to invent things (the transistor and the microchip were, after all, created in the US), they merely had to build products beautifully to suit the customers' needs and prices, market them well and provide good after-sales service. Elementary, really.

Nowhere has the success of this formula been demonstrated so well as in the car industry. Once again, underestimation ruled. In 1968, *Business Week* offered its opinions, *'With over 50 foreign cars already on sale here, the Japanese auto industry isn't likely to carve out a big share of the US market.'*

Today, General Motors has seen its market share halved in a generation. It is the same with Ford and Daimler Chrysler. Toyota, Nissan and Honda are becoming the industry leaders. In Britain, it is worse. There is no British car industry – except foreign-owned. Rover was even turned down by the Chinese.

In a world that is rapidly becoming starved of oil, it is once again the Japanese who have taken the lead. Toyota's Prius, a 'hybrid' that achieves 65 mpg by combining petrol and electric power, is beginning to look like the 'cool' future, while the huge and once profitable SUVs begin to languish. And Toyota has even produced a Prius which parks itself.

Never underestimate the Japanese.

David Beckham, Posh & their curious world

Whether you like it or not, we have all been subjected to the explosive phenomenon that is 'Posh and Becks'. Ever since a brilliant young footballer from London's East End started dating the 'Posh' Spice Girl in 1998, the media, with the couple's enthusiastic help and obsession for celebrity, has relentlessly pushed their image almost down our throats.

David Beckham could hardly avoid football. His father, Ted, a kitchen fitter, and his hairdresser mother, Sandra, would regularly take him to Old Trafford by coach to watch their beloved team, Manchester United. So it was natural for David to sign on with United, where his prodigious talent soon made him a household name.

Victoria Adams had a smarter background. Indeed, her father even drove her to work in a Rolls-Royce. No wonder that when she joined the manufactured pop group, 'The Spice Girls', she was dubbed 'Posh'. In contrast to the easy-going David, she also seemed driven by a relentless ambition. She may have come from Hertfordshire, but for many of us, she seems an 'Essex Girl' *par excellence.*

At their wedding in an Irish castle, they sat on red and gold thrones, while 437 staff attended to their guests. The £500,000 bill was slightly reduced by the exclusive deal with OK magazine for the photographs. The claim that they were now the second Royal Family was reinforced by their website, on which Victoria gave a tour of an electronic 'Beckingham Palace.'

Beckham became the highest-earning footballer in the world, his huge wages dwarfed by the even larger sponsorships. The 'Beckham Brand', backed by the image of a glamorous and fashion-conscious marriage, became a money-making machine worth £20 million a year.

And yet this golden couple and their curious life have suffered more than their share of banana skins. Even on the pitch, Beckham has had his problems. You did not have to be a football enthusiast to notice him kicking Diego Simeone of Argentina, being sent off and helping to eliminate England from the 1998 World Cup. 'TEN HEROIC LIONS,

ONE STUPID BOY', screamed the *Daily Mirror*, featuring Beckham's face on a dartboard. Worse, his effigy was burned outside a London pub. Perhaps because of Victoria's influence, his relationship with United's manager, Alex Ferguson, began to deteriorate. He missed training, apparently to look after his seriously ill son, Brooklyn, but Ferguson saw 'Posh' that same evening on TV, happily attending the London Fashion Week. Why wasn't she at the child's beside? Furious, he fined 'Becks' £50,000.

Two years later, Beckham sported a plaster under his eye, the result of a football boot kicked in frustration by Ferguson. Not surprisingly, Real Madrid signed him up, not least for the incredible merchandising he brought with him.

For 'Posh', Madrid would prove a dangerous challenge. As the only Spice Girl not to make it as a solo artist, she was determined to try to revive her career, and therefore elected not to join 'Becks'. David, unable to speak Spanish, was left alone in a strange city. Well, not exactly alone. It was Rebecca Loos, assigned to look after him, who was the first of several women to reveal to the tabloids that she had enjoyed *'the most explosive sex I have ever had.'* Victoria cannot have enjoyed reading how *'he did things to me which he wouldn't have dared to ask to try with his wife.'*

She would have hated even more Sarah Marbeck's revelation that Beckham now *'hated his wife's stick-like body.'*

Faced with all this, the Beckhams presented a united front. 'Ludicrous'. 'Absurd'. Not many people believed them. They even sued the *News of the World*, who claimed in an article, 'POSH AND BECKS ON THE ROCKS', that their marriage was a sham, kept together only by sponsorship's needs. Two years later, they have humiliatingly dropped the case, at a cost of £250,000. It is obvious to their friends that they dare not stand up and face the likes of Rebecca Loos across the courtroom.

It may well be, to misquote a famous saying, that those who 'live by celebrity' may yet 'die by celebrity.'

ghastly gaffes & blurted blunders

'And once sent out,
a word takes wing
beyond recall.'
Lord Halifax

'Man does not live by
words alone, despite the
fact he sometimes has to
eat them.'
Adlai Stevenson

Gerald Ratner & the prawn sandwich

Before his famous and fatal slip of the tongue, Gerald Ratner was one of the most successful tycoons in Britain. He had built his family business into the largest jewellery chain in the world, with 2,500 stores – popular haunts of the lucrative wedding market for those all-important engagement and wedding rings, and strongly associated with affordable quality. The visible results were a chauffeur-driven Bentley, a helicopter, a yacht, luxury homes and frequent invitations to Downing Street.

'Cheaper than a prawn sandwich.'

In April 1991, he addressed 6,000 fellow members of the Institute of Directors and made the most expensive joke in corporate history. He claimed that his stores 'sold a pair of earrings for under a pound, which is cheaper than a prawn sandwich from Marks & Spencer – but probably wouldn't last as long!' Not content with this he went on to describe his sherry decanters as 'crap.'

Gerald has since insisted that he had told such jokes before, normally just provoking friendly laughter. But he had not allowed for the presence of the *Daily Mirror*, which was on an unfair crusade against Britain's business 'fat cats.' The resulting media frenzy meant that, in two minutes, the reputation of a company which had taken years to nurture was in tatters: £500 million was wiped from its stock exchange value, the 'romance' of a Ratner ring was in ruins, and with it, a long-term emotional attachment to the name. Gerald Ratner personally lost £6 million and his £600,000 a year job, and the company had to be re-branded 'Signet' to stave off total disaster.

While Gerald Ratner has recently made a successful come-back selling jewellery on-line (geraldonline.com), his gaffe has meant that 'doing a Ratner' is now regularly used to describe similar statements, as with Barclays Chief Executive Matt Barrett. In 2004, Barrett told a Commons Treasury Select Committee that he would never use a Barclaycard because 'it was too expensive', adding that he had advised his children accordingly. An even more cryptic and amusing 'Ratner' was by Topman boss David Shepherd, who described his customers as 'hooligans or whatever' and whose suits would only be bought 'for

their first interview or first court case.'

Sometimes it is better to resist temptation, and avoid that flip remark which seems so funny at the time.

Prince Charles & the microphones

It should have been a smooth and happy public relations event. Just before his marriage to Camilla Parker-Bowles, Prince Charles agreed to do a photo-opportunity on the ski slopes with his sons Prince William and Prince Harry. Early in the morning, when everyone had been out late, they faced a posse of cameras and media people, some of whom placed their microphones at the feet of the royal party to pick up their responses clearly.

Prince Charles was plainly ill-at-ease and appeared not to notice the dangerous microphones, which easily picked up his opening remark, 'I hate doing this. Do I put my arms around you?' William was more assured than his father, 'Keep smiling,' he advised. 'This is so much fun', added Harry sarcastically. Then, inevitably, came a pleasant and innocent question from the BBC's Nicholas Witchell, a journalist with whom Charles had had problems

in the past. 'Eight days now to the wedding, how are you, William and Harry feeling at the prospect of marriage?' The whole world heard the Prince's next sotto-voce remarks to his sons, 'Bloody people, I can't bear that man. I mean he's so awful, he really is.' While some people apparently share Charles' views on Witchell, the press corps was none too pleased at the Prince's confirmation of his attitude to them. The views of the public may be more charitable, knowing just how intrusive and cynical the media can be.

Prince Charles is a charming, hard-working and well-meaning man. He has suffered decades of unfair, spiteful media attacks, not least because of the media's almost hysterical adulation of Princess Diana – an adulation selfishly enhanced by her ability to sell newspapers and TV

'I can't bear that man!'

footage.

Charles has also inherited the rather robust and non-PC attitude of his father, Prince Philip. People may have a sneaking admiration for a man who can ask a Scottish driving instructor, 'How do you keep the natives off the booze long enough to pass the test?' or asking Tom Jones, 'What do you gargle with, pebbles?'

Princes should be very careful with their words.

Beau Brummell & his fat friend

He single-handedly created Savile Row.

The days when a man could cheerfully insult his sovereign were over by the beginning of the nineteenth century: a court jester had to know his place. The story of Beau Brummell and his spectacular fall from favour provides a tragi-comic object lesson on the dangers of criticising your kind, patronising your patron – or, indeed, defecating on your doorstep.

From 1811 to 1820, Britain was governed by the Prince of Wales. George III was in the grip of a disease later identified as Porphyria, a rare condition characterised by erratic behaviour and purple urine. The Prince, also called George, assumed control of the government as the Prince Regent. This period, known as The Regency, is now remembered for its splendid architecture, wild living, and above all, impeccable taste. And Beau Brummell, sardonic and effortlessly stylish, was its apostle and epitome.

He rose unconventionally. His grandfather had been a shopkeeper who leased his rooms to aristocrats. His father was Lord North's Private Secretary. By the standards of the time, therefore, he was an unlikely companion for a prince, but Brummell had an innate talent for self-reinvention. At university he became so renowned for his wit that word of this prodigy reached the ears of the Prince of Wales, who secured him the post of Captain in the Tenth Hussars and the unofficial post of confidant. Until his fall in 1816, Brummell was given a free hand to direct the course of courtly fashion. The Prince was a great lover of dress, and a great hater of anything associated with the reign of his father.

It was Brummell who almost single-handedly created what we now call 'Savile Row', the Earl of Burlington's estate, north of Piccadilly, itself named after the ornate Elizabethan shirt collar – the 'pickadil'. He encouraged tailors to gather in Cork Street, Old Burlington Street and Savile Row to create elegant, bespoke tailoring in wool. Thanks to Brummell, Savile Row is now so famous that the word for a suit in Japanese is 'Sebiro'.

So the eighteenth century fop gave way to the Regency dandy. The style of the fop was openly and avowedly effeminate: perfume was liberally used, wigs were the norm, and men wore breeches and stockings. Under the influence of Beau Brummell, the arch-dandy, breeches were eschewed in favour of trousers, wigs were abandoned and perfume became anathema. Indeed, Brummell has some claim to be regarded as the man who reintroduced the classical idea of cleanliness to the scented but stinking world of upper-class English society. And men could adorn themselves while remaining masculine. In this sense, as in others, he was the inventor of modern male fashion.

When his father died, Brummell inherited £30,000 (one and a half million today), enabling him to found a salon in Mayfair and fund a ferocious gambling habit. His witticisms amused

Beau Brummell

the prince (or 'Prinny' as he was nicknamed), but also tended to irritate him.

And there was one issue on which the Prince was particularly, and understandably sensitive: that of his considerable bulk. In the latter days of the Regency, the poet and critic Leigh Hunt was to be imprisoned for describing the Prince as 'a corpulent Adonis.' But while Hunt achieved a measure of glamorous notoriety through his mini-martyrdom, Brummell was destroyed by his own. One day, the Prince, offended by some sally of Brummell's, publicly 'cut' him. An amused Brummell turned to his neighbour and loudly asked, 'Alvanley, who's your fat friend?'

It wasn't the wittiest of one-liners – but it was enough. Brummell was effectively banished from court by the apoplectic Prince. The timing could not have been worse: he now had no protection against his creditors. Baffled and frightened, he fled to France in 1816. Not everyone abandoned him. He became British consul at Caen as a result of his friends' efforts, but the post was abolished after two years. The prophet of

The Prince was very sensitive about his bulk.

hygiene gradually sank into squalor. One visitor recalled meeting the erstwhile dandy dressed in a faded kaftan and picking morosely at his one remaining tooth with a slip of carob root. Poverty and disgrace overthrew his mind and he died in the Asylum du Bon Sauveur in 1840.

His is a sad tale, but he would not have wanted us to dwell on his tragedy, caused by one blurted blunder. And we *do* now all wear trousers.

Bush, Quayle & friends

With the speed of modern communications, the spoken banana skin is instantly recorded, and sadly for the speaker, easily retrieved to remind us all over again.

Among American politicians, the all-time champion of the verbal banana skin must be Dan Quayle, U.S.Vice-President from 1989 to 1993. After just a few gaffes, he tried to brush off his unfortunate tendency. 'The American people would not want to know of any misquotes that Dan Quayle may or may not make.'

How wrong he was. The American people could not get enough of him. Probably, his most famous mistake was to make some schoolkid spell 'potato' as 'potatoe'.

Sometimes his support for his President, George Bush Senior, was less than helpful. 'This President is going to

Dan Quayle

lead us out of this recovery'. Then again, he weakened his support for the Christian Coalition to help with AIDS when he said, 'My friends, no matter how rough the road, we can and will never, never surrender to what is right.'

Those who looked to Washington for an understanding of financial matters might wish to look a bit further than the Vice -President: 'Bank failures are caused by depositors who don't deposit enough money to cover losses due to mismanagement'. The environmental lobby was also not getting much help: 'It isn't pollution that's harming the environment. It's the impurities in our air and water'. Geography was also not Quayle's strong point: 'I love California. I practically grew up in Phoenix.' (Unfortunately, Phoenix is in Arizona). Abroad it would get worse. 'On a tour of Latin America, my only regret is that I didn't study Latin harder in school, so I could converse with those people.'

But he did retain his confidence: 'This isn't a man who is leaving with his head between his legs'.

One might feel that an amiable and lightweight Vice-President could just about be allowed such foibles. But George W. Bush is a top contender in today's verbal banana skin ratings. For him, pushing education is always a bit risky: 'Rarely is the question asked: Is our children learning?'

Maybe he blamed the system. As he said on NBC: 'First I would like to spank all the teachers'.

For him, mixing metaphors is likely to cause problems too: 'I think there is a Trojan horse lurking in the weeds trying to pull a fast one on the American people.' Perhaps he had been meeting his brother too often in alligator-filled Florida. Before Bush embarked on the Iraq war he might have pondered his own sage remarks, 'It is clear our nation is reliant upon big foreign oil. More and more of our imports come from overseas.'

The most powerful man on earth will tend to worry people over his policies when he says, 'I have opinions of my own

– strong opinions. But I don't always agree with them.' Perhaps he was right when he claimed 'I think they have misunderestimated me.' A Pentagon audience surely did when he stated, 'Our enemies never stop thinking about new ways to harm our country and our people, and neither do we.'

The gaffes of other politicians vary from the ignorant, as in 'A zebra does not change its spots' (Vice President Al Gore), to the cynical, 'If two wrongs don't make a right, try three.' (President Richard Nixon)

We can even rely on local politicians to follow the wonderful idiocies of Washington. Mayor of New Orleans, Vic Schiro, no doubt meant well when he stated, 'Don't believe any false rumours until you hear them from me,' and Mayor Marion Barry of Washington DC did not do himself any favours: 'There are two kinds of truths. There are real truths and made-up truths.'

Maybe they should have all kept their mouths shut.

John Lennon & Jesus

'Lennon was very aggressive, then as later.'

Fans had screamed for Elvis, they had screamed for Buddy Holly, but the British pop group The Beatles aroused a screaming that was incessant, desperate. It was to be the backdrop to their live performances for three years. The phenomenon was called 'Beatlemania', and it had no precedent. Then a casual comment by the group's leader changed the tone of the screams: cries of rapture turned to howls of hate, before sinking into silence. John Lennon, eccentric leader of the Beatles, who was later to claim that 'anything that gets a reaction is good', doomed Beatlemania in America. His group would never again attain the height of adulation it had known in 1965. And fifteen years later, his flippancy would bear dark fruit.

The Beatles were an unlikely success for the early sixties. Their hair was too long for a start. None was conventionally good-looking. So, they were the subject of one of the music industry's great banana skins when on New Year's Day 1962, Decca's Dick Rowe famously turned down the Beatles in favour of Brian Poole and The Tremeloes, 'because they lived closer.' (George Harrison was kind enough to save Rowe's reputation a year later by talking him into taking on a new group called The Rolling Stones.) In spite of the Decca set-back, The Beatles, with their exuberance on stage and their phenomenal talent – they were once compared to Chopin – conquered Britain and later America. The world soon followed suit.

Of the 'Fab Four', John Lennon was always the most interesting and also the most blunt and outspoken. Veteran British jazzman George Melly recalls meeting him first at The Cavern, where Melly had allowed Lennon and 'The Quarrymen' to play in the intervals. 'John Lennon was very aggressive, then as later. Brutally he said, 'You old farts are standing in our way.'

He could be equally cynical and acerbic about his fellow Beatles. Asked if Ringo was the best drummer in the

world, he shot back 'He's not even the best drummer in the band.'

So it was hardly surprising that he quite casually managed a real banana skin. He alienated the American bible-belt.

It started back in Britain when he was interviewed by London's *Evening Standard* on 4 March 1966. He drawled 'We're more popular than Jesus now; I don't know which will go first – Rock 'n' Roll or Christianity.'

In relatively secular Britain, his words hardly caused a ripple. But when the media in the United States picked up his words, Middle America rose in fury. There were vague death threats. Radio stations told fans where to burn 'Beatles trash'. Brian Epstein, the Beatles' manager apologised on television. Lennon retracted, genuinely hurt by America's response to his quip.

After the adulation and hysteria of the Beatles' earlier tours, it would have been easy for him to underestimate the deeply conservative element in America. Not just short hair and button-down shirts, but more important, the deeply held religious views of the same people who years later propelled George W. Bush to the White House. Of such voters, according to a 2005 CBS poll,

67% did not believe in evolution.

Thus in America the unquestioning adoration shifted and Beatlemania had died. The group went on to record albums of unequalled originality and power, but the days of screaming girls were over. A young chubby-cheeked loner, a worshipper of the Beatles, listened to Lennon's remarks and his face darkened. Until then, he had known two great loves – the Beatles and Jesus. He felt he had to make a choice.

In December 1980, while Lennon was recording what remains by common consent, his

John Lennon and Mark Chapman

finest solo album, the same young man, Mark David Chapman, a born-again Christian, asked him to sign a copy of the album, *Double Fantasy*; Lennon obliged. On leaving the Dakota building, where he lived and recorded, Lennon heard a soft, courteous question: 'Mr Lennon?' Five shots rang out. Flowers are still placed there.

For Ron Atkinson, it was to prove a gaffe too far. He was in Monaco at the end of commentating on a semi-final of the European Cup, when he turned to his colleague and, believing he was off the air, referred caustically to Chelsea captain, Marcel Desailly, 'He is what is known in some schools as a fxxxxxg lazy, thick, nxxxxr.' Unfortunately for him, two Middle Eastern stations were still getting the feed, and complaints started rolling in. It was an unforgivable remark, which lost him his ITV job and cost him about £1 million.

Ron Atkinson

It was all the sadder, because Atkinson had a distinguished record over the years as a team manager who helped and promoted black players, many of whom now rallied to his support.

Since becoming a soccer pundit, his career had been peppered with less dangerous, but nevertheless bizarre, comments:

'I would not say that David Ginola is the best left-winger in the Premiership, but there are none better.'

'He sliced the ball when he had it on a plate.'

'I'm going to make a prediction – it could go either way.'

'I never comment on referees and I'm not going to make an exception for that prat.'

'He dribbled a lot and the opposition don't like it – you can see it all over their faces.'

Sport seems to have brought out the best or the worst in both participants and commentators. Father of them all must be the great 'Yogi' Berra, the New York Yankees and Mets baseball hero, later a coach. It was he who first uttered the sports truism, 'It ain't over, till it's over.' He also managed, 'This is like déjà vu all over again.' and 'If you don't know where you're going, you'll wind up somewhere else.' One could have some sympathy with, 'It was impossible to get a conversation going. Everyone was talking too much.'

Probably Britain's best-loved and most verbally accident-prone TV commentator would be veteran Murray Walker, who so enlivened he world of Formula One Grand Prix racing. His autobiography was appropriately named, *Unless I'm very much mistaken.* He very frequently was, much to the entertainment of his TV listeners. Consider these gems:

'The lead car is absolutely unique, except for the car behind, which is identical.'

'There is nothing wrong with the car, except it's on fire.'

'This is an interesting circuit because it has inclines. And not just up but down as well.'

'A sad end, albeit a happy one.'

'Tambay's hopes, which were previously nil, are now absolutely zero.'

'Do my eyes deceive me or is Senna's car sounding a bit rough.'

'Young Ralf Schumacher has been upstaged by the teenager, Jensen Button, who is twenty.'

David Coleman, dubbed 'Colemanballs' by the satirical magazine *Private Eye,* has never been far behind: 'I don't think he's ever lost a race at 200 metres, except at 400.'

'There goes Jaunterena, opening his legs and showing his class.'

This last announcement shows how the pressure of sports commentating 'live'

can give rise to some unfortunate sexual innuendoes. For instance, Radio 4's situation report, 'The batsman's Holding, the bowler's Willey' was all too easily misunderstood. As was, 'The most vulnerable area for goalies is between their legs.'

'Your first instinct when you see a man on the ground is to go down on him', was actually a comment on some new Rugby rules. The technique of slipstreaming in cycle racing could also have been better described, 'The girls in front are breaking wind.' Some comments work in the printed media, but not on the radio: 'The wife of the Cambridge President is kissing the cox of the Oxford crew.'

Participants are just as productive as the pundits; witness Sam Torrance at the Ryder Cup, 'If you had offered me a sixty nine this morning, I'd have been all over you'.

And Greg Norman celebrated his win in the World Match play championships by breathlessly announcing, 'I would like to thank my parents – especially my father and mother.'

Finally, a boxer who had just lost his fight in Chicago was asked by a concerned reporter, 'What state were you in at the end of the fight?' Puzzled, he replied, 'State? Illinois.'

Neville Chamberlain & his piece of paper

'How horrible it is that we should be digging trenches because of a quarrel in a far away country between people of whom we know nothing.'

In one of his ruder moments, Winston Churchill complained that 'the trouble with Neville Chamberlain is that he looks at the world down the wrong end of a municipal drainpipe.' He was basing his opinions of Chamberlain's unworldly and parochial attitudes on his five-year stint as Mayor of Birmingham. He could have based it equally well on Chamberlain's first job – managing his father's banana plantation.

Neither would qualify Chamberlain to negotiate successfully with a mercurial, cunning, treacherous and ruthless opponent like Adolf Hitler – a lowly former corporal, who after all, had used dogged willpower and the ability to cheat and lie his way to the undisputed leadership of one of the most hierarchical and conservative nations on earth.

In March 1938, Germany had annexed Austria, the *Anchluss*, in direct contravention of the Treaty of Versailles. Czechoslovakia, another neighbouring country which was actually created by Versailles, was plainly going to be next. Hitler used as his excuse the 2.5 million Germans living in the Sudetenland, which also held the vast Skoda armaments works and all of Czechoslovakia's defensive positions.

Chamberlain, ill-equipped as he was, decided to intervene on foreign policy. On September 15, 1938, he flew to meet Hitler and agreed to 'self-determination' for the Sudetenland. Czech Prime Minister Benès announced to his colleagues, 'We have been basely betrayed.' Seven days later, Hitler said the proposals 'were no longer any use.' His invasion, *Fall Grun* (Operation Green) was ready to roll, in spite of the anxieties of his military advisors about the combined forces of Czechoslovakia, France and Britain. As Britain prepared for war, Chamberlain quavered pathetically on the radio, 'How horrible, fantastic, incredible, it is that we should be digging trenches and trying on gasmasks here because of a quarrel in a far away country between people of whom we know nothing.'

That very night a welcome telegram, proposing a conference, arrived from Hitler. He had been persuaded by Mussolini, his reluctant ally, who knew that Italy was hopelessly unprepared for war. And so it was that Hitler, Mussolini, Chamberlain and France's Edouard Deladier met in Munich. The Czechs were even not allowed to attend. Chamberlain arrived, a rather bizarre figure with his old fashioned wing collar and carrying his umbrella. What other world leader would have, as his main fashion accessory, an umbrella? Certainly not Hitler, Mussolini or Stalin. It was but a symbol of the naïve approach that the British Prime Minister brought to the Munich table. He had never met, or wished to meet, a personality like Hitler, who would see any well-meaning generosity as mere weakness. (If Chamberlain had taken the simple precaution of asking his civil servants for a précis of Hitler's brutally and clearly-stated intentions in *Mein Kampf*, he might have been better prepared.)

The four leaders duly sold Czechoslovakia down the river, and the Sudetenland was handed over. Hitler appeared, of course, to be reassuring, telling his own people, 'I assured Chamberlain, and I repeat it here, that when this problem is solved, there will be no more territorial problems for Germany in Europe.' Chamberlain had arrived back at Heston aerodrome to crowds of cheering, ecstatic people. He waved his famous piece of paper signed by Hitler, ending his speech, 'My good friends, for the second time in

history, a British Prime Minister has returned from Germany bringing peace and honour. I believe it is peace for our time. Go home and get a nice quiet sleep.'

The euphoria did not last long. Hitler's true intentions were contained, three weeks later, in his secret directive to Field Marshal Keitel, *'Liquidation of Czechoslovakia. It must be possible to smash at any time the remainder of Czechoslovakia.'* Of course, the promises were broken and the rest of Czechoslovakia swallowed up. A disillusioned Chamberlain now rather quixotically pledged future support for Poland, Hitler snarling 'I'll cook the British a stew they'll choke on.' Hitler was also not going to be cheated of warlike glory a second time by a man with an umbrella. He told his generals, 'Now Poland is in the position in which I wanted her. I am only afraid that at the last moment some Schweinehund will make a proposal for mediation!'

When Germany did attack Poland,

'Go home and get a nice quiet sleep.'

nine days later, it was a thoroughly chastened Chamberlain who had to declare war. His fumbling leadership ensured that he was soon replaced. Churchill was asked to form a National Government, including the Labour party and the Liberals. Hitler was now to face the opponent that he least wished and most deserved.

POLAND

David Niven & his new regiment

Among actors on both sides of the Atlantic, there was one who had no trouble playing the role of 'an officer and a gentlemen'. That is because he was an officer and a gentlemen before ever he went to Hollywood.

There is no doubt, however, that David Niven's life was full of banana skins – many self-inflicted and all of which he found very funny.

Leaving the Royal Military Academy at Sandhurst in 1929, he had set his heart on joining the famous Argyll and Sutherland Highlanders, and was faced by a War Office form which requested:

'Name in order of preference three regiments into which you desire to be commissioned.'

As he later recorded in his wonderful book, *The Moon's a Balloon*.

'I wrote as follows:
- The Argyll and Sutherland Highlanders
- The Black Watch

and then, for some reason which I never fully understood, possibly because it was the only one of the six Highland Regiments that wore trews instead of the kilt, I wrote:
- 'Anything but the Highland Light Infantry'.

Somebody at the War Office was funnier than I was, and I was promptly commissioned into the Highland Light Infantry.'

What he did not know was that the same joker had told his new regiment. Luckily, its Adjutant kindly filed the letter away for ever.

There are innumerable stories of the slip-ups that punctuated David Niven's life. A very typical one was told to the author by Niven himself over dinner in the 1970s, (Niven and the author's father had been great friends at school).

As a young officer, David was on a lonely hillside during a TEWT (Tactical

Exercise Without Troops). He had stashed a couple of bottles of beer down a rabbit hole and was dozing in the hot afternoon sun. Suddenly, he scrambled to his feet as the visiting General and his party of officers approached. The General then said, 'Well, Mr …?'

'Niven, Sir'.

'Suppose, Mr Niven, you were to attack that hill over there. Which method would you use?'

Niven hadn't the slightest idea, so he blurted out the first thing that came into his head 'The Middle Method, Sir.'

The General was puzzled. He had never heard of 'The Middle Method' but was also somewhat unsure of himself, lest this 'Method' be some new, bang-up-to-the-minute product of the Staff College. He probed further.

'Why would you use the Middle Method, Mr Niven?'

Niven could do nothing but bluster on. 'Well it would be, er, shorter than 'The Outer Method', sir, and, er, at the same time more, shall we say, more flexible than 'The Inner Method.'

The General was becoming impatient and turned to his staff. 'What is this Middle Method?' he asked.

One of them dryly responded, 'I rather think it's a product of Mr Niven's fertile imagination.'

The General, perhaps reluctantly, ordered, 'Place that young officer under arrest.'

David Niven, always the charming gentleman

Lady Docker & Monaco's flag

Only in one decade could a couple like the Dockers have become quite as famous. The fifties were a time for austerity for the British. Rationing was still in place, few people had cars or money and income tax could reach 83%. None of this seemed to apply to the glittering Dockers.

Sir Bernard Docker was very rich. He had made his money out of Anglo-Argentine Tramways, Midland Bank and Thomas Cook. An old Harrovian, he had been married before, to Jeanne Stuart, an actress – against furious opposition from his family. His wedding present to Jeanne was a magnificent 860-ton yacht, the *Shemara*. The marriage lasted only a few months, but at least Jeanne had the grace to give back the boat.

Lady Docker (National Portrait Gallery, London)

At this point Sir Bernard met Norah Collins, a former dancer at the Café de Paris, and from then on the couple were never out of the headlines. Indeed, there was nobody to compare. The real aristocrats were either broke, being taxed to death or living modestly and keeping their heads down. There were, of course, some heroes for the public to admire; test pilots, actresses and footballers. But the equivalent of David Beckham would have been paid a pittance. There were no 'celebs', no *OK* or *Hello* magazines.

In the drab 1950s, the Dockers stood out, with Bernard seemingly going along with Norah's determination to spend, spend, spend– often as tastelessly as possible. It was not just the furs and the champagne, it was the cars. Sir Bernard was the Chairman of Daimler, then the Royal Family's choice of transport, and Norah persuaded him to build a series of fabulous Daimlers. Visitors to the 1951 Motor Show, lucky if they could afford a Ford Popular on hire purchase, were treated to the incredible sight of a huge black Daimler, covered in gold stars and with all its chrome work plated in real gold. This was followed in 1953 by 'Silver Flash' with red crocodile-skin seats; 'Stardust', with lizard skin in 1954 and 'Golden Zebra' in 1955. Nominally the cars were meant to raise the company's profile, which they certainly achieved, but Norah then proceeded to use them as her personal transport. She was even to arrive in her Zebra-upholstered Daimler with a team to compete in the traditional Castleford 'Taws' or marbles competition in 1955. The next year she brought cricketers Len Hutton and John Wardle and football star John Charles. She also kept *Shemara* firmly in the news, now magnificently appointed and with a crew of 35.

When at last the shareholders of Daimler lost their tempers with this extravagance and fired Sir Bernard in 1956, the *Shemara* became one of the Dockers' homes, frequently moored on the French Riviera and in the tax haven of Monaco. And it was there, in 1958, that Norah was to slip on her worst banana skin. At the famous Casino, she publicly criticised Prince Rainier and his family and dramatically tore up the flag of Monaco. Rainier expelled them from Monaco forever.

Norah was defiant, 'As far as I am concerned Rainier can go and jump in the sea. Monte Carlo is a dump. I've actually banned myself.' A few days later a formal expulsion order was delivered to their hotel in Cannes, banning them from the whole of the Riviera.

In 1967, the couple moved to a modest bungalow in the tax haven of Jersey, Bernard commenting that it would be a good base for *Shemara*. Not for long. It had to be sold the next year, to property tycoon Henry Hyams.

Without their yacht, the Dockers did not seem to enjoy themselves too much in Jersey, with Norah commenting on her neighbours, 'They're the most frightfully boring, dreadful people that have ever been born.'

Quite a few observers probably thought the words applied rather well to the Dockers.

James Callaghan & his 'crisis'

Looking back from the reasonably stable and prosperous Britain of the twenty first century, one struggles to recall, understand or even believe the mess of the 1970s. The Labour government of Harold Wilson and then James Callaghan was an economic disaster, with years of crippling inflation peaking at 27% in 1975, wiping out savings and ruining livelihoods. The trade unions had been allowed to become far too powerful, with 'wildcat', unofficial strikes used to ransom whole industries at a moment's notice.

Faced by the real loss of earnings eroded by inflation, it was not surprising that the unions demanded and achieved huge wage increases, further fuelling the cycle of inflation. Desperately, Prime Minister James Callaghan, himself a product of the trade union movement, tried to create an incomes policy, the 'Social Contract', with the support of the Trades Union Congress. A 'five per cent guideline' for wage increases was announced in July 1978, and Callaghan also announced he would not call a General Election that autumn but would serve through the winter so that the economy would be in better shape for electoral success in the spring. It was a fateful decision, because all hell broke loose.

Ford, the usual benchmark for private industry, dutifully offered its workers 5% and was rewarded with an immediate unofficial strike in September, soon made official, with 57,000 workers downing

Inflation at 27% led to crippling strikes.

tools. Ford eventually settled at 17%. It and 220 other companies were threatened with sanctions which were then blocked by Labour's own backbenchers and the Conservatives.

Free from risk, petrol tanker drivers struck for 40% and settled for 15%, but in January all lorry drivers struck. Petrol stations closed, as did the ports. Hardship and recriminations mounted. (The author failed to get to his father's deathbed through lack of fuel.) A million people were thrown out of work.

This was the moment on January 10 1979 when James Callaghan arrived back at Heathrow from a summit meeting at Guadeloupe. His press secretary, Tom McCaffrey told him to say nothing, but his political advisor, Tom McNally, thought the image of a Prime Minister returning 'to grip the situation' would appeal to the public. But to McNally's dismay, a tanned and beaming Callaghan, 'Sunny Jim', adopted a confident and jocular tone, boasting that he had been swimming in the Caribbean and blaming the media for exaggerating. *The Sun* said it all with its famous headline, 'CRISIS? WHAT CRISIS? Rail, lorry, jobs chaos – and Jim blames press.'

This banana skin moment would haunt Callaghan, and the slip became a slide because things soon went from bad to worse, in the so-called 'Winter of Discontent.' Train drivers started wildcat strikes, then ambulance drivers. The army tried to cope, but hospitals went on an 'emergency-only' basis. Gravediggers struck, and bodies piled up. The newspapers, at home and abroad, focused symbolically on pictures of mountains of refuse filling Leicester Square and Britain's parks.

The political fallout was not long in coming. Margaret Thatcher had outlined her plans for restricting trade union power. Now the Conservatives could use the 'CRISIS?' WHAT CRISIS?' words against images of mounting industrial chaos. Labour's opinion poll lead went from 5% in November to a Conservative lead of 20% in February. In April 1979, Margaret Thatcher swept to power. For James Callaghan and his trade union friends, life would never be the same again.

'Crisis? What crisis?'

Henry II & his turbulent priest

We have all publicly cursed a friend who has let us down. We have all later wished we could retract our words. But it is unusual for one's outburst to be construed as public incitement to murder. Such was the fate of England's King Henry II. His foolish words not only caused the death of his closest friend, but also the humiliation of public penance.

Henry II (1154–89) was a strong and energetic ruler of an English kingdom that extended from the Alps to the Scottish borders. He restored order after years of civil war and anarchy under King Stephen, when as a chronicler memorably observed, *'Christ and His Saints were asleep'*. He brought secure peace, removed foreign mercenaries and reformed English law, reigning in the power of the barons, whom he taxed with scutage or 'shield money' to raise an army (his own, not theirs), and strengthening the judicial influence of the monarchy.

He was aided by the close support of another most able man, the slightly older Thomas of London, son of a Norman merchant called Becket. From 1155 Thomas Becket was the King's Chancellor, at that time more a Private Secretary than member of the judiciary. The two men became close friends, who enjoyed talking, feasting and riding together, some comparing them to the biblical David and Jonathan. Thomas even helped Henry tax the church for his wars in France, and he himself commanded a company of knights in the campaign of 1159–60. Second only to the king, he became a very wealthy man.

Then in 1162, eager to extend his reformed rule of law to the English church, Henry appointed Thomas (already a deacon, but a most secular one) as Archbishop of Canterbury. Thomas was a worldly man; arrogant, charming, ambitious and materialistic, although with a strong sense of sexual sobriety and moral decorum. The church had expanded its power under Stephen's weak and ineffective rule, and had sought to bring all aspects of law for clerics (a large proportion of the population was in some sort of holy orders), under the ecclesiastical courts – even for serious offences like rape or murder. Thomas was most unhappy with the King's plans

'Who will rid me of this turbulent priest?'

The murder of Thomas Becket

to curb the power of the clergy, and warned Henry that it would damage their friendship. It did indeed lead to bitter feud and ultimately tragedy.

Thomas knew he could not serve two masters, Henry and God, and he resigned as Chancellor. Instead, he took his new role seriously, seeing himself as serving God for the good of the church and asserting the rights of the clergy in competition with the earthly power of the king. He built up his office, accepting no compromise to his prestige and influence. He and Henry had several legal stand-offs, relations deteriorated badly and Thomas fled into exile in France. There he enjoyed Papal protection and worked hard to force Henry to accept the independence of the church in all matters of law.

At last in 1170, Henry, forced into reconciliation by the Pope, permitted his return to England. Thomas, having landed at Sandwich and travelled to Canterbury to the acclaim of the people of Kent, made it clear that nothing had changed and continued to oppose Henry and harass his supporters. Less than a month later, Henry, at his court in

France, and enraged by Thomas's persistent obstinacy and power, raged openly: 'Who will rid me of this upstart clerk?' (some say his words were 'turbulent priest'.) Four knights of his court – Richard Brito, Reginald Fitz Urse, Hugh de Morville and William Tracy – slipped away and made haste by ship to England, thence to Canterbury. On 29 December 1190 they caught up with Thomas, who had sought sanctuary in the Cathedral. They struck him down with their great Norman swords, an act of homicide and desecration that horrified Christendom. Local people dipped pieces of cloth in his blood, rumours of miracles circulated, a martyr was created, a legend born. In 1172, the Pope canonized him.

In 1174, Henry faced his darkest hour, with rebellion in France and the north of England, an incursion by the Scots, and temporary collapse of his authority. He came to Canterbury, where he sought out Thomas's shrine, now a place of pilgrimage. Henry spent the night in prayer, and in the morning had monks scourge him as a penitent.

Ever since, pilgrims and tourists alike flock to visit the spot where foolish words ended the friendship between two powerful, proud and determined men.

Captain Nolan & the Light Brigade's guns

For many of us, just to get up on to a horse requires some courage. The concept of galloping that horse towards thousands of well-armed enemies, whether cavalry, infantry or artillery, would require courage bordering on the foolhardy. So it is not surprising that cavalrymen were regarded as supremely brave and, sadly, often very stupid.

In the British army, this was compounded by the way that rich and aristocratic officers could purchase their commissions, or even furnish whole regiments. All of this combined to create the disaster immortalised as the 'Charge of the Light Brigade.'

At the battle of Balaclava, during the Crimean war, the British commander, Lord Raglan, looking down from high ground, could see Russians removing guns from some heights. He wrote out a loosely worded order, unfortunately delivered by a young officer, Captain Nolan, himself an ardent advocate of the cavalry arm. Lord Lucan and Lord Cardigan received the apparently suicidal order '*to attack the guns*' with stupefaction, because the only guns they could see were those at the end of a long 'valley of death' where the Light Brigade could be fired on from three sides. Lucan

was scarcely on speaking terms with his brother in law, Lord Cardigan, whose career had been dogged by scandal and disgrace, and whom *The Times* had once even called '*the plague spot of the British army*'. However, any understandable hesitation by the two bemused officers was swept away by Nolan, pointing wildly in the wrong direction and shouting imperiously the fatal words, 'there is your enemy! There are your guns!' So off they went.

Half a league, half a league
Half a league onward
All the valley of Death
Rode the six hundred.

After a few hundred yards, Cardigan was infuriated to see Captain Nolan cutting across head of him. Nolan was almost certainly trying to undo his dreadful mistake, and to warn the Light Brigade that they were heading in the wrong direction and to destruction. We will never know, because Nolan, 'with a horrible scream', was killed in the saddle by a shell.

The gallant 600 did reach the guns, but faced by massive Russian forces, the survivors were forced to limp back down that same shot-swept valley. The end

Lord Cardigan

result was a tragedy that destroyed a brigade, spoiled the earlier successes of the Heavy Brigade and the Highlanders and prolonged the war into a ghastly winter.

'C'est magnifique, mais ce n'est pas la guerre', said a French General watching with horror.

Unfortunately, it was the kind of war that cavalrymen indulged in quite a lot.

The Charge of the Light Brigade, by C.E. Stuart (courtesy: The Cavalry and Guards Club)

William Fetterman & Crazy Horse

'Give me 80 good troopers and I will ride through the whole Sioux nation!'

It is doubtful that William Fetterman had ever heard of the fate a decade before of the Light Brigade, let alone Captain Nolan. But he fits the profile of the brave but foolhardy calvary officer perfectly. He had boasted frequently, 'Give me 80 good troopers and I will ride through the whole Sioux nation!' In December 1866, sadly for his men, he was to be given his chance.

The latest attempt to steal Indian land started with a conference presided over by Civil War hero General William Tecumseh Sherman. A road up

Red Cloud

the Bozeman Trail was to be built straight through Indian hunting grounds, protected by three forts. Red Cloud of the Oglala Sioux was the first to jump up and correctly accuse Washington of deceit, 'I prefer to die fighting rather than by starvation'. He led all the Chiefs from the conference, warning that there would be war. Foolishly, the US government started to build the road and the forts anyway, but tried to do it on a shoestring, because continuous Indian fighting had been bankrupting the tiny US Army. The key fort was to be Fort Phil Kearny nestling beside the Bighorn

Mountains – soon to be a familiar name to Americans. Colonel Henry Carrington, its builder and commander was a good man for fort building. A middle-aged engineer, he was a poor choice for a fighting commander, ordered to spend the Civil War on the supply staff and away from the regiment he had raised, and was thus unfairly denigrated by his fellow officers, who had endured brutal fighting. From the start, his 350 men and women in the fort were virtual prisoners, under-provisioned and surrounded by hostile tribes who attacked anyone that tried to travel up his 100 miles of the Bozeman Trail. This frustrating situation was too much for Carrington's right hand man, Captain William Fetterman. An outstanding and brave young officer in the Civil War, he had not enjoyed the lucky breaks that had propelled George Custer to become a Brigadier General at 24, and was itching for a fight that would make his reputation. He despised the Indians for their hit and run tactics, and fumed at Carrington's patient approach, even plotting and speaking against him. Red Cloud's waiting warriors had just the right enemy and just the right leader to deal with him – Crazy Horse.

Fetterman

The 'Achilles Heel' of the fort was its need for timber five miles away – the wood-cutting parties were constantly being attacked. On December 21, 1866, the last party of the winter was planned, and Carrington ordered a steady officer, Captain James Powell, with 79 men, to relieve the wood-cutters.

But Fetterman grabbed Carrington by the arm and demanded, as the next senior officer, to be given the command. After weeks of harassment by his brash young deputy, Carrington weakly acquiesced, but gave him a written order ending '*Under no circumstances pursue beyond Lodge Trail Ridge*'. As he loudly repeated the order twice, Fetterman's cocky friend Captain Fred Brown, vowing to 'bring back Red Cloud's scalp', joined the party. Fetterman now had exactly eighty men.

Crazy Horse and a small group lured Fetterman on, using the oldest trick in Plains warfare, the classic Indian decoy game. Keeping just out of range, Crazy Horse rode slowly, pretended his horse was lame, dismounted several times and even appeared to give up, building a small fire and letting the other decoys 'abandon him.' At the last minute, he mounted

and rode after his braves. It was all so realistic that Fetterman fell for it and steadily pursued, against orders, over Trail Lodge Ridge out of sight and to his doom. At a signal from Crazy Horse, two thousand Sioux, Cheyennes and Arapahoes rose from where they had been quietly hiding in the grass along the flanks of Peno Creek and charged the tiny force. In twenty minutes all the infantry were dead. Only a few more minutes saw the end of the cavalry further up in the rocks. Almost all were killed by the 40,000 arrows that rained down. Before the end, Fetterman and Brown stood up, counted to three, and shot each other to avoid a tortured death. With most of his fighting men gone,

Carrington was fearful for the fort and that the ten women and several children would fall into the hands of the Indians. Calmly, he prepared the magazine to explode and to kill them all. Luckily, a freezing blizzard started and the Indians moved away to shelter from the driving snow.

The 'Fetterman Massacre' shook the army and the nation. The Bozeman Trail was closed down, but the cynical wars to oust the tribes from their homelands continued. Nine years later that other firebrand, George Custer was given command of the Seventh Cavalry.

He was to show that he had learned nothing from Fetterman's fate.

George Custer & the Little Bighorn

With his long fair hair, and his exuberant if arrogant personality, George Custer was both glamorous and popular. History records that he was also one of the most dangerous men with whom to go into battle. With reckless courage, his heroic exploits in the American Civil War certainly earned him wide publicity and the rank of General at the age of just 26, but often at the expense of needless losses.

So it is hardly surprising that when

Custer arrived at a sleepy stream called the Little Bighorn, disaster was about to strike. After many exhausting days riding, Custer looked down and could see only part of what was a very sizeable camp of Sioux and Cheyenne. He therefore sensed an easy, surprise victory – mostly against women and children – like his dubious exploit at the Massacre of the Washita. Against specific orders to wait for reinforcements from the infantry,

Custer cried, 'We've got them this time!' and impetuously split his forces and plunged 225 tired cavalrymen down towards the camp, to realise – at once and with horror – that 4,000 united, prepared, fresh and well-armed braves were thundering up towards and around him. Losing the race for protection from the nearest hill, Custer was trapped between Gall and Crazy Horse, Fetterman's nemesis. Custer was killed, as was every man in his command, all of them overwhelmed by heat, exhaustion and superior firepower.

A brush fire in 2001 revealed 9,000 artefacts of the battle, which showed that the Indians were using 40 types of rifle and had more than enough Winchesters, while some of the unfortunate cavalrymen had not even had time to fire their weapons.

While a new monument is being erected to honour both sides, The Little Bighorn still remains a symbol of the excellent old military maxim, 'Never underestimate your enemy'.

Crazy Horse

Brendan Behan & his poem

In 1960, an elegant equestrian statue in Dublin's Phoenix Park was blown up. Lord Gough, Anglo-Irish hero of wars in China and India, but now rather an ancient symbol of the British, went skywards. Soon a poem was circulating in Dublin, its first verse opening:

Neath the horse's prick, a dynamite stick
Some gallant hero did place
For the cause of our land, with a light in his hand
Bravely the foe he did face.

Many may feel that this does not represent some of the finest poetry in the English language but that was not the reason that the poet wished to remain anonymous. In fact, the poet was Brendan Behan, and he had his reasons to hide his disdainful views of the IRA's latest triumph, which he thought frankly moronic.

His connections with the Irish Republican Army had been very important to Brendan since he was nine years old. He had, at sixteen and a half, quixotically left Dublin for England in 1939 on a madcap, unauthorised bombing mission, to 'blow up a battleship.' He was caught at once, and found himself in a Borstal in Suffolk. His

As with many literary geniuses, the drink did for Brendan.

stay provided him with inspiration for *Borstal Boy*. On his release, he was involved in something much more serious and was jailed in Dublin for trying to shoot an (Irish) policeman. Mountjoy Prison gave Brendan *The Quare Fellow*, the play that first made him famous. One final prison stretch preceded his IRA based *The Hostage*. His attitude to his IRA comrades could always be somewhat cynical, 'When I came back to Dublin I was court martialled in my absence, and sentenced to death in my absence, so I said they could shoot me in my absence.'

His wit and literary drive overcame his anxieties about IRA reprisals, possibly fuelled by his real nemesis, alcohol. After all, he had described himself as a drinker with writing problems.' Drink was to kill him aged just 41.

So to cheer the reader up, here is the rest of his poetic masterpiece.

Then without showing fear, he kept himself clear
Excepting to blow up the pair
But he nearly went crackers, all he got was the knackers
And made the poor stallion a mare.

This is the way our heroes today
Are challenging England's might
With a stab in the back and a midnight attack
On a horse that can't even shite.

Show business & its predictions

Irving Berlin once said, 'There's no business like show business'. Quite right. The world of entertainment has always attracted people who will sound off about their industry or about their colleagues at a drop of a hat. It is a world that can be self-centred, over-paid and hysterical, and our modern love affair with 'celebrities' has made it even more frenetic.

Ever since Cecil B. de Mille turned down New Mexico in favour of a Los Angeles suburb called Hollywood, show business has been surrounded by hype and ill-judged opinions.

Many of the future titans of the cinema thought that it was 'not quite proper' compared with the lofty ideals of the theatre. In 1914, Charlie Chaplin considered that the silver screen was little more than a passing fad. 'It's a canned drama. What audiences really want is to see flesh and blood on the stage.'

An obvious way for movies to be more like the stage soon presented itself – sound. Al Jolson burst on to the screen in *The Jazz Singer*. Amazingly, even a pioneer of sound, Thomas Edison could intone in 1925, 'People will tire of talkies. Talking is no substitute for the good acting we have in silent pictures.' Harry Warner even blurted out, 'Who the hell wants to hear actors talk?' Director D. W. Griffith, famous for *The Birth of a Nation,* went further, 'We do not want now, and shall never want, the human voice in our films.'

If the film industry was contemptuous of innovation, it could be equally incompetent in spotting talent. How many potential stars must have been turned down by studio idiots? After his first audition, Fred Astaire's interviewer reported as follows: *Can't act, can't sing, slightly bald. Can dance a little.*

The eccentric Howard Hughes was even more dismissive. He called James Cagney 'a little runt' and referred to Clark Gable as an actor 'whose ears make him like a taxi cab with both doors opened.' The producers of the Bond films were very reluctant to hire Sean Connery because 'he looks like a bricklayer.'

Clark Gable and his ears

Even a non-human potential star called Mickey Mouse was turned down by Louis B. Meyer, because 'every woman is frightened of a mouse.' *Snow White* was at first scoffed at and dubbed 'Disney's folly.'

Even some who were to benefit hugely from success at first tried to resist it. Francis Ford Coppola complained that Paramount wanted him to direct 'this hunk of trash.' Luckily, his father told him to stop whining about making art films and to get on with it. Thus, we have the *Godfather* series.

Marlon Brando is The Godfather

One film alone, *Gone with the Wind*, has contributed several legendary banana skins. Louis B. Meyer luckily ignored his producer who said, 'No Civil War film ever made a nickel.' But, Bette Davis turned down the part of Scarlett O'Hara because she thought 'it would be a flop'. The director, Victor

Fleming, agreed, refusing to take a share of the profits in such a 'white elephant' – although he won an Oscar for it. Gary Cooper was, for a short while, delighted he had turned down the part of Rhett Butler, 'I'm glad it's going to be Clark Gable who's falling on his face and not Gary Cooper.'

The advent of television brought a new crop of foolish words. C. P. Scott, the editor the of the *Manchester Guardian* started on a lofty and classical note of disapproval, 'No good will come of this device. The word is half Greek, half Latin.' *The Listener* wrote in 1936, 'television won't matter in your lifetime or mine.'

However, Sam Goldwyn, that fount of splendid show business quotes, understood television's threat to the cinema, 'Why should people go out and pay money to see bad films, when they can stay home and watch bad television for nothing?'

Pop music has its fair share of foolish words and false predictions. Frank Sinatra scorned the new music which would sideline many and sweep the world, 'Rock 'n Roll is phoney and false, and is sung, written and played for the most part by cretinous goons.'

As we have seen, future mega stars, like The Beatles have been turned down only too easily (page 148) Even Elvis Presley was told by the Grand Ole Opry in Nashville, 'You ain't goin' nowhere son. You ought to go back to drivin' a truck.'

No doubt the same kind of advisor would have told J K Rowling to go back to the kitchen.

Robert Fulton & Napoleon's invasion

Napoleon still ranks as one of history's geniuses - intelligent, courageous and innovative. But all his triumphs were on dry land.

At sea it was a different matter. Britain and her Royal Navy had thwarted Napoleon's ambitions several times. Nelson had even made it very personal in 1788 when he stranded a furious Napoleon in Egypt for months, after destroying his ships at the Battle of the Nile. Napoleon recognised that to eliminate Britain he would have to invade her– by crossing the tantalisingly narrow Straits of Dover, blocked by a well-trained and superior Royal Navy.

However, new technology offered Napoleon a solution. The American

Robert Fulton was in Europe, bustling with ideas. His own first effort was the submarine, which he offered to Napoleon. After trying to blow up the blockade ships of the English, Fulton eventually abandoned his submarines as too advanced for the technology of the day. He turned to steamboats, which would make him famous. By 1803 he had initiated the world's first commercial passenger steamboat service, in New York. Another was operating in Paris.

So an idea struck him that might solve the problem for the French. He proposed it to Napoleon: 'Why not use steamboats to tow invasion barges rapidly across the Channel, when the English ships were against unfavourable winds?'

Napoleon, normally one of the world's great innovators, lost his chance with the memorable reply: 'What sir, would you make a ship sail against the wind and currents by lighting a bonfire under her deck? I pray you excuse me, I have no time to listen to such nonsense.'

In 1805, Napoleon with his huge invasion force waited and waited at Boulogne for Admiral Villeneuve's fleet to join him. It was destroyed at Trafalgar.

Napoleon was doomed by his technological prejudice, while Fulton returned to America to become the ' father of the steamboat.'

Guy Fawkes & the giveaway letter

All over Britain, on November the fifth, bonfires are lit, usually topped with a grotesque figure of Guy Fawkes. 'Remember, remember the fifth of November, with gunpowder, treason and plot'.

The plot, in 1605, was to blow up the houses of Parliament, killing King James I, his government and the whole ruling aristocracy. Had it succeeded, it would have been the political and social equivalent of 9/11, Kennedy's assassination and the French Revolution all

rolled into one. We would certainly not be celebrating it with cheerful victory bonfires. However, many things conspired against the conspirators.

The plot was hatched by a group of provincial Roman Catholic landowners who were bitterly disappointed with James's unexpected crack down on Catholicism. They planned to replace him with his infant daughter Elizabeth. The ringleader, Thomas Catesby, turned to Guy Fawkes because of his military and explosives expertise. A cellar was

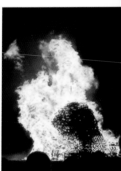

Guy Fawkes

'They shall not see who hurts them.'

rented under the Houses of Parliament, and 36 barrels of gunpowder, nearly 3 tons, was smuggled in and hidden behind piles of wood.

The State Opening of Parliament was delayed time and again, and more people were brought into the conspiracy. Finally, it was announced that Parliament would sit on 5 November, 1605. All was ready. However, one of the newcomers got cold feet about the intended carnage. Francis Tresham decided to tip off his Catholic cousin, Lord Monteagle, and, on 26 October, wrote him a letter warning him not to attend because, *'They shall receive a terrible blow, this Parliament, and yet they shall not see who hurts them.'* Monteagle, who had been treated well by the government, did not burn the letter as instructed, but showed it to Robert Cecil, James's Secretary of State, an anti-Catholic spymaster. Writing the letter was a bad enough mistake, but the real blunder was that knowing it had been sent so foolishly, the conspirators still decided to carry on with the plot.

On the night before the planned attack, Guy Fawkes was duly caught red-handed by Cecil's men, arrested and, by order of the King, tortured. Many of the plotters galloped north, and were caught at Holbeche House in Staffordshire.

Their defence against the King's troops was weakened because several of them had been injured trying to dry out gunpowder in front of an open fire (they were plainly missing Guy Fawkes' explosive skills.)

All the conspirators were hanged, drawn and quartered – except one, the letter writer, Francis Tresham. He was locked up alone in the Tower of London and died in mysterious circumstances six weeks later. The mystery remains.

King James ordered that bonfires be lit every 5 November, topped by an effigy of the Pope – later replaced by Guy Fawkes. Of the plotters, his name is the only one we remember. Indeed, his first name, starting in America, slowly became changed from a 'person of grotesque appearance' to just another name for a man. Even in Britain, Guy is replacing 'bloke', 'fellow' or 'chap.'

Whatever the murderous, if blundering, intentions of the plot, Guy Fawkes seems to command some respect and affection. He was recently voted into the BBC list of 'One Hundred Greatest Britons', and JK Rowling gave his name to the phoenix in *Harry Potter*.

So cynical have people become about politicians, that some have joked, 'Guy Fawkes was the only man to go to Parliament with honourable intentions.'

sloth & inattention

'*Oh! How I hate to get up in the morning!*'
Irving Berlin

'*An idle brain is the devil's workshop.*'
Proverb, 17th Century

Bill Gates & his flying friend

He could have been the richest man on earth. But Larry Kildall decided to go flying and let his wife handle things. It was the largest and most tragic business blunder in history.

The world of computing was changing fast. Gone were the days when IBM's Thomas Watson estimated that perhaps five computers in the world would suffice, or when Kenneth Olsen of Digital would stop any development of personal computers because he did not see 'any reason why anyone would want to have a computer at home.'

Intel's invention of the microprocessor or chip changed everything. Now computers did not have to weigh tons and fill whole rooms. In 1974, young kids with long hair and/or beards met on Wednesdays at the 'Homebrew Computing Club', a hall rented from Stamford University in what would become 'Silicon Valley'. Young men like Steve Jobs and Steve Wozniak of Apple and 19-year old Bill Gates and Paul Allen of Microsoft shared their triumphs. Soon the Personal Computer or PC was on its way – out of their garages and into millions of homes and offices.

Now IBM, the world's leading mainframe manufacturer, wanted to get into this booming PC market and they wanted to do it secretly and fast. One August day in 1980 they called Bill Gates and said they were flying in to Seattle and would like to come in next day 'to talk about Microsoft products.' This was like a visit from the Queen or the Pope, so Gates quickly looked for a suit to wear. Jack Sams of IBM described arriving, *'We were waiting in the front and this young fella came out to take us to Mr Gates' office. I thought he was the office boy, but, of course, it was Bill Gates.'*

After agreeing to sign IBM's standard non-disclosure agreement (swearing them to secrecy), Bill Gates then had to reveal that he did not have one of the key things IBM was looking for – an operating system. But in a spirit of friendly collegial cooperation, he recommended that he call his friend Larry Kildall at Digital Research. 'I'm sending some guys down. Treat them right, they're important guys.' So next day, the three IBM executives flew south and turned up at a small house in Pacific Grove, California, the headquarters of Digital Research. But Larry Kildall, the genius who had created the CP/M (Control Program/ Microcomputer)

Three years before the IBM meeting, a young Bill Gates, booked for a traffic violation

ALBUQUERQUE NMEX
APD 105 519
12 13 77

operating system, was not there to greet them. He had gone flying. And his wife Dorothy refused to sign the non-disclosure agreement. Jack Sams of IBM recalls the chaotic, frustrating day in the tiny house, *So we spent the whole day in Pacific Grove debating with them and with our attorneys and her attorneys and everybody else about whether or not she could even talk to us about talking to us. We left.'* And they went back to Bill Gates.

This time, Gates did not hesitate. He agreed to find them an operating system and turned to Tim Patterson, who quickly wrote QDOS (quick and dirty operating system), which IBM called PC DOS 1.0. Gates paid just $50,000 dollars for the rights. It was based on Larry Kildall's CP/M and months later, when he discovered, there was a furious confrontation at a Seatttle restaurant between the two friends. But Kildall knew he could not sue Microsoft without suing IBM, a daunting task. So, to avoid trouble, he agreed to licence his system to IBM at a high royalty. But when IBM's PC was launched, he was stupefied to find that IBM was charging $240 for his CP/M and just $40 for Bill Gates' DOS.

The result was inevitable; hundreds of millions of computers running Microsoft's software, and Bill Gates becoming the richest man in the world, worth $40 billion and climbing. Larry Kildall sold his company for $120 million and died aged 52 on the floor of a bar.

If only he had not gone flying.

> *It is worth recalling the second banana skin relating to the story of Bill Gates and Larry Kildall. IBM made the fateful decision to opt for hardware rather than software and then to give away the software field to Microsoft. Microsoft is now twice as big as IBM.*

Ferdinand de Lesseps & the mosquito

There have been few more successful projects than the Suez Canal. Built on plans first surveyed by Napoleon in 1878, 'the stagnant ditch' as it was cynically called, was completed in 1869 and immediately had a huge effect on both world trade and strategic power, making possible, among other things, the British Empire.

Suez was a triumph for the French engineer, Ferdinand de Lesseps, who became an international hero. So it was with great confidence that he approached his next project in 1879, a canal across the isthmus of Panama, the crossroads not only between the Atlantic and the Pacific but also of North and South America.

In spite of his fame and stature, de Lesseps was almost immediately in

trouble. Financially, he limped from crisis to crisis. He had attempted to raise 400 million francs, but had only managed to obtain 30 million, a feeble eight per cent of the total needed. This meant that de Lesseps, now in his seventies, was forced to travel back to France several times to scrape up funds – taking out a number of loans – and even using a lottery to raise capital.

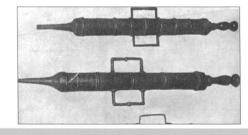

Then his confidence as an engineer was dented. He insisted at first on trying to repeat a flat, sea-level canal like Suez, with no locks. But Panama was mountainous with hard volcanic rock, and with the huge barrier of the Culebra Mountain.

But what really brought the engineering hero down was a tiny creature – the mosquito. The French had paid scant attention to the efforts twenty years earlier of the British botanists at Kew to cultivate the *Cinchona* tree to make life-saving quinine. Nor had they realised the crucial need to install screens on houses and to eliminate the breeding grounds of stagnant water – indeed they planted pretty trees round their houses in bowls of water!

The result was unimaginable disaster. Nearly 30,000 of de Lesseps' workers died of malaria and yellow fever.

By 1889 de Lesseps was transformed from the 'Hero of Suez' to the 'Villain of Panama'. He and his shareholders were ruined, his son was jailed and even his friend, the great engineer Eiffel, was heavily fined. The project had failed, as had its founder, who died a broken man in 1894.

Twenty years later a team of West Point engineers built the Canal, with proper finance, massive locks to conquer the mountains and the right methods to beat the mosquitoes.

Sir Thomas Bludworth & The Fire of London

Charles II had become increasingly worried about the risk of a major fire in London, and had repeatedly written to the Lord Mayor, Sir Thomas Bludworth, who had done nothing to improve the city's feeble firefighting capability and pathetic water syringes.

The London of 1666 was, in many ways, a huge accident waiting to happen. The skyline was magnificent, with the old St. Paul's Cathedral and 109 parish churches pushing their spires above the houses, but a closer look presented a desperate picture.

While there were large halls and mansions built by nobles, merchant adventurers, wealthy traders and the guild and livery companies, much of the city was mean and squalid, with tortuous alleys, dark and smelly. Crowded, densely packed timber-framed dwellings were built on a web of cobbled streets, and an open channel ran down the centre of lanes into which householders threw their kitchen water and refuse. Worse, the overlapping storeys above these evil-smelling streets meant that there was often only a narrow shaft of daylight piercing through to the foetid scene below. Little wonder that the Great Plague had killed 56,000 people in the city of London alone.

On the night of Sunday, 2 September, the inevitable happened. In Pudding Lane, a narrow line of tottering timber houses running down to the Thames, the King's baker, Thomas Farynor, had gone to sleep thinking that his oven had been safely damped down.

However, at two o'clock in the morning he awoke with his house full of smoke, and he and his wife and daughter escaped by climbing through a window and across a roof to reach a neighbouring house. His maidservant – not as brave – remained behind and became the first victim of the fire.

At first, the fire went slowly, but after an hour, hay in the yard of the Star Inn opposite blazed up. Gradually the flames moved down Pudding Lane and Fish Street Hill towards the Thames river quays, engulfing the first church. That was when Sir Thomas Bludworth, much irritated to be got out of bed, arrived to make his second fatal mistake. He thought the blaze could be easily

extinguished like some of the small regular fires, and has gone down in history with the memorable, if inelegant remark: 'Pish, a woman might piss it out!'

'Pish, a woman might piss it out!'

Sir Thomas did not realise that the flames were carried by a rising wind down to Thames Street. Here was the perfect place to start a dangerous conflagration – in the cellars and warehouses full of tallow, oil, spirits and hemp, and on the open wharves with their hay, timber and coal. The fired raged on. The Lord Mayor was then faced with his last possible chance: to pull down houses to create fire breaks. But wringing his hands with meanness and indecision, he hesitated, stammering, 'But who would pay to renew them?'

He lost his chance. The fire became unstoppable and eventually even St. Paul's Cathedral was consumed, its stones splitting apart in explosions. Molten lead poured from the six acres of lead on its roof and ran down the streets in a red stream. The bankers got their gold away from Lombard Street but the shopping area of Cheapside was gone in hours.

The great diarist Samuel Pepys met Bludworth in Canning Street, now crying out like a fainting woman. 'Lord, what can I do? I am spent; people will not obey me; I have been pulling down houses but the fire overtakes us.' Luckily the King himself intervened to provide decisive action with troops, sailors and gunpowder to create the firebreaks. It was his brother, the Duke of York, who did Bludworth's job, saving some of the city by his exertions.

There is a famous epigram that says 'the Fire of London began in Pudding Lane and ended at Pie Corner'. Unfortunately, not true. The fire burned a long way after Pie Corner had been levelled to the ground.

The Great Fire of London raged for four days and nights, but the wind dropped, and on the Thursday the sun rose over a still-smoking city – covered in ash and dirt inches thick. Some four hundred and fifty acres were devastated, over 13,000 houses were destroyed in 400 streets, and 87 parish churches. So many people were ruined or made destitute that four debtors' prisons had to be built – although by a miracle only six people died.

Today, the City of London is almost unrecognisable, with glass and steel monuments marking it as one of the world's leading financial centres. Only the names on streets and tube stations remain to remind us of the city that burned down, partly because of the unworthy behaviour of its Lord Mayor.

Kermit Tyler & Pearl Harbor's radar blips

There were tens of thousands of young Lieutenants in the US forces of World War II. We probably know the names of just two of them – the hero Audie Murphy and the poor, unfortunate Kermit Tyler.

Kermit was not to know that, for a few brief seconds, he was America's very last line of defence – and that he held the outcome of a crucial battle and the history of his nation in his hands.

On Sunday morning, 7 December 1941, over a hundred ships lay at anchor at Pearl Harbor, including eight battleships moored alongside Ford Island. Vast fuel storage tanks, repair facilities and dry docks were theoretically protected by hundreds of fighters and even some new radar sets.

Some 235 miles to the north of the sleepy Hawaiian islands, after an undetected voyage of 4,000 miles, six Japanese aircraft carriers had turned into the wind and launched 350 dive bombers, torpedo bombers and fighters.

There should have been plenty of reasons to be alert. With a new war faction in Tokyo, Japan and America were plainly on a collision course. The US had cut off supplies of vital scrap metal and, more importantly, oil if Japan did not withdraw from China, which the Japanese had no intention of doing. Intelligence reports from all sources were pouring in, not least from the threatened British and Dutch. Furthermore, a 14 part signal to Japan's embassies had been decoded by US code breakers, plainly indicating an imminent raid, and therefore, war. But, as so often, Army and Navy did not co-ordinate. Ships at Pearl Harbor lay with no torpedo nets out, ammunition was locked up and planes were parked on their airfields wing-tip to wing-tip.

There was just one last chance to avert disaster. Six new radar sets had been set up on the islands. At 7.02 am, just after the normal time to switch off, the two private soldiers operating the set at Opana Point detected a huge, unusual

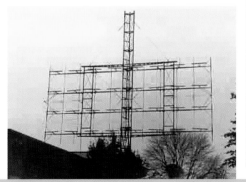

'Well, don't worry about it.'

TONY COWLAND

Japanese dive bombers pounce on Pearl Harbor

in to the Information Center, to be answered by a tired, young Kermit Tyler, a fighter pilot who had hardly been briefed and had never seen a radar set. Just imagine if he had swung into action. Ships would have raised steam, anti-aircraft crews been alerted and, above all, hundreds of American fighters would have been swarming above Pearl Harbor. But no. Tyler just assumed that the incoming blip was 12 B-17 bombers due in from San Francisco. He told the operators to switch off and get some breakfast, adding one of the most memorable lines in warfare: 'Well, don't worry about it!'

The rest, as they say, is history.

'blip', denoting at least 50 planes coming in from the north. They urgently phoned

Houdini & the punch

The most famous escape artist of all time could have escaped his death by paying more attention to his health and less to his showmanship.

Harry Houdini was actually born Erich Weiss back in Budapest in 1874. Four years later, Samuel Weiss brought his family to Appleton, Wisconsin, and became its Rabbi. The four sons and the daughter were brought up both poor and poorly educated, but Erich was extremely athletic and burning to succeed.

It was a travelling magician who first fired the boy's interest in magic and at just seventeen, to avoid manual labour, Harry teamed with a friend to form 'The Houdini Brothers.' (The name was inspired by Jean Eugene Robert-Houdin, the most famous magician of the age.) Later his brother Hardeen and then his wife, Bess, would become his stage partners.

For five years, magic proved a real struggle. Houdini's card manipulations, illusions and box escapes failed to excite the public – all except the 'Needle Trick', where he swallowed dozens of needles and pieces of thread, then regurgitated the thread with the needles neatly threaded on. Disillusioned with magic, he nearly gave it all up, unsuccessfully advertising to sell his tricks and secrets for just $20. But in 1898, Houdini hit on the 'Challenge Act', escaping from any handcuffs the audience produced – including the ones jammed by policemen trying to catch him out. The 'Challenge Act' made him famous.

Then a visit to a friend, a psychiatrist, inspired him to use strait-jackets from which to escape, often upside down high above the crowd. His 'Challenge Act' soon expanded to exotic variations – escaping from jail cells, padlocked crates thrown into rivers, locked mail sacks, milk churns and even a bronze coffin for his 'Buried Alive' act.

This daring pioneer was also the first man to fly an aeroplane in Australia, to create a new diving suit and to start a movie company, performing his own stunts. He was also so impressed with the way a young Vaudeville actor, Joseph Keaton, managed to fall downstairs that he called him 'Buster.'

Houdini was a driven performer and his very professionalism led to his premature death, coupled with the inattention to health that many men display, in contrast with women. On tour in 1926, he began to suffer severe stomach pains, but refused to see a doctor lest he miss some shows and disappoint his fans. A few days later he was in Canada. In his dressing room, an admiring McGill University student, Gordon Whitehead, decided to test Houdini's legendary ability to withstand blows and suddenly hit him in the stomach. Houdini did not have time to tense his muscles and doubled over in pain. Probably already suffering from appendicitis, he still did not check in with a doctor. A week later, Houdini collapsed on stage in Detroit and was rushed to hospital. For the next six days, his wife Bess, who was also ill, was wheeled in to be with him.

At last, he whispered to his brother Hardeen, 'I'm tired of fighting', and died. The cause was peritonitis, caused by appendicitis and the stomach punch.

It would have been worthwhile for Houdini to pay less attention to his audiences and more to his health and, for that matter, to those who were let into his dressing room.

Houdini preparing for one of his escapes from water

By 1550, the town of Cremona in Northern Italy was already well known for its violins, but it was a varnish that really made it famous.

The violin saw its origins in Islam, where the Arabs had developed stringed instruments like the rebab, which had then evolved in Spain during the Moorish invasion with

A superb 'Messiah' Stradivarius violin made in 1716, complete with its varnish from Cremona. (Courtesy of the Museo Civico Cremona)

rebecks, viellas, violas, lyres and 'fidulas' – hence the name for the fiddle.

By the XVII century, the violin had become the most important instrument in any orchestra and three Italian cities, Venice, Brescia and Cremona, became the world centres for the craft of violin making. Andrea Amati founded the tradition in Cremona, and it was his grandson Nicola who passed on his skills to two of his most brilliant students, Antonio Stradivarius and Andrea Guarneri.

In addition to their superlative skills in creating the shape and quality of their violins, the Cremonese had also developed a thin, non-greasy, slow-drying varnish to be placed on top of a special mineral-rich grounding. And it was this varnish that the master violin makers, including Antonio Stradivarius, used on their violins. The result was a mellow sound that has never been rivalled.

In 1704, when he was sixty, Stradivarius was the only person who thought it might be a good idea to write down the composition of the golden-red Cremonese varnish, and he duly recorded it on the inside cover of his Bible. What a tragic banana skin. The Bible was later lost, and with it, the priceless secret.

However, that is one reason why the 600 surviving violins, 60 cellos and 17 violas inscribed 'Antonio Stradivarius Cremonensis' now change hands for nearly two million dollars. Fine if you are selling one, but sad for the rest of the world's music lovers.

Adolph Eichmann & the Wannsee folder

It was all decided in a couple of hours over polite cakes and cognac in a pleasant villa, overlooking the lake of Wannsee, near Berlin. It was no less than the plan for the 'Final Solution of the Jewish Question', the blueprint of the Holocaust.

On January 15 1942, one of the most evil Nazis of all, Himmler's deputy, SS-Obergruppenführer Reinhard Heydrich, convened a meeting of fifteen young, bright civil servants, SS officers and police officials to review how to solve the question of the Jews. Why? After all, brutal anti-Jewish measures had been in place since *'Kristallnacht',* the traumatic night of the looting of shops and burning of synagogues in 1938. German Jews had been progressively removed from public life. The notorious Nuremberg Laws had made life impossible. Many, the 'lucky' ones as it turned out, had been forced to emigrate. Others were already in concentration camps.

With the invasion of Poland in September 1939, her two and a half million Jews had been quickly herded into ghettos and starved. After the 1941 attack on the Soviet Union with its five million Jews, killer squads from

Heydrich's mobile *Einsatzgruppen* were now shooting Jewish men, women and children in their thousands every day.

However, from the Nazi standpoint, this was not good enough. The maniacal destruction of their racial enemies was all too 'muddled and slow'. There were 27 different agencies dealing with Jewish matters. Thus Heydrich, backed by his efficient and faithful henchman, Adolph Eichmann, determined to sort everything out, and moreover, exclusively under SS control.

Heydrich opened the Wannsee conference by coldly reviewing the 'struggles against the enemy, the Jew' and discussing the 'storage problem'. The meeting was then given a list of the European countries and their eleven million Jews, including those in Britain and Ireland, to be involved in the *Endlosung* or 'Final Solution'. This proposed 'Evacuation to the East', a euphemism for promised mass killing on an unimaginable scale. After just three hours of calm and genial discussion over food, wine, cigars and brandy, the

Eichmann, the smiling technocrat

The horrific list of those planned to be killed	
A.	
Germany proper	131,800
Austria	43,700
Eastern Territories	420,000
Poland (GG)	2,284,000
Bialystok	400,000
Bohemia & Moravia	74,200
Estonia	free of Jews
Latvia	3,500
Lithuania	34,000
Belgium	43,000
Denmark	5,600
France/occupied	165,000
France/unoccupied	700,000
Greece	69,600
Netherlands	160,800
Norway	1,300
B.	
Bulgaria	48,000
England	330,000
Finland	2,300
Ireland	4,000
Italy	58,000
Albania	200
Croatia	40,000
Portugal	3,000
Romania	342,000
Sweden	8,000
Switzerland	18,000
Serbia	10,000
Slovakia	88,000
Spain	6,000
Turkey (European)	55,500
Hungary	742,800
USSR	5,000,000
Ukraine	2,994,684
White Russia	446,484
Total over 11,000,000	

decisions were made, the meeting was closed and the delegates all drove off into the snowy evening.

The effects of Wannsee were immediate. Within the next 12 months the new gas chambers and the huge extermination camps like Auschwitz became operational, and half of the Holocaust's victims perished.

From then on, until even the last chaotic days of the collapsing Third Reich, Adolph Eichmann and his men diligently 'combed Europe from West to East', as he had been directed at Wannsee. Six million Jews eventually died, the greatest, most methodical and horrific mass murder in history. But, of course, the cruel and cynical planning of all this was meant to be an absolute secret. Even when the Germans appeared unstoppable, the perpetrators realised there *just* might be future risks. So Eichmann had stressed to each Wannsee delegate that he must, at all costs, destroy his copy of the stenographer's minutes, the *Wannsee Protokoll*.

However, one day in 1947, an American officer, preparing for the Nuremberg War Crimes Tribunals, was rummaging through files in the old German Foreign Ministry, only to come across a strange folder; *Protokoll* copy number 16. Somebody at Wannsee had blundered: the Under Secretary at the Foreign Office with the unlikely name of Dr Martin Luther. Inattentive in the weeks after the conference, he had forgotten the strict order to destroy his folder. Bizarrely, he was then unable to do so, because in 1943 he was evicted from his office after he had tried to oust his boss, von Ribbentrop, and (pure irony) he spent the rest of the war in Sachsenhausen concentration camp. His

Russian liberators were not to know his true role, and he luckily died before he was discovered.

However, Dr Luther's banana skin of inattention and disobedience was the only way we thankfully know exactly what happened in that villa, giving the world the evidence, word by word, of the most clinically appalling conference in history. As for Eichmann, the most clinical of them all, when he was tracked down in South America and brought back to face trial in Israel, it was that missing folder that sealed his fate.

The last folder sealed his fate.

Ian Woosnam & his clubs

Sport in today's world is not really sport any more, it is business. And like all businesses where the financial stakes are enormous, the temptation to cheat or to behave 'unsportingly' can be irresistible. So German racing drivers have been known to push 'Brave British Boys' off the track and out of the Championship; footballers take 'dives'; boxers can be bribed to win or lose; skaters can be assaulted; horses can be doped; as can, of course, athletes in every sport; tennis players can distract; results are altered to benefit gambling syndicates and entire cyclist teams kicked out of the Tour de France. The list is depressingly endless.

But there is one sport that recognised the threat from its inception and decided that the players should police themselves, with, sometimes, rather peculiar results.

Ever since 1744, when the Royal and Ancient Golf Club at St Andrews was founded and first created the rules, golf has dictated that the players are on their honour to play fair. They not only check on each other, but are expected to guard their own behaviour even when hidden from view in the deepest wood.

The rules can be arcane and strict – and the task of self-regulation under pressure can lead to banana skins of inattention that can be disastrous.

For instance, Ian Woosnam noticed that he had one extra club in his bag at the 2001 Open at Royal Lytham St Anne's. It was his caddy's fault, but he still received a two-stroke penalty, so only finished third.

Worse, Padraig Harrington was disqualified completely from the Benson and Hedges International Open in 2000, despite a five-stroke lead, after

his playing partner signed Harrington's score card by mistake. Mark Roe and Jesper Parnevik did not remember to swap score cards before their third round in the Open at Royal St George's in 2003, and were both disqualified.

Craig Stadler didn't want to get his trousers dirty at the Andy Williams Open in 1987, and knelt on a towel to play a stroke from under a tree. He was disqualified for illegally *building a stance.* In February 2005; Retief Goosen was a few minutes late for his 6.40 am Pro-Am tee-off at the Nissan Open and was disqualified from the whole $4.8 million main event.

Most golfers would agree with P. G. Wodehouse that this unique self-regulation is also a unique test of character.
'Golf is the infallible test. The man who can go into a patch of rough alone, with the knowledge that only God is watching him, and play his ball where it lies, is the man who will serve you faithfully and well.'

Thomas Bouch, Marx, Engels & The Tay Bridge

The Tay Bridge was to create two banana skins. One was of purely engineering interest, and the other was to rock the world.

We might have known Thomas Bouch as one of the great engineers of the Industrial Revolution, with a reputation to match that of Brunel, Telford and the Stephensons. Bouch thought he was reaching a pinnacle in 1873 when he opened his great bridge over the River Tay, the longest railway bridge in the world. Queen Victoria and her Royal Train used it a year later, and she knighted the proud engineer. Now 'Sir Thomas Bouch', he looked forward to the ultimate accolade – his next assignment, which was to build a huge bridge across the Forth.

But on the Tay Bridge, engine drivers had begun to complain that their trains were swaying as they crossed, and that bolts were loosening. On the night of 28 December 1879, in a terrible storm, the Tay Bridge collapsed into the river taking a complete train with it. The disaster was recorded by that famously ridiculous Scottish poet, William McGonogall:
'Beautiful Railway Bridge of the Silv'ry Tay!
Alas! I am very sorry to say

That ninety lives have been taken away
On the last Sabbath day of 1879,
Which will be remember'd for a very long
time.'

However much people may have sniggered at McGonogall's description, the tragedy and its effect on Sir Thomas Bouch were hardly laughing matters. He was disgraced for faulty design, poor workmanship and materials and promptly dismissed from the Forth Bridge project – to die within months, apparently of a broken heart.

However, a much more important banana skin for the rest of the world was created by two people missing the fateful train. Karl Marx was staying with his friend and collaborator Friedrich Engels. They were booked to travel on the doomed train, but became so engrossed in a heated discussion that they managed to miss it.

Had they both died, the revolutionary and influential book, *Das Kapital*, that they were both creating, might never have been published, and but for *Das Kapital* and 'Marxism', the world might never have been doomed to endure Communism.

Karl Marx, saved from disaster by his long talk with Engels

The bridge designers & 'Galloping Gertie'

It is not often that bridges become celebrities. But one did. Most of us have seen the famous grainy, black and white film; a bridge twisting like a ribbon before collapsing into the river.

The Tacoma Narrows Bridge was built in 1940 to connect Washington State in America's Pacific North West with her Olympic Peninsular. It was a prime example of the finest design of suspension bridges at the time; light, graceful and flexible.

However, something was very wrong. Even in a light wind, the bridge began to twist up and down like a roller coaster. It was soon called 'Galloping Gertie' by the

The bridge twisting, moments before its collapse

amused public, and became a popular tourist attraction. But it was a major worry for the Washington Toll Bridge Authority.

So, on November 7 1940, the bridge was being filmed by engineers with several 16mm cameras to study its peculiar motion and to try to find a cure. The wind began to rise. Soon the roadway was twisting and writhing like a mad animal, with the sidewalks rising 18 feet above each other. One car was on the bridge and the driver, terrified, ran back down the roadway. He was only just in time, because the whole span suddenly collapsed into the water. His dog, unfortunately trapped inside the car, was the only sad casualty of the much sadder engineering disaster, all captured on film.

This very public banana skin was a dramatic lesson for the world's bridge builders on the effects of 'resonance', and how a bridge's roadway can have the lift of an aircraft wing. From then on, all new bridge designs were tested in wind tunnels. Factored in nowadays are the effects of vibration, aerodynamics, wave phenomena and harmonics. That is the theory anyway.

However, things still seem to go wrong. In 2000, in celebration of the millennium year, a new foot bridge, costing £18 million was built across the Thames between London's St Paul's Cathedral and the Tate Modern Gallery. From the very first day, it became notorious for an unsettling, swaying motion which made anyone crossing the construction feel sick. Within two days of its inauguration, the bridge was closed and it took months and millions of pounds to correct this unfortunate phenomenon.

Engineers and architects seem no better than the rest of us at learning from past slips of judgement.

Brian Boru & his bodyguards

Clontarf, now a suburb of Dublin, was, on April 23 1014, a wooded brushland leading down to a sea full of Viking ships. It witnessed the most fateful battle in Ireland's history, and the tragic death of her greatest High King, Brian Boru.

Brian seems born to be a hero. He was the younger brother of Mahon, King of Munster, who had tried to live peaceably with the Vikings. As with the English, who paid off the fierce Norsemen with 'Danegeld', the Irish had offered no coherent resistance to the invaders. Dublin was now second only to Yorvic (York) as a Viking settlement.

Unlike his brother, Brian hated and distrusted the Vikings, having seen his mother killed in one of their raids. He conducted continuous and successful guerrilla warfare, and encouraged, Mahon joined him in expelling the Viking King of Limerick, Ivar. But ten years later Ivar had his revenge, returning in 975 to encourage his allies, treacherously to capture and assassinate Mahon. He paid with his life in personal combat with Brian, who then gradually built up alliances, notably with Malachy, King of Meath, while taking over from him the position of 'Ard Ri', High King.

He earned his name Brian Boru (Brian of the Tributes) by collecting taxes from other rulers and restoring the ravaged monasteries and libraries. Brian's military prowess seems to have been matched by sexual enthusiasm - he had 30 concubines and four wives, of which one, the beautiful and treacherous Gormblaith, was to prove his nemesis and his first banana skin. When he rejected her after four years, she summoned the traditional enemy, the Vikings, for assistance.

Brian, now an old man, marched across Ireland gathering his armies, although slightly weakened by the absence of his son Donough's contingent, away fighting in the south. Not all the Irish would join Brian - he had many jealous enemies. Some would stand aside, some would fight for the Vikings, some would fight for him. At dawn, while Gormblaith, her son, and in agony,

When he rejected the beautiful Gormblaith, she turned to the enemy, the Vikings

'The Death of Brian Boru' by Thomas Ryan RHA

Brian's loyal daughter watched from the walls of Dublin, the two armies began their massive battle. Brian carefully noted the state of the tide and directed the battle, while for once, not participating.

Vicious hand to hand raged fighting all day. Brian's son Murrough, and most of the leaders on both sides fell. The Vikings finally broke and tried to make it through the surf to their ships. Few succeeded, because as Brian had planned, the incoming tide meant that the boats were now half a mile out to sea.

Irish victory turned to tragedy.

Brian's bodyguards, seeing the Vikings in retreat, rushed off to loot. This stupid inattention meant that he was unprotected when the Viking King Brodir of Man found Brian Boru praying in his tent and felled him with his axe. But the dying King, aged seventy three, amazingly struck back and killed Brodir. Their bodies were found together.

While the Vikings were beaten militarily and eventually integrated into Irish society, the sudden removal of the great unifying influence of Brian Boru as High King fatally weakened Ireland. The invasion and domination by Normans and English for centuries might never have occurred.

Nome, Alaska & the map maker

There are places in the world which regret their names because they are unsuitable or have become embarrassing.

There are others that have received their names for strange reasons like Truth or Consequences, New Mexico, which voted to change its name to that of America's most popular radio show.

But consider the Alaskan town of Nome only a few miles from the Bering Strait and Siberia. It has seen its ups and downs. The height of its fame and prosperity was when in 1900 it had its own gold stampede to rival that of the Klondyke. It briefly took its population up to 20,000, with the normal mixture of prospectors, saloon-keepers, gamblers and prostitutes. The rip-roaring town even attracted a well-known figure from Tombstone, Wyatt Earp, who briefly ran a saloon called the 'Dexter' that made him more money than most miners.

The people of the town wanted to call it Anvil City, but a map-making banana skin was to thwart them. A British naval Captain was surveying the coast to create a map. He did not know the name of a nearby cape, so he wrote 'Cape Name?' beside it on the map. Forgetting to follow up the enquiry, he sent it off to the map printer in London, who thought he meant 'C. Nome' or 'Cape Nome' and marked it in. When the townspeople protested that they would much prefer Anvil City, the US Post Office said it was too difficult to change and threatened not to deliver the mail. So, reluctantly, the town has been Nome ever since.

The Archduke's driver & the wrong turn

All of us who drive have occasionally missed a turning and then have had to reverse. The normal result can be a bit of abuse by other drivers and some criticism from our passengers– especially wives and husbands. But one such driving slip was to have much more catastrophic consequences.

In June 1918, Archduke Franz Ferdinand, heir to the throne of the Austro-Hungarian Empire, was to visit Sarajevo in Bosnia-Herzegovina to inspect army manoeuvres. He was not to know that members of Serbia's secret 'Black Hand' were waiting to assassinate him.The designated killers were suffering from tuberculosis and had been told to kill themselves after their attempt.

Franz Ferdinand arrived at the railway station on Sunday 28 June and his cavalcade set off for a reception at City Hall. Seven members of the Black Hand were in the crowd along Appel Quay. One of them threw a grenade at the Archduke's car. The driver took evasive action and the grenade bounced off the back of the Archduke's car and rolled underneath the next car. It exploded and wounded two of its occupants.

The assassination appeared to have failed, and a furious Franz Ferdinand interrupted the Mayor's speech of welcome. 'What is the good of your speeches? I come to Sarajevo on a visit, and I get bombs thrown at me. It is outrageous!'

After the reception, the Archduke insisted on visiting the injured at the city hospital. His host, General Potiorek decided that the motorcade should take an alternate route to the hospital, avoiding the

A furious Archduke returns to his car

Princip was captured seconds after the shooting.

city centre. However, the driver of Ferdinand's car, Franz Urban, was not told of the change of plan and so took the original route.

Turning into Franz Joseph Street, General Potiorek, now a passenger in Ferdinand's car, noticed that the altered route had not been taken. He shouted at the driver who stopped the car and then began to reverse slowly out of the street.

There, sitting in a café was Gavril Princip, one of the young assassins, consoling himself over the morning's failure. He could not believe his luck. He rushed out with his revolver and shot at Franz Ferdinand, hitting him in the neck. His second shot killed the Duchess Sophie, who had flung herself across her dying husband to protect him.

Europe went into shock, and it was nearly four weeks later that the Austrians presented impossible demands to the Serbian government. Britain offered to mediate, which the German Kaiser decided was 'insolent.' The Austrians, encouraged, declared war on the Serbs. Russia, Serbia's ally, mobilised, as did France and Germany. In every country, 'mobilisation' now meant huge and complex railway plans. Once they were ordered, they were almost impossible to stop. Europe began to chuff to war.

On 1 August the Kaiser declared war on his cousin Czar Nicholas. Two days later he declared war on France, and just 24 hours later the *Schlieffen Plan* sent German troops into Belgium, and Britain came back from the August Bank Holiday and was amazed to find herself at war with Germany.

The world had lurched into the most horrible war in its history. It would kill millions, wiping out the flower of Europe's youth. It would engulf monarchies, destroy the Austro-Hungarian and Ottoman Empires, bring Communism to Russia and then the world and lay the seeds of Fascism and the Nazis.

Because he was only 19, Gavril Princip languished in jail for four years, slowly dying of his T.B. He must have wondered what he had unleashed. But at least he was deliberately sent to create havoc. A simple mistake by poor Franz Urban, the driver, was the most terrible traffic banana skin in history.

Icarus & the wrong flight plan

Dædalus was the son of Erechtheus, King of Athens. He was the most ingenious artist of his age, credited with the invention of the wedge, the axe, the gimlet, the level and many other mechanical instruments, and made lifelike statues, which moving of themselves, seemed to be endowed with life. When his nephew looked to rival him as an inventor, he killed him (actually throwing him out of a window) and with his son, Icarus, fled to Crete where the King, Minos, gave them sanctuary.

By now Minos had been given a beautiful big white bull by the god of the sea, Poseidon, which he was supposed to sacrifice to the god. But he decided to hang on to it. Poseidon was furious, and in revenge arranged for Minos' wife Pasiphae to fall in love with the animal. Dædalus, the master carpenter, to quote Lemprière's Classical Dictionary, then; *'prostituted his talents in being subservient to the queen's unnatural desires and, by his means, Pasiphae's horrible passions were gratified'.* The result, half man, half bull, was called the Minotaur, and lived in a labyrinth at Knossos also constructed by Dædalus.

Every nine years, the Athenians, having lost a war to Minos, had to send him as tribute seven young men and seven young virgins, who, if approved, were then eaten by the Minotaur. However, Theseus, one of the young men on the picnic menu, volunteered to kill the Minotaur – which he did with his bare fists – escaping from the labyrinth with the help of the king's daughter Ariadne and a large ball of string. But the labyrinth was not wasted. Dædalus, his part in the 'Queen's Affair' having come out, was imprisoned in it with his son Icarus.

In the labyrinth, Dædalus decided on escape. Tunnelling from an island being impractical, he made two sets of wings with feathers and wax. Wearing these wings, Dædalus and Icarus set off from Crete in the general direction of Greece, but the heat of the sun melted the wax on the wings of Icarus, who had soared too high, (not having listened to his father at briefing). Dædalus went on to Cumæ, on the north side of the Bay of Naples and then Sicily, where

CHAGALL

he was kindly received by King Cocalus.

Minos, of course, had set off after him, and Cocalus, thus threatened with war by Minos (who was good at wars in a grisly sort of way), decided he preferred to hang on to the gifted carpenter. So he had Minos killed instead. (He was duly entertained for so long in a hot bath by Cocalus' two daughters that he fainted, after which the girls rounded off the day by suffocating him).

What has never been satisfactorily explained is why Icarus, shortly after take-off, set off in a totally different direction from his father. The accident report is understandably non-committal.

ACCIDENT REPORT

Site of accident:	5 miles north west of Crete
Date of accident:	approx 750 BC
Aircraft Type:	Homebuilt, Man-Powered (ultralight class)
Injuries:	1 (fatal)
Date of Report:	1/1/0001

Details of Accident

Considerable delay has occurred between the accident and the investigation, but the following facts that have been established. The aircraft was a homebuilt ultralight of original design, one of two. It was constructed from a range of novel composite materials, including wax and feathers. The accident occurred on the first flight of the type. Icarus, the pilot, was the co-designer of the aircraft, and had a total time of 25 minutes (all on type). The wind was 180/3kts and cloud cover was 0/10 at all altitudes.

There are no records of pre-flight inspection, indeed the indications are that none was performed. Witnesses report the aircraft to have successfully taken off from Crete, the pilot having announced the intention of making for Greece (although no flight-plan had been filed). The flight was in company with another aircraft of the same type flown by the co-designer and father of the pilot, Dædalus. The second aircraft was also on its maiden flight. Approximately 25 minutes into the flight, some 5 miles north west of Crete the aircraft was observed to climb to a considerably higher altitude than its partner. At this point it appeared to suffer a substantial structural failure, followed by a departure from controlled flight; the aircraft entered a dive from which it did not recover before impact at sea.

There was no post-impact fire. No search was attempted due to lack of facilities, but the circumstances of the accident suggest that the pilot would have died on impact. The second aircraft proceeded successfully to its destination.

Analysis of Accident

The novel composite structure of the aircraft was known to be the subject of physical restrictions on operating temperatures. These had been carefully explained to the pilot. When the pilot climbed to a higher altitude, the levels of ambient solar radiation probably led to these temperature restrictions being exceeded, resulting in a thermal degradation of the basic wax structure. Pilot error must be the obvious cause.

'Lord Haw-Haw' & his passport

For the beleaguered British awaiting the Nazi onslaught in 1940, there was one person even more hated than Hitler. He was 'Lord Haw-Haw' the insidious voice on the radio – 'Germany calling, Germany calling,' sounding more like 'Cheermoney calling!' That man was William Joyce.

The Joyces are one of the celebrated 'tribes of Galway,' but William's father emigrated to the United States; thus William was born in Brooklyn in 1906. Three years later, the Joyces returned to Ireland, then part of the United Kingdom. They were staunchly pro-British even when Ireland began to fight for her freedom, so in 1921, they wisely came to England. William was now a patriotic schoolboy, good-looking, intelligent, blue-eyed and fair-haired.

The saga of his nationality begins when he tried to join the Officers Training Corps. His father assured the authorities that, while William was born in New York, the whole family was British.

In 1924, Joyce joined an anti-Labour, anti-Communist movement called the British Fascisti, and in a fracas in Lambeth, a 'Jewish Communist' (as he claimed) tried to cut his throat but missed – scarring Joyce's face for life.

Despite all this, he obtained a First in English at Birkbeck College and a wife, Hazel. Soon, however, he fell under the spell of Sir Oswald Mosley and joined his British Union of Fascists. In the hope of visiting Hitler with Mosley, Joyce made what was to be a fatal error. He falsified his passport application, declaring he had been born in Galway. Little did he realise what this banana skin, Passport no. 125943, would do to him years later.

Soon Joyce was appointed Propaganda Director by Mosley at a salary of £300 a year. He also began to make his name as an orator, and not just on street corners. At a smart Blackshirt event at the Park Lane Hotel in 1933, a witness recalled, *'Never before have I met a personality so terrifying in its dynamic force, so vituperative, so vitriolic. We listened in frozen hypnotism to this cold, stabbing voice.'*

At one meeting in Scotland, a young girl, Margaret White, was fascinated by Joyce speaking. She little knew she would soon share her life with him. After his divorce from Hazel, they were married in February 1937, but it was not plain sailing. The British Fascists began to lose political ground

Joyce, 'a cold, stabbing voice'

and income as British liberal opinion recoiled from Mussolini's attack on Abyssinia, the Spanish Civil War and Hitler's increasing belligerency. Joyce lost his job, and Margaret and he became language tutors. Joyce still made his speeches, increasingly anti-Jewish and pro-Hitler. He also joined the Right Club, a disgraceful anti-Semitic secret society.

It was not his German passport, but his British one, that would catch him out.

As war clouds gathered, Joyce realised that as a security suspect he would be interned, and agonised between Southern Ireland and Germany. Fatally, he decided to renew his passport and to leave for Germany. After an exhausting train ride to Berlin, they discovered that his German friends were not quite sure what to do with them – until someone suggested the radio which was being used by the Propaganda Minister, Josef Goebbels, to undermine the morale of foreign countries. At the *Reichsrundfunk,* he met Norman Baillie-Stewart, the Seaforth Highlander 'officer in the Tower', who had been jailed for five years for spying in England. They hated each other. It was Baillie-Stewart, with his upper-class accent who was really the first 'Haw-Haw', identified by Jonah Barrington of the *Daily Express.* 'A gent I'd like to meet is moaning periodically from Zeesen. He speaks English of the haw-haw, dammit-get-out-of-my-way variety.' But soon Joyce had eclipsed the rest of the team beaming propaganda towards Britain. With his clever scripts and effective delivery, he had become *the* 'Lord Haw-Haw' for his large numbers of listeners, at one stage reaching 14% of the British population. More impressive were the mass of Britons who claimed to know what Haw-Haw had said – the individual buildings to be blitzed, the local roads to be 'widened' by bombs and, above all, his uncanny knowledge about which clocks were wrong. As the Luftwaffe wrecked Britain's cities, 'Haw-Haw' quickly went from a public joke to public enemy. Hitler, Goebbels and Goering were distant cartoon figures. 'Haw-Haw' spoke to the British, sneeringly and threateningly, in their own homes. Simple people even thought he was personally directing the war against them. Little wonder that he was the most hated person in Britain.

For William Joyce and Margaret the war dragged on – in increasing strain as Germany began to lose and the bombs fell on Berlin. They were even divorced and remarried. As the discomfort, danger and depression increased, it was scant consolation that Joyce was awarded the *Kriegsverdienstkreuz* (War Service Cross) with the certificate personally signed by Hitler. On April 30 1945, he made his last broadcast. Obviously drunk, he slurred, 'you may not hear from me again for a few months. I say, Ich liebe Deutschland! Heil Hitler, and farewell.' When the war ended, the couple found

themselves in Flensburg in the British zone of occupation, and there Joyce made a last foolish gamble – deciding to talk to some British officers in French. One was sharp-eared, and recognised the famous voice. In a scuffle, Joyce was shot and wounded and was soon on his way to England.

Now that British passport, obtained 'for holiday touring' in 1939, doomed him at last, as a British and not an American citizen. Found guilty of treason by the High Court and by the House of Lords, this hated but fascinating man was hung in January 1946.

The Marquis de Portago & his racing priorities

The Mille Miglia was undoubtedly the most dramatic and dangerous of motor races. Its creation in 1927 was an act of revenge by the Auto Club di Brescia, who had seen the Italian Grand Prix, which they had pioneered in 1921, 'stolen' from them the next year by the Automobile Club of Milan and held at Monza. With the help and permission of the Fascist Party, a dramatic new race would bring prestige back to Brescia. The Mille Miglia was driven round a thousand miles of Italian roads, closed to traffic but not to people. In the dark of the evening, starting with low-powered

sports cars driven by virtual amateurs, every minute a car would roll down the ramp at Brescia, with the fastest cars leaving at dawn.

Over the years the race, mostly dominated by Italians, would have some strange moments. Gianni Marzotto once won in a smart double-breasted suit, and another winner's car was found full of cigarette ash and empty brandy bottles. The German Rudolf Caracciola sneaked up behind three Alfa Romeos with his lights off and

Every minute, a car would leave the ramp.

became the first foreign winner.

By the 1950's, superfast works teams from Maserati, Ferrari and Mercedes were screaming down the narrow roads, blasting past the slower cars. It was dangerous enough driving along narrow roads and through typical Italian towns and villages. For the drivers, it was doubly terrifying because the uncontrolled spectators crowded on to the road, only leaping back when the cars came through. So it often seemed that they were driving at 170mph straight at a solid wall of people.

In addition, it was almost impossible to memorise the thousand mile course. The most successful method of knowing what on earth lay beyond the crowd was devised by Dennis Jenkinson, who acted as navigator for Stirling Moss in his Mercedes in 1955. After a careful reconnaissance drive, he created an 18 foot scroll, resembling a toilet roll, on which every corner, bridge or bump on the route had been noted, and for a thousand miles he shouted instructions in Moss's ear, 'Second gear, hump-back-bridge, saucy one left, dodgy one right…' They broke the tradition that 'he who leads at Rome never wins at Brescia.'

But inevitably, a much less careful and attentive character was to put paid to himself and the race. In 1957,

running fourth, Spain's glamorous sportsman and playboy, Marquis 'Fon' de

Portago, pulled in to refuel. He had hit a bank and his Ferrari mechanics shouted to him that a wheel was damaged and needed changing. Impatiently, he waved them away and howled back into the race, only to skid to a halt after fifty yards for a passionate kiss with his beautiful girlfriend, the Hollywood actress Linda Christian.

His romantic and Latin sense of priorities had tragic results. 10 miles down the road his tyre burst and his car ploughed into the crowd, killing him, his navigator and ten spectators.

Under pressure from the Vatican, the Mille Miglia was never run again.

Right: 'Fon' de Portago and his film star girlfriend, Linda Christian

One of the Mille Miglia's most spectacular winners, Stirling Moss

Admiral Gensoul & the missing clause

In July 1940, Britain had her back to the wall. Above London, her pilots were fighting to the death against the Luftwaffe in the Battle of Britain, many of her ships had recently been sunk – first off Norway and then Dunkirk, invasion was expected any day and France had capitulated.

But Winston Churchill had to focus on a port in Algeria, because much of France's fleet, the fourth largest in the world, was now moored in the harbour of Mers el-Kebir, a port near Oran. It was vital that this fleet should not fall into the hands of the Germans. If it had, Britain might have lost control of the Mediterranean, the Middle East and its oilfields, and perhaps even the war.

'Force H', a British fleet, arrived off Mers el-Kebir, commanded by a reluctant Vice-Admiral Sir James Somerville, who sent Captain Cedric 'Hooky' Holland in to negotiate with the very Anglophile French Admiral Gensoul. The negotiations had every chance of succeeding because Holland was very pro-French, spoke the language excellently – having been Naval Attaché in Paris – and was even involved with a French woman.

In Gensoul's stifling cabin, Holland put four options on the table:
- Sail the ships to British harbours and join the fight alongside Britain.
- Sail to a British port, from which the crews would be repatriated to France.
- Sail to the West Indies, with the ships entrusted to the neutral United States for the duration of the war.
- Scuttle the ships.

Something disastrous then happened. Somehow, by an oversight, Admiral Gensoul's signals officer did not include the attractive 'West Indies' option when it was sent to the anti-British Admiral Darlan, who ordered French ships to resist and to rally to Gensoul – a signal immediately intercepted by Britain's code-breakers.

At 5:15 pm, Somerville was forced to give a 15-minute ultimatum; 'ACCEPT, OR I MUST SINK YOUR SHIPS'. At 5:54 pm, the battleships *Hood*, *Valiant* and *Resolution* opened fire with huge 15-inch shells. In ten minutes, several of the French ships had been sunk in the harbour, with 1,300 Frenchmen dead. The battle cruiser *Strasbourg* and five destroyers escaped to France where, ironically, in 1942, the Vichy government kept its promise and scuttled them.

Churchill was distraught. Tears were

propaganda value to the full. Somerville wrote to his wife, *'An absolutely bloody business, the biggest blunder in modern times.'*

However, after reflection, the Free French leader, General Charles de Gaulle, in his broadcast to the French people, called the action 'deplorable et detestable', but added that it was better that the ships be sunk than that they should join the enemy.

There was however, a positive effect of this banana skin, actually in America. The very ruthlessness of the decision against a former ally and friend convinced Roosevelt and his government of Britain's absolute determination, and strengthened their desire to help.

'A hateful decision'

streaming down his cheeks when he described the action to the House of Commons: 'A hateful decision, the most unnatural and painful in which I have ever been involved'.

The incident horrified everyone but the Germans, who exploited its

Chernobyl, botched test & fatal silence

When the news of a nuclear catastrophe at Chernobyl in 1986 gradually filtered out, there were many for whom it was no surprise. Soviet Russia was slowly changing under the new Premier Mikhail Gorbachev, but old habits die hard. Years under Stalin's iron rule had left a legacy of a strange mixture of industrial success and failure.

The same country that had put the first man in space and had produced gigantic industrial complexes was also bizarrely inefficient – incapable of producing effective washing machines, let alone calculators – and dogged by shortages of materials and supply bottlenecks. Her huge industrialisation programmes had been achieved at terrible human cost, with millions dead or placed in slave camps. Output figures were regarded as all-important, but were often phoney, with real production way behind the official figures. Even Stakhanov's famous feat of hewing 102 tons of coal instead of his allocated seven tons a shift, was a cheat. (Stakhanovites were given extra perks). Crash programmes, *'shturmorshchina,'* created erratic and inefficient production flows, and quality was constantly sacrificed for output control. When Krushchev boasted to the West 'We will bury you', he was deluding himself.

Electricity was vital for growth, but Soviet power stations could not keep up with demand. Only nuclear energy could bridge the gap. The power stations of Chernobyl were a product of this situation. The RBMK reactors were relatively simple, but there were potential flaws.

On the night of 25 April, a planned test to create a new safety procedure was postponed for a fairly typical Soviet reason. The Kiev grid controller suddenly insisted that he needed a few more hours of power. So when the Chernobyl technicians finally initiated the test, they were tired and made a series of drastic slips. Frantically, the emergency AZ-5 button was pressed to shut down the reactor, but all too late. The power shot from 200 thermal megawatts to 360,000 megawatts, one

hundred times more than the reactor could cope with. All hell literally broke loose. The huge 1,000 ton steel plate was blown right off the reactor, and a second explosion blasted uranium fuel, burning graphite and sending huge clouds of deadly radioactive steam and dust high into the air.

Incredible bravery by ill-equipped local firemen contained some of the fires, many of whom knew they were doomed by radiation, as did the helicopter crews who for days flew low over the burning reactor to seal it by dropping 5,000 tons of sand, lead, clay, dolomite and boron carbide. Local hospitals were swamped with radiation victims.

After the appalling technical crisis that caused the explosion, there were now two self-inflicted banana skins – both products of the old Soviet system. The first was inefficiency. The 35,000 people from the area of Chernobyl and Pripyat were evacuated with painful slowness, with children sometimes taking weeks to find their parents. Panic then occurred in Kiev, the Ukraine's capital, with 250,000 children suddenly being taken away from the city.

However, this was no local problem. Radioactive 'plumes' drifted across East and West Europe, causing widespread agricultural and social damage, and not least prompting thousands of women to opt for abortions. Now came the second banana skin – lack of honesty. In spite of Gorbachev's desire for 'glasnost' or openness, the disaster was shrouded in true old-fashioned Soviet secrecy. The authorities gave out little real news, and even that was too late for appropriate action. This lack of frankness caused fury both in the Soviet Union and in the countries that were affected by the fallout.

Chernobyl was a setback for the nuclear industry we now really need, because climate change is being accelerated by coal-fired stations. It was also a crisis for the Soviet Union which helped to speed her break up. It was a real medical and economic problem for her neighbours, and a continuous threat, with the leaking plant now requiring a huge, billion dollar 'hangar' to be built and slid into place.

Stray dogs were all that were left in Chernobyl.

The plumes of radioactive dust spread across the globe.

> *'A fool and his money are soon parted.'*
> Proverb

naivety & gullibility

> *'There's a sucker born every minute.'*
> Phineas Barnum

The 'Fake Sheik', Sophie & Sven

They should have known better. One was a public relations professional and part of the Royal Family. The other was the most senior sports figure in England. But both were taken in by one of the media's most mysterious figures, in the guise of a 'Fake Sheik.'

Mazher Mahmoud has been an undercover reporter for the *News of the World* for many years. Few people know what he looks like, and he needs to keep it that way. He claims to have successfully trapped over a hundred dubious characters, including drug dealers, immigration racketeers, arms dealers and paedophiles. High profile victims of his 'stings' have included Blue Peter's Richard Bacon, the DJ Johnnie Walker, the Earl of Hardwicke, Prince Harry, Princess Michael of Kent, John Fashanu and Lawrence Dallaglio. Together with his large salary he has an enormous expense account (as *Time* magazine put it, *'he must be one of the few tabloid journalists who can get away with expensing cocaine.'*) He was named Reporter of the Year at the 1999 British Press Awards but, of course, did not get up to receive this, his award being collected by a figure dressed as an Arab Sheik, actually his friend, Kelvin Mackenzie, former editor of *The Sun.* It was very appropriate because the 'Fake Sheik' disguise has worked only too well – and especially with Sophie, Countess of Wessex and Sven Goran Eriksson.

In February 2001, Mahmoud was actually not after Sophie, but rather her business partner, Murray Harkin, for some vague and never substantiated business irregularities. But Sophie decided to attend the meeting arranged with an 'Arab looking for a PR firm.' She was completely taken in by Mahmoud's disguise, and talked rather too much and too unwisely. Her remarks, which did not appear in the *News of the World* but the *Mail on Sunday* and *Sunday Mirror*, included not only her boastful chat about her Royal connections but also frank comments about politicians like Tony Blair, ('too presidential') and his wife, Cherie ('horrid, horrid, horrid.') However much Buckingham Palace protested about 'inaccuracies', the net effect was that Sophie was compelled to give up her role in her PR firm and that

Sophie, Countess of Wessex

she and Prince Edward were forced to devote themselves to 'Royal Duties.'

Sven Goran Eriksson had even less excuse than Sophie for his gullibility. He has been in the media spotlight for years, and not just in his role as England's football Manager. His high profile sexual relationships have included not only his girlfriend, Nancy dell'Olio, but TV presenter Ulricka Johnnson and Football Association secretary, Faria Allam, whose favours he shared with the FA's Chief Executive, Mark Palios.

Even professionally, he should always have been on his guard because his every move is watched, as at his 'innocent' meetings with Roman Abramovich, Chelsea's owner, and its Chief Executive, Peter Kenyon.

When Sven was invited to Dubai, he was not alone. He had with him his agent Athole Still and his lawyer, Richard Des Voeux. All three of them took their host, in Arab dress, at face value as they sat and talked in one of Dubai's magnificent hotels and on a sumptuous yacht (no wonder Mahmoud's expense account was so lavish). The trio never seemed to have felt that a little checking in the business community of Dubai about the 'Sheik' might have been worthwhile. But no. Sven was to open up a treasure trove of

Eriksson. He should have known better.

damaging quotes and opinions. They discussed the Sheik's desire to buy Aston Villa with Sven as Manager, including disparaging remarks about Villa's incumbent Manager, David O'Leary, and Chairman, Doug Ellis. Sven also boasted he could lure David Beckham away from Real Madrid, and criticised many prominent players and key Managers, like Manchester United's Alex Ferguson and Chelsea's Jose Mourinho, the main co-operative suppliers of key players for his England squad. Above all, he casually revealed that England's transfer market was a 'cesspit', and that three prominent clubs were involved in 'bungs' with managers pocketing money from transfers.

Once all this had exploded over the pages of the *News of the World,* Eriksson's position became extremely difficult – to say the least. The Football Association did not fire him, but his contract was now cut back from 2008 to just after the World Cup in the summer of 2006.

There are many who feel that Mahmoud's methods are sneaky and dishonourable, but there is no doubt that he gets results. It will be interesting to see whether the 'Fake Sheik' scam continues to work, or whether celebrities can curb their gullibility for long enough.

Richard Dimbleby & the spaghetti harvest

In the 1950s, *Panorama* was one of the BBC's flagship programmes, its anchor presenter being the portly and portentous Richard Dimbleby, whose sonorous tones had led us through the first televised royal wedding in 1953. It was in black and white, but the world watched entranced as Elizabeth and Prince Philip were married in Westminster Abbey.

Thus the public was familiar with Dimbleby and his distinguished style of delivery, and expected *Panorama* to cover important matters all over the world.

In 1957, the viewers of *Panorama* watched Dimbleby in Switzerland, where the camera followed him as he strolled through an orchard of trees festooned with strands of spaghetti. Apparently, the annual spaghetti harvest was going well enough, but when he interviewed the farmers they grumbled about the prices they could obtain. For listeners, the voice-over explained that the reason was a matter of volume, 'Cultivation in Switzerland is not on anything like the scale of Italian spaghetti farms. Many of you will have seen the huge spaghetti plantations in the Po Valley.' So this was obviously a serious economic and social crisis, to which Dimbleby listened sympathetically.

Hundreds of viewers did not notice the irony in Dimbleby's sign-off, 'And that is all from *Panorama* on this first day of April', and quickly called in to find out how to grow spaghetti at home. A spokesman for the BBC advised them to 'place a sprig of spaghetti in a tin of tomato sauce and hope for the best'.

In fairness to such viewers, it must be pointed out that in 1957 most people did not travel abroad and spaghetti was regarded as rather exotic and foreign. So perhaps the stuff really did grow on trees?

The banana skin was for the public and not for Richard Dimbleby, who did not seem to suffer too much in public esteem from his momentary lapse into the frivolous.

The Guardian & the lovely islands of San Serriffe

The advertising world is full of banana skins. Campaigns that have bombed, products that failed ('You're never alone with a Strand', 'Nothing sucks like an Electrolux' in the US, Coca Cola's Dasani Sidcup tap-water, 'Dinners for one', suggesting loneliness).

One of the most curious must be the Volvo poster featuring a dinosaur, which was banned after the British Dinosaur Society complained to the Advertising Standards Authority 'that the dinosaur had lasted 45 million years, rather longer than even the sturdiest Volvo.'

But it is seldom that an advertising banana skin is created for no commercial purpose, and just for a bit of fun.

The readers of Britain's *Guardian* newspaper who rang in to find out more about lovely San Serriffe in 1977 could be forgiven. After all, it was featured in a special anniversary seven-page supplement full of interesting articles and lively advertisements. Many were travel agents looking for business, curious that the travel trade had not heard about these beautiful islands in the Indian Ocean before.

However, anyone in the advertising, journalism and print worlds should have smelled a rat – if they had noticed that the country was divided between two islands, Upper Case and Lower Case. Others should have paid much more attention to the date – the first of April.

Regarded as one of the best April Fool's jokes ever, San Serriffe was cooked

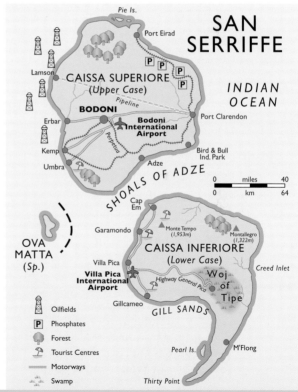

up between the London office of the leading advertising agency, J. Walter Thompson, and its client *The Guardian.* The agency's master stroke was to persuade several of its other clients to actually pay for advertisements. Thus, British Airways proudly announced new direct flights into Bodoni International Airport; Texaco offered a holiday competition and Kodak asked readers to send in their San Serriffe holiday snaps.

The supplement featured articles of welcome, apparently by the Minister of Tourism and the country's President, General Pica (a size of type). The detailed map listed towns like Bodoni, Clarendon, Garamondo (all popular typefaces). The northern cape on Lower Case, Cap Em, overlooked the body of water called Shoals of Adze. Tourists were invited to visit the Woj of Tipe, or stroll along the beach of Gill Sands (another typeface). Boats could visit Ova Mata ('over matter' or too much copy) or sail round Thirty Point (the type size of a newspaper headline).

Nowadays, readers might have sued the newspaper and advertisers. The Advertising Standards Authority would never allow something like this to appear – in that the product does not exist.

But in the more relaxed 1970s, everyone shrugged off the banana skin and had a good laugh.

Piers Morgan & the Iraq photographs

It seemed a perfect scoop. Just after America and her forces in Iraq had been rocked by the humiliating photographs of mistreated Iraqi captives in Abu Ghraib prison, Britain's *Daily Mirror* published similar photographs. On Saturday May 1, 2004, the newspaper's front page featured a hooded captive apparently being urinated on by a British soldier. 'VILE' screamed the headline, 'but this time it's a BRITISH soldier degrading an Iraqi.' Other pictures apparently showed a captive being hit in the groin by a rifle butt. The photographs went all over the world, incidentally earning the *Daily Mirror* £100,000, and had an immediate and devastating effect in the Middle East, where is was not difficult to assume that the British were just as bad as the Americans.

And yet almost as quickly doubts were raised. The prisoners and the soldiers looked too clean, there was no dust or sweat, and the pictures looked professionally lit – unlike the snaps from the kind of camera a soldier might carry in his knapsack.

It soon emerged that the paper had paid two unknown soldiers £5,000 each for the photographs, and for the story of how the Iraqis had been abused 'for up to eight hours'. And the Editor, Piers Morgan, was sticking to his guns that the pictures and the story were genuine.

Piers Morgan was himself a colourful and enigmatic figure. Formerly a show-business editor, at 36 he had been the youngest editor in Britain for 50 years, at the *News of the World.* At the *Mirror,* his career had not been without controversy. He had been forced to apologise for an 'Achtung! Surrender' headline before an English soccer match with Germany, and had been mixed up in a stock market scandal. Paradoxically, Piers Pughe-Morgan had been a fan of Margaret Thatcher, but now edited a Labour-supporting tabloid with an anti-war stance, while his own brother, a Major, was serving in Basra. Above all, Morgan had an ego 'the size of the Grand Canyon,' and his judgement could go out of the window at the hint of a scoop. He was well-liked by journalists, but the *Mirror's* management was becoming worried by circulation figures drifting downwards – partly due to the anti-war posture of Morgan.

After two weeks of mounting crisis, the Queen's Lancashire Regiment launched its own counter-attack. At a televised news conference, Colonel David Black proved decisively that the pictures were taken in Britain. He ticked off new anomalies, wrong items of dress, wrong rifles and wrong trucks. His concluding words were devastating. 'These photographs are a recruiting poster for Al Qaeda and every other terrorist organisation. They have made the lives of the Armed Forces that much more difficult and dangerous. It is time that the ego of one editor is measured against the life of a soldier'.

Only Piers Morgan's ego resisted the tide of evidence. But others had watched the news conference with mounting concern, not least the American investors in Trinity Mirror plc. Always anxious about *The Mirror's* anti-war and anti-American stance, they now put their views forcefully to the *Mirror's* Chief Executive, blonde Sly Bailey. She and the Board acted with swift, cold resolve.

On Friday May 14, at 5.45 pm, just as Piers Morgan was about to give a leaving present to his personal assistant, Kerrie Hutton, his phone rang. On the 20th floor, Sly Bailey simply said, 'The Board has lost confidence in you. That's it. Your

DAILY Mirror

WORLD EXCLUSIVE

VILE

...but this time it's a BRITISH soldier degrading an Iraqi

CAPTIVE TORMENT

MORE SHOCKING PHOTOGRAPH

contract is terminated'. He was escorted from the building, and a tearful Kerrie had to rush down his jacket and his mobile phone. He even had to convince the security guard that the Mercedes 500 was his own before driving away. The next day the *Daily Mirror* said, SORRY. WE WERE HOAXED.

Since then British troops have continued to die in Iraq, a Territorial Army soldier has been charged with

faking the pictures, and Piers Morgan has done rather well. His payoff from the *Daily Mirror* may have been about £2 million, he has signed a £1.2 million book deal for his story and he has his own television show. He recently said '*The Mirror* apologised, I do not.' His defiance may have a point, because the world's TV screens have now been filled with real British soldiers beating real Iraqi teenagers.

'La Grande Thérèse & the strong box

'She lied as a bird flies.'

She started out as a little girl in Toulouse who kept her family amused with her fantasies about fabulous castles and grand houses – and ended up by actually living out those fantasies and becoming one of France's and the world's greatest swindlers.

Thérèse Daurignac was born in 1856 to parents who were both illegitimate. Her mother died early and her father Guillaume became eccentric, wandering the streets, muttering something about 'legacies in locked boxes'. Thérèse had to look after her brothers and sisters, becoming famous locally for her wonderful stories told with wide-eyed

innocence and a charming lisp. 'She lied as a bird flies', said a friend. But all her talk of future inheritance could not save the family from bankruptcy and poverty.

What did save them was that her aunt Marie-Emilie had married a rising star in the legal profession, Gustave Humbert. In 1878, in a double ceremony, Thérèse married his son Frederick, and her sister wed his brother Lucien. It was not long before the 'Chateau Marcotte' surfaced as a property for which Gustave Humbert, now a Senator, arranged large mortgages. After that came a fabulous 'estate of cork trees in Portugal' apparently left to Thérèse by a grateful but mysterious

Robert Henry Crawford, part of a colossal inheritance of 100 million francs (£200 million today), only the interest of which she could touch. The scale, grandeur and audacity of the lies were key to their success, added to the fact that her father-in-law (and uncle) was now the revered Minister of Justice. With the money borrowed on these fictitious properties, Thérèse started on a buying spree that included the purchase of the chateau owned by the Toulouse-Lautrec family.

Soon Thérèse installed herself at the magnificent 65, Avenue de la Grande Armée, where all of Paris attended her magnificent social events. Among her friends were no less than three Presidents and five Prime Ministers. The whole financial edifice was propped up by vast loans enthusiastically lent to the 'heiress.' Some privileged people were granted a titillating glance at the bulky packages of bearer bonds in the strong box on the third floor. The heart of the scam was provided by an entirely real court case with real lawyers against the entirely fictitious 'Crawford nephews', a dispute which dragged on relentlessly and appeared to explain why Thérèse could never lay her hands on her capital and seemed to need continuous credit.

For years, La Grande Thérèse dominated the social scene of Paris, but trouble was slowly brewing. The old Senator died, however his prestige propped things up for a while. However, more and more people were trying to get their money back. In February 1895, a desperate Paul Girard, President of the Girard Bank, owed millions, even tried to shoot Thérèse. He missed, so he eventually shot himself – the first of several of her cynically named *'carnet suicidés'*. Jewels lent on approval (and promptly pawned) kept things going for a while, but by 1901 trouble closed in once again. Creditors began to panic, and it was then that Thérèse made a fatal slip.

When the judge in the long-running Girard coroner's investigation asked her where the 'Crawfords' actually lived, she blurted out the first address that came into her head – 1302, Broadway, New York. When no Crawfords were found there, the judge ordered the famous strong box to be opened. After a last champagne dinner, the Humbert family simply disappeared. Two days later, ten thousand people gathered

The legendary strong box is removed for inspection.

out in the street. The box was lowered by crane and broken open.

The ashen-faced witnesses found that it contained an old newspaper, an Italian coin and a trouser button.

Six months later the Humberts were discovered in Madrid and brought back to justice, to huge public excitement in Paris. Thérèse and her husband Frederick served five years in jail and then disappeared forever.

With the humiliating realisation of how many prominent people had been taken in, it is not at all surprising that France wanted to forget about the Humbert Affair as quickly as possible.

Rudolf Hess & the Duke of Hamilton

Quite late into the evening of May 10 1941, a bulky package was delivered to the Führer in his study at the Berghof, high above Bertchesgaden, with its magnificent views over the Bavarian Alps. Adolf Hitler was very busy with his preparations for 'Operation Barbarossa', his attack on Russia, so he pushed it aside. It was, no doubt, nothing but another of Rudolf Hess's long-winded, boring memoranda.

Hess was once Hitler's closest Nazi party confidant, a loyal fanatic who had helped him to write his testament, *Mein Kampf,* and to gain power. 'Hitler ist Deutschland und Deutschland ist Hitler!' he had shouted at Nuremberg rallies. But since the war had started, Hess had grown a trifle irrelevant and plainly felt it, showing distinct jealousy towards the war leaders and generals who now crowded round his beloved Führer.

At almost exactly the same time that evening, Wing Commander The Duke of Hamilton and his staff at RAF Turnhouse near Edinburgh were puzzling over a lone Messerschmitt 110 which had entered their fighter sector's airspace. Where on earth had it come from, and why? A few minutes later, its pilot shut off its two engines, rolled the aircraft on to its back to avoid hitting its tail and parachuted into the darkness.

Next day, Prime Minister Winston Churchill was at Ditchley in Sussex, restlessly alternating between watching a

'Just another boring memo from Rudolf?'

Marx Brothers film and going outside to gaze at the heavy bombing of London. Suddenly the telephone rang. The caller was a personal friend, the Duke of Hamilton, who had almost incredible news of 'cabinet importance': Hitler's deputy had managed to fly all the way from Augsburg to land just ten miles from the Duke's house in Renfrewshire, and was demanding to meet him to discuss 'peace proposals between Germany and Britain.'

Back in Germany, with the package still sitting on his desk, Hitler was interrupted by an Adjutant of Hess who handed him a slim envelope. Hitler glanced at the two pages and then slumped into a chair, bellowing, 'Oh My God, My God! He has flown to Britain!' Hysteria and speculation gripped the Berghof. Perhaps Hess had crashed? Or, much worse, the British had him and he might reveal Hitler's plans for Russia? Goering, who had been brutally ordered to report in, thought – together with his Luftwaffe chiefs – that Hess could not have managed the audacious flight. Hitler thought otherwise. And he was right. Hess had prepared well for what was actually his fourth attempt, persuading Willy Messerschmitt into lending him the long-distance fighter, using the 'Y-beams' system that guided German bombers, and

'A deluded, deranged and muddled idealist, riddled with hallucinations'

arranging for two radio stations to make a broadcast to fix his position. After an amazing solo flight of 850 miles, he landed in the dark almost within walking distance of the Duke's Dungavel House.

With silence from Britain, the Germans became frantic with worry, and after ten drafts, issued a communiqué stating that this star of National Socialism had become *a deluded, deranged and muddled idealist, riddled with hallucinations traceable to war injuries.*

While the planning and execution of the flight was a brilliant feat, its purpose was a banana skin of miscalculation. Hess was sincere, but ridiculously naïve. He assumed that the Duke of Hamilton, whom he had met casually at the 1936 Berlin Olympics, was some kind of leader of an 'opposition party'. As 'Lord Steward', he 'presumably dined with the King every night and could persuade him to make peace in spite of Churchill's war-mongering clique.' (In fact, the Duke was one of four brothers gallantly serving as pilots in the RAF). Hess did not even seem to know the names of any 'opposition leaders', nor realise that after two years, Britain was united in her hatred and defiance towards Hitler's Nazis.

To the Duke and to other questioners, Hess insisted he was 'on a mission of humanity', that 'Hitler admired Britain and only wanted a free hand in Europe' in exchange for Britain's 'free hand in its Empire', that Germany was bound to win the war anyway and that, by the way, Hitler would not negotiate with 'Churchill and his clique who had planned the war since 1936.' He must have been shocked and amazed when he did not meet the King nor the 'opposition party', and was quietly locked up by Churchill in The Tower of London for the duration of the war.

Hitler ordered that his old friend should be shot if he ever returned, and went back to planning his treacherous attack on Stalin – who was to be forever suspicious that Hess and Churchill had been plotting against him. Hess was to meet many of his colleagues again in Nuremberg, scene of so many past rallies and triumphs alongside Hitler. But now he was in the dock for 'crimes against peace' for which he was to serve 41 years, ending as the lone 'Prisoner Number Seven' in Spandau.

In 1987, aged 92, he appeared to hang himself with an electric cable. Some, including his son, thought he was murdered. Whatever the truth, it was a sad end for an idealistic man who, in one scatterbrained slip of judgement, sought to eclipse his political enemies and finally impress his Führer with his devotion.

Orson Welles & The War of the Worlds

If you mention *War of the Worlds*, most people will think of Steven Spielberg and Tom Cruise. Back in 1898, the brilliant novel of H. G. Wells would spring to mind. In his remarkable look into the future, Welles has his frightening Martian invaders targeting first his own town. *'I completely wreck and sack Woking, killing my neighbours in painful and eccentric ways – then proceed via Kingston and Richmond to London, selecting South Kensington* (where he used to teach) *for feats of peculiar atrocity.'*

But it was forty years later in America that *War of the Worlds* really became part of history. Radio had become the dominant and exciting new medium. Columbia Broadcasting Service was locked in a rating war with its rivals ABC and NBC, and CBS had been faced with filling the 8 p.m. slot on Sundays against NBC's hit, *The Chase and Samborn Hour*, with the wildly popular wise-cracking dummy Charlie McCarthy. So they had resorted to dramatising well-known literature like *The Count of Monte Cristo* and *Dracula*, thus positioning themselves as 'patrons of the arts'. October 30, 1938 was Halloween Night. For the brilliant young Orson Welles,

just 23, the idea of reviving the old H. G. Wells classic, but moving it to familiar places in America, seemed a good idea at the time. He was only worried that 'such an improbable tale might be too boring'. However, both he and CBS vastly underestimated the gullibility of the American public of that time.

Admittedly, it was a time of great tension. A new world war had just been postponed by the Munich Agreement, but Nazi Germany was definitely on the march (more radios were sold that October than in any other month). Recent vivid radio descriptions of the bombings in the Spanish Civil War had heightened the worry. Listeners had grown used to following

Orson Welles during his broadcast. Outside the studio, chaos was building up.

dramatic real events like the Lindbergh baby kidnapping, and also to the words 'We interrupt this programme…' Only months before, the nation had been

In spite of the implausibility of a Martian attack in the first place, and its amazing progress in only about 15 minutes, a quarter of the six million audience thought they were listening to reality, enhanced by real places and 'real people'. Half the listeners had only tuned in when they grew bored by an opera singer on the rival *Charlie McCarthy Show*, so they had missed the introduction, as they did the repeated reassurances during the programme that it was only fiction. After thirty minutes, Associated Press issued a notice to the newspapers that the attack was not real, as did the clattering teleprinters of the New York and New Jersey Police Departments. It did little good. Phone lines had become jammed and police switchboards were overwhelmed by weeping women (and men), adding to the general sense of panic.

All over the country, mass hysteria affected thousands of people. In Indianapolis, a woman ran into a church screaming 'New York is destroyed! It's the end of the world! You might as well go home to die.' In Harlem, where one man insisted that he had heard the President, churches began to hold 'end of the world' services. In Pittsburgh, one man just managed to stop his wife taking poison, as she screamed, 'I'd rather die

'It's the end of the world! You might as well go home to die!'

gripped by the almost hysterical reporting of the *Hindenburg* airship disaster in New Jersey. This was a broadcast whose breathless immediacy Welles was to copy deliberately.

At 8 pm, after a brief introduction (which many people missed) some routine dance music was apparently interrupted by an announcer reporting a 'gas explosion on Mars'. More music, more bulletins, 'A flaming object falling in New Jersey…Thirty yards in diameter… A humming sound… Something wriggling out…' Things grew worse. 'Poisonous black smoke… Death rays …Police and army wiped out… Monstrous Martian machines landing everywhere…people lying dead in the streets…'

this way, than like that.' In New Jersey, a woman was interrupted by her neighbour, banging on the door, 'I've got my seven kids in the car. Come on, let's get out of here!' Nearby, traffic was blocked by hundreds also trying to flee by car, many with wet towels round their faces to ward off the gas 'which they could already smell'.

Some men, made of sterner stuff, decided to 'get their guns to join in the defence of Grover's Mill', a real and perfectly calm little New Jersey hamlet selected from a road map by the scriptwriter as the site of the first Martian landing.

It was not just the gullible public who reacted. Thousands of medical and military personnel attempted to organise. 'Where can I volunteer? We have got to stop this awful thing!'

With the chaos at full pitch outside, at the end of the programme Orson Welles intoned mischievously, 'And if your doorbell rings and nobody's there – it was no Martian. It's Halloween'.

It may have launched Orson Welles' career, but lots of people thought it all very unfunny, including the Federal Broadcasting Commission, who told the networks not to do anything like it again.

Not many radio stations have tried a repeat. Probably wise. In 1950, a Caracas station did. It was stormed and burned to the ground. Venezuelans didn't think it funny either.

'We have to stop this awful thing!'

Cartier & the Australian

In the summer of 1932, a striking figure became quickly familiar in Mayfair. He was a tall Australian, very goodlooking, immaculately dressed, and judging from his taste in luxury goods, also very rich. He bought his shirts at Turnbull & Asser, his shoes at Lobb and his Savile Row suits at Henry Poole, and was staying at Claridges for the Summer Season.

One Saturday morning, he dropped in to Cartier in Bond Street, in the company of a beautiful French girl. Taking the assistant aside, he quietly asked, 'I noticed the wonderful diamond and ruby necklace you have out there in the front window. How much is it?'

'Three thousand pounds, sir.' (about £36,000 today.)

'I'll take it. I presume a cheque will be alright?'

'Well sir, I'm afraid we'd have to let the cheque clear before we could give you the

necklace – perhaps on Monday?'

'No, that's hopeless. I'm flying to Paris with my friend for the weekend, if you know what I mean. But you can check my credit with shops all over the West End. Try Turnbull's, Lobb, Henry Poole – or for that matter, Claridges.'

The Cartier staff quickly did just that, and were told that Mr Phillips was indeed an excellent customer, who always paid at once on Glyn Mills cheques (in marked contrast to the tardy payment of some of their snooty English clients.) So after suitable apologies for the delay, the necklace was wrapped and the pair strolled out, with the pretty girl clinging appreciatively to her generous escort.

About half an hour later, the telephone rang. It was a friendly jeweller further down Bond Street.

'A funny thing, but an Australian fellow came in and said he didn't want a necklace he had bought. He sold it to us really cheaply – a thousand pounds in cash. When he'd gone, we suddenly remembered it was that terrific one we'd all admired in your window. We thought we ought to tell you. Bit strange.'

The Cartier team was shaken to the core. 'Good grief! It may be a con trick. Check with Claridges and see if he's still there.'

'They say he's checked out early, in a hurry. Catching a plane at Northolt.'

'Right, it *must* be a con. Tell the police. We may not be too late.'

Indeed they were just in time. The Dragon Rapide was warming up its engines when two police cars, bells clanging, came bumping across the grass. A protesting Australian and his tearful

girlfriend were manhandled from the plane, to their huge embarrassment and to that of the other well-heeled passengers. (The Paris flight was like Concorde.)

The pair were brusquely delivered to Ruislip police station, to wait in the cells until Monday morning when they were due before the Magistrate.

Except that on that very same Monday morning, Glyn Mills honoured the cheque.

The defamation case was quietly settled out of court for £50,000, about £600,000 today.

An expensive case of jumping to the wrong conclusions – for the right reasons, an all too common slip.

The Trojans & the wooden horse

One morning, the citizens of Troy woke up to find something very peculiar outside their gates: a huge wooden horse, with no Greeks to be seen. It seemed, at first glance, to be the end of a ten year siege.

Homer, writing in 850 BC, four hundred years after the event in his *Iliad,* tells us that it all started when Helen of Troy, the most beautiful woman who ever lived, born of Zeus himself, was given to a human called Paris, for judging that Aphrodite was the 'fairest of the gods'. Helen, unfortunately, already had a husband, Menelaeus, whose brother was inconveniently Agamemnon, king of the Greeks. Unaware of the gods' divine involvement, the Greeks plainly considered Paris a mere seducer and kidnapper, and pursued him back to his home city, Troy. Thus, Helen was famously said to have had 'a face that launched a thousand ships'.

The siege had destroyed many of the heroes on both sides, including Achilles – who had been dipped as a baby in the river Styx to make him invulnerable. By bad luck, his heel, by which his mother dipped him, remained untouched by the magic river – and that is exactly where he was later fatally wounded by an arrow shot by Paris.

So, when they found the wooden horse outside the gates, described by the Greek 'deserter' Sinon, as a gift to the gods from the departed Greek army, it must have been quite a dilemma for the Trojans. However, after such a long and bitter war, you would have expected them to show a touch of prudent cynicism and suspicion.

The Trojans debated furiously. Should they destroy it or leave it for a few days, sitting in the hot sun of Asia Minor? Either way, Ulysses and his small team of volunteer Greek fighters concealed inside the horse would have perished, and Troy would have survived. A Trojan priest, Laocoon, was adamant. 'Do not trust the horse! Whatever it is, I fear the Greeks, even when they bear gifts.' When mocked, he threw a spear at the horse. His only reward was for him and his children to be eaten by two serpents that rose from the sea. After this grisly spectacle, even the most hardened sceptics were subdued.

Nor was it any use that Cassandra, King Priam's daughter, agreed with Laocoon and warned against the horse. Unfortunately, she had been blessed by Apollo with the power to foresee the

'I fear the Greeks, even when they bear gifts.'

orgy of drunken celebration, left it unguarded.

The concealed Greeks slipped out and opened the gates for their now returned army. The sack of the city itself was so violent that the Gods themselves were said to be joining in. '*Neptune has loosened the foundations with his great trident and is shaking the walls.*' (Virgil, *Aeneid.*)

Nearly all the Trojans were killed, with their aged King Priam murdered on his own altar and Cassandra sold as a concubine.

All in all, it would have been much better if the Trojans had been rather more suspicious.

future correctly, but also cursed that she would never be believed. She had foretold the sack of Troy, but as usual, nobody believed her, leaving her raving to herself in frustration.

In a banana skin of gullibility, the Trojans then foolishly dragged the wooden horse into the city, and in an

Victor Lustig & the Eiffel Tower

Victor Lustig's whole attitude to life made him the perfect confidence trickster. 'I really don't understand honest people. They lead desperate lives, full of boredom.' It was a view which would lead him to forty five aliases, fifty arrests in the United States alone and one of the best-known con tricks of all time – and, eventually, to Alcatraz.

Born in Bohemia, now the Czech Republic, in 1890, Lustig became fluent in five languages and an excellent player of billiards, bridge and poker. He first applied his wits and charm to fleece the rich on the magnificent liners on Transatlantic cruises. When the first World War intervened, Lustig went to the United States where he became a European 'Count'. In Missouri he bought a farm with Liberty Bonds, persuading the bank to give him cash for some of the bonds, switching envelopes and escaping with the bonds and the cash. Arrested in New York, he then persuaded the bank to 'avoid a run on the bank', release him and to give him another $1000! It was one of dozens of such brazen con tricks and cucumber cool escapades.

But it was in May 1925, back in Paris, that Lustig was to dream up the scam which made him famous. He read in a newspaper that the Eiffel Tower, one of the great landmarks of the world, was costing the French government so much to paint and maintain that it was exploring the idea of dismantling it.

It was the work of only hours before a forger friend had created letterheads from '*The Deputy Director-General of Posts and Telegraphs*'. Lustig wrote to six leading scrap metal dealers inviting them to a meeting to 'discuss a government contract'. At the prestigious Hotel Crillon, he explained that the Eiffel Tower, part of the 1889 Paris Exposition, had never been intended to be permanent. It was now costing so much that it had to be scrapped. But, of course, this might be highly controversial and unpopular, so they were all sworn to secrecy. 'The Deputy Director-General' then drove them in rented limousines to inspect the Eiffel Tower with its 15,000 pre-fabricated parts. He soon noticed that

André Poisson, anxious to be in the big league of Parisian business, was the most gullible and over-eager, and it was Poisson whom he chose as the 'mark', invited back four days later to be awarded the contract. At the meeting, Lustig also discussed the lifestyle that a Minister was expected to lead, and revealed 'how little he was paid'. Poisson understood and quickly supplemented the $125,000 contract cheque with a hefty bribe. Lustig and his accomplice, 'Dapper Dan' Collins, were on the train to Vienna that very evening. For a month, they scanned the French newspapers for news. There was nothing. Insecure and humiliated, poor André Poussin had decided it was better to absorb his loss and keep quiet.

Then Victor Lustig did something that was both unbelievable and typical. He returned to Paris and *repeated the whole scam* with six new scrap merchants. But this time the 'mark' did go to the police, and Lustig only just made it back to America.

There he graduated from selling his 'Rumanian Boxes' which appeared to transform paper into $1000 bills, and went into serious counterfeiting, but was caught by the FBI in 1935. After a daring escape, he was finally sent to Alcatraz for twenty years, but died of pneumonia after twelve.

However, his name will live on as the man who sold the Eiffel Tower – twice.

The Mitford Sisters & the Nazis

It was the ultimate nightmare which ended a decade of foolish dreams. A young aristocratic English girl, Unity Mitford, obsessed with Hitler, was brought back to England with a gunshot wound to her head. Her sister Diana was already in Brixton Prison.

Surprisingly, Unity and Diana Mitford were not tearaway renegades from the family of Lord Redesdale – but rather the products of it. Their story also reflects one of the most disgraceful episodes in British history.

David Freeman-Mitford, Second Baron Redesdale, after a military career, went to Canada and purchased the Swastika Gold Mine. It was an omen for the future, because on returning to Britain he became very right-wing and joined several Fascist and anti-Semitic organisations, even though in upper-class British circles, he was not alone.

Of his four daughters, Deborah became a Duchess, Nancy became a famous writer and Jessica became a Communist. But Diana and Unity Valkyrie fell under the thrall of Fascism and Nazism.

Diana was one of England's great beauties, her perfect features adorning fashion and society magazines and her portrait painted by Augustus John. One of her many admirers, Evelyn Waugh,

A cynical heckler once broke the spell by shouting 'All right, Mosley, you may be excused.'

even dedicated *Vile Bodies* to her. While married to the extremely rich Hon. Bryan Guinness, she had been watching with fascination the career of another star, Sir Oswald Mosley. Mosley, elected Conservative MP for Harrow aged just twenty one in 1920, had that same year married Lady Cynthia Curzon at a glittering wedding attended by King George V. The golden couple had shocked society when first Oswald and then Cynthia defected to a rather bemused Labour Party. Soon he was to change again – and founded the New Party, and more importantly, the British Union of Fascists.

Such upper-class political antics were not as surprising as they seem now. All sorts of people had extreme right wing views. Lord Rothermere in his *Daily Mail* had thundered 'HURRAH FOR THE BLACKSHIRTS.' Lord Redesdale himself was a prominent member of the secret Right Club, started by Captain Archibald Ramsay MP, 'to oppose International Jewry.' Its members included William Joyce (later the hated, traitorous broadcaster to England, 'Lord Haw-Haw'), but more disgracefully, the Duke of Westminster, the Duke of Wellington and 230 others whose names were later never published because it would have been so dangerous to British

Unity (left) and Diana with SS troopers at the 1937 Nuremberg rally

society. More openly, distinguished people attended the smart 'Blackshirt Ball' at the Savoy in 1934.

When Cynthia Mosley then unexpectedly died, Diana left her husband to join Mosley in his quest to create a genuinely influential British Fascist movement. Blackshirt parades, marches, riots and bloodshed in the Jewish East End of London became commonplace.

But the gullibility of the Mitford sisters had taken a new turn. They were invited to attend the first of Hitler's Nuremberg rallies and were intoxicated. Unity, aged nineteen, insisted on returning – and for weeks she hung around Hitler's favourite Munich restaurant until he noticed her on February 9 1935, *'the most wonderful and beautiful day of my life.'* She became part of his intimate circle, and she and Diana were soon familiar figures at rallies and then at the 1936 Berlin Olympics as the guests of Propaganda Minister Josef Goebbels.

Unity had subtly changed with a new poise and beauty. She became quite close to Hitler, meeting him 140 times – often

'The most beautiful day of my life'

arrested, but its treasurer had escaped to France with the books. The Chancellor of the Exchequer, who had supported the Company in Parliament, was imprisoned in the Tower of London and his effigy burned by angry mobs.

Robert Walpole, who had constantly warned against foolish speculation, came to power and helped to restore some confidence. But centuries later, the story of the 'South Sea Bubble' is still recalled in history lessons. Unfortunately, too many of us ignore what we are taught at a tender age.

Charles Dawson & 'The Piltdown Man'

Between 1912 and 1917, a number of fossils were found by an amateur archaeologist called Charles Dawson in the Piltdown quarries in Sussex. As the findings were collected, it became increasingly apparent that the site contained the remains of an animal with a large, human cranium, but also the long jaw of an ape. Furthermore, some of the teeth were worn down in the manner of human teeth, not that of an ape. Though many scientists were sceptical, particularly French and American palæontologists, the 'Piltdown Man's mix of features seemed to fulfil all the expected criteria of the long-awaited 'missing link'. The new genus was named *Eoanthropus dawsoni*.

However, as other remains of early man were found around the world, such as Peking Man, the Piltdown Man increasingly failed to fit into the growing picture of humanity's evolution. By 1950, it was being largely ignored by the scientific community, and in 1953 it was barely mentioned at the International Conference of Palæontologists.

Nevertheless, though attention to the fossil was dwindling, nobody had guessed at the possibility of outright forgery. However, a new dating technique, called the 'fluorine absorption test' had become available in 1949, and in 1953 it revealed that the bones were not old enough for Piltdown Man to be an ancestor of humans. Furthermore, upon microscopic examination, the teeth were found to have a criss-cross artificial scratching pattern. It turned out that the skull bone was from a human, the jaw from a modern orang-utan, and the bones had been soaked in a solution which aged them convincingly.

This most famous of hoaxes threw up a long lists of suspects, starting of course, with Charles Dawson himself, together with W.J. Solass, a professor of geology at Oxford, and even Arthur Conan Doyle, the creator of Sherlock Holmes and author of *The Lost World*. However, the evidence for each is very circumstantial, and today we are no closer to discovering the true perpetrator of the hoax.

Whoever created the Piltdown Man must have had a comprehensive understanding of palæontology and biology, and he or she must have planted the evidence diligently over a number of years. Almost more intriguing is the lack of conventional motives, such as the desire to make money by selling the fossil, or to confirm the theories of a researcher. This makes it even harder to theorise as to the daring culprit.

So why was the deception, this banana skin for the whole scientific community, so very successful? First, scientists were not actually allowed to examine the evidence. The bones themselves were locked away in the British Museum, and anyone wanting to look at the Piltdown Man had to make do with plaster moulds, which gave nothing away. Second, the age of the bones could not be precisely fluorine tested until after 1949.

However, the reasons behind the long life of the hoax were probably not only

A curator from the British Museum finally pronounces that the Piltdown skull comprises the remains of a quite modern human and an orang-utan.

practical and scientific, but psychological too. The scientific community was simply not prepared to believe that someone would be so malicious. Furthermore, scientists wanted to believe that the 'missing link' had been discovered; it fitted every theory of evolution that they had espoused, and especially seemed to confirm that man's large brain had evolved before any of his other features, casting intelligence as the factor which has allowed humanity to evolve so far.

The Piltdown Man lived a long, illustrious life as one of the world's most famous, successful and mysterious hoaxes.

Stern magazine & 'Hitler's diaries'

In January 1983, the managers of *Stern*, one of Germany's most famous magazines, thought they had pulled off one of the world's great publishing coups. It was the fiftieth anniversary of Adolf Hitler's accession to power and they had obtained a gem: his private, handwritten diaries. Not only was *Stern* going to publish them every week, the rights had been profitably sold for syndication in newspapers all over the world.

However, within weeks the whole scheme had collapsed with maximum embarrassment and financial loss. A simple hoax had created a perfect case of *Schadenfreude*, that special German word for 'the malicious joy in the misfortune of others.'

It all began with a petty forger, Konrad Kujau, appropriately nicknamed 'Konni'. Born in East Germany, he was a small time crook and had enjoyed several spells in prison – one, rather pathetically, for forging ten pounds' worth of travellers cheques. Near Frankfurt, he and his wife set up a window cleaning company, but also went into the business of selling Nazi mementoes, smuggled illegally out of East Germany – including flags, uniforms, medals, guns and swords.

He told his friends that 'his brother was an East German general' and decided he would earn more money if he could prove authenticity. So he simply forged the relevant documents and then went on to fake Hitler's drawings and paintings skilfully, complete with notes in Hitler's handwriting.

Fritz Stiefel, a local businessman, started buying 'Hitler's paintings' in 1975, together with speech notes, poems and letters. Then, in 1978, 'Konni' thought up the idea of copying out Hitler's movements from a 1935 Nazi Party yearbook into a school notebook. Stiefel was more than pleased to buy this volume of 'Hitler's private diary'. Two years later, he happened to show it to Gerd Heidemann of *Stern* magazine.

Heidemann, who had been in the Hitler Youth, was fanatically interested in the Nazis. He had driven himself into debt restoring Reichsmarshall Hermann Goering's yacht, *Carin II,* and even had an affair with Edda, Goering's daughter. When Heidemann saw the diary and was told there were 26 more, he perceived a way out of his financial difficulties. After talking to 'Konni' on the telephone, he persuaded the editorial board of *Stern* to start parting with hundreds of thousands of Deutschmarks for the diaries 'being smuggled out of East Germany in pianos'. 'Konni' obligingly forged three more diaries, with red wax seals and a fake authenticated letter from Rudolf Hess.

The diaries were boringly banal, and surprisingly, revealed a rather amiable Hitler, seemingly unaware of his regime's atrocities. However, the team at *Stern* was convinced, and over the next two years steadily paid out 85,000 marks per volume. What they did not know was that, every time, 35,000 marks were going straight into Heidemann's pocket. 'Konni' settled down to a routine. Using 600 reference books to assemble his information, he could produce a 'diary' in less than five hours. Heidemann then managed to persuade *Stern* to pay 200,000 DM per volume, because the 'East German general was having to pay heavy bribes.' Soon he was able to move to two apartments in Hamburg's smartest street and to buy two villas in Spain, sports cars and all sorts of other luxuries.

In the spring of 1983, *Stern* prepared

'Konni'

for publication in Germany, while its directors were delighted that foreign rights had been sold for millions.

It seems remarkable that no real effort had been put into checking that the diaries were authentic. There had been some technical anxieties about the date of the paper used, but at the same time handwriting experts had all vindicated the diaries and Sir Hugh Trevor-Roper (Lord Dacre), Assistant Editor of *The Times* and an expert on Hitler, had been won over by a visit to the Zurich bank vault where the diaries were kept. Next day his proprietor, Rupert Murdoch, also went there and then bid for the English language rights.

On Monday, 25 April 1983 in a fanfare of publicity, *Stern* published the first diary, with Rupert Murdoch's *The Sunday Times* actually printing the day before. However, the doubts were emerging, first publicly voiced by David Irving, author of Hitler's War. That did not stop *Newsweek* publishing on the Tuesday, and *Paris Match* on Wednesday. Frank Giles, Editor of *The Sunday Times,* told Murdoch that Lord Dacre was now getting cold feet, but he was overruled on

No real effort had been made to check that the diaries were authentic.

the telephone by Murdoch from New York, who apparently said, 'F*** Dacre. Publish!' So, that weekend, the second diary was published by *The Sunday Times*, whose circulation jumped by 60,000 copies.

But the very next day, Monday 2 May, a bombshell hit *Stern*. Berlin's Federal Institute of Forensic Investigation belatedly delivered its detailed findings. Chemicals found in the diaries' paper and bindings were not available until years after they were supposedly written. Suddenly four more handwriting experts declared the diaries as fakes. 'Konni' Kujau fled, but both he and Heidemann were arrested and later jailed for four and a half years.

The financial losses for *Stern* probably topped 19 million marks or £8 million. Much more serious was the severe embarrassment and loss of reputation. The judge piled on the agony by declaring that the magazine had acted with 'such recklessness' that it was effectively an accomplice to the hoax.

Han van Meeregen & the 'dangerous Vermeer'

Works of art were ruthlessly looted by the Nazis from every country they conquered. The greatest and greediest looter of them all was Reichsmarschall Hermann Goering. So as the Second World War ended, the victorious Allies were on the lookout for mountains of treasure and piles of art works. Hidden in a salt mine in Austria, they found what they were looking for. In the 'Goering collection', art experts found a Vermeer, *'Christ with*

the Adulteress', *(left)* which they had never seen before. The painting was traced back to an Amsterdam nightclub owner, and the Dutch police began to interrogate Han van Meeregen very carefully. Selling national treasures to the occupying Germans was regarded by the Dutch as collaboration, and worse, treason, which *carried the death penalty*. Van Meeregen was in very deep trouble.

After several days, he revealed the astounding truth. He had painted the 'Vermeer' himself. The police did not believe such a ridiculous line of defence, so he set out to prove it. In three weeks, under the amazed supervision of the police, he created another wonderful Vermeer, *'The Young Christ teaching in the Temple',* and while he worked, he revealed his motives for a brilliant career of art forging.

As a young painter with classical leanings, he had been savaged by local critics and had decided to embarrass them – especially Dr. Abraham Bredius, a leading expert on Vermeer. He used 17th century canvasses, specially created paints, authentic brushes and a phenol and formaldehyde mixture which caused the paint to harden and crack. He then baked the paintings, and rolled them over a drum to crack them with a wash of black ink to fill in the cracks. His first triumph was *'Christ at Emmaus',* which fooled the whole art world, including, to his delight, his enemy Dr. Bredius. But having achieved his objective, the painting was suddenly sold for millions and he had second thoughts about his 'big revelation'. So he began to paint and sell more 'Vermeers', as well as false works by Frans Hals and Pieter de Hoog. The chances of his forgeries being discovered were much reduced by the war, occupation, and the black market. Then, in 1942, one of his 'Vermeers' was sold for 1.6 million guilders, making it one of the most expensive paintings ever sold. Goering, who normally just stole things (page 84), paid a huge price for his 'Vermeer' – but then paid the dealer in counterfeit money, which was poetic justice.

Left, van Meeregen painting under police supervision

After he appeared in court, his hoax made him immensely popular.

After three weeks painting, while chatting away to his guards, van Meeregen revealed a fabulous new 'Vermeer' for the world to see, and the charge was dropped to forgery. During his trial in October 1947, he became the second most popular person in Holland. He was sentenced to two years in prison, but failing health meant he was sent straight to hospital, where he died peacefully in December.

He had succeeded in fooling the art world and the Nazis, becoming rich, then an international celebrity and finally a local hero.

Not bad for a fellow who just started out with a grudge.

We all agreed. Of all the speakers who had ever addressed the International Hotel & Restaurant Association, none was more unusual and fascinating than a middle-aged American called Frank Abagnale, who stood up in Seville and warned us of the havoc that crooks and fraudsters like him could wreak on the world's hotel industry. Then, none of us had ever heard of him. It was to be twelve years before Leonardo DiCaprio would portray him in *'Catch Me if you can.'*

Frank grew up in the New York suburb of Bronxville, and at a young age became streetwise hanging about with his divorced father. Looking ten years older than fifteen, when his father gave him a car, he used it to pick up girls. But he still needed money, and now used his father's Mobil card to raise cash for spare parts he never took away. So, sadly, the first person he ever conned was his own father, for $3,400. His father forgave him, but his mother did not, and sent him to a monastic school. But Frank decided to leave both school and home. One day, he sat

down next to a beautiful brunette on a beach. 'Who are you?' she asked. 'Anyone I want to be,' he replied. It summed up his next few years perfectly. An extraordinary eye for detail and ability to learn like lightning together with his attractiveness to women, would serve him only too well.

After a few weeks of passing dud cheques on his own bank account backed by an altered driver's licence, Frank decided he needed a bigger stage. A revelation solved his problem standing outside New York's Commodore Hotel. A flight crew emerged. The men in their uniforms were handsome and confident, the stewardesses lovely. So Frank decided 'to become an airline pilot.' By guile, he acquired a smart Second Officer's Pan Am uniform and wing badges and then forged a FAA licence and a Pan Am identification card, cleverly finished off

with a logo from a model aircraft kit. He then started to 'dead head', a reciprocal arrangement whereby pilots can travel for nothing in the cockpit of other airlines all over America. In each city he visited, he cashed lots of quite small dud cheques. Indeed by now, he was an ace 'paperhanger.' In his pilot's uniform, nobody ever suspected or checked until he was long gone. His appearance created pre-conceived ideas and gullible trust, time and again. 'The FBI was now looking for a cool well-dressed con man of about twenty nine. I was seventeen.' He netted thousands of dollars, but became rattled when his identity was at last questioned by airline officials in Miami. The wily Frank got away with it, but decided to lie low.

In Atlanta, because he had casually put 'Doctor' on a resident's application form, he found himself button-holed by a neighbour, the head of the local

children's hospital, and was offered a job as its Supervising Paediatrician, which he miraculously held down for eleven months before he became really scared that his ignorance might kill a child. Then in Louisiana, Frank posed as a Harvard Law School graduate, and was suddenly and amazingly recruited on to the Louisiana Attorney General's staff of prosecutors, having (genuinely) passed the State Bar exam. He lasted nine months, before decamping once again to become 'a teacher' in Utah.

Then it was back to the cheque scams, but this time with forged PanAm pay cheques 'apparently mailed to him' in forged PanAm envelopes. As a test, he stung every bank in Eureka, California for $500 each. It was just the beginning. Frank started flying all over the country again, now with a complete TWA identity to supplement his PanAm one. Soon, he had to rent safe deposit boxes to stash his bulging suitcases of money.

Frank then fell in love, but when his girlfriend Rosalie starting planning the wedding with her mother, he felt that he just had to tell her that he was not a twenty-eight year old pilot, but a crook of nineteen. She did not take it too well, and he found police cars in her parent's driveway. The net was closing. He did not know that back in Washington, FBI

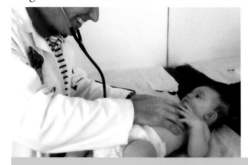

Leonardo learns from the master.

'temporary' account.

Now, armed with an intimate technical knowledge of how to forge cheques to go slowly round the banking system, Frank began indulging in a blizzard of 'paperhanging.' He was a millionaire, and not even twenty one.

Deciding that things were getting too hot in the US, after a brief but a profitable stay in London, he arrived in France – where once again a girl gave him an opportunity. Her father was a printer in Paris. Frank, posing as a purchasing agent, persuaded him to print 10,000 PanAm cheques for him. He showered Paris with them, and then New York. He very nearly got caught in Boston, and a furious O'Riley turned up to discover that Frank had bailed himself out only hours before. His most spectacular coup was recruiting a team of eight PanAm hostesses to tour the world on a 'recruiting drive', in fact a front for more paperhanging all over the world.

Inspector Sean O'Riley had decided to take a special interest in the elusive young man who kept moving on.

A chance meeting with another girl, a cheque designer, set him on a seriously ambitious course – counterfeiting, with a special camera and a printer, cheques on an industrial scale. He left Las Vegas $39,000 richer after just two days. On a visit to a bank, he also noticed that people nearly always forgot to put their account number on the deposit slips which were left on the counter. So he stole a bunch of them, entered his own account number, put them back and found $43,000 had been quietly transferred by the bank's computer to his

However, it was in sleepy, provincial France that Frank, in retirement at just twenty, was caught at last, surrounded by armed police in his local Montpellier supermarket. He was sentenced to one year in prison. This doesn't sound too serious? It was. Because for six months, he lay naked and unwashed in a bare, stone cell with no human contact and moreover, *completely without light*. When he emerged, two Swedish female police inspectors were appalled by the half-blind, bearded, filthy and emaciated figure they had to fly to Malmo.

During his six months in the comparative comfort of an open prison in Sweden, he was horrified to hear about the queue of countries waiting to jail him in considerably less comfort. Just in time, he was extradited to the United States. Amazingly, using his aviation knowledge as his plane landed, he removed a toilet assembly and squeezed through a tiny floor hatch to drop unseen to the ground, and run off across a darkened JFK airport – to the fury of O'Riley who was meeting the plane. He was arrested, but bluffed his way out of a jail and then from a motel surrounded by police led by O'Riley.

But it was not to last, and four years in a Virginia jail finally brought him to some lateral thinking. With his unique knowledge of white collar crime, why not put it to good financial use?

For thirty years, Frank has been one of the world's experts on beating such crime. He works with the FBI's Financial Crimes Unit, and lectures to the world's police at the FBI's Academy. He has helped 14,000 financial institutions.

All of which is why he came to talk to us in Seville, and why a fresh-faced Leonardo DiCaprio starred so successfully in his film.

The Captain from Köpenick

As we have seen with La Grande Thérèse and Frank Abagnale, impersonators can fool people for years. And in a few glorious moments, a middle-aged cobbler and petty criminal in Berlin created one of the world's classic impersonations – all based on the German respect for a uniform.

Fredrich Wilhelm Voigt was born in 1849, and at the age of 14 attracted a prison sentence for theft, the first of six which would ensure that he would spend half his life in jail and very little at his nominal trade as a shoemaker.

After his last stint in jail, Voigt came to Berlin to live with his sister. But it did not take long for the local police chief to list him as *'a person dangerous for public safety and morality.'*

But Voigt, now 57, had a last card to

play. Visiting various local second-hand shops, he carefully assembled the uniform of a Captain of the First Regiment of Foot Guards. On October 16, 1906, he collected it from the Beussel Strasse station's left-luggage locker and went to dress up in the local park. He then arrived in the suburb of Köpenick. At noon, he accosted a Sergeant and four soldiers, who crashed to attention. Voigt showed the Sergeant a forged 'Cabinet Order,' and told him to report back to barracks. He then marched the four soldiers off until they met six more soldiers coming off a shooting range. He now ordered them all to follow him to Köpenick Town Hall, where he posted them at the entrances. He also instructed local police 'to keep order'. They clicked their heels and obeyed.

Voigt then strutted into the building and arrested the Mayor and Town Clerk. He ordered the cashier to collect all the cash in a box and signed a receipt for it. The town officials were then sent off to Berlin under military escort, and Voigt disappeared with the money box and 4000 marks.

For those who contend that the Germans have no sense of humour, the press reaction is refreshing. 'A plot cunningly and impudently devised and daringly carried out' (*Köpenicker Tagesblatt*.) 'A robbery story as adventurous and romantic as any we can remember from a novel. It's overwhelmingly funny, what can be done in our country with its unlimited respect for uniforms, a military one with which an old, bow-legged individual had so successfully draped himself.' (*Berliner Morgenpost*.)

Voigt was arrested after ten days and later sentenced to four years jail for *the unauthorised wearing of a uniform, offences against public order, wrongful deprivation of personal liberty, deceit and heavy falsification of a document*. It seemed that German seriousness had reasserted itself. Except that the Kaiser heard about it and was sufficiently amused to intervene personally. Voigt was out in two years.

He made it to America where he was a theatrical success, then became the subject of a waxwork in Madame Tussauds' in London, and wrote a book that made him rich. He then retired to Luxembourg and featured in satirical plays and films for years.

And all because the Germans love a uniform.

Titus Oates & his Popish Plot

Many of those who profit from the gullibility of their fellows have a certain attractiveness. One can admire their charm, acting skills, nerve and sheer gall. However, Titus Oates does not qualify. He was one of the most unpleasant rogues in history.

First, he was physically repulsive, resembling a squat pig. He was sexually depraved and was duly expelled for sodomy from two schools, and for the same offence, sent down from Cambridge, dismissed as a Master from a Hastings school, and in 1677 nearly hung from the yardarm as a perverted Chaplain of a Royal Navy ship. Foul-mouthed and insulting, he was completely dishonest and a born liar. It was this undeserving miscreant who just escaped naval justice to hide with the Jesuits. He was to repay his Catholic benefactors strangely for their kindness.

Titus was then to fall in with another misfit, the Reverend Dr Israel Tonge, an almost mad anti-Catholic fanatic. In their apartment, they invented and rehearsed the 'Popish Plot.' This bizarre fiction envisaged the Jesuits combining with the English Catholics and the French king Louis XIV to assassinate Charles II and to place his brother James on the throne, to massacre all Protestants and to welcome a French invading army.

At first the King, quite rightly, refused to take the 'plot' seriously, regarding Tonge as a lunatic and Oates a charlatan. Unfortunately, he handed the matter over to a much more gullible Earl of Danby and the King's Council who, on 28 September 1668, heard and actually believed Oates' story of a huge and fantastic plot involving priests and Catholic nobles. Soon, with the Council's authority, Titus Oates, with a troop of soldiers, began rounding up innocent Catholics, even (or especially) those who had befriended him. Hysteria and fear mounted, and veracity was given to the 'Popish Plot' by the chance murder of Sir Edmund Berry Godfrey, the magistrate who had first taken Oates's disposition under oath. Sinister and self-serving impetus was added by the Earl of Shaftesbury, who for political ends, seized the chance to embarrass the King and perhaps to exclude his brother from the succession.

The frenetic surge in anti-Catholic

feeling in London began to resemble the anti-Jewish fever in Hitler's Berlin three centuries later, and with just as little justification or truth. The Queen, Catherine of Braganza, and James, the Duke of York, were publicly assailed, and Charles' position – to his impotent fury – was threatened. England was swept with false rumours of French landings.

Soon the prisons were packed with Catholics, and the first executions – by hanging, drawing and quartering began. Titus Oates strutted around London, now a rich man. The judicial murders included old scores being settled, with Oates watching old friends and enemies die horribly at Tyburn.

But after two wretched years of this collective banana skin of gullibility, a reaction set in. The populace had seen enough. Politicians and judges quickly sensed the changed mood, and prisoners began to be released. In August 1681, the King made his first move and ordered Oates from his luxurious Whitehall apartments, but instead of realising the game was up and escaping abroad, Titus Oates overreached himself. He attacked the King, and his brother whom he accused of 'being a traitor', for which he was fined £100,000. Then, failing to pay, he was put in prison.

Much worse was to befall him when Charles died, and his brother (whom Oates had tried so hard to ruin) became King James II. Revenge was sweet. Oates was tried and convicted of perjury. After being placed in a pillory and pelted with eggs, he was then 'whipped from Aldgate to Newgate.' This was, by specific order of the newly crowned

Oates in the Pillory.—From a Contemporary Print.

King, repeated the next day, almost killing him. Oates stayed in prison for three years until William and Mary came to the throne in 1688.

Considering the harm he had done to the country, the Royal Family and thousands of innocent Catholics, including thirty five horribly killed, Titus Oates was very, very lucky to die peacefully in his bed years later.

lies &treachery

*' The broad mass of a nation
will more easily fall victim to
a big lie than a small one.'*
Adolf Hitler

*' One of the most striking
differences between a cat and a lie
is that a cat has only nine lives.'*
Mark Twain

Tony Blair, George Bush & their WMDs

Blair had a chance to stop the war, but said nothing.

British Prime Minister, Tony Blair, faced the House of Commons on 24 September 2002 and declared on television, 'Saddam has existing active and military plans for the use of chemical and biological weapons, which could be activated within 45 minutes.'

Remembering Saddam's gassing of the Kurds, his chilling words convinced a sceptical Parliament and public. Britain trustingly followed America into war with Iraq. We now know that there were no such 'weapons of mass destruction', but rather that George W. Bush seemed intent on finishing off Saddam Hussein as his father had failed to do in 1992. We also have the devastating evidence of Britain's Ambassador to the US, Sir Christopher Meyer, who had been crudely instructed by Blair's staff to 'get up Washington's arse and stay there.' He tells us that Tony Blair could have used his unique influence to hold back Bush, but failed to speak up at the critical moment.

Tony Blair had enjoyed a wonderful, even euphoric, relationship with Bill Clinton, so he and his team were shaken when Bush narrowly beat Al Gore. But after the horrific tragedy of 9/11, Blair's fervent support for America won over the Bush team. From then on, Blair appeared to want to keep the American 'special relationship' at almost any cost.

As America prepared for war, little attention was paid to what might happen when the shooting stopped. Secretary of State Colin Powell sensibly warned the President, 'You do know that you are going to be *owning* this place?' But Bush's advisor, Condoleezza Rice admitted America's aversion to peacekeeping, 'The 82nd Airborne is not trained to escort grandmothers across the road.' The feeble preparation for the aftermath of the inevitable victory was to be one of the war's greatest flaws.

Britain insisted on United Nations' approval and, in November 2001, UN Resolution 1441 did indeed demand that Saddam disclose his weapons. Iraq's leader let in Hans Blix and his team of 250 inspectors, but they found nothing. Bush did not believe them. Blair repeatedly told the Commons that Saddam was developing weapons of mass destruction. As evidence, he produced Britain's own intelligence report, later dubbed the 'Dodgy Dossier', which turned out to be plagiarised, partly from the work of a post graduate student in California.

Many of Blair's political team were against the impending war, and not just Foreign Secretary Robin Cook and Clare Short, who resigned. Most of them did not buy into Blair's insistence that toppling Saddam had something to do with 9/11. The Conservatives reluctantly swallowed the WMD evidence. The Liberal Democrats did not. Countries like France, Germany and Russia were also doubtful and demanded more inspections.

However, Bush himself appeared to be on a crusade. In his January 2003 State of the Union address, he proudly announced, 'This call of history has come to the right people.' The reality was that America was desperate for the support of at least one ally. Two days later, Blair had a unique chance of holding back a unilateral attack on Iraq. But flattered by Bush's insistence that 'Tony has *cojones* (balls)' and seeming to be on a mission himself, he missed his chance. According to Christopher Meyer, at a decisive meeting in Washington, Bush had written down an acceptable wording for a second UN Resolution. However, Blair and his team said nothing to urge him to use it. There was silence. The moment passed. Two months later America and Britain went to war.

The campaign was short, and the victory – thanks to vastly superior technology – was overwhelming. However, the inspection teams that followed the troops found no weapons of mass destruction at all. Weeks of searching followed. Still nothing. Tony Blair, visiting the troops, tried to keep up the myth. 'The Iraq Survey Group has already found massive evidence of a huge system of clandestine laboratories, workings by scientists, plans to develop long range ballistic missiles.' Embarrassingly, the American Paul Bremer, who was by then running Iraq, retorted, 'I don't know where these words come from, but that's not what ISG chief David Kay has said.'

Bush had proudly announced, 'Mission Accomplished.' However, the reality is more bleak. After 23 years of Saddam, Iraqis expected a lot from his fall instead, but landed up with a ruined country. The most basic infrastructure remains wrecked. Three years on, 87%

Moments after the key meeting, Bush and a rather worried Blair face the media.

Tony Blair tries to reassure the troops.

still have no sewage or clean water system, and 53% seldom get electricity. Even in 2006, a Baghdad woman said bitterly, 'During Saddam's time, we always had power, clean water and better food than we have now.' Unemployment has soared, as have prices. Much worse is security, with bombings, kidnappings and shootings that have killed at least 30,000 innocent civilians and 60,000 'insurgents.' Little wonder that most feel less secure and would like their 'liberators' to leave.

Outside Iraq the results are no less dire, with British and American prestige damaged amid evidence of US torture and 'rendition', with terrorism increased worldwide, Hamas elected in Palestine and rampant Muslim fundamentalism affecting friends like Egypt and potential enemies like Iran, whose real plans for WMDs may now be difficult for a dispirited America to challenge.

Amazingly, Blair and Bush, who waged a 300 billion dollar war using the kind of spurious pretexts that Hitler might have admired, were not impeached or even punished by their electorates. Both are still in power. It is not just Iraq that has paid the price.

Jeffrey Archer & his life of fantasy

There's an old saying that 'truth is stranger than fiction.' Never has it been more apt than when describing Jeffrey Archer. There has always been some confusion about his early life, particularly his 'university' career at Oxford. What is not in doubt is that he was elected a Conservative Member of Parliament at 29, claiming, falsely, to have been the youngest MP ever. Hoping to make a quick fortune, he then became embroiled in a fraudulent Canadian

investment scheme which brought him to the brink of bankruptcy, and he was forced to stand down as an MP at the general election in 1974.

This would have driven most people to despair. However, Jeffrey had an extraordinary ability to bounce back. Reinventing himself as a writer, his first novel, *'Not a Penny More, Not a Penny Less'*, was a great success. Reincarnated as a famous novelist, he was able to re-enter political life as Deputy Chairman of the Conservative Party. Talking of parties, he used to host one during the Tory Party Conference for politicians and the glitterati, serving vintage Krug champagne and shepherd's pie, an odd combination, but one which attracted publicity, so essential to Jeffrey's life. All seemed to be going swimmingly for the millionaire novelist and politician, when strange rumours began to circulate. In September 1986, a witness saw Monica Coghlan, a prostitute, leaving a Victoria hotel with her third client of the evening. A potential fourth client was waiting in a car and flashed his headlights. Monica went over to the car - and then back into the hotel with him. She always claimed subsequently that it was Archer.

As a major figure in British public life, leading a charmed and glamorous existence, Archer knew that if the truth about his private life was aired in court, his political career would flounder. Because there was not just Monica. He had, in fact been living a double life, keeping a mistress, Andrina Colquhoun, and several girlfriends in London and returning to his beautiful and highly intelligent wife Mary for weekends at the Old Vicarage at Grantchester, where the poet Rupert Brooke used to live. Thus, he decided to fight back.

First he and his friends tried to buy off Monica Coghlan. This backfired,

with a media 'sting.' On 26 October, the *News of the World* detailed a meeting between Monica Coghlan and Archer's friend and 'fixer' Michael Stacpoole at Victoria Station. Coghlan was wearing a hidden microphone, which picked up Stacpoole offering her £2,000 in £5 banknotes to leave the country. The newspaper did not allege that Archer and Coghlan had had sex, but the implication was clear. Archer denied any knowledge of this event, but still resigned as Deputy Chairman of the Conservative Party. A few days later, the tabloid *Daily*

Lord Archer and his 'fragrant' wife,

Star alleged that Archer had picked up Coghlan at the hotel in Victoria and paid her £70 for 'perverted sex.' Archer decided to sue for libel.

His next ploy was to pay Michael Stacpoole £40,000 to leave the country. But then, he had to prepare an alibi. The *Star* asserted that he had had his assignation with Monica Coghlan between midnight and one on the night of September 8/9. Archer claimed that he had dined with his literary agent Richard Cohen and Cohen's wife at Le Caprice, a popular West End restaurant, and that they had parted company at about 11.0 pm. Two hours still needed to be accounted for. Another friend popped up to fill the gap. Terence Baker, his film rights theatrical agent, now claimed that he had gone to Le Caprice at about 10.45pm and sat at the bar with Archer for two hours.

Once Baker had agreed to the phoney alibi, Archer was fairly confident of winning his case. Then fate took a hand in the form of a simple mistake about dates in the *Star's* defence, which stated that the encounter between Archer and Coghlan had taken place on 10 September, a day later than the initial allegation. This meant that Archer had created an alibi for the wrong day/night.

Undaunted, in January 1987 Archer

Monica Coghlan

He had created an alibi for the wrong night.

covered himself by asking his friend Ted Francis, a freelance TV producer, to say that he had dined with him on the evening of 9 September. Francis agreed because he thought he was providing an alibi for a 'marital embarrassment.' By April 1987, the date error in the *Star's* defence was identified and the allegation reverted to September 8/9. 'Oh what a tangled web we weave, when first we practise to deceive.'

Archer's PA, Mrs Peppiatt, helped him to create the false alibi for both dates, by agreeing to write up a duplicate copy of his diary, altering the dates and meetings to match his statement. But she became worried that she was getting trapped in a conspiracy, and to protect herself, photocopied the false entries and recorded a statement about what she had done.

The case went to the High Court in July 1987 in a blaze of publicity, and Archer perjured himself by swearing an affidavit on the diary and in court. Monica Coghlan was unfairly denigrated by the court, crying out in despair, 'He's a liar and he knows it. He's even putting his wife through it.' Famously, Mary Archer was described by the judge as 'fragrant.' So the jury believed the alibis and found against the Star, which had to pay Archer a record £500,000 damages, plus £700,000 costs.

Now with a peerage, 'Lord Archer of Rebound' carried on living the high life and glorying in his power and influence with the Conservative Party for twelve years, only marred by suspicions over a windfall profit in shares in Anglia TV, where the 'fragrant' Lady Archer happened to be a Director. Then he was selected as the Party's candidate for the new office of Mayor of London. This was just too much for Ted Francis, who felt that such high office going to a flagrant liar was a step too far. In the Autumn of 1999, he called Max Clifford, a publicist known for placing scandalous stories with the media. Clifford called the *News of the World*.

The paper again decided to use a 'sting', arranging for Francis to call Archer, saying that 'a journalist had discovered the false alibi.' During the course of the recorded conversation, Archer incriminated himself. When the paper called and confronted Archer with its evidence, he initially denied it and then pleaded with them to play it down. He knew he would have to pull out of the Mayoral race and did so on 20 November, admitting that he had 'procured a false alibi.' Curiously, he thought that his main problem was a sex scandal. But it was much more serious. Scotland Yard investigated and arrested him for 'perjury' and 'perverting the course of justice.'

The trial took place in July 2001, and as a result of evidence from Ted Francis and Mrs Peppiatt, Archer was convicted and jailed for four years.

Responses to the verdict varied. Sir Bernard Ingham, once Margaret Thatcher's Press Secretary, said, ' I think it is a personal and political tragedy. His is yet another terribly wasted talent. I think he was an almost obsessive chancer. He relived his books.'

Lord Archer, as he still was, was released from open prison on 23 July 2003. Many felt that he should have resigned, or been stripped of, his peerage. As Michael Gove of *The Times* wrote, *'After his conviction, one might have expected a degree of penitence, even humility, or at the very best, circumspection. But not a bit of it. The Archers continue to insist, in defiance of all the facts, that his incarceration was the result of a terrible miscarriage of justice. They are determined to elbow their way back into the limelight, as though that were the only place they were truly alive.'*

As usual, Archer had lied, this time involving his wife, his mistress, his P.A. and his friends. A slippery slope indeed.

'An almost obsessive chancer, he re-lived his books.'

Cambridge & its upper-crust traitors

The Soviets triumphed by recruiting a whole group of influential young men.

It was 1930, just after the 'Wall Street Crash', with the Great Depression engulfing the world. But England's Oxford and Cambridge Universities remained bastions of privilege. Their undergraduates could indulge themselves outrageously, not least in political views. While the Oxford Union was to debate 'That this House will not fight for King and Country', at Cambridge, 'city of dreaming spires' and punts and parties on the river, something more sinister quietly occurred. Disillusioned by the collapse of Ramsay MacDonald's Labour government in 1929, students shifted further to the left, towards Communism. Their mentor was Maurice Dobb, an economics lecturer, who in 1932 stood up to propose to the Cambridge Union 'That this House sees more hope in

Moscow than in Detroit'. His attentive listeners included Donald Maclean, Guy Burgess, up from Eton and already notorious for his homosexual exhibitionism, Anthony Blunt, the present Queen's cousin, and the smooth and charming 'Kim' Philby, son of the famous Arabist, St John Philby.

Kim Philby only became a Communist on his very last day at Cambridge. Cleverly, Dobb did not send him to the Communist Party office in Covent Garden but told him to join up in Paris. It was to be brilliant advice, because Philby would have no record in Britain when he later joined her intelligence service. The first cover for Britain's greatest traitor was in place.

We still do not know quite how it came to pass or who the real Russian recruiter was, but the Soviet secret service had achieved its ambition: the nearly impossible triumph of recruiting a whole group of well-educated, influential young men, capable of a lifetime's supreme duplicity of betraying their country, families and 'class' by becoming 'penetration agents'. They were all to succeed – but none more spectacularly than Philby.

Back in London, Philby cleverly erased his Communist past by joining the right-wing, pro-Nazi Anglo-German Fellowship, and then going to report on the Spanish Civil War for *The Times* on the Nationalist (Fascist) side. When he was wounded by a shell, General Franco even gave him a medal, increasing his credentials and influence. Some thought he was working for British intelligence, but he was, in fact, feeding information to his real masters in Moscow.

After Germany attacked Poland there were months of 'phoney war,' and Philby could do little but act as a correspondent at the front in France, but Donald Maclean, now Third Secretary at the British Embassy in Paris, was able to pass invaluable material to Russia. When the Germans invaded France, both found themselves back in Britain. Philby met two old friends, Burgess and Blunt – both now working for British intelligence. Blunt shook Philby when he remarked quietly, 'I know what you're doing. Well, I'm doing the same.' It was Burgess who finally landed Philby his job with the SIS (Special Intelligence Service). Now the serious penetration of Britain's creaking security establishment could begin. The key role Philby was to play was to alert the Soviets about attempts by Britain to create a separate peace with Germany and, indeed, to block such moves – prolonging the war and enabling the Soviet Union to engulf Eastern Europe.

The achievements of the 'Cambridge spies' after the war were even more significant. Maclean became First Secretary in Washington, regarded as the 'Golden Boy of the F.O.' There he was able to help Stalin outwit the West by passing President Truman and Churchill's correspondence to Moscow.

Philby scored the triumph of manoeuvring himself into being appointed head of 'Section 9.' This meant he was not only able to protect Russian penetration agents, including himself, but also to reveal to Moscow all British operations mounted against the Soviet Union. Hundreds of SIS and CIA-recruited agents were to disappear behind the Iron Curtain. 'I do not know what happened to them, but I can make an informed guess, ' he was to comment drily later. Awarded the OBE, in Washington he was put in charge of the sensitive liaison between the SIS and CIA. Philby was even being groomed to be the next 'C', head of the SIS.

But the banana skin of allowing the Cambridge traitors to do such damage was now balanced by a banana skin of their own. Guy Burgess arrived in Washington, a 'last chance' posting for

Confident and smooth, Kim Philby

'What do you mean, worse? Goats?'

the drunken, blatant homosexual. Fatally, he went to live with the Philbys, not only creating a terrible strain for Kim's wife Aileen, but breaking an elementary rule of Soviet espionage. Philby knew the danger his friendship could cause, but tried to excuse Burgess. 'It could get worse.' Their boss retorted, 'What do you mean worse? Goats?' All this was very risky because, in spite of his own alcoholic breakdown, Maclean was head of the American Department of the Foreign Office where he was providing Moscow with vital secrets, not least that the Americans would not use atomic bombs in Korea. However, Philby knew that the FBI was closing in on a British spy called 'Homer'. This was Maclean, who was now forced to escape, which he duly did on May 25, 1951. What shook

Philby to the core was that Burgess went with him, a disastrous and unplanned move that now exposed Philby himself to suspicion, especially from the furious Americans. He was subsequently able to beat off British and American charges that he was the 'Third Man' for years, but now he never made it to the top, eventually escaping to Russia via Beirut in 1963.

Kim Philby was decorated with the Order of Lenin and lived out his life on a KGB pension in Moscow, following the cricket scores and doing the crossword in *The Times*. Outliving Maclean and Burgess, he was awarded a state funeral in 1988, with a brass band and a guard of honour. People are still wondering if there were any more traitors from Cambridge.

Studio 54 & an old enemy

There has never been a nightclub to match it, a perfect symbol of the flamboyant hedonism of New York in the seventies.

In April 1977, two young entrepreneurs, Steve Rubell and Ian Schrager, hit on the idea of transforming a old theatre, casino and television studio, calling it Studio 54 because it was at number 254, West 54th Street.

Pandering to the excesses of the time, they created the first 'superclub', huge in size, ambition and reputation. What made it really famous was Rubell's method for ensuring its amazing popularity – keep the 'grey people' out. The red velvet rope at the entrance marked an elitist selection parade, which Rubell and his cohorts monitored vigorously. Indeed, he was dubbed 'Mr

Outside'. It didn't matter if the approaching hopeful was a millionaire or a film star, if Rubell didn't think a person was 'happening' enough for that night, he turned them away. To get in, women sold their bodies and men sold their women. Amazingly, anyone who wanted to prove they were 'someone' would line up for endorsement – from Cher or Rod Stewart to Andy Warhol. The group 'Chic' wrote their disco hit 'Le Freak' as a protest, furious when they were turned away by mistake.

Warhol described the experience as 'dictatorship at the door and democracy on the floor,' because once inside, nothing was off limits, including a large 'man in the moon' puppet dangling from the ceiling, that would receive nightly doses of fake cocaine via an oversized spoon, to raucous applause from the people taking real cocaine below.

Everyone who was 'someone' could be seen at Studio 54 – Diana Ross, Liza Minnelli, Calvin Klein, Elton John, Bianca Jagger, Christopher Reeve, Michael Jackson, Brooke Shields, Warren Beatty, the Trumps, Truman Capote, Margaux Hemingway and Madonna. Such celebrity success was matched by financial success, with the club grossing seven million dollars in its first year.

It is ironic that the club was

Eager hopefuls crowd round the entrance.

threatened not by the blatantly obvious, the rampant drugs, the public sex or even the obstruction of the sidewalk and street. No, it was that old enemy of the famous – the taxman. Steve Rubell was bragging all too openly about how much money they were taking. Every night, thousands of undeclared dollars were being stuffed carelessly into garbage sacks. Inevitably, in December 1978 they were raided by Internal Revenue Service agents and in June 1979 charged with tax evasion. In December, things became even more serious. 50 IRS agents burst in tipped off by a disgruntled former employee and a boastful article that had appeared in *New York* magazine.

Rubell and Schrager were defended in court by an old friend and one of the

Thousands of dollars stuffed into garbage sacks

club's best customers, Roy Cohn, who was once Senator McCarthy's notorious side-kick during the anti-Communist 1950s. But to no avail. On 1 February, the pair went off to jail, the morning after one final all-night party crammed with celebrities. Just one month later, the liquor licence expired. Sylvester Stallone downed the last legal drink, and after thirty-three momentous months, the club closed.

Steve Rubell died of AIDS in 1989

and Ian Schrager has now become a successful hotelier. Their mistake had been to join the long line of celebrities whose banana skin was not filing an honest tax return – Al Capone, Leona Helmsley, Lester Piggott, Willie Nelson, Richard Prior, Ken Dodd, Chuck Berry, John Travolta, Mike Tyson, Spiro Agnew and Sophia Loren. Some were more guilty than others.

Lord Chelmsford & the Zulus

Lord Chelmsford

How often is it that an unfortunate friendship can ruin two reputations and doom a proud and successful nation? Frederick Thesiger, later Lord Chelmsford, and Sir Henry Bartle Frere first met in India, where they were both affected by the Indian Mutiny of 1857. They resolved never to have a powerful 'native' army able to threaten 'white rule'. In Africa, twenty years later, this attitude was to have fateful consequences.

Now with Frere as British High Commissioner and Chelmsford the Army commander, together they resolved to destroy the Zulu nation, for many years a friendly ally, in order to create a confederation of white states.

Not only was this in direct disobedience to British Government instructions, their iniquitous intentions were obvious to many worried British officials in Africa. Trying to avert disaster, Sir Henry Bulwer convened a Boundary Commission in 1878 at Rorke's Drift on the Buffalo River, a place soon to become very famous indeed.

Frere was mortified when after five weeks, the Commission ruled in favour of the Zulus. So he locked up the report. The Zulus were then summoned to Rorke's Drift on 11 December, expecting a favourable verdict, and were dismayed to hear an ultimatum from Frere insisting that they dismantle their military machine, an impossible demand that had huge social implications.

One remarkable man, Shaka, had created the Zulu nation with its 50,000 warrior army. It was he who transformed inter-tribal warfare from the equivalent of village cricket to ruthless conquest (page 364). He had personally perfected the deadly stabbing assegai, the *iXwa*. He had also trained his men to be so physically fit that they could run down a horseman, and manoeuvre smoothly in regiments, with the tactics of the 'head' and the 'enveloping horns', and the 'loins'. Furthermore, he had imposed mortal discipline that no African (or European) had ever known. Frere and Chelmsford should have known better than to underestimate the Zulus, but now they were on a mission.

It was once again at Rorke's Drift, on 12 January 1879, that an illegal invading British Army under Frere's confident accomplice Lord Chelmsford crossed into Zululand. Chelmsford, an energetic, likeable and well-respected officer, was convinced that not even the Zulus would face European firepower. A quick and easy victory could surely be achieved. The classic military mistake of 'under-estimating your enemy' was about to take its toll.

Under the mountain at Isandlwana, the British made camp, and Chelmsford made his first slip, overruling his officers and not bothering to dig trenches and laager the wagons, in direct contravention of *Regulations for the Field Forces in South Africa.* As one officer noted, 'It was as defenceless as an English village'. In one sense, he was wrong. For riflemen, the houses and walls of a village would have provided better defence than the sprawling open camp.

The next day Chelmsford made his second fatal error. He divided his command and took half his army to seek out the Zulus, whom he was anxious 'would not give battle'. He need not have worried. At noon, firing from back at the camp alerted him that something was wrong, although telescopes revealed that 'bodies of men were moving about and the tents were standing'. But at 3 pm, in galloped Commandant Lonsdale with dreadful news. Despite their discipline and courage and the firepower of their Martini-Henry rifles, backed by artillery and rockets, the 1,700 defenders at Isandlwana had been overwhelmed by 25,000 well-coordinated Zulus in less than an hour.

That evening, fighting from the buildings and walls of nearby Rorke's Drift, a handful of British soldiers

'As defenceless as an English village'

held off 4,000 Zulus, a truly heroic action which caught the public's imagination and somewhat mitigated the earlier disaster.

Victoria Crosses were showered on the defenders, and Chelmsford later managed to defeat the Zulus. But it did not really redeem his reputation, nor that of his friend Frere. They would always be regarded as the pair who caused the greatest Victorian defeat, and in hindsight, the deliberate and squalid destruction of a great nation.

Governments & tobacco

Roosevelt with cigarette holder at its usual jaunty angle

Take a look at any photograph of the 1920's or 1930's and the chances are you will see people smoking - from New York 'Society' and the glamorous in Hollywood to humbler industrial workers, and from the Royal Families of Europe and political leaders like Roosevelt and Churchill to gangsters like John Dillinger and Bonnie and Clyde. After World War 1, during which reliable provision of tobacco to the troops was regarded as important as food and ammunition, 92% of British men smoked. It was much the same everywhere.

Ever since Sir Walter Raleigh brought back tobacco to England from the New World, it became fashionable and even essential. Most governments not only allowed it, they became the principal supporters of the tobacco industry - indeed in many countries, also the only suppliers. Many of these national monopolies have only recently been sold off for huge sums to a few of the big international tobacco companies – notably British American Tobacco and Philip Morris. By using the huge profits from tobacco sales, these have expanded to become colossal enterprises. Philip Morris, now Ultra, owns Kraft and Jacobs Suchard, and is America's sixth largest corporation and its fourth most profitable. Moreover, all the while governments, where they did not own tobacco companies, certainly taxed them. For instance, the British Government levies 75% tax on every packet, thus effortlessly collecting £12 billion. It then spends just £750 million on 'smoking-related' health problems.

However, this cosy arrangement between government and tobacco shifted irrevocably in the 1950's when medical researchers began to discover and reveal the health risks of smoking. This was to be the first banana skin for the tobacco industry, because it either denied the risks or suppressed the evidence. It was 'economical with the truth', to say the least.

However, note that governments faced by the evidence have not banned tobacco as a dangerous substance or drug. Electorally and financially they would not dare. Instead, they have banned cigarette advertising, slapped on health warnings, and of course, continued to collect their huge taxes. They have acted more like secret business partners than adversaries or watchdogs.

Tobacco's second banana skin came in 1998 when the heads of all the main companies solemnly swore on television to a Grand Jury in Washington that 'smoking was not addictive', at least according to their own definition.

However, over one issue, the tobacco industry has not lied – but governments and health authorities *have* stretched the truth to suit their agendas. In their laudable efforts to reduce smoking, governments have turned pressure on the 'innocent bystander' and have given them the name 'passive smokers'. However, in nearly all circumstances, the danger of 'passive smoking' is actually a myth. Except in the case of asthma or small children, tobacco smoke in the air is so diluted as to pose a minimal threat, especially when compared with many other substances in the air. A hi-tech study published by Britain's respected Hazleton Institute in 1998 measured for the first time the real exposure of non-smokers to tobacco smoke by using filters attached to the people tested. In England this was found to be the equivalent of smoking half a cigarette a month. In Sweden, exposure was close to undetectable. A seven-year study by the World Health Organisation

It's hard to imagine anyone telling Harold Wilson or Winston Churchill not to light up in the Members' Bar.

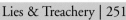

found the risk from passive smoking to be statistically insignificant. The fact is that all modern buildings have to filter and clean the urban 'fresh air' they use. So we should really worry much more about the diesel engines in the street than the smokers at the next table.

But following the questionable epidemiology of the U.S. Environmental Protection Agency (who has now admitted it lied) governments have imposed public smoking bans not only in the workplace but, by extension, into hotels, bars and restaurants. The pub industry of Ireland, which recently spent millions on new ventilation systems may be crippled forever, with part of the traditional Irish lifestyle being destroyed. Smoking bans are now arriving all over the world.

Britain has followed suit, Parliament turning down compromises and banning smoking in all bars 'to protect the staff.' Except, of course, in the bars in the Houses of Parliament!

Tobacco and government are still locked in a mutual embrace of mendacity. Like many couples, they deserve each other.

Teddy Kennedy & Chappaquiddick

Teddy was probably the least gifted and most flawed of the three Kennedy brothers. He was prone to cheating, lying, drinking and making easy decisions. However, since all his brothers had died (Joe Junior in a bomber and Jack and Bobby by assassination), the political ambitions fostered by old Joe Kennedy now rested on this last unlikely candidate. In fact, he was not doing too badly, having taken over JFK's seat in the Senate in 1962 and in fact becoming the youngest ever majority whip in 1969. But that year something happened which blunted his career forever.

On 19 July 1969, two people out fishing reported that a car was upside down under Dyke Bridge, on Chappaquiddick Island, near Martha's Vineyard, Massachusetts. At 8:20 am the local Police Chief, James Arena, was informed. At 8:45 John Farrer of the Fire Department dived down with scuba gear and, to his horror, found the body of a young woman, Mary Jo Kopechne, which floated to the surface in a cloud of bubbles. Word quickly spread, not least to Edward Kennedy and his friends Paul Markham and Joseph Gargan, who pretended they had just heard about the accident. At about ten, Kennedy went to the police station, where he and his team blocked the two telephone lines calling for help from lawyers and advisors. Eventually the Police Chief turned up and took down the following statement:

John Farrer finds Mary Jo Kopechne's body.

```
Official Police Statement

On July 18, 1969 at approximately
11:15 pm on Chappaquiddick Island,
Martha's Vineyard, I was driving my
car on Main Street on my way to get
the ferry back to Edgartown.I was
unfamiliar with the road and turned
right onto Dyke Road instead of
bearing left on Main Street. After
proceeding for approximately a half
mile on Dyke Road I descended a hill
and came upon a narrow bridge. The
car went off the side of the
bridge.There was one passenger in the
car with me,a former secretary of my
brother Robert Kennedy. The car
turned over and sank into the water
and landed with the roof resting on
the bottom.I attempted to open the
door and window of the car but have
no recollection of how I got out of
the car. I came to the surface and
then repeatedly dove down to the car
in an attempt to see if the passenger
was still in the car.I was
unsuccessful in the attempt.I was
exhausted and in a state of shock.I
recall walking back to where my
friends were eating. There was a car
parked in front of the cottage and I
climbed into the back seat.I then
asked for someone to bring me back to
Edgartown.I remember walking around
for a period of time and then going
back to my hotel room.When I fully
realized what happened this morning,I
immediately contacted the police.
```

From that moment, most of America has thought that Kennedy's statement was a lie, and have punished him for it politically ever since.

At the very least, by waiting for nine hours before reporting the accident, he may have caused Mary Jo Kopechne to die, because she had not in fact drowned but was found in what had been an air pocket, with virtually no water in her lungs. The poor young woman had clung on for two or three hours in the freezing dark while the oxygen turned to deadly carbon dioxide. If Kennedy had reported the accident within minutes, or even an hour, she might have lived. An autopsy was blocked by her parents, her bloodstained clothes were destroyed and the car was bought by a Kennedy lawyer and crushed. All the local investigations were dominated by the Senator's influence. He even escaped the mandatory manslaughter charge normally incurred when one walks away from a fatal

If Kennedy had reported the accident, Mary Jo might have lived.

accident without reporting it – bad enough to ruin his political ambitions.

And in 1989 Kenneth Kappel came out with an even more startling theory in his book *Chappaquiddick Revealed. What Really Happened.* His scenario: Kennedy left a party and crashed his car on the bridge. This damaged the roof, hood and doors and gave Mary Jo Kopechne a blow on the back of the head, covering her with blood and knocking her unconscious. At midnight Kennedy came back to the party, then returned to the scene with Gargan and Markham. They thought the girl was dead and that the Senator's political hopes would be doomed by his drunk driving. So they pushed his Oldsmobile off the bridge and into the water and spent the rest of the night alerting friends, preparing alibis, and of course, enabling Kennedy to sober up. If this is true – and the three of them actually killed Mary Jo by mistake – it is, of course, even more of a damning disgrace than anything postulated before. Neither Kennedy nor his two friends have ever challenged Kappel's book.

Teddy Kennedy finally threw in the towel for the presidential nomination in 1979, ten years after that fatal night which was to doom his hopes forever.

Gleiwitz & the excuse for war

In August 1939, Hitler was poised for his next triumph. Without firing a shot, he had taken over the Rhineland, merged Germany with Austria, and split up and then destroyed Czechoslovakia, absorbing its munitions factories into his war effort. Now it was Poland's turn. As with all his political and military ventures, all was clouded with deceit.

In January, he had announced in the Reichstag, 'During the troubled months of the past year, the friendship between Germany and Poland has been one of the most reassuring factors in the political life of Europe'. But only weeks later in May, he was brutally specific to his Generals at a secret military conference: 'There is therefore no question of sparing Poland, and we are left with the decision to attack Poland at the first suitable opportunity. We cannot expect a repetition of the Czech affair. There will be war.'

Furthermore, only days before his attack, he seemed mainly worried that he might be robbed of his war. 'Now,

Poland is in the position in which I wanted her … I am only afraid that at the last moment some Schweinehund will make a proposal for mediation!'

Germany's official quarrel with Poland was the 'Polish Corridor' to the sea at Danzig, ceded to Poland at the Treaty of Versailles and which separated Germany from East Prussia. The secret and real objective was naked expansion eastwards, making the Poles into slaves and exterminating her huge Jewish population. To pull this off, Hitler at first pretended to ally himself, temporarily, with the Soviet Union in the cynical, and to the British and French, shattering, Non-Aggressive Pact signed just seven days before his planned attack on Poland.

However, Germany still needed a pretext. This was duly cooked up by Himmler and his scheming side-kick Heydrich, together with the Gestapo. Reinhard Heydrich called in Alfred Naujocks of the *Sicherheitsdienst (SD)*. Naujocks has been described as an 'intellectual gangster'. He had already helped Heydrich with his brilliant plan to discredit Soviet Marshall Tukhachevsky, which ended with the almost unbelievable result of Stalin wiping out his own officer corps.

Now he was ordered to fake an attack

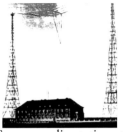

on the German radio station at Gleiwitz, near the Polish border. On 31 August, 12 Polish concentration camp prisoners (code named 'Canned Goods') were dressed in Polish uniforms, with weapons and identity cards, given lethal injections and then shot at the radio station in a way to simulate battle wounds. A member of Naujock's team then broadcast, 'This is the Polish rebel force. Radio station Gleiwitz is in our hands. The hour of freedom has struck'. The station then went off the air.

The press, German and foreign, were duly taken next day to Gleiwitz to view the dead bodies and the 'evidence'. The problem was that the Panzers and Stukas had already attacked Poland hours ago. As a propaganda coup, this bizarre, crude and murderous pantomime was a real slip of credulity. Not even the most gullible or stupid newsman could possibly believe that an incident at 8 pm could, hours later, unleash a million and a half

'Some Schweinehund might make a mediation proposal'

German troops, 4,000 aircraft and 3,400 tanks. Such an invasion would plainly have taken months of careful planning and weeks of secret troop movements.

Not only was the phoney attack a banana skin, the results were too. When told that the British and French were to declare war, Hitler turned on his Foreign Minister, Joachim Ribbentrop, who had led him to believe that they would abandon Poland, and snarled, 'What now?'

Hitler now had the war he so desired. But it would be a war that would be an increasing disaster, would kill him, destroy Germany and wreck the world.

Randolf Hearst & the Maine

'You furnish the pictures. I will furnish the war.'

Only once in history has a war been fought and an empire created by a newspaper proprietor.

In 1898, there had been agitation for months in America to intervene in Cuba, even after Spain had recalled her brutal Governor General, 'The Butcher' Weyler, who had created 'reconcentration camps' as a policy of 'salutary vigour' in her colony. Spain now made moves to give Cuba home rule. But William Randolph Hearst, the powerful publisher of the *New York Journal* and other papers, had been rabidly advocating war. His objective still seemed distant when his man in Cuba, the famous Western artist Frederic Remington, complained by telegram, 'EVERYTHING QUIET, NO TROUBLE HERE. THERE WILL BE NO WAR. I WISH TO RETURN. REMINGTON.'

He received the cynical response,

'PLEASE REMAIN. YOU FURNISH THE PICTURES AND I WILL FURNISH THE WAR. HEARST'

An excuse for war was provided, quite unexpectedly. On February 16 1898, the cruiser USS *Maine* was at anchor in Havana for three weeks, ostensibly 'showing the colours' as a sign of friendship with Spain. At 9:40 pm a huge explosion ripped out the bottom of the ship, killing 252 officers and men.

We now know that it may not have been a mine that sunk the *Maine,* but probably a coal-dust explosion that set off its magazines, a disastrous accident. But, of course, that was not how Hearst and his papers would see it, 'WHO SANK THE MAINE?'

On April 2 the United States eventually declared war – a war which Spain certainly did not want. President McKinley, a gentle man, was pushed into

it by public opinion, fuelled by newspaper barons like Pulitzer, Gordon Bennett (the eccentric sportsman who sent Stanley to find Dr Livingstone) and, above all, Hearst. 'We'll whip the Dagos until they howl' was a typical cry of thousands of volunteers who flooded the recruiting stations.

In the far away Philippines, Admiral Dewey annihilated the Spanish fleet riding at anchor in Manila Bay. In Cuba, led by the bellicose future President Theodore Roosevelt and his 'Rough Riders,' charging to cries of 'Remember the Maine', US forces overcame the outnumbered Spanish at San Juan Hill. 'Fighting Joe' Wheeler, an elderly former Confederate commander, appeared to be somewhat confused when shouting 'The damn Yankees can't stop us.'

'HOW DO YOU LIKE THE JOURNAL'S WAR?', gloated Hearst's headlines. The Americans were in a hurry. They knew that the wet season was coming, and with it, the threat of yellow fever and malaria. In July, they surrounded the city of Santiago, and with no prospect of relief from Spain, it surrendered. Exclaimed Roosevelt: 'A grand time to be alive. A bully time'.

Bully may be the right word. The United States had effectively obtained an empire on the cheap. Her expansionist faction forced Spain to give up not only Cuba, Puerto Rica and Guam, but also insisted on the whole of the Philippines, which President McKinley actually needed a map to locate.

For America, her empire was a banana skin. An Anti-Imperialist League arose protesting the acquisition of foreign colonies. The Filipinos, hoping for independence, were less than happy to trade one colonial power for another rather sanctimonious one, and rebelled. Soon 56,000 US troops were fighting there for two years before the rebellion was crushed.

Cuba, too, would always be a problem, either as a Mafia haven or the pivot of the Cold War, with The Bay of Pigs failed invasion, the Cuban missile crisis and Fidel Castro there as a danger and irritant, seemingly for ever.

Hearst, having created his war, retreated to his magnificent house at San Simeon, California, the inspiration of Orson Welles' film *Citizen Kane*.

'How do you like the Journal's war?'

Richard Nixon & the Watergate tapes

When young journalist Bob Woodward of *The Washington Post* was woken by the telephone on June 17 1972, he was not best pleased; to have to go in on a Saturday morning to cover a routine burglary was not what he was looking for. But this was no ordinary local burglary. First, it had taken place at the Headquarters of the National Democratic Committee in the Watergate complex. Second, the five burglars were very unusual. They were dressed in business suits with wallets stuffed with new bank notes, armed with surgical gloves, a walkie-talkie, two cameras, lock-picks, tear-gas guns and even bugging devices. They had stayed the night at the Watergate Hotel, eating lobster together in the dining room. Unusual burglars indeed.

Burglars in business suits, eating lobster

In court, the somewhat jaded Woodward woke up when one of the burglars, James McCord, claimed 'he was ex-CIA.' Thus began one of the most brilliant journalistic investigations in history. Both Woodward and Karl Bernstein, backed by the *Washington Post* owner Katherine Graham and Executive Editor Ben Bradlee, would gradually peel away layer after layer of lies and subterfuge from the Nixon adminis-tration. The desperate two-year cover-up would eventually bring down all Nixon's top advisers: Former Attorney General John Mitchell, Chief of Staff Bob Haldeman and Presidential Assistant John Ehrlichman (The 'Prussian Guard'), Patrick Gray, Head of the FBI, Richard Kleindienst, the Attorney General, (and highest law officer in the land) and dozens of smaller fry. Many went to jail. Only Henry Kissinger, the Secretary of State, would emerge unscathed. Eventually it would even force Richard Nixon out of office, under threat of impeachment or worse.

It emerged that the clumsy and stupid Watergate burglary, which was, in fact, a return visit to 'improve the sound quality' of the bugs successfully planted there days earlier, was just one of many illegal and reprehensible dirty tricks of burglary, harassment and subterfuge carried out by Nixon's lieutenants against the Democratic Party in the run-up to the 1972 Presidential Election. The question must be: why?

After four years in power Nixon was a comfortable nineteen points ahead of his hopelessly weak Democrat rival, Senator George McGovern, and would, in November, win every state except

Massachusetts and with more popular votes than in any election. This triumph was soon to be destroyed by the apparently ridiculous and unnecessary risk of the Watergate burglary.

The answer lies in Richard Nixon's extraordinary personality, with his insidious insecurity and self-pity. He was paranoid about his perceived enemies, including political opponents, 'the bureaucracy who are here to screw us,' and 'the goddamned intellectual élitists'. 'None of those Harvard bastards in my Cabinet,' he had ordered Haldeman. He was obsessed with leaks, especially after *The New York Times* had published 'The Pentagon Papers', the leaked secret history of the Vietnam War. He had the suspected source, Daniel Ellsberg, bugged and even the ordered the burglary of Ellsberg's psychiatrist.

This was the tip of the iceberg. His young aide, Tom Huston, had created an 'enemies list' and had mooted a comprehensive programme of bugging, wire-taps, mail theft and burglary, which was only blocked by the FBI's J. Edgar Hoover out of prudence and jealousy. Nixon, nevertheless, persisted in his own appalling way. 'We're going to get those sons-of-bitches, those cock-suckers, those rich Jews.'

Thus, at the very moment of his greatest international acclaim, his presidential visit to China, Nixon was placing his fate in the unlikely hands of 'The Plumbers', men like Howard Hunt, a 'James Bond with butterfingers' and gun-nut Gordon Liddy, whose 'Gemstone' programme had proposed kidnapping Democrats and trapping them with call-girls', while bugging their National Headquarters.

When these unsavoury characters were caught doing just that, Nixon's team first tried to bluff it out, with John Mitchell threatening, 'Kate Graham is going to get her tit caught in a big fat wringer.' Then Nixon blamed others, even trying to pay off Hunt with a million dollars. 'I don't give a shit what happens, stonewall it!'

When most of his team had gone to jail or oblivion, Nixon first appeared to have weathered the storm. Then came his final banana skin. On July 16 1973, it was revealed by chance that he had taped his own office. He could have burned the tapes, but somehow thought they

> *'We're going to get those sons of bitches.'*

would vindicate him. Instead they revealed a guilty, foul mouthed, suspicious, weird and unworthy incumbent in the White House. A tantalizing 18 minutes of the tape 'erased by accident' was the final nail in Nixon's political coffin.

Richard Nixon finally resigned in August 1974, two years after the Watergate burglary. It is ironic that the great wire-tapper's final slip was the poetic justice of tapping himself.

The Protocols, cruel hoax & 'Big Lie'

There have been forgeries ever since man learned to write. Some have been used to inherit wealth or titles, others to cheat financially, and yet more to discredit or outwit an enemy. But only one has been used to engineer and justify the greatest crime in history, the Holocaust, Hitler's attempt to annihilate the Jewish people.

The *'Protocols of the Elders of Zion'* were meant to be the sinister record of a secret meeting during the first Zionist Congress in Basel in Switzerland in 1897, revealing the Jewish leaders plotting to take over the world.

In fact, the *Protocols* were written by Pyotr Ivanovich Rachovsky, an agent of the Okhrana, the Russian Czarist secret police in about 1897. He had copied them from a satirical novel attacking Napoleon III by Maurice Joly called *'A dialogue in Hell between Montesqieu and Machiavelli.'*

They were indeed anti-Semitic, but also had the purely domestic purpose of trying to discredit the modernising Russian Minister of Finance, Sergie Witte. Their twenty-six chapters range from the sinister, 'use violence and intimidation' to the slightly silly, 'make the people unhappy by banning drinking.' Whatever the limited Russian purposes of the forgery, the *Protocols* became a 'Pandora's box' when they were published in 1905 by another secret police agent, Sergei Nilus. After the Russian Revolution in 1917, Russian expatriates spread the *Protocols* as proof that the Jews were responsible for the fall of the Czar. One of these was Boris Brasol, who influenced America's Henry Ford in his own famous brand of anti-Semitism. Ford's newspaper, *The Dearborn Independent,* serialised the *Protocols* in 1920 under the banner *'The International Jews: The World's foremost problem',* and then reproduced the series in half a million books and several foreign languages. More and more countries were flooded with copies.

In Britain, Robert Wilton of *The Times* and Victor Marsden of *The Morning Post* pushed the Jewish conspiracy theory. *The Morning Post* published eighteen articles with the introduction: *'The Jews are carrying their schemes out with steadfast purpose, creating wars and revolutions to destroy the white Gentile race, that the Jews may seize the power during the resulting chaos and rule with their claimed superior intelligence over the remaining races of the world, as kings over slaves.'*

However, it was *The Times* which investigated and then exposed the *Protocols* as complete forgeries in August 1921, printing extracts from Joly's book

side by side with extracts of the *Protocols* to show how they had been plagiarised. Most sensible people now dismissed them as forgeries.

Thus when Hitler was shown them by Alfred Rosenberg, he knew perfectly well that they were not authentic. But he also knew that they ideally suited his own fantasies and purpose. He used them for much of the philosophy of his 1923 book *Mein Kampf,* (my struggle), linking economic hardship to a secret plot and ultimately to Bolshevism. The *Protocols* became the chief weapon in the Nazi hate campaign against the Jews masterminded by Joseph Goebbels, the Propaganda Minister, who printed millions of copies in dozens of languages. It did no good for a Swiss judge in 1933 to rule 'For all the harm they have already caused and may yet cause, they are nothing but ridiculous nonsense.' After all, Hitler had also written in *Mein Kampf* his memorable and cynical view: *'The broad mass of a nation will more easily fall victim to a big lie than to a small one.'* He now had his big lie. Without the deadly influence of the *Protocols,* it is highly unlikely that the Germans could have been whipped up into such a frenzy of anti-Semitism, so that hundreds of thousands of ordinary people could willingly participate in the

They perfectly suited Hitler's fantasies and purposes.

methodical extermination of Jews. The Holocaust might never have been possible, and we might never have heard of Auschwitz.

Amazingly, the *Protocols* are still being used as factual truth by anyone in the world who wants to continue the myth of a Jewish conspiracy, including fanatical groups in the United States. There are 50 books in the Middle East based on them, so it is not surprising that extreme Muslim groups have embraced their veracity.

In 1964 a Senate Judiciary Committee repudiated them again: 'every age and country has had its share of fabricated 'historic' documents, which have been foisted on an unsuspecting public for malign purpose. One of the most notorious and most durable of these is *The Protocols of the Elders of Zion.*'

Sadly, the *Protocols* are a lie that will still not slip away.

Alfred Dreyfus & the forged papers

On Saturday morning, January 5 1895, in the courtyard of the Ecole Militaire in Paris, an artillery captain was marched out in front of the parade. A general on his horse intoned, 'Alfred Dreyfus, you are unworthy to bear arms. In the name of the French people, we degrade you.' The prisoner shouted back,

'Soldiers, you are degrading an innocent man. Vive la France! Vive l'Armée!' A tall sergeant stepped forward, stripped the insignia and buttons from the captain's uniform and finally broke his sword over his knee. The huge crowd outside screamed, 'Death to the traitor! Death to the Jew!' Within weeks, Dreyfus was on tiny Devil's Island off South America, his only companion a guard who was not allowed to speak to him. There, tropical fever or madness would quietly dispose of him – or so the French army fervently hoped. But this travesty of justice was not to be covered up so easily. Indeed, it was to wrack France for twelve years.

Everything started with the French spying on the German Embassy through its cleaning lady, Madame Bastian, regularly bringing the contents of its wastepaper baskets to the French Army's 'Statistical Section'. In September 1894, a memo, or *bordereau,* was unearthed by the Section's Major Hubert Henry, listing French military information for sale. Henry surmised that the spy who wrote it must be an artillery officer on the General

Staff. Captain Dreyfus seemed to fit the bill. Somewhat pompous and stiff, he was nevertheless keen, hardworking, well-off and a very promising officer, and was also the first Jew ever to be posted to the General Staff. And for Major Henry and an anti-Semitic officer corps, the Jews were hated and threatening outsiders.

After a ridiculous charade of being forced to take dictation, Dreyfus was arrested. The most unreliable of the 'handwriting experts' was Alphonse Bertillon, whose famous body measurement system for criminals was about to be swept away by fingerprinting (see page 77). The court martial in December was propelled to its verdict by the howls of the rabid anti-Semitic press. Major Henry pronounced, 'The traitor is sitting there.' Asked to explain, he icily replied, 'There are secrets that an officer does not even share with his hat.' Only too true, because a few months later, he had a new chief, Lt. Col. Picquart, an honourable officer who was not only worried about the verdict but, to his horror, discovered that the spying had not stopped. Another letter was intercepted, this time to a Major Esterhazy. Picquart had him followed twice to the German

Embassy and, even more convincing, his handwriting was identical to that on the famous *bordereau,* the only piece of evidence offered against Dreyfus. But Picquart's military superiors told him to keep quiet, while Henry decided he should forge more false evidence. Esterhazy was cleared at a court martial and Picquart was dismissed from the service, both influenced by Henry's secret subversion.

Then, the famous novelist, Emile Zola, changed everything. Across the front page of *L'Aurore*, he wrote to the President of the Republic the most famous open letter of all time, 'J'ACCUSE!' He named many of the officers involved in the cover-up. As a result, Zola was prosecuted for criminal libel and fled to England. Now France became bitterly divided over the 'Dreyfus Affair', with friends, families and even business partnerships breaking up about the case.

For the army, the affair began to unravel when Major Henry broke down and confessed to his crude forgeries, was arrested and eventually killed himself in his prison cell. Esterhazy fled to London and there admitted his guilt. Dreyfus, after nearly five years in his tropical hell, was brought back for a re-trial. Amazingly, he was once again found guilty of treason but, ludicrously, *'under extenuating circumstances'*. In a strange compromise, he was pardoned ten days later. It took another seven years for his supporters to have the second verdict overturned. In 1914, Dreyfus ended up the only one of the affair's protagonists to fight for his country against the Germans – as a Colonel of Artillery.

There have been more books written in France about the Dreyfus Affair than on any other subject. The latest, by Jean Doise, claims that the disgraceful treatment of Dreyfus and the highly prolonged 'Affair' were all part of a disinformation campaign to disguise the arrival of France's great secret weapon, the famous 75mm field gun. It may even be that Esterhazy, who lived on comfortably in London until 1923 on a mysterious pension, was a double agent.

Whatever the truth, the 'L'Affaire Dreyfus' was a terrible banana skin for France, dividing the nation and actually weakening the country, because politicians now so distrusted the General Staff and everything they said.

The CIA & Gary Power's U-2

May 1, 1960, 'May Day' was beautiful and sunny all over the Soviet Union, perfect for celebrating the most important day in the Communist world. In Moscow, Soviet Premier Nikita Khrushchev was looking forward to presiding over the traditional May Day parade in Red Square, a parade rather less military than usual in deference to Khrushchev's planned Nuclear Disarmament Conference with the Western leaders in Paris.

Unfortunately for all concerned, America's Central Intelligence Agency had chosen that very day to attempt its first reconnaissance flight by a U-2 across the whole of Russia. The Lockheed U-2 was regarded almost as a strategic weapon. Dubbed 'The Angel', it flew at a modest 450 mph, but its enormous wingspan of 80 feet took the aircraft to 75,000 feet. From there, its cameras could read a newspaper 14 miles below, secure in the knowledge that Soviet fighters and missiles could not, at that height, get anywhere near it. The steady intrusion by U-2s into their airspace for the purpose of spying was an insult to the Soviet leaders, who now embarked on a race to improve their missiles.

The U-2 pilots sensed that things were getting dangerous. Bob Erikson had nearly been shot down himself, so it was with some trepidation that he briefed

Gary Powers. He handed him a pistol, packets of dollars and roubles and the famous 'Silver Dollar', with its needle tipped with deadly curare poison so a pilot could kill himself if captured.

After two hours pre-breathing oxygen, Powers took off from Peshawar in Pakistan for Norway, reaching 60,000 feet in just ten minutes. He switched off his radio link to Erikson and switched on his cameras. Soviet radar picked him up, and at 6 am Khrushchev was woken. In spite of his recent public relations triumph visiting the United States and the looming summit meeting, the Soviet Premier was so insulted by the CIA's intrusion on a national holiday that he ordered that every attempt should be made to shoot Powers down. 'I told them that it was a scandal that after all the resources poured in, they still couldn't bring the U-2s down!'

So when the alarm sounded in Sverdlovsk, it was not surprising that Major Mikhail Voronov swung frantically into action. About to be retired, he was putting up May Day decorations and preparing to spend the holiday with his family when the sirens went. But soon his three SA-2 missiles swung round as radar tracked an unsuspecting Gary Powers. Desperate not to leave his command in disgrace, Voronov gave the order to launch. To his horror, only one missile hurtled into the sky. But it was enough. At 75,000 feet it exploded just close enough to cripple the U-2.

Powers landed by parachute and was picked up with severe concussion and ringing ears. The helpful peasants naturally assumed he was Russian until they found his American pistol.

On the saluting stand in Red Square, Khrushchev heard the news with grim satisfaction. Powers was rushed to Moscow for trial and sentence. The Paris conference was wrecked, but not before Britain's Harold MacMillan, France's de Gaulle and President Eisenhower were hectored by Khrushchev, 'A person should not shit where he's about to eat. That's elementary!' Some felt that he was right. The CIA's over-enthusiasm and deplorable timing set back the thawing of East/West relations for years.

Voronov received the Soviet Order of the Red Banner. Powers was later swapped for Soviet master spy, Rudolf Abel. Bob Erikson went on to be the U-2 pilot who discovered the Soviet missiles in Cuba in 1963, precipitating the 'Missile Crisis' that eventually caught out and brought down Khrushchev in disgrace. Poetic justice.

'It was a scandal that they couldn't bring the U-2s down.'

The 'Young Turk' & his battleship

We call thrusting business people 'Young Turks.' In 1913, the 'Young Turks were a political party who staged a coup, three 'Pashas' setting up a military dictatorship. One, Ismail Enver, became the dominant force.

Enver Pasha admired the Germans, but he knew, that faced by the threat of Russia, he must seek an alliance where he could. So he was happy to play on the enthusiasm of Winston Churchill, who sent three naval missions to try to help build Turkey's navy. Enver Pasha decided Turkey needed some heavy weapons, and quietly purchased two battleships in January 1914. One was nearly completed on Tyneside, and she was the most heavily armed warship in the world. The Turkish crew arrived on July 27 to collect the *Sultan Osman 1* five days before the First World War broke out.

Enver knew that when Austria threatened Serbia, the Russians would mobilise. He had to turn to someone for protection. Germans were at first not interested. What on earth could Enver offer to tempt them? The answer was the two battleships which, under German control, would be a formidable threat.

Churchill could see this at a glance, and after checking the legality (or rather illegality) of such a move, rushed in Marines, appropriating them.

Enver, negotiating desperately with the Germans, knew his ships were doomed, but pretended all was well. On August 1, he signed his secret treaty with the Germans. Three days later he received a cable from Churchill stating that the two ships had been seized. As they had been partly paid for by public subscription, this piratical action raised the Turks from lukewarm confusion about the war to fury with the British.

The clever Turkish bluff did Turkey and Enver little good. Despite the excellence of her soldiers, of generals like Kemal Ataturk, and Turkey's victory at Gallipoli (page 343), she was defeated.

And when the Great War ended, Turkey then lost more than anyone. Her ill-judged alliance with Germany and Austria saw the once mighty Ottoman empire reduced to the Turkey we know today.

If Turkey had remained neutral, in an age of oil, she would now be a huge empire of 250 million – controlling the oil reserves of the Gulf, Iraq, Iran and Saudi Arabia. This would have been a powerful combination indeed.

Enver Pasha

anger & revenge

'Anger is never without an argument, but seldom with a good one.'
Lord Halifax

'You can't be fuelled by bitterness, it eats you up but it cannot drive you.'
Benezir Bhutto

The Victorians delighted in the sensational, and in the libel suit taken out by Oscar Wilde against the Marquess of Queensberry they found it in lurid abundance. Wilde was the most celebrated dramatist of his time, and Queensberry, a fierce and contrary Scottish peer who had invented the boxing rules that still bear his name. It was, in a sense, a somewhat unlikely

Wilde, combination of bohemian arrogance and despairing fatalism

feud, since on the one occasion when the two men talked, they got on perfectly well. But the irresponsible and easygoing Wilde had allowed himself to become the catspaw in the deadly battle between Queensberry and his son 'Bosie', Lord Alfred Douglas, who was Wilde's lover. The trial was to lead to Wilde being imprisoned, separated from his children, bankrupted and even unofficially exiled. Perhaps most sadly, the man who made late Victorian

England laugh at itself was never able to write comedy again. And none of this need have happened.

Our story begins with a calling card. Queensberry was furious at what he saw as the debauchery by Wilde of his son, and had been 'stalking' both Wilde and Douglas for over a year, on one occasion leaving a bizarre bouquet of vegetables on the opening night of *The Importance of being Earnest*. But the spoiled, unstable 'Bosie' took dark delight in continuously provoking his father, and acted with no thought for Wilde's safety or reputation.

Wilde was in financial straits when he tried to leave the Avondale Hotel in Piccadilly on 28 February 1895. Douglas's extravagances were partly to blame, but he could hardly tell that to the hotel staff when they refused to allow him his bags until he had paid his bill. It was a position at once humiliating and intensely inconvenient. It was also very upsetting, because 'Bosie' had now left in a huff with a boy and written him a cruel letter. Then Wilde went to the sanctuary of his club, the Albermarle, to find a card that had been waiting for ten days. It was from the Marquess of Queensberry and was addressed to *'Oscar Wilde, posing somdomite* (sic)'. He returned to his hotel, thinking to escape to Paris, but once again could not take his luggage. Furious, frustrated, hounded – as he saw it – as much by 'Bosie's' aggressive affection as by Queensberry's implacable rage, Wilde made a fatal slip. He saw no way out but to sue for libel.

Though homosexuality at the time was illegal, so was libel. Douglas was delighted; here, he thought, was his chance to disgrace his loathed and loathsome father. Wilde and his friends had their misgivings, but Douglas would not hear them. Wilde was himself to blame, however; he was a paradoxical combination of bohemian arrogance and despairing fatalism.

Thus everything Wilde had driven so hard to hide came to light. Queensberry had proved himself far more resourceful than either had expected, and Wilde's true sexual nature was aired from the mouths of rent-boys and hotel maids. His libel suit collapsed and the findings were sent to the Director of Public Prosecutions.

The inevitable criminal trial which followed condemned Wilde to two years of imprisonment in what were generally regarded as the worst prisons in Europe. His spirit was broken, his muse forever crippled.

On his release, Wilde composed *The Ballad of Reading Gaol*, a magnificent, though occasionally purple, tale of a prisoner who had *'killed the thing he loved/and so he had to die'*. Sadly, it was a swansong. He died in poverty in 1900.

Of the many things this kindly, brilliant, self-destructive man must have regretted in the last moments, one must surely have been the moment when he picked up a card from a mad, savage aristocrat, and acted upon it.

His spirit was broken, his muse forever crippled.

George Patton & the slapped soldier

One day in Sicily in August 1943, a young man was slapped by an older one. Nothing particularly unusual in that. However, there are some who feel that the result of that slap, that slip, that impulsive act of sudden anger, was to affect the shape of Europe, the destiny of the United States and would cost literally millions of lives.

George Patton was an American anachronism, seeming to belong to the nineteenth century – or even earlier. Born into a rich, landed and military background, he had longed to be a soldier since his father had read him Homer. He could read a military map at age seven. At West Point he became an expert fencer and polo player, and his football aggressiveness earned him three broken noses and two broken arms.

Patton even came fifth in the Modern Pentathlon at the 1912 Stockholm Olympics, missing a medal by insisting on using a big military .38 revolver for the shooting part. His stint at the French Cavalry School at Saumur made him so expert at fencing that he became the 'U.S. Army Master of the Sword,' and even designed the army's new cavalry sabre.

'A man of diffident manner will never inspire confidence.'

When World War I started, he tried to enrol with his friends in the French cavalry, but had to content himself with joining 'Black Jack' Pershing's expedition against Pancho Villa in Mexico, where he personally shot a general with his revolver.

America's entry into the war in 1917 saw Pershing promote Patton to lead the new tank arm, and after many daring and gallant actions in France, he was wounded as the fighting ended.

Between the wars he learned to fly and honed his military knowledge with 600 books which he carefully annotated, from Caesar, Alexander the Great and Napoleon right up to works by his future panzer foes, Guderian and Rommel.

Indeed, it was Rommel's vicious blooding of the U.S. 2nd Corps at Kasserine in February 1942 which saw Eisenhower giving the Corps to Patton, who ruthlessly gripped its battered and demoralised troops. He also started to dress extremely flamboyantly, with full medals and ivory-handled revolvers. 'A man of diffident manner will never inspire confidence', he said.

His 2nd Corps helped to throw the Axis out of Africa, and then his 7th Army in Sicily beat Montgomery to Messina, starting a poisonous and childish rivalry.

But it was not just the strange and obsessive Montgomery and the more amenable British commanders who disliked the talented but intemperate Patton. His American colleagues also resented the flashy profanity and even the successes of 'Old

Blood and Guts'.

It was while visiting a field hospital in Italy that a tense Patton slapped an unwounded but shell-shocked soldier, calling him a 'coward'. A few days later in another hospital he did it again. When news leaked out, he was forced to apologise publicly. But the long-term results were much worse. In spite of the support given to 'Georgie' by his old and exasperated friend Dwight Eisenhower, the Supreme Commander, he was effectively demoted, and Omar Bradley, his subordinate, became his boss. Patton did not land on D-Day, and the Germans, refusing to believe that the Americans had disciplined and sidelined their best combat general for such a tiny offence, were more easily convinced by an elaborate 'phantom 10th Army', led by the 'Patton Bogeyman' which appeared to be about to attack at Calais. The Germans held back huge forces to receive him.

In fact, after participating in this useful deception, Patton had been given the 3rd Army and was placed south of the 'action' in Normandy. He then made his army into one of America's greatest fighting forces and broke out and thundered across France, advancing 600 miles in two weeks. But his supplies kept running out, often diverted (to Patton's fury) to Montgomery further north. Several times in the drive towards Germany he was held back by the cautious Bradley and Eisenhower, allowing the off-balance Germans to reorganise.

There are some who argue that if Patton had not lost his temper and slapped the two soldiers, he would have been commanding a whole Army Corps, and, with his reckless courage and drive, he might well have cut right into Germany in 1944. Thus, no Russians in Berlin, no Iron Curtain and perhaps millions of lives saved.

Some Patton sayings:

'The object of war is not to die for your country, but to make the other bastard die for his.'

'A good plan today is better than a perfect plan tomorrow.'

'A pint of sweat will save a gallon of blood.'

'If a man does his best, what else is there?'

'We're going to go through the enemy like crap through a goose.'

Tonya Harding & Nancy Kerrigan

In one of the most legendary sporting rivalries of all time, two US figure skaters were battling it out to be the nation's Number One. Nancy Kerrigan was glamorous, media-friendly and tipped as the favourite for the 1994 Winter Olympics. Her rival, Tonya Harding, had come from humble roots to be one of the country's greatest skaters. Though some disapproved of her athletic 'unladylike' style, she was the first American woman to land a 'triple axel' in competition, winning the National Championships in 1991 which established her as a fearsome competitor.

No-one could have predicted the events of 7 January 1994. Leaving the ice after a practise session, Nancy Kerrigan was dramatically attacked by a mystery assailant, who clubbed her brutally on the knee with a blunt object – a clear attempt to ruin her skating career. The world was horrified by the footage of her curled up in agony on the floor, crying out 'Why me?' over and over again. The incident threw up disturbing echoes of the on-court assault on tennis player Monica Seles the previous year, and it seemed a certainty that Kerrigan was out of the Winter Olympic trials, and therefore the competition.

Rivals pretending to be friends. Nancy (right) and Tonya

Tonya Harding's main rival was out of her way, and the obvious benefits to her began to foment suspicion that she might have had a hand in the attack. Indeed, the investigations soon led to Jeff

Gilloly, who happened to be Harding's ex-husband. She herself was repeatedly accused of obstructing the inquiry (an offence for which she later pleaded guilty) which by now had resulted in Gilloly's arrest, along with three other men. Horror gripped the nation, as the

realisation dawned that the attack on Kerrigan was a direct attempt to pave the way for Harding's success. This sport had never had been so sensationally tarnished, and the reputation of figure-skating would arguably never be the same again.

Throughout the affair, Harding always insisted that she would still compete in the Winter Olympics, and it seemed that her long-time rival, too injured to participate in the trials, would be no obstacle. But the saga was far from over. Through a loophole in the Olympic rules, Kerrigan was still allowed to take part in the competition. In a remarkable display of courage, the nation's skating darling managed to return to training and recuperate sufficiently to compete on 25 February 1994. The stage had been set for a phenomenal spectacle – one skater, having miraculously recovered, competing with the woman who may well have tried to cripple her.

For Tonya Harding, the scandals of the previous seven weeks had taken their toll. Progressively dissolving into tears, the former National Champion missed her first jump, restarted her routine, and failed to attempt her trademark triple axel. Her Olympic day was over.

Nancy Kerrigan's performance was quite different. Lifted by the obvious support of the crowd, she never wavered and pulled off a difficult display, showing that she had conquered both the physical and mental scars inflicted on that dark day in January. As she concluded her routine, a torrent of flowers rained affectionately upon her; her display and her recovery had captivated audiences across the world. Though she was pipped to the Gold Medal by the Ukraine's Oskana Baiul, she seemed ecstatic with her Silver: 'I think I skated great. I was smiling, I was happy, I was enjoying myself. I had fun. I mean, how can I complain?'

Tonya Harding's fall had only just begun. Nearly six months after the attack, the US Figure Skating Association stripped her of her former National Championship and banned her from the organization for life, stating: 'Ms Harding's actions as they related to the assault on Nancy Kerrigan evidence a clear disregard for fairness, good sportsmanship and ethical behaviour.'

She had fallen from being one of America's leading athletes to a national disgrace. Years later, she hit the headlines again when she was accused of battering her boyfriend with a hubcap – a far cry from the glamour and finesse of the Olympic ice.

When Iraq was invaded in 2003 by the United States and Britain, the decision was on the pretext that Saddam Hussein not only possessed 'weapons of mass destruction' but was imminently about to use them. When this was found not to be the case, the Americans switched the reasons for the invasion to the appalling behaviour of Saddam, his sons and his regime, including what went on in his prisons. The most notorious was Abu Ghraib, a 280 acre complex where thousands of Iraqis had been killed and tortured over the years.

To demonstrate that a prison could be run in an humanitarian way, Abu Ghraib was started up again by the Americans. General Janis Karpinski, its new Commandant, was proud of her assignment, 'This is international standards. It's the best care available in a prison facility.' She showed Defence Secretary, Donald Rumsfeld around, later reporting to the press, 'Living conditions now are better in prison than at home. At one point we were concerned they wouldn't want to leave.' President Bush boasted, 'Iraq is free of rape rooms and torture chambers.'

Not quite. In November 2003, the Red Cross reported that all was not well at Abu Ghraib. The US authorities merely responded by telling the Red Cross to make appointments before arriving (in direct contravention of the Geneva Convention). One month later the US Army had quietly investigated and discovered a truly horrible litany of appalling abuses on Iraqi prisoners. Not only had the prisoners been subjected to torture and sexual humiliation, but the many incidents had actually been photographed and videotaped like triumphant holiday snaps, souvenirs for loved ones back home. If it is hard to imagine what on earth these American men and women thought they were doing, it is even more extraordinary that they thought they were being clever recording it: smirking soldiers pointing and gawking at naked Iraqis; prisoners forced to simulate sex; men on leashes; prisoners attacked by dogs; even prisoners hooked up to electric torture devices. Saddam himself would have been proud of them.

The US Army sat on its own secret damning report for months – another banana skin, even when it knew the media were on to the photographs.

When CBS television programme *Sixty Minutes II* was ready to transmit, General Richard Myers, Chairman of the Joint Chiefs of Staff, asked CBS to delay for two weeks, but he then did nothing to prepare for the storm. The whole world recoiled when the programme went out, and hit the printed press as well. The pictures were indeed appalling. But when *The Baltimore Sun* showed the photographs to the mother of Lynndie England, the grinning girl who appeared most often, she responded 'Stupid kid things – just pranks.' This was the kind of mindless, ignorant, 'trailer-trash' attitude that had caused the abuses in the first place. Worse, it also confirmed that the abuses were not part of some kind of official 'softening up process before interrogation', but the simple bullying of helpless prisoners.

The Bush administration's response was also woeful. George W. Bush admittedly said, 'That's not the way we do things in America. So, I didn't like it one bit.' But then it was revealed that neither he, Donald Rumsfeld, the Theatre Commander or General Myers had yet to even read the army's own damning report.

Whatever effect it may have had in America and Europe, the real deadly result was, of course, in the Middle East. All the good intentions of the Allied forces, their combat bravery and tenacity, all the efforts of the new Iraqi government to rebuild the country were wrecked by a few stupid corporals and private soldiers, apparently totally unsupervised or restrained by their superiors to obey the law. To photograph what they were doing was an apparent act of real insanity. Those pictures must have recruited hundreds of suicide bombers and been responsible for thousands of deaths – from Iraq to Bali, from Madrid to the London tube bombings.

A pregnant Lynndie England and her lover Corporal Granger (right) and others were duly courtmartialled and sentenced to short terms in jail. Their trial produced one last question. How can a reservist corporal end up with more medals on his uniform than Britain's fighting commander, General Sir Michael Jackson? It says it all.

Jean-Paul Marat & Charlotte Corday

The scene has been preserved for ever by his friend and fellow revolutionary, the painter Jacques Louis David. Marat lies in his bath where Charlotte Corday has stabbed him to death.

At first glance, Jean-Paul Marat seems a rather unlikely revolutionary. Born in Switzerland and educated at Neuchâtel College, he found himself in Britain studying medicine, graduating from St Andrews in Scotland in 1775. Back in France, he saved the life of the Marquise de Audespine, and with her influence started a lucrative practice whose patients included the Guards Regiment of King Louis' brother, Comte d'Artois. But his travels to Britain had convinced him that conditions in France needed to be changed. In 1788, he became so ill he thought he was dying, but the next year the Convocation of the States General galvanised him, and he threw himself into the French Revolution aided by his newspaper *L'Ami du Peuple*. Several times he had to flee, once into the sewers of Paris, increasing his fervour and hatred of authority. Such fanaticism meant that many of the excesses of the Revolution can be blamed upon him.

The French Revolution was far from being a simple matter of overthrowing an *ancien regime* of a monarch and some aristocrats. It was long, complex and bloody, eventually devouring its own heroes like Robespierre and Danton. One of its greatest struggles was between Marat's Jacobins and the more moderate Girondins, who favoured regional power. The Girondins brought Marat to trial in April 1793, but he escaped the guillotine to plan his revenge. The 29 Girondin Deputies were proscribed and fled to Caen. There a young, beautiful and idealistic Charlotte Corday, from an impoverished aristocratic family, had been appalled by the brutal behaviour of the Jacobins and their 'Reign of Terror', which had killed 40,000 people. She had been known to write continuously on slips of paper, *'Shall I, or shall I not?'*

By July she had made up her mind. She arrived in Paris, purchased a kitchen knife and on 18 July knocked on Marat's door, saying she had information about 'the runaway Girondins in Caen.'

Marat was working in his bathtub where he spent much of the day, cooling with herbal water his raging eczema – contracted years before in the sewers. In such dangerous times, it was madness not to check on

Charlotte's credentials, or even to search her for weapons. But such was his driving desire to track down his Girondin enemies that he foolishly let her in, and began to note down the names. Charlotte suddenly stabbed him in the neck.

At her trial, she calmly stated that she had acted alone for the good of the country. The tribunal wanted her declared insane to steal her aura of patriotism, and her lawyer cleverly compromised by stating: 'This incredible calm, this complete tranquillity and abnegation which in their way are sublime, are not natural.' In July 1793 she went to the guillotine anyway.

Her revenge was in vain. Marat was martyred, the Girondins were crushed and the Terror continued. But Marat's overconfidence and rage had provided the French Revolution with its most heroic and dramatic act of resistance.

The death of his friend, Marat, was recorded by artist and revolutionary Jacques-Louis David.

John Maxwell & the Easter Rising

'A dead fanatic is the only one to extend any sympathy to.'

If you were looking for early signs of arrogant and callous indifference to those John Maxwell despised, the Sudan and the battlefield of Omdurman in 1878 would provide them. There, in belated revenge for 'Gordon of Khartoum's', death, 26,000 Mahdists dervishes had been killed or wounded, with only 48 British fatalities: the result of firepower, because, as Rudyard Kipling wrote:

Whatever happens we have got
The Maxim gun and they have not.

A young Winston Churchill, who had just taken part in one of the world's last cavalry charges, vehemently objected to Major Maxwell's orders not to help the wounded dervishes, but to 'finish them off or let them die.' Maxwell contemptuously replied, 'a dead fanatic is the only one to extend any sympathy to.'

Eighteen years later Maxwell was to indulge himself again, but with more far-reaching effects. In April 1916, the Easter Rising had occurred in Dublin, when after hundreds of years of British occupation, the Irish had risen in armed revolt. They seized key buildings in Dublin and defended them against the British garrison which, recovering rapidly, poured in 30,000 troops and tightened a cordon round the city centre. Four days later, Sir John Maxwell, now a Major General, arrived to take 'firm charge', promising maximum severity with indifference to damage. After five days of shelling and machine-gun fire, the insurgents in the General Post Office and the other battered buildings decided to surrender to avoid more bloodshed.

Initially, the feeling among Dubliners was that these men and women were at best misguided, and at worst, traitors to the thousands of Irish fighting for the British against the Germans. Indeed, the prisoners being marched off to be shipped out to England were cursed by the crowds and pelted with vegetables.

Unfortunately, however, Maxwell followed his usual instincts which changed everything. After rudimentary, secret and illegal courtmartials, he began to shoot the 'ringleaders' at Kilmainham Gaol – a few every day. Public horror began to mount. James Connolly, too badly wounded to stand, even faced the firing squad strapped in a chair while Joseph Plunkett was shot just ten minutes after being married to his fiancée. 'It was like watching a stream of blood coming from beneath a closed door.'

'All changed, utterly changed'

The British Cabinet saw the political danger and began to protest. Too late. In Ireland, a wave of revulsion gradually translated into fervent nationalism.

W.B. Yeats echoed the mood in his memorable poem: *'All changed, utterly changed. A terrible beauty is born.'*

The willingness to die galvanised the country. As Yeats also put it:
'There's nothing but our own red blood
  Can make a right Rose Tree.'

He later wrote a letter to warn the British about Ireland's passionate and shifting emotions, quoting a neighbour, *'The young men are mad jealous of their leaders for being shot.'*

After more years of warfare and bloodshed, Ireland indeed obtained her liberty. Maxwell's unfeeling actions started a process of unravelling, in just fifty years, a British Empire that had taken three centuries to build.

The Krays & 'The Blind Beggar'

The Krays were the closest Britain has ever been to organised crime. The twins, Ronnie and Reggie, and their brother Charlie grew up in the East End of London, dominated by their doting mother, Vi. Being rather good boxers, the twins' army careers during National Service lasted only for a few minutes, when they simply punched the first Sergeant to shout at them. Then, after serving time in military prison, they came back to the East End to begin a life of extreme violence, eventually running nearly thirty drinking and snooker clubs, providing protection rackets and stealing almost anything they could get their hands on.

'The Firm', as it was called, even started making inroads into the fashionable West End, for example with the nightclub 'Esmeralda's Barn' in Knightsbridge, fronted by the aristocratic sixth Earl of Effingham (whose title was rather more respectably earned by Thomas Effingham's role in the defeat of the Spanish Armada).

The Krays loved their new social connections and were publicly photographed with film and sports stars. National notoriety increased when Ronnie's gay friend, Lord Boothby, actually asked questions in the House of Lords about why the Krays were being treated unfairly.

So everything was going pretty well for the Krays until they carried out two crazy acts of anger and revenge.

There was only one other publicly known gang in London, the Richardsons, who certainly did not need to quarrel with the Krays. However, one member of this rival gang, 'Mad' Frankie Fraser, stepped out of line and there was a confused and botched shoot-out in March 1966 at the East End 'Battle of Mr Smith's Club', in which a cousin of the Krays was killed.

Ronnie Kray lost his temper and decided on revenge. On 9 March, he coolly walked up to George Cornell, a Richardson gang member in the East End pub 'The Blind Beggar', and shot him three times in the head.

After years of instilling real fear in the East End, no witnesses dared to come forward to identify Ronnie. It was not surprising that the Krays became even more confident. But they were wrong to do so. Public disquiet was growing, and nemesis was at hand. Frances, the childhood sweetheart and now wretched wife of Reggie, cracked after months of misery and killed herself. Reggie became crazed with grief and drink, and embarked on an orgy of public violence. Goaded by his brother's constant boasting about his 'Blind Beggar' killing, he brutally knifed to death another small-time gangster, Jack 'The Hat' McVitie, who cried out, 'Why are you doing this, Reg?' 'Kill him now', snarled Ronnie, and Reggie complied.

Enough was enough. The authorities finally struck back. Both brothers went to prison in 1969, eventually to die there. Throughout, their mother Vi never ceased to insist that 'They were such good boys!'

Napoleon & his attack on Russia

By 1811, Napoleon Bonaparte was at the pinnacle of his career. At last he had a son and heir, 'The King of Rome', by his wife Marie-Louise, daughter of his reluctant ally the Emperor of Austria. If he had, at this point, sat back and rested on his achievements, he might well have lived to a ripe old age as the contented Emperor of the most powerful nation on earth.

Born in Corsica in 1797 and trained for military service in France, Napoleon was in the right place and at the right time to benefit from the French Revolution, helping to beat off the vengeful monarchies of Europe, and after a series of victories, he became Emperor in 1804.

Napoleon was an organisational and military genius, and battles like Ulm, Austerlitz, Friedland and Wagram ensured that his continental enemies, Prussia, Austria and Russia, were subdued. Only Nelson's naval victories at The Nile and Trafalgar and Wellington's successes in far-off Spain cast a shadow on his aura of invincibility and success.

But having failed to invade England because of Trafalgar, Napoleon tried to strangle her economically with his 'Continental System'. When Russia opened her ports to neutral (in reality English) shipping, he decided to punish her. Such an angry quest for revenge was to be a fatal and, in some ways, an inexplicable slip.

Napoleon's attack on Russia was, on the face of it, well prepared and organised. His *Grande Armée* was 530,000 strong, comprised of twenty nations, with 1,000 guns, 30,000 wagons and 170,000 horses. Furthermore, in splendid French style, his massive baggage trains and depots contained 28 million bottles of wine and two million fortifying bottles of brandy. But his Russian campaign began slowly to unravel. In the primitive conditions, his normally efficient supply system broke down, so his advancing troops and horses actually starved. In spite of many small battles and a horribly costly and marginal victory at Borodino, the Russians were not destroyed and Napoleon lost far too many men and horses as well as good officers, including no less than 35 Generals. Worse, he captured a deserted Moscow to find no Czar with whom to negotiate, and much of the city then suddenly burned down. Meanwhile, the notorious Russian winter approached.

Exasperated, at the end of October 1812, Napoleon decided to retreat, very slowly, owing to his initial decision to leave nothing behind. This succeeded only in exhausting the horses, which had but one week's feed. On 2 November the snow came, and the struggling army, now 105,000 strong and harassed by Cossacks, began to lose guns, wagons, horses and men in the freezing conditions.

Several Russian armies closed in, and in spite of courageous improvisation in bridge building which enabled the pathetic remnants of the *Grande Armée* to escape back across the Berezina River, 400,000 perished. Napoleon, faced by a political crisis in Paris, was forced to leave his men to their fate. 'From the sublime to the ridiculous, there is but one step,' he commented bitterly.

Napoleon never really recovered from the disastrous loss of veteran soldiers, vital horses and prestige. From then on, he was on a slippery slope. He used all his old resourcefulness and military skill in a series of battles, but the one at Leipzig in 1814 (The Battle of the Nations) was to lead to the invasion of France and Napoleon's eventual abdication and incarceration on Elba.

His comeback – the 'Hundred Days' that culminated at his defeat at Waterloo – was all part of a process that started with his vengeful and foolhardy decision to attack Russia.

In 1811, he should have left well alone.

'From the sublime to the ridiculous, there is but one step.'

Indira Gandhi & her bodyguards

The Sikhs make up only three per cent of India's population. Yet, for centuries they have been one of the country's most independent, religious and uncompromising people. They are also one of the most warlike, a strength appreciated by the British, who, when India was 'the Jewel in the crown' of their Empire, regarded them as some of their finest soldiers.

Founded in 1577 by the guru Ram Das as the holy city of the Sikhs, Amritsar has been in the news for tragic reasons only too often. On 13 April 1919, under British rule, after rioting against new British security laws had grown out of hand, the police asked for military support from Lahore. General Dyer arrived, and ordered his troops to open fire on the demonstration. Several hundred in the crowd were shot, trampled to death or died trying to escape down a well, including many women and children. Unsurprisingly, this massacre and Dyer's unfeeling attitude did little for the long-term prospects for British rule over the huge subcontinent.

When the British did eventually leave in October 1947, the tensions between Moslems and Hindus forced the partition of India, and Amritsar was the site of several of the worst sectarian massacres that followed.

But the next time that the Sikhs and their holy city hit the headlines was due to a strictly Indian political struggle. Mrs Indira Gandhi had been involved in politics since childhood. The daughter of Nehru, India's first Prime Minister, she was photographed with the great Mahatma Gandhi at his bedside after one of his fasts, although she was not related. She was Prime Minister twice, first between 1966 and 1977 and then 1980 to 1984. While she demonstrated extraordinary political skills and tenacity, there was, however, an authoritarian streak in her make-up. There were also long-standing animosities between Mrs Gandhi's Brahmin Hinduism and Sikhism. Her eldest son, Sanjay, did little to damp down some of the

Indira Gandhi, under pressure in 1984

hatreds and tensions that were inevitable in such a huge and diverse country.

In her second term, Mrs Gandhi had to face the problems in the state of Punjab – where a militant sect of Sikhs led by Jarnail Singh Bhindranwale had conducted a campaign of extreme violence to obtain an independent state of Khalistan. Several thousand people had already been killed. Her hand was suddenly forced in June 1984 when Bhindranwale and a fanatical and heavily armed group took over the Golden Temple of Amritsar, the very holiest of shrines, under whose gold and copper dome is kept *Adi Granth*, the sacred book.

Always a staunch defender of Indian unity, Mrs Gandhi was forced to take action and to order an army assault, 'Operation Bluestar'. The battle against the well-prepared defenders proved unexpectedly fierce, and over 100 soldiers and 712 extremists died. Inevitably, some of the sacred buildings were damaged.

For once, Mrs Gandhi failed to grasp just how strongly the Sikhs felt about her unintended sacrilege on their holiest place. Otherwise, she would have changed her bodyguards.

On October 31 while she walked in her garden, two of those guards, both Sikhs, took their revenge and shot her sixteen times. The result of her overconfidence was not only her own death, but thousands of other casualties in the riots which followed.

After twenty years, the tensions between the Sikhs and the rest of the nation have eased. Indeed, there has now been a Sikh President and Prime Minister. Sonia Ghandi, Indira's daughter-in-law and the leader of the Congress Party, has played a major role in the reconciliation.

Nevertheless, and perhaps pointedly, Sonia has not appointed Sikhs as her bodyguards.

The Golden Temple

Arthur Scargill & Margaret Thatcher

Coal was king in Britain for over a century. It powered the factories, the mills, the steam locomotives and the ships that made Great Britain great for a while. But it had to be mined from deep below the earth, and the stalwart and rugged miners were a breed apart. In 1920 there were more than a million of them, living and working in close-knit communities where the mine was the only employer. It was not for nothing that they were called 'the shock troops of organised labour', especially after the General Strike of 1926, called out in their support.

In the years that followed, coal gradually lost some of its industrial and domestic importance. By the 1970s, natural gas was supplanting both coal gas and coal in homes and factories, and steam locomotives, which once used 60 million tons a year, had now disappeared from the railways. However, coal still generated nearly all of Britain's electricity, and in 1973 it proved that it was still king. A passionate and articulate former Communist, the militant leader of the Yorkshire miners, Arthur Scargill, confronted the Conservative government of Ted Heath, by slashing coal reaching the power stations, reducing Britain to black-outs and a '3-day week', and ending up bringing down the government. Miners became the highest paid industrial workers in the country. In 1981, Scargill became President of the National Union of Mineworkers, with the Communist Mick McGahey as his Vice-President. Three years later, a confident Scargill decided to take on the government again.

However, things had changed. Scargill seemed not to have noticed that Margaret Thatcher had just won the Falklands War against General Galtieri, who had plainly underestimated her determination. A woman who could send a task force 8,000 miles and ruthlessly torpedo the *Belgrano* was not to be trifled with. She was determined to reduce the overweening power of the unions in Britain, and was now ready to act. Thatcher had appointed a tough American, Ian McGregor, as Chairman of the National Coal Board, who proposed the closure of 20 pits, which were 'uneconomic', with the loss of 20,000 jobs. Unofficial strikes broke out,

Scargill seemed not to have noticed the fate of General Galtieri.

and in March 1984 Scargill declared a national strike. However, he had acted illegally, because he had not balloted his members, perhaps because polls showed that 60% of miners were against striking.

This lack of a secret ballot was his first slip, because the Trades Union Congress and many important unions did not support the miners. Moreover, the NUM's funds were sequestered. But Scargill's overconfidence led to plenty of other mistakes. It was pretty foolish starting a strike in the spring, with electricity demand tailing off and coal prudently stockpiled by the Government at the power stations. Railway workers and lorry drivers continued to deliver coal, which, disastrously for Scargill, was supplied by the Nottingham miners who had decided to keep working and to split from the NUM. Above all, he underestimated both Margaret Thatcher and her determination. Unlike in 1973, his 'flying pickets' were now confronted by thousands of determined police, and the coal kept flowing. The continuous violence sickened the public, especially when a taxi driver delivering a working miner was killed by a block of concrete. Scargill also made few friends when it was discovered that he tried to obtain cash from Libya's Colonel Gadaffi.

The months of confrontation continued, with real hardship growing in the mining communities (the film, *Billy Elliot*, depicts the tensions well). Gradually, more and more miners, desperate and disillusioned, drifted back to work. Arthur Scargill's defiant rhetoric could do nothing to halt the slide. After a year, the strike was called off. Margaret Thatcher duly set about dismantling the rest of union power.

For the miners, the strike was a disaster. The pits that it was meant to preserve were closed, and the jobs lost. Many customers were also lost forever. Cheaper open-cast coal was imported from abroad, and the Government decided to go for its 'dash for gas.'

When the strike started there were 185,000 miners, today there are 9,000. Having seen his once-mighty NUM ejected from the TUC Council because it was now too small, Arthur Scargill created the Socialist Labour Party, but lost twice trying to become an MP.

Scargill's ideological anger at the Tories was to lead to their revenge against him, and the wrecking of a once proud union and industry.

The Japanese & the Kwai railway

The story is now quite well known, and many of us have seen it in a sanitized film version in *The Bridge over the River Kwai* starring Alec Guinness and William Holden.

In spite of their earlier victories, the Japanese had lost control of the sea off Burma, and so were forced to build a railway through the rugged jungles from Bangkok to Burma to supply its armies which were trying to break into India at Kohima and Imphal. In peacetime, this would take five years, but they could do it in one if, illegally and against all the rules of war, they used their thousands of prisoners of war as slave labourers.

The experience of 'F' Force was typical. In April 1943, 7,000 British and Australian prisoners were told by their Japanese guards at Changi camp on Singapore that they were 'to go up country to a nice place in the mountains' where their 2,000 wounded could recover. Lulled by this pleasant picture, they even decided to take their grand piano. But they were cruelly deceived. After a long train journey, they abandoned their piano, and even more seriously, their medical supplies, as they faced a terrible 200 mile march over 17 nights. They arrived totally exhausted at a filthy campsite to start work the next day, in appalling conditions.

Illness, brutality, lack of food and medicine soon reduced fit young men to human wrecks. The Japanese were frantic. 'Speedo, speedo', they kept repeating to the sick, hollow-eyed skeletons staggering in the jungle dressed in loincloths, threatening, 'It will be built even if it is over the dead bodies of each and every one of you'. The brutality of the Japanese should have come as no surprise – they treated each other just as brutally, and also their Korean allies. They had already committed major acts of bestiality – with 200,000 civilians slaughtered in 'The Rape of Nanking' in 1938, and 6,000 Chinese slain in Singapore. Gang rape was regarded as soldierly bonding, as was bayonet practice on prisoners. Only 4% of allied prisoners died in German camps, but in Japanese camps the figure was 29%, and for the Australians an appalling 36%. Half the Australians who perished in the war against Japan died as helpless prisoners.

But on the Thailand-Burma Railway along the River Kwai it was even worse. 12,000 allied prisoners were to die, 29% of the British and no less than 69%

Prisoners slave in Hintok Cutting, as depicted by Australian artist, Jack Chalker

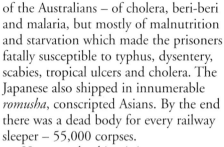

The monument at his home town of Benalla to Lt Col. 'Weary' Dunlop, the legendary surgeon on the railway who became one of Australia's great heroes

Kohima, the battle the Japanese lost because the railway was so late (Imperial War Museum)

of the Australians – of cholera, beri-beri and malaria, but mostly of malnutrition and starvation which made the prisoners fatally susceptible to typhus, dysentery, scabies, tropical ulcers and cholera. The Japanese also shipped in innumerable *romusha*, conscripted Asians. By the end there was a dead body for every railway sleeper – 55,000 corpses.

However shocking it is to contemplate such a story, what is truly extraordinary about the 'Death Railway' is its banana skin – the sheer stupidity of the cruelty and neglect. Because, given enough food and medicines, the prisoners would have built it so much faster. But with their workforce sick and dying, the schedule fell months behind. Practical mistakes added to Japanese inefficiency. Wrong surveys meant that laboriously dug cuttings and embankments had to be changed. One leaking radiator on a compressor, instead of being simply repaired, required three precious elephants to bring water to keep slowly filling it up. Barrels of concrete, already wet from river water, were hauled by two prisoners uphill to the railway, with the concrete hardening and already useless.

When the lines from Thailand and Burma finally and belatedly met, the Japanese made a propaganda film of the 'last spike' ceremony. The film crew were appalled by the appearance of the naked, emaciated men, and quickly gave them costumes – which they snatched back when the filming was over.

The idiocy of the brutal behaviour was one of the greatest blunders of the war. Because it was built so late, the railway never achieved its purpose of supply. At Kohima, after 64 days of knife-edge battle, General Sato signalled to his superiors in despair, *'Since leaving the Chindwin, we have not received one bullet from you, nor a grain of rice'*, and he ordered withdrawal, which became a horrific and unheard of retreat, and the greatest disaster in Japanese military history. Scant satisfaction for those destroyed or scarred for ever by the 'Death Railway.'

A Japanese engine still rusts in the jungle

Wyatt Earp & the OK corral

Apart from that at Bethlehem, no stable is perhaps as famous as the OK Corral. Moreover, there has certainly never been a more famous gunfight than the one that erupted there.

In 1879, Tombstone in Arizona, became one of the most spectacular mining centres on earth. Once silver had been found, the population mushroomed with bizarre suburbs like Hog-em, Goug-em and Stink-em. Soon the town had thousands of residents and was booming, with a brewery, two banks, two newspapers – *The Nugget* and *The Epitaph* – a hospital, a school and lots of restaurants, gambling halls and saloons. There were two theatres, Schieffelin Hall and the much racier 'The Bird Cage', where *Uncle Tom's Cabin* was once being performed when a drunken cowboy shot dead the (real) bloodhound so that Eliza could escape!

Tombstone also had one of the world's most famous graveyards, Boot Hill, named for the many who had died violently – with their boots on. Indeed the other thing that marked out Tombstone was its lawlessness, not helped by smuggling and rustling problems with nearby Mexico, with which even US President Chester Arthur

became embroiled. But what was to propel Tombstone into the headlines was the feud between a cowboy faction, the Clantons and McLowerys, backed by Town Sheriff John Behan and the five Earp Brothers. Virgil Earp was City Marshall, and his more famous and dominant brother Wyatt had been a saloonkeeper, cardsharp, policeman, churchwarden and bigamist. His best friend was the tubercular gambler, Doc Holliday.

What happened at the OK Corral on October 26 1881 has been glorified by Hollywood several times, notably with Burt Lancaster as an upright Wyatt Earp and Kirk Douglas as Doc in *'Gunfight at the OK Corral.'* The truth was much closer to a vindictive act of revenge, an overconfident ambush of unprepared, defenceless men. A witness, John Gray was to testify:

> 'The Earps — Wyatt, Virgil and Morgan — and Doc Holliday had stepped suddenly out on to Fremont Street from the rear entrance of the OK stable lot and immediately commenced firing on the cowboys who were preparing to leave town. Frank McLowery was sitting on his horse and at first fire fell mortally wounded. The other two cowboys lay dead in the street. Tom McLowery had his hands up when a load of buckshot cut him down. It was all over almost as soon as begun. A play enacted by the Earps to wipe out those cowboys under the pretence of enforcing the law — and carried out under the manner of shooting first and reading the warrant to the dead men afterward. But in this case I doubt if there was ever a warrant issued. The Earps called out, "Hands up" and began firing simultaneously.'

This virtually blatant murder was a banana skin for the Earps. Far from being praised by the Tombstone residents and becoming respectable pillars of society, they were despised for their action. Citizens draped the coffins with a banner declaring 'MURDERED IN THE STREETS OF TOMBSTONE'. The town turned against the Earps.

Six months later Morgan Earp was ambushed and shot and, moments after his funeral in Tucson, Wyatt gunned down his killer. Indicted for murder, he had to flee Arizona forever, re-emerging all over the West and later running a bar in the gold rush town of Nome, Alaska.

The OK Corral had exacted its own revenge.

miscalculation & ill-judgement

'*It is worse than a crime, it is a blunder.*'
Antoine Boulay de la Meurthe

'*I don't think we have failed, we have just found another way that doesn't work.*'
Andy Elson, balloonist

Prince Harry & the fancy dress party

In January 2005, two of the best-known young men in the world were going to a fancy dress party, with the theme of 'colonials and natives'. So Prince William and Prince Harry wandered into 'Cotswold Costumes' with their friend Guy Pelly. From the 2000 costumes available, William chose a reasonably appropriate leopard skin leotard, and Pelly a dress which plainly imitated the Queen, but Harry perused a rack of Nazi uniforms. The black SS uniforms were too small, so Harry chose an approximation of an Afrika Korps one, with a (completely incorrect) Nazi party red armband and a rather crude black swastika.

At the party, one of their fellow revellers took a photograph, which quickly found itself on the front page of *The Sun*, with a headline HARRY THE NAZI. The lethal combination of royalty and Nazism created a media feeding frenzy – much of it pretty facile.

However, there are all sorts of reasons why Harry's actions showed almost unbelievable stupidity and insensitivity.

First, only three weeks away was the 60th anniversary of the liberation of Auschwitz-Birkenau, the most notorious of the death camps, which killed 60,000 victims a day. Visitors to the snow-swept camp were due to include his uncle Prince Edward, Queen Beatrice of the Netherlands, US Vice-President Dick Cheney, Russian President Putin, German President Horst Köhler, French President Jacques Chirac, Italian President Silvio Berlusconi and Israeli President Moshe Katsov. You would think Harry might notice.

It could be argued that young Harry was no different from most young people in Britain. A recent poll showed that 60% of them had never even heard of Auschwitz. But then, privileged and royal Harry was meant to be different. As was pointed out by his former headmaster, Eton has an Auschwitz Essay Prize and is visited by survivors every year. Naturally enough, the world's Jewish community was up in arms.

Some might also argue that people often mocked the Nazis and this could be funny – Charlie Chaplin in *The Great Dictator,* John Cleese in *Fawlty Towers,* and Mel Brookes with his film *The Producers,* now a West End hit. But

Harry was not trying to be funny, he was just not using his brain.

Some of the media also dwelt on the sensitivity of the German roots of the Royal Family, which had tactfully changed its name from Saxe Coburg Gotha in 1917 at the height of the First World War – against the Germans. What is more, the last Prince of Wales, later Edward VIII, had boasted, 'There is not a drop of blood in my veins which is not German.' As Duke of Windsor, the Germans intended to install him as the logical King, once they had successfully invaded Britain. Even in 1970 he had the crass nerve to state, 'I never thought Hitler was such a bad fellow.' The Duke of Edinburgh (from the family of Schleswig-Holstein-Sonderburg-Glucksburg) was formerly Louis Mountbatten, again from a family which had changed its name from the German-sounding Battenberg. His brother-in-law, Prince Christoph of Hesse, was an SS officer, as was Princess Michael of Kent's father, Baron Gunther von Reibnitz. So all in all, drawing attention to such connections was not very bright.

But then Harry has lived in a not very bright world, surrounded by not very bright, out-of-touch, privileged young friends. As the *Pittsburgh Post-Gazette* pointed out, *'Harry is either the last truly innocent white man left in Britain or that nation's biggest moron.'*

The simple answer is probably that poor young Harry did not think. We all hope that the Royal Military Academy at Sandhurst has taught him to do so – for the sake of the soldiers under his command. But the report that, a week before his commissioning, he spent the night in a lap-dancing club in Slough makes one worry.

Drawing attention to German connections was not very bright

John F. Kennedy & The Bay of Pigs

In 1960 an attractive young John Kennedy and his beautiful and charismatic wife Jackie entered the White House. This promised to be a new, fresh and exciting era for America. The omens were good, but all was very nearly spoiled by a bizarre adventure in Cuba.

During the Presidential campaign of 1960, Senator Kennedy cynically and repeatedly accused President Eisenhower of 'not doing enough about Cuba', knowing perfectly well that the Republican administration of Eisenhower and Nixon was indeed hatching a coup against Fidel Castro, but could not reveal it.

By the end of the fifties, America was obsessed with Communism. The vicious and out-of-control anti-Communist witch hunts by Senator Joe McCarthy and his Un-American Activities Committee had only just ended, J. Edgar Hoover was devoting an inordinate amount of FBI time to domestic Communism, and the Central Intelligence Agency was certainly not going to be outdone in paranoia.

'They tried to make Castro's beard fall out!'

Imagine the horror of the United States and its government when, in 1959, Castro overthrew the corrupt Mafia-linked Batista regime in Cuba. While it was no tragedy that the Mafia and its casinos were kicked out of Cuba, Communism was now on America's doorstep, just 90 miles away.

With the approval of President Eisenhower, in 1960 the CIA started to try to discredit Castro. Ludicrous plans included spraying LSD into a TV studio or even making Castro's trademark beard fall out! The CIA was even working with the Mafia on actual, if hardly more credible, murder plots.

More seriously and practically, Eisenhower had approved a CIA plan and a budget in March 1961 to attack and overthrow Castro, using US-trained and armed Cuban exiles. When Kennedy was elected, he endorsed the plan, except that he made the fatal slip of changing the landing place from the more suitable town of Trinidad to the Bay of Pigs in a risky night assault.

Not surprisingly, there was honourable and justified opposition to the whole idea by many inside and outside the Administration. On 29 March, William Fulbright wrote to Kennedy, *'to give this activity even covert support is of a piece with the hypocrisy and cynicism for which the United States is constantly denouncing the Soviet Union in the United Nations and elsewhere. This point will not be lost on the rest of the world – nor on our own consciences.'*

Kennedy and his team, buoyed up by infectious optimism and overconfidence in their own luck, ignored such opposition and he gave the go-ahead.

In the darkness of the night on 16 April 1961, 1,500 armed men waded ashore at the 'Bahia de los Cóchinos'. Everything went wrong. Bombing raids by poorly disguised US B-26s failed to destroy the Cuban airforce, which immediately sank two vital support ships. The Cuban people did not rise to join the invaders. The Cubans were well organised and competent, and Castro displayed calm and impressive leadership.

After four American pilots had been

killed in desperate last minute air strikes, Kennedy pulled off the air cover, finally dooming the operation after three days. The last radio message from Brigade 2506 said : 'We have nothing left to fight with. How can you people do this to us, our people, our country?' A good question.

Two hundred of the invaders were killed and 1,197 captured, later to be ransomed privately for 53 million dollars' worth of food and medicine.

While publicly taking responsibility, Kennedy made the CIA scapegoats. As he admitted to Richard Bissell, the principal architect of the Bay of Pigs fiasco, 'If this were the British parliamentary government, I would resign and you, being a civil servant would remain. But in our Government, you and Dulles have to go and I have to remain.'

Neither the Kennedys nor the CIA had learned their lessons well enough. The Kennedys, with their exaggerated competitiveness and feeling that they had lost a round in a game, then authorised 'Operation Mongoose', a series of new, illegal and sometimes ridiculous attempts by the CIA to 'eliminate' Castro. These included poison pens, exploding cigars and contaminated wetsuits. Moreover, the Kennedys became further involved in the unholy alliance with the Mafia, and one of the tasks of John Kennedy's mistress, Judith Exner, was the very dangerous one of asking her other boyfriend, Sam Giancana (the head of the Mafia), for help over Cuba.

Much more important for the rest of the world, the Bay of Pigs fiasco also led to Soviet Premier Nikita Khrushchev embarking on the equally reckless idea of placing missiles in Cuba and the resulting 'Missile Crisis', which very nearly brought the world to nuclear war. Cuba then turned out to be Khrushchev's own banana skin. The Soviet Praesidium dismissed him a year later, quoting his 'harebrained scheming, hasty conclusions, rash decisions and his actions based on wishful thinking.'

We still do not know if Cuba led to Kennedy's assassination in Dallas in 1963, but the feelings of multiple betrayal ensured that the many candidates for suspicion included pro-Castro Cubans, anti-Castro Cubans, the CIA and the Mafia.

A furious Castro would prove defiant for decades.

'How can you do this to us, our people, our country?'

Margaret Thatcher & the Poll Tax

Perhaps a greater knowledge of English history might have warned Margaret Thatcher that a poll tax might not be such a good idea.

After all, it had been tried before, no less than six hundred years before. In the time of the child King Richard II, three poll taxes were imposed in 1377, 1379 and the last a 'tallage of three groats' in 1380. However, the huge resentment directly resulted in Wat Tyler's 'Peasants' Revolt' the very next year, with an invasion of London only just resisted with great bloodshed.

In 1974 the frugal daughter of a shopkeeper, Margaret Thatcher, had decided that if she was ever elected, she would replace domestic rates with a simple per capita tax. Inserted in the Conservative manifesto, this was to be a poll tax, only faintly disguised as a 'community charge.' She had a point, in that individuals mostly used local services equally, and that some owners of big houses paying high rates actually used them less. But now in power, she was opposed by a very worried Treasury and especially by Nigel Lawson, her Chancellor of the Exchequer. But he was stubbonly over-ruled, and the tax was introduced in 1991.

It was Thatcher's banana skin. The Poll Tax was hugely unpopular and regarded as very unfair to poorer people. Huge riots rocked London. Margaret Thatcher had at last offended her new type of supporter, 'Essex Man'.

A Prime Minister who had been immensely popular after her victory in the Falklands War and who had won three General Elections was fatally damaged by the Poll Tax. Her own party turned against her, and Michael Heseltine, one of the ex-ministers she had offended, stood against her for the leadership of the Conservative Party. His bid failed, but she was so wounded by the contest that she was forced to step down in favour of John Major.

Margaret Thatcher, Britain's first woman Prime Minister, had transformed Britain beneficially in so many ways. But, like many successful leaders, she began to suffer from hubris and arrogance and the fatal fault of not listening, either to others or to the lessons of history. The Poll Tax, sadly, was to be her undoing.

Nigeria & her cement fleet

In 1975, Nigeria was ruled by the military under General Gowon. As part of his Third National Development Plan, the Ministry of Defence decided it needed a huge construction programme of barracks, roads and airfields. Various people all calculated how much cement they needed. Totalled up, it came to nearly twenty million tons. And, even though it was a five-year programme, they ordered it all at once. One reason was that officials planned to use the bonanza's currency variations to shift money abroad.

Probably because they were soldiers and not sailors or engineers, they failed to realise that Nigeria's three ports could only unload 5 million tons – if they were lucky. There were no cement silos, and all other exports and imports had to go through those ports.

So, by April, 105 ships were moored off Nigeria; two months later it was 455.

The horizon was filled with ships from all over the world.

The ports were completely jammed, so imports now had to come by road, and the cement in bags was spoiling in the damp heat. Adding to the chaos was the expense, because once a ship was delayed from unloading for more than ten days, the Nigerian Government had to start paying $4,100 day demurrage for each vessel. It came to $300 million because some ships were stuck there for a year, with the crews growing mutinous while the owners grew very rich.

The Lagos Sunday Times made the obvious suggestion: *'The only constructive course is for the Government to calculate how many ships it can use within the next six months and tell the rest to dump their lousy cement in the Atlantic Ocean and go away, now!'*

Which, after a while, is exactly what they did.

The British & their aviation giveaways

There is an old theory that the British are great at inventing things, and then blow it by not being able to go on develop and to manufacture them. There is no greater and more tragic example than Britain's aviation industry after the Second World War. But in this case, the blame can be laid firmly at the door of a succession of ignorant, cowardly or dishonest decisions by governments –

both Labour and Conservative.

During World War II, Britain created the second biggest aircraft industry in the world. Under-resourced, under fire and under siege, Britain managed to build 125,000 planes. The United States, five times bigger, safe from bombing and with huge resources, built 300,000. Even more remarkable was the advanced nature of Britain's scientific achievement – far ahead in radar, electronic navigation, specialised weapons and jet engines, all of which was shared with its larger ally.

In 1943, for instance, the Miles Aircraft Company was issued by the government with an amazingly advanced specification. Working with Frank Whittle's Power Jets Ltd, Miles was asked to produce an aircraft which could fly at 1,000 mph at 36,000 feet. (This at a time when a Spitfire could manage 430 mph, and Germany's secret jets could just top 500 mph). By 1946 the Miles M52 was ready to fly. Then a shattering note to cancel the whole project arrived from Sir Ben Lockspeiser, the government official who had first commissioned it. It was ostensibly on cost grounds, but Sir Ben later revealed that he privately believed that planes could not fly supersonically, and might never do so! He

It could have been a British triumph, but it was Chuck Yeager (right) and his Bell X-1, who first broke the sound barrier.

also said publicly that, 'he had not the heart to ask pilots to attempt it', in spite of a crowd of enthusiastic test pilots who volunteered, including a German former Messerschmitt 262 test pilot, then a prisoner of war.

In the usual spirit of friendly co-operation, Miles sent all the M52's test data to the United States. Just one year later, benefiting from this wonderful technical windfall, Chuck Yeager rocketed the Bell X-1 to Mach 1.06,

76,000 feet above New Mexico.

The Miles M52 incident was sadly typical of the pattern of what was to come. Rolls-Royce, with its Nene and Derwent jet engines, was way ahead of the world. The Russians were desperately trying to catch up, unsuccessfully using captured German engines which suffered from lack of power and reliability. Imagine their

amazement when Britain offered to sell her technology. As usual, Soviet dictator Josef Stalin was highly suspicious, fearing a trick, 'What a fool one must be to sell one's own secrets'. What fools indeed! First, Soviet scientists were given free access to visit all Britain's aviation factories, especially Rolls-Royce. One of them, V. Klimov, did a 'soft-shoe shuffle', picking up metal filings on his special boot soles. S.T.Kishkin even managed to slip a Nene turbine blade into his pocket to copy its advanced Nimonic 80 metallurgy. They need hardly have bothered, because a few months later, dozens of complete Rolls-Royce engines were sold, crated up and shipped to Moscow with all their maintenance manuals. The result was

that Russian aviation jumped two years, all its engines exact copies of Rolls-Royce Nenes and Derwents. Indeed, battles in the skies above Korea were filled with transonic fighters, Russian MIG15s or American F-86 Sabres, all using British technology. Only the British did not have such a modern fighter in the Korean War.

For the next two decades, the litany of British Government vacilations and cancellations at the very last minute continued, and with them the gradual destruction of a great industry. The Hawker P.1081 fighter was not taken up, nor the thin-wing supersonic Hunter. In 1956, Britain amazed the world when its delta-winged Fairey FD research plane beat the world's speed record by reaching 1,132 mph. It was, of course, not put into production – but soon the French Dassault Mirage was. It was almost identical. Even the Harrier, Britain's world-beating vertical take-off fighter had its supersonic version cancelled.

As with military aircraft, this sorry story was repeated in the commercial market. Just as long haul and transatlantic passenger traffic was really opening up, Britain's best contender, the Vickers V1000/VC7, was cancelled, thus leaving the way open for the massive success of the Boeing 707 and DC8.

Rolls-Royce engines powered a decade of Soviet aircraft.

Among smaller airliners, the DH121 and the AVRO 776 were cancelled. Soon the Boeing 727 dominated that market. Even helicopters were not immune, with several Westland projects cancelled, so everyone uses American Chinooks and Hueys.

If the double decker VC10 had not been cancelled, it might well have rivalled the Jumbo Boeing 747. Several British transport planes were scrapped, so we now only use the C130 Hercules.

Probably the greatest tragedy was the TSR.2, a super fast bomber and reconnaissance aircraft miles ahead of its time. One of its enemies was naval enthusiast Lord Louis Mountbatten, who publicly favoured upgrading Buccaneer carrier aircraft instead. Finally, after years of development, the first successful flights and with production actually under way, Prime Minister Harold Wilson decided to cancel TSR.2. Its proposed replacement, the American F-111, then arrived years late and at a cost *actually higher* than the TSR.2. The prototypes of TSR.2 were broken up for scrap and one was taken out and used for target practice on a beach, a humiliating and disgraceful end.

The terrible thing is that nearly all of these cancellations by successive governments occurred at the last minute, when all the work was done. They cost a fortune and wrecked a superb export industry.

The brilliant TSR.2, now preserved at the Imperial War Museum, Duxford

Princess Diana & her sad legacies

Diana, Princess of Wales, was one of the great icons of the twentieth century. Fairytale Princess, fashion leader, caring mother, wronged wife, champion of the under privileged – take your pick. Love her or hate her, she exerted an enormous influence. It is therefore sad that her two legacies have been tainted by two banana skins – one of them highly slippery and the other a fall of judgement.

After Diana died there was a great debate about a suitable physical monument. Perhaps a statue, maybe a fountain. Eventually it was decided to commission the American designer Kathryn Gustafson, who decided to create, at a cost of £3.6 million, a large oval in Hyde Park - part fountain, part paddling pool. Opened by the Queen in July 2004, the Princess Diana Memorial Fountain slid into trouble the very next day.

After heavy rain, leaves blocked the pumps, creating huge puddles. It happened again a week later, so it had to be closed for cleaning once a week. A week later, three people were taken to hospital after slipping up. Paddling was banned. By August, resurfaced, paddling was allowed again with 'paddle police' supervision. On August 21, the monument was a mudbath and another woman was injured. Royal Parks admitted that they must spend £140,000 a year on cleaning, and allocated £150,000 for immediate improvements, for which the site was closed for four months in January 2005. The Hyde Park Estate Association described it as 'a laughing stock.' The local MP called it a 'pig's ear, which has turned out to be staggeringly expensive.' A friend of Diana's sighed, 'It's a total disaster and not what she would have wanted.'

What she would have wanted even less is the saga of the Princess Diana Memorial Fund, set up to give money to her favourite charities. This started well enough, with £20 million donated by the public and nearly £57 million from the sales of Elton John's *Candle in the Wind* and the

Adding to the farce: Bryan Ferry's son, Otis, leads a protest in the Commons, chased by guards with ceremonial swords.

Right: Kate Hoey with a bird of prey

young people. Some hunts have used another loophole designed to preserve hawking. Many hunts now arrive with a huge bird of prey. These are seldom actually let off, 'it might take a hound or a child off the back of a pony,' said one cautious bird handler. Another occasion was rather costly – they did let an eagle off and it did indeed kill the fox, but the hounds then unfortunately polished off the pair of them, costing £5,000 for the highly trained bird.

In the meantime, many more foxes are quietly being killed by farmers, who are desperate to keep down their numbers and to reduce their damage to livestock and poultry.

One of the more vociferous critics of the hunting legislation is Kate Hoey, the Labour MP for Vauxhall, an inner-city constituency, and surprisingly, the Chairman of the Countryside Alliance. She was shocked by her own party's attitudes. Tony Banks finally did admit that it was all about class. David Lammy, our Culture Minister, no less, said to a Labour group that 'all members of the Countryside Alliance look alike, as a result of in-breeding.' Kate Hoey

correctly pointed out, 'You couldn't say that about a black person, an Asian person or a disabled person, but country people are fair game.'

One Cabinet Minister, at least, has admitted privately that the ban has been a complete waste of time. 'It was the Labour Party talking to itself, rather than doing what the voters wanted.'

Indeed, he may be voicing the worry that there may be long-term and unforeseen dangers in pandering to a large group of Labour backbenchers to buy off their support for other laws. The Party seems to have earned the implacable hatred of significant numbers of previously non-political folk.

They might just tip the electoral balance next time round.

Nicolae Ceausescu & Timishoara

One of the most unsettling qualities of the tyrant is sentimentality: the butcher is often the puppy-lover. Nicolae Ceausescu, the Communist dictator of Romania, was one such example. He was genuinely hurt when the Hungarians of Transylvania compared him with the terrible Vlad Dracul, the fifteenth century Wallachian prince upon whom Bram Stoker based his Dracula. He felt curiously misunderstood and even rather ill-used. The fact that he had obliterated hundreds of Hungarian villages in Transylvania simply seemed not to register. It was therefore fitting that Transylvania proved his undoing.

His own people had little reason to love him. While living in a huge palace, Ceausescu had destroyed the economy to horse-drawn subsistence level, and had caused untold human anguish by banning divorce, birth control and abortion to boost the birthrate – which indeed doubled. However, without similar increases in maternity facilities, infant mortality rocketed. This Ceausescu simply covered up by not issuing birth certificates for a month. Soon, the country was flooded with unwanted babies, many of whom were to die of an AIDS epidemic from contaminated blood given 'to strengthen them'.

After a visit to North Korea, he was inspired to pack the mental hospitals with any dissidents, most of whom never emerged again. He banned typewriters in 1983 as a form of censorship, and even destroyed Bucharest's main hospital. The reason? His dog, 'Corbu', had been made a Colonel in the army and rode around in a limousine. On a visit to the hospital, the black labrador got into a fight with one of the hospital cats, kept to keep down the rats. The dog itself had been given a gift from the British Liberal leader David Steel, one of many foreign politicians who had amazingly honoured the mad dictator, although Queen Elizabeth was certainly not too pleased when the obsessive Ceausescu was seen cleaning his hands with disinfectant after shaking her hand!

HUMPHREY STONE

While his people starved, Ceausescu built this vast and overblown palace for himself.

It was one town that provided Ceausescu's fatal banana skin. In south-western Romania, in the region once known as the Banat, lies the town of Timishoara, or Temesvar to the Hungarians. It has always had a strong Lutheran tradition, and one of its most celebrated pastors was Laszlo Tokes. Tokes belonged to the proud Hungarian minority in Transylvania, a region acquired by Romania after the treaty of Trianon in 1922. To the Hungarians of Transylvania, their homeland was rightfully part of Hungary. Ceausescu knew this, and lost no opportunity to dilute their presence. He destroyed villages, intimidated community leaders, and, in the final insult, moved thousands of Romanians into Transylvania to consolidate a Romanian majority in that region. However, neither he, nor the biddable church leaders in Timishoara,

had reckoned with Tokes. In sermon after sermon, this indefatigable preacher spoke out against the evils of the regime. Finally, the *Securitate* secret police moved against him. Enraged Hungarians took to the streets in protest. Many were killed. Days after the event, Ceausescu summoned a rally in Bucharest to celebrate his 'victory.' But amid all the dreary pomp of a Communist rally, something was clearly wrong. The crowd was sullen, and silence greeted the dictator's words. Then an ominous chant began, 'Timishoara! Timishoara!' The incredible had happened: Romanians had taken up the cause of their loathed Hungarian fellow-citizens.

Ceausescu seemed bewildered. He glanced anxiously around – as well as he might. In the event of trouble, *Securitate* snipers were meant to open fire on the crowd from a hidden bunker. But one by one, they caught the mood, put down their rifles and walked quietly away. In panic, an aide signalled that Ceausescu should leave on his waiting helicopter. But he was soon caught, out in the countryside, and he and his equally unfeeling wife Elena we re shot. The last Eastern Eu ropean Communist tyrant was brought down by a little town that most of us have never heard of.

Coca-Cola's last cock-up, Sidcup's tap water

By any standards, Coca-Cola has been one of the great marketing successes of all time. First created by John Styth Pemberton in Atlanta in 1886 as 'an intellectual beverage and temperance drink', it was apparently capable of curing stomach upsets and headaches. This may well have been because of its cocaine ingredient.

Three years later Asa Briggs Candler bought the rights, and his bookkeeper Frank Robinson first used the distinctive typeface that has been its logotype to this day. As its popularity grew, there were legal complaints against the cocaine which was replaced in 1906 with caffeine. However, its success seemed unstoppable, becoming synonymous with the American way of life. In 1944, the billionth gallon was produced, as all

over the world, a huge network of independent bottlers churned it out to its secret formula.

However, success has not come without problems. First there were the imitators led by Pepsi, the upstart rival that was created by Caleb Bradham in 1898 in North Carolina. It was Pepsi that was to inspire one of Coca-Cola's great self-inflicted banana skins. By the 1980s, Pepsi had achieved a younger image, and its rather sweeter product was continuously beating Coke in blind tests. Head of Marketing, Sergio Zyman, who had the successes of Diet Coke and the 'Coke is it' campaign under his belt, decided on something radical. In April 1985, the Coke everybody knew and loved was withdrawn, and a sweeter 'New Coke' was launched. It was a disaster. The Atlanta headquarters received 1,500 angry calls a day and sales plummeted by 15 per cent. By July, traditional Coca-Cola was back on the shelves under the face saving name 'Coca-Cola Classic.'

There have been plenty of other bloomers. In 1990, the so-called 'MagiCan' was withdrawn after just three weeks. This was a promotion whereby some Coke cans had 10-dollar bills inserted into them. A flight attendant had tried to pour one out for a passenger, and she panicked when nothing came out. The San Francisco bomb squad was rushed to the airport to meet the plane. Then, in 1999, Chairman Douglas Ivester had to resign when sick customers were rushed to hospital in Belgium. Coca-Cola was forced to recall millions of bottles and lost $200 million. It hardly helped when a spokesman tried to say, 'It may make you feel sick, but it's not harmful.'

But it was in Britain that one of the most spectacular of Coca-Cola's banana skins occurred. In February 2004, the company launched Dasani, already the second best-selling water brand in the United States. It was to be a double-whammy. First, the media got wind of the fact that this water did not come from some ancient pristine spring or Alpine glacier like its competitors Perrier, Evian, Volvic or Highland Spring. No. Unfortunately it came right from the mains supply in suburban Sidcup. The cynical newspapers lapped it up, *'Real Thing or Rip-off'*, *'Eau de Sidcup.'* Coca-Cola countered by saying that they added minerals to Sidcup's water. They did indeed. That's when the Foods Standards Authority revealed that Dasani contained twice the legal level of bromate, which 'could cause an increased cancer risk from long-term exposure.'

Half a million bottles of Dasani were pulled from the shelves, and the brand was withdrawn from Britain at a cost of about £10 million – with knock-on effects in Europe. A rival water producer put the boot in. 'It's typical Coke arrogance. They assume they can replicate what they have done in the US. Well, they can't.' *Marketing Week* underlined the damage to the brand, *'The idea that, when you buy a Coca-Cola product you buy quality, has been kicked away.'*

Americans may be more gullible and brand-conscious, but in Britain you do have at least to pretend that bottled water comes from somewhere attractive.

Stalin & the Berlin airlift

Josef Stalin had always felt a sullen resentment about Berlin, the city which he had at last conquered at the cost of 300,000 Red Army soldiers, after a bitter and horrific war defending against Germany, which had cost Russia twenty seven million lives, over half civilians. Now Berlin stood miles behind the Iron Curtain, an island of freedom in a sea of Soviet dominance. Germany had been divided up into four zones, Russian, British, French and American, and so had Berlin. By 1947, Stalin certainly did not like what he saw in Germany. The British and Americans had merged their occupation zones into an economic area called Bizonia. The French were to follow. A free, capitalist, federated West Germany was in the offing.

At least one comfort for Stalin was that the western zones had been kept back economically by the currency, the old, worthless Reichsmark, which he kept undermined by flooding in counterfeit notes. The black market was the only one thriving, and cigarettes were the only hard currency.

So he was appalled when, in complete secrecy, 20,000 cases of new bank notes were flown in from the United States, (Operation Bird Dog). On June 18,

1947, the Deutschmark was revealed, which was to transform West Germany. Overnight the black market and the barter system vanished and the economic miracle began. As a result, collaboration between the victors of World War II quickly evaporated. By March, the furious Soviets had walked out of the Control Commission, and soon they began inspecting trains to Berlin and interrupting telephone links. It was becoming crystal clear where the blow was going to fall. On June 16, 1948, the Russians walked out of Berlin's 4 power *Kommandatura*. Two days later the Deutschmark was launched in Berlin. That very evening, all traffic from West Germany to Berlin by road and rail was stopped at gunpoint by the Russians and electricity was cut off. Two million men, women and children were now threatened, as General Lucius Clay, the US commandant put it, by 'one of the most ruthless efforts in modern times to use mass starvation for political coercion.'

The Allies rejected as totally unacceptable the abandonment of Berlin, but were also wary of a dangerous military confrontation with the massive Soviet forces still

The cause of the trouble with the Russians, the new Deutschmark

Grateful German children greet planes of food.

The rush to unload flour

in East Germany. Instead, they opted for an idea put forward by General Wedemeyer, whose forces in China had been supplied by air over the Himalayas from India. They too would attempt an 'airlift.' Many, initially including General Clay, were sceptical that a major city could be supplied by air. (Stalingad in 1943 had not been a brilliant precedent.) They gambled that Stalin's fighters would not actually shoot down the Allied planes. The Soviet leader was cautious, suspecting that the quickly arriving US bombers were carrying atomic bombs, of which the US still had a monopoly. (He was dead right. In the event of real trouble, the US had detailed plans to drop 133 atom bombs on 70 Soviet cities – including eight on Moscow.)

To survive at all, Berlin would need 4,500 tons of food and fuel a day. On June 26, the first 70 aircraft brought in 225 tons – not a very hopeful beginning.

But soon General William Tunner, another veteran of the China air bridge, arrived and took charge, commenting, 'It's well-meaning, but a real cowboy operation. Total confusion.' But Tunner, ably supported by a British deputy, Air Commodore Meren, soon gripped the situation.

Aircraft would now arrive every three minutes, day and night, around the clock with excellent air traffic control. Twin-engined Dakotas and C47s flying down the three air corridors were soon joined by larger C54 Skymasters and British Avro Yorks. By July, daily tonnage hit 2,226. By October, 400 aircraft were bringing in 4,760 tons a day, exceeding the minimum requirement. When winter arrived, to stop the city freezing to death, the British even used converted airliners to ship in 20 million sacks of coal and 300,000 barrels of oil. Cargoes included lightweight food, seedlings to re-grow trees, newsprint paper to keep the newspapers going, even food for the animals in the zoo. 175,000 sick children and patients ill with tuberculosis were also taken out, together with goods labelled 'Made in blockaded Berlin.'

On Easter Day 1949, General Tunner mounted his 'Easter Parade' of 1,398 flights with 13,000 tons. The Russians got the point. Days later, they caved in.

'Finals at Gatow',
by kind permission of
Charles Thompson
GAvA; ASAA

It had been a massive miscalculation on Stalin's part. He had not only looked powerless and foolish. The blockade and airlift had damaged East Germany's economy and revived that of West Germany. Much more important, it made the Germans feel that their former enemies were now their firm friends, a position which has lasted to this day.

It would take many years, but Stalin's miscalculation would eventually destroy the 'Iron Curtain', liberate Eastern Europe and destroy the Soviet system.

McDonald's & the environmentalists

It is not often that legal and public relations professionals agree. But they are certainly in one mind that the 'McLibel' trial was one of the greatest P.R. banana skins in corporate history.

The story all started when a little group of environmentalists calling themselves London Greenpeace (nothing to do with International Greenpeace) started to distribute leaflets to McDonald's customers criticising the poor nutritional value of the food in its 600 outlets in Britain. When the leaflets' copy started to be quoted by others, McDonald's infiltrated the movement, discovered the names of five activists and threatened them with legal action. But two of them would not desist, David Morris and Helen Steele, both unemployed.

Someone in McDonald's, no doubt egged on by its lawyers, then made a

*David Morris
and Helen Steele*

fatal mistake, deciding to sue the pair for libel. McDonald's then compounded the error by producing a leaflet *'Why McDonald's is going to court'*, which effectively called the activists liars. This caused the 'McLibel 2' to counter-sue, so both sides had to defend their claims.

In the High Court, McDonald's was represented by a huge legal team led by Queen's Counsel Richard Rampton. The environmentalists, denied state 'legal aid' for a libel case, had to represent themselves – which they ended up doing rather well. The trial was expected to last three weeks. It ended two and half years later, making, as the Wall Street Journal scoffed, 'the O.J. Simpson murder trial look like a quick take-out.'

Quite apart from its laborious length and huge expense, the trial opened up a 'Pandora's Box' of damaging information about McDonald's. Their own expert witnesses were forced to admit that their products could damage health. An extraordinary combination of critics and potential enemies were drawn into the trial – nutritionists, environmentalists and trade unionists. Even Prince Philip's public contention that McDonald's was helping to destroy the Brazilian rain forest to breed cattle was admitted by a McDonald's witness. A side effect was another crisis brought on by an American witness called by the pair, the Assistant Attorney General of Texas. He decided to investigate further, and this resulted in a stinging attack on advertising by McDonald's in their States by the Attorney Generals of Texas, California and New York.

The trial dragged on and on, with 20,000 pages of transcripts, 40,000 of documentary evidence and 130 witnesses. All in all, it cost McDonald's £10 million. In June 1997, the judge delivered a verdict which was devastating for McDonald's, ruling that the company 'exploited children' with 'misleading advertising' was 'culpably responsible for cruelty to animals', was 'antipathetic to unionisation' and 'paid its workers low wages'. However, as Helen Steele and David Morris had not legally proved all their points, they were ordered to pay £60,000 damages, which McDonald's was sensible enough not to try and collect. An appeal lasting another 23 days reduced the sum to £40,000.

In image terms, one would have thought that things could not get any worse. But now the case moved to the European Court of Human Rights in Strasbourg. Once again things went badly for the company. The judges ruled that because the 'McLibel 2' had been denied legal aid, 'they did not have a fair hearing' and that the British courts 'had failed to produce a measure of procedural fairness and equality of arms' – and that 'the damages were disproportionate.'

They awarded the pair £84,000 damages.

The whole long and sorry saga has damaged McDonald's worldwide, and probably even more important, has thrown the company right into the firing line in the next great health battle – the issue of obesity.

We can all bet that the company wishes it had left the pair alone as they handed out their little leaflets to bemused McDonald's customers.

Tolpuddle & its martyrs

A harsh and poverty-stricken existence faced farm workers in nineteenth century rural England. In the towns, the Reform Act of 1832 had legalised trade unions for factory workers and had secured better wages and conditions. But in the countryside, a rigid social structure still locked the poor into subservience to wealthy landowners.

In the sleepy Dorset village of Tolpuddle, farmhand George Loveless, who had taught himself to read and write, persuaded the vicar to approach the landowners on behalf of local farm workers. This was initially successful, resulting in a weekly wage increase from a paltry 9 to 14 shillings. But the

triumph was short-lived. Landowners reverted to the previous wages and threatened to cut them if workers complained. By 1834, the wage was back to just 6 shillings. Tolpuddle was desperate.

Hoping to seek justice through affiliation with the 500,000 strong National Consolidated Trades Union, Loveless and his brother James – with Thomas Stanfield and his son John, James Hammett and Joseph Brine - formed the 'Tolpuddle Lodge of the Agricultural Labourers' Friendly Society.' They met beneath a sycamore tree in the village and at Thomas Stanfield's cottage, where they swore a solemn oath of

'Punished,
not for
anything
they had
done, but
as an
example
to others'

secrecy and brotherhood. In a climate of illiteracy, downtrodden spirits and religious fear, such oaths were common in forming trades unions. Appealing to workers' superstitions was virtually the only way to impress upon them the significance of their undertaking. However, it was this oath which was to prove the Martyrs' downfall.

When news of the Friendly Society's attempts to undermine their diktat reached the Dorset landowners they were outraged. Was the whole rural class system in jeopardy? Might it lead to a workers' revolution, as in France? Particularly incensed was James Frampton, an influential magistrate and landowner, who wrote for advice to the Home Secretary, Lord Melbourne, stating that labourers were being encouraged to *enter into combinations of a dangerous and alarming kind, to which they are bound by oaths administered clandestinely.*

Melbourne knew that the Friendly Society was not illegal. Therefore he advised Frampton to invoke a long forgotten law against 'Unlawful Oaths,' originally passed to suppress naval mutinies, punishable by seven years transportation. Notices warning that *'anyone taking unlawful oaths would be prosecuted'* were posted in Tolpuddle on 22 February 1834. Just two days later the six men were arrested and charged.

At Dorchester Assizes on 17 March, Judge Williams, biased and hostile, informed the carefully chosen jury of squires and rich farmers that 'trades unions were evil,' and that 'the use of secret oaths made the defendants guilty of sedition and treason.' He added, 'If you do not find them guilty you will forfeit the goodwill and confidence of the Grand Jury.' Sentencing, he had the revealing gall to say that the punishment was 'not for anything they had done, but as an example to others.'

Within weeks the 'Tolpuddle Martyrs', a little group of well-meaning farm workers, were sailing to seven years transportation in Australia, a punishment second in severity only to death. Worse, they were shackled and chained like criminals of the most murderous and depraved kind.

But if the landed gentry thought that the matter was closed and that country workers had learned their lesson, they were soon disabused. The event became a huge political and social banana skin. Public outrage grew. Petitions pleading for the sentences to be overturned soon poured in to Parliament from every quarter, with direct protests made to

King William IV. At first, Melbourne stood his ground, hoping that the fuss would die down. A year later, however, no such thing had happened. An election and cabinet reshuffle in 1835 saw him become Prime Minister. His successor as Home Secretary was Lord John Russell, who now argued that 'if being members of a secret society and administering secret oaths was a crime, the reactionary Duke of Cumberland, as head of the Orange Lodges, was equally deserving of transportation.'

In March 1836 the Government finally backed down and agreed to full pardons. The ordeal of the martyrs, however, was not yet over, because, unbelievably, they were not informed, the Governors of New South Wales and Tasmania making no attempt to trace them. If George Loveless had not seen the news by chance in a copy of an old London newspaper, they might well have remained in Australia in ignorance. They returned to England and farms were bought for them, but such was their disgust with England, all but one emigrated to Canada.

The landowners had thought that they could break the Martyrs. Instead, their own stranglehold was broken. At the Tolpuddle Martyrs' Museum, a Festival takes place every year. On the nearby Green, where only the stump remains of the sycamore tree, a commemorative seat provides a place to sit down and dwell on this momentous shift in history.

The Print Unions & advertising

It is difficult now to remember, or even imagine, the destructive grip the trade unions used to have on British life: constant strikes and stoppages, the car industry plagued by the likes of 'Red Robbo', overseas trade paralysed in the docks, the Heath Government actually brought down by the miners.

Then, in the early 1980's, things changed. It was partly thanks to new technology. Containerisation, for instance, meant there were no more docks. There was also a huge political shift. Margaret Thatcher's determination to break the arbitrary power of the unions saw the virtual destruction of Arthur Scargill's National Union of Mineworkers, when he foolishly tried to repeat his past triumph against Ted Heath. But now it was the wrong time and against the wrong woman.

Nowhere was the change more dramatic than in the printing industry. Newspapers and magazines had been in the thrall of arcane featherbedding posing as craftsmanship. Production was constantly halted or made more expensive. Union resistance even meant that *The Financial Times* had to be printed on ancient 1898, hot metal,

Police on their way to Wapping, and a picket harranging the workers being bussed in

Linotype machines in London, while it was printed electronically in Frankfurt.

Three strokes of fate emerged at once. One was Thatcher. The second was new technology, with desk-top publishing taking typesetting and artwork from the hands of the print unions to those of journalists and even secretaries. The third was the public sale of the news agency Reuters, owned by hundreds of newspapers large and small. With their share of the huge windfall cash, newspapers and magazines could now invest in the new technology. The resistance to furious union picketing by Eddie Shah and his little freesheet company was then mirrored by Rupert

Murdoch's 'Fortress Wapping', with *The Times* and *Sun* production besieged in their Docklands plant by 7,000 pickets in 'The Lost City of the Inkies'.

Murdoch was to win, and Fleet Street became just words, a memory.

That is when the print unions, competing for falling dues and membership, decided to target the advertising industry. They picked on Collett, Dickinson and Pearce, then the most respected advertising agency in the UK, the biggest creator of print advertising, and importantly, with no American parent to help out financially. Frank Lowe of CDP received a letter from SLADE (the Society of Lithographic Artists, Designers, Engravers and Process Workers). It demanded that all CDP staff join the union, and not just those in production, which might have had some logic, but, ridiculously, even creatives, secretaries, account handlers and management. The message was stark. If they did not all join, all work would be 'blacked' and no CDP advertisements would be printed.

Faced by this threat, CDP sought help from its trade body, the Institute of Practitioners in Advertising, 'which was useless and cowardly', as Frank Lowe puts it. While the top ten agencies pledged their support, led by J. Walter Thompson, Lowe also polled his agency,

Frank Lowe

very properly using the Electoral Reform Society for fairness and for secrecy. 200 staff refused to join the union, one single unknown person agreed.

Frank Lowe was then visited at his office by SLADE. When told of the poll results, the union leaders, confident of their power, made a fatal slip by being extremely threatening. However, Frank Lowe tape-recorded the confrontation, 'for some curious reason'. When he later received a letter from SLADE virtually menacing him physically, Lowe decided to turn to the media. He took along a panel of his staff to an interview on Thames Television. Then, momentously, he played his tape. On national television, the brutal, first-hand evidence was shocking to hear.

The tape was replayed at interviews several times over the next two weeks, and on the very day the 'black-out' was due to take place, CDP received a letter saying the matter had been 'called off'.

Thus the advertising industry was never unionised. How very fortunate that Frank Lowe made that tape recording – 'for some curious reason'.

Israel & the 'conkers'

Each Autumn, all over Britain, children pick up shiny brown horse-chestnuts, drill holes in them, attach them to string and then try to smash the 'conkers' wielded by their friends.

The conker, which arrived in western Europe from Turkey in 1576, appears a harmless enough fruit. The conker tree or Horse Chestnut *(Aesculus hippocastanum)* is a native of mountain valleys in Greece, Albania and Bulgaria, all then under the sway of Turkey's Ottoman Empire. In the four centuries since its introduction to England in early Jacobean times, this handsome tree – so conspicuous in bud, leaf, flower, fruit and autumn colour – has become an evocative icon of countryside, parks and streets, providing the ammunition for innumerable 'conker fights.' Yet the fruits have also played a part in more violent human affairs – via the munition factories of World War I. And, by a strange irony of history, the Islamic world should rue the day they reached the West.

The story is a curious one that starts three and a half centuries after the tree arrived in western Europe. From dawn on 1 July 1916, waves of British soldiers attacked firmly entrenched German lines at the tragic Battle of the Somme. One reason for their failure to break through, despite weeks of subsequent fighting and horrific casualties, was the inability of the artillery to destroy the German barbed wire. Many shells fell short, or failed to explode. Minister of Supply, David Lloyd George, desperately needed to source more and better munitions, especially cordite, the smokeless propellant of artillery shells, of which Britain would eventually fire off 258 million. He needed a large quantity of acetone, a solvent essential for its manufacture, of which there was then a serious shortage.

Lloyd George and Winston Churchill, who, in charge of the Navy, was equally anxious about shell quality, turned for help to a 'boffin.' Zionist and chemist Professor Chaim Weizmann of Manchester University took up the challenge. He used his process of bacterial fermentation that he had discovered in 1912 to ferment maize starch to yield acetone. But now Britain's stocks of maize were running low, as the successful German U-boat campaign against merchant shipping had badly hit imports from North America. Weizmann needed a new source of starch – and conkers were free and plentiful. Soon a national collection campaign was underway, and in the autumn of 1917 children from all over the country gathered sacks of the precious fruits for the processing factories at Poole, Dorset, and King's Lynn, Norfolk, sending their conker parcels to government offices in London for secrecy. Acetone was now available, cordite production assured and, in November 1918, Germany surrendered to the victorious Allies.

In reality, the fermentation of conkers yielded only a small proportion of acetone. Nevertheless, a grateful Lloyd George, by now Prime Minister, wanted to reward Weizmann. Even before war's end, he had rashly asked the Professor (Herod and Salome spring to mind) if there was anything he could do for him, no doubt thinking of a Knighthood or even a Peerage. Yes, there was. Weizmann would like help to establish a homeland for the Jews in Palestine. Thus, the Prime Minister introduced him to Foreign Secretary Arthur Balfour to take the matter forward. And that, wrote Lloyd George, *'was the fount and origin of the Balfour Declaration'* that established in principal the modern state of Israel and *'left a permanent mark on the map of the world.'*

Chaim Weizmann, university professor and future President of Israel, with his fellow scientist Albert Einstein

The problem was that the fledging state of Israel, the product of an almost casual gesture, then grew too slowly. In vain did Weizmann appeal in 1920, 'Jewish People, where are you?'. Few Jews in Europe, especially in Germany, where they were prominent and influential, had any intention of abandoning their successful lives for a poor, hot, barren settlement. So most were later trapped and died in the Holocaust. As a result, Israel grew so slowly that it became the focus of resurgent Arab nationalism. Since 1948, when Chaim Weizmann duly became its first President, the laudable concept of Israel's 'promised land' has sadly spawned wars, permanent refugee camps, terrorism, oil crises, suicide bombers, Al-Qaeda, 9/11 and conflict in Iraq.

There are some who, perhaps unfairly, feel that it might have been better if the conker had never reached Britain.

'A peerage? No, I'd like a homeland for my people.'

Saddam Hussein & the outside world

Ruthless and brutal dictators tend to have a special problem. People do not dare to tell them the truth. The inevitable result is that leaders begin to delude themselves, and then make serious and disastrous miscalculations. Even in such exalted company as Stalin and Hitler, Saddam Hussein stands out as an arch miscalculator.

Saddam became President of Iraq in 1979 and surrounded himself with sycophantic advisors from his hometown of Tikrit, a move hardly likely to enhance his grip on world affairs. Now, only a year into power, he opportunistically attacked much bigger Iran, then ruled by Ayatollah Khomeini. Fresh from their setback in the region of losing their ally the Shah, and the humiliation of U.S. President Jimmy Carter over the Embassy hostage crisis, the Americans now regarded Saddam as the lesser of two evils, and supplied him with arms. In spite of this, Saddam failed to conquer Iran and involved his country in a murderous slogging match for eight years, the longest war in the 20th century. He now had the fourth largest army in the world, but in the meantime he had bankrupted Iraq – his expenditure was twice his oil revenue.

The world and the Americans were now waking up to Saddam's true nature, especially when in 1988 he killed 5,000 Kurds in the town of Halabja with poison gas. The pictures of contorted women and children did fatal damage to his reputation.

Driven by pride to solve his economic problems, Saddam decided to use force and take over oil-rich Kuwait. His dilemma was gauging the possible reaction of the United States. Now, his propensity to miscalculate was helped by April Glaspie, the U.S. Ambassador, who did not bluntly warn him against a move against Kuwait. Instead she said, 'We have no opinion on the Arab-Arab conflict, like your border dispute with Kuwait.' Saddam took this as a green light, and a week later invaded Kuwait on August 2, 1990. He seemed mightily surprised to find himself facing a United Nations coalition of 32 countries with 700,000 troops. Then, given the option of

Saddam Hussein and his equally unpleasant sons, Uday and Qusay

withdrawing, Saddam fooled himself again. He thought his own huge army with its 7,000 tanks and 3,000 artillery pieces could resist. He simply had no idea of the technological advantages against him, especially from the air. In spite of setting fire to Kuwait's oil wells (another public relations disaster), his forces were overwhelmed in just 100 hours, losing 100,000 men to just 274 Allied deaths.

Unfortunately, President Bush stopped the battle 44 hours early and Saddam survived, together with his Republican Guard – who were brutally able to put down U.S.-inspired revolts by the Kurds and the marshland Shiite Arabs.

By now, one would have thought that Saddam might have learned some lessons – but no. With his country subjected to crippling sanctions and no-fly zones, Saddam was not finished with his intransigence. He allowed the world to think he was developing weapons of mass destruction. He also convinced himself that he could block inspections and that America would not attack, perhaps confining herself to a bombing campaign. If he had been up against Bill Clinton, he might have been right, but he was facing a belligerent George W. Bush who seemed determined to complete his father's unfinished business.

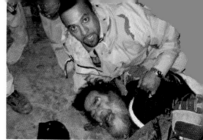

Once again, Iraq's forces were obliterated by American and British technology. Despite the laughably unrealistic announcements of the Information Minister, 'Comical Ali' (see panel), the Iraqi government collapsed and fled. Saddam Hussein, bearded and dirty, was dragged by an American soldier from a hole in the ground in Tikrit. He had lost his sons, his country, his power and even his dignity. His career of miscalculation was over.

The sayings of 'Comical Ali' (Mohammed Saeed al-Sahhaf)

The Cruise missiles do not frighten anyone. We are catching them like fish in a river. Over the past two days, we managed to shoot down 196 missiles.

They are trapped in Umm Qasr. They are trapped near Basra. They are trapped everywhere.

As our leader Saddam Hussein said, 'God is grilling their stomachs in hell'.

I can say, and I am responsible for what I am saying, that they have started to commit suicide under the walls of Baghdad.

Britain is not worth an old shoe.

They are not even 100 miles from Baghdad. They are not anywhere. They are like a snake moving in the desert.

They are sick in their minds. There is no presence of American infidels in the city of Baghdad at all.

We surrounded their forces with our special Republican Guards and we are finishing them off.

The Americans are going to surrender or be burned in their tanks. They will surrender.

These cowards have no morals. They have no shame about lying.

Rusting boats line the channel desperately dug to try and save the fishing industry.

water. Millions of tons of salty sand blow into the air. Even the irrigated farmland has become too salty for crops. The winters are colder and the summers can reach 49 C. This is desertification on a huge scale.

The human cost has been terrible too. The former fishing port of Muynak is now land-locked. It once employed 60,000 of its inhabitants to catch or process fish. Locals now face poverty and malnutrition, with the Red Cross and Red Crescent sending food parcels. Their health is also irreparably damaged by the corrosive salty dust that blows in from the wide barren wastes around the shrunken sea. Drinking water is polluted. Tuberculosis, typhus, lung

and oesophagal cancer are rife. Infant and maternal mortality rates are as bad as anywhere in the world. Climate change, with hotter and drier conditions, has exacerbated the problem, and heavy fertilizer and pesticide residues contribute to an appalling ecological and human disaster. Nature has once again struck back, demonstrating that even a structure as large as an inland sea is vulnerable – and that it is certainly unwise to see it as another piece of state property.

Meanwhile, government scientists in the surrounding and now independent countries are agreed that more water must be allowed to reach the Aral Sea. But some suggestions, such as diverting other rivers, may now inflict worse ecological damage. And the sea will never be the same.

Peter Stuyvesant & the nutmeg tree

It was extremely unlikely that Peter Stuyvesant had ever even heard of Nathaniel Courthope, but both men were linked in one of the greatest banana skins in history. In what was a legendary bargain, in 1626 the Dutch purchased Manahatta (the 'small island' or 'hilly island') from the Menates tribe for 24 dollars worth of trinkets, naming the island 'New Amsterdam.'

The remaining Indian tribe, the Lenapes, introduced the new settlers to maple, sugar, tobacco, maize and corn. Oysters generated the shiny shells they used for currency, and at what is now the Battery, the Dutch built a fort which could dominate both the Hudson and East Rivers and pushed the tiny settlement up an old, wide Indian trail which they called *De Heerewegh*, or

Broadway, protecting themselves by a wall at Wall Street.

Manhattan was always going to be dominated by events back in the Old World. The Protestant Dutch were escaping from the oppression of the Catholic Spanish and French after the St Bartholomew's Day Massacre of 1572. The English victory over the Spanish Armada in 1588 had made it suddenly possible to challenge Spain everywhere, including the New World. The Jews were expelled from Spain and Portugal, and had moved to Holland and then to Brazil. When the Portuguese recaptured Pernambuco in 1654, the first penniless Jews arrived in New Amsterdam.

Above all, the riches of the East meant that Europe was sending explorers to find a short sea route to the east, the fabled but non-existent 'North-West Passage'. Verrazano tried to reach Cathay. Jacques Cartier got as far as present-day Montreal. Henry Hudson failed, by trying to go west up the river that now bears his name. However, his report to the Dutch of the area's abundance of valuable furs led to their own arrival.

Peter Stuyvesant did a good job of building up the Dutch colony, but suddenly lost everything when in 1664 four British naval ships arrived in the name of Charles II – and renamed the island New York after his brother the Duke of York. Stuyvesant was not to realise that, bizarrely, the English attack was the direct result of bitter struggles over the nutmeg spice, four decades earlier and ten thousand miles away.

Today, it is hard for us to grasp the huge economic and political importance of spices in the past, the later equivalent of gold and now oil. Two thousand years before Christ, the spice trade from the East was already fully developed. In 950 BC, the Queen of Sheba visited King Solomon. Why? She was worried his fleet would bypass her kingdom (now Yemen), ruining its wealth on the spice route. The trade of Egypt, Rome, Venice, Genoa and Constantinople was also crucially dependent on spices, as was later that of Portugal and Spain. Soon the English and Dutch entered the market and were competing and fighting, especially over the 'Spice Islands' of Molucca and Banda, and it was nutmeg that provoked the New Amsterdam confrontation and one of the strangest twists of fortune in history.

On the other side of the world, the tiny island of Run, covered in sweet-smelling nutmeg trees, was ceded to the British in 1616 by the Bandanese islanders. As the only Spice Island not under their control, it was besieged by

Nutmegs and other spices were like gold or oil today.

the furious Dutch. Cut off, a British hero, Nathaniel Courthope, led the defence for three long years until he was trapped and killed. His followers and many other British traders were then horribly tortured by the Dutch at the 'Massacre of Amboyna'. The atrocity created hatred and a desire for revenge; hence Manhattan's capture by the English, part of an exhausting war that had dragged on for years. Finally, both sides met at Breda in 1667. After weeks of argument, the Dutch decided to exchange Manhattan for what they considered to be the much more valuable little island of Run.

A banana skin indeed, for Run today is a tiny sleepy island, now even without nutmegs. New York is a little more important.

Claus von Stauffenberg & his misplaced briefcase

The staff car wound its way through the sultry, dank forests of Poland, carrying a one-eyed Colonel with a yellow briefcase. He had come to kill Hitler.

An aristocratic, religious and family man, the handsome Count Claus von Stauffenberg's military ancestry went back to the 13th century. He had fought bravely and loyally in all of Hitler's campaigns, but the atrocities he had seen in Russia had appalled him and convinced him that Hitler was the 'anti-Christ', an incarnation of evil. 'Is there no officer in HQ capable of shooting that beast?' In North Africa fighting the

British, he had lost an eye, a hand and two fingers. He was now the key figure in one last conspiracy to get rid of Hitler and the Nazis before it was too late. Germany was now in real trouble. By that fateful day, July 20 1944, the Allies were advancing from their Normandy beachhead and the Russians were only 60 miles from German soil. In deep despair, hundreds of army officers were now part of *Operation Valkyrie,* a plan to take over Berlin, Paris and Brussels, arresting the SS and Gestapo and making peace with the Allies. This was their third attempt to kill Hitler with a bomb.

A fatal complication was that Stauffenberg was no suicide bomber, nor just the assassin. He had to survive. Because, as Chief of Staff of the Replacement Army, he also had to lead the revolt and win over the fainthearted. When he arrived at Rastenburg's *Wolfsschanze* or Wolf's Lair headquarters, he was given bad news. The Führer's briefing would be held in a wooden hut with open windows – but not nearly as deadly in an explosion as the still-unfinished concrete bunkers. It was also to be held early, so Hitler could welcome his fellow dictator, the recently rescued Mussolini. So, they had to move quickly. He and his adjutant went to 'freshen up' and carefully to assemble and prime the

two bombs they had brought, made no easier by Stauffenberg's missing hand and fingers. They were suddenly interrupted and told they were late for the briefing, so duly decided that one bomb must suffice. The Colonel hurried to the conference, knowing that acid was eating away at a ten-minute fuse. He placed his briefcase under the wooden table only a yard from Hitler's feet, and awaited a pre-arranged 'urgent telephone call' which gave him the excuse to leave the room. Then something terrible happened, an unforeseen banana skin that changed the course of history. Colonel Heinz Brandt, who was actually one of the conspirators but who knew nothing about the bomb plot, became irritated by the briefcase at his feet, and reached down and lifted it to the other side of the stout wooden table support. When the bomb exploded, Hitler was thus saved from most of the blast by the thick oak support. He staggered out blackened and shaken, but he survived and was soon able to show Mussolini the wrecked room. 'Duce! I have just had the most enormous good fortune!' He did not know how good.

Stauffenberg was convinced he had

Claus von Stauffenberg, German hero

A few inches saved Hitler's life.

Stauffenberg (left) at Rastenburg with Hitler and his generals, a few days before the bomb plot

killed Hitler, and after a three hour flight, was appalled to find that nothing had been done in Berlin. Frantically, he arrested his wavering boss, General Fromm, and began to work the telephones. It was too late. Goebbels, the Propaganda Minister, had telephoned a key figure, Major Otto Remer, Berlin's Guards' commander, with Hitler at his side. 'Do you recognise my voice?' shouted the deafened Führer. He persuaded Remer to start arresting, not supporting, the Berlin conspirators, while the Wolf's Lair's teleprinters counter-manded their well-planned orders. In Paris, the army was about to shoot the SS and Gestapo. Then came the final proof, Hitler's unmistakable voice on national radio. 'A miniscule clique of ambitious, unscrupulous officers of criminal stupidity have been plotting to get rid of me and to liquidate virtually the entire German command staff....'

The game was up. Fromm escaped, arrested Stauffenberg and his comrades and, to try to hide his own equivocal position, quickly had them shot in the courtyard. Stauffenberg's last words were 'Long live sacred Germany!' Fromm's cowardly action did him little good. Hitler's suspicions ran deep and wide, and his revenge was terrible. Fromm joined nearly 5,000 people, not just officers but civil servants, professionals and clerics, who were executed, some by slow strangulation hanging by piano wire, with Hitler gloatingly watching the filming each night.

Colonel Brandt, who had saved Hitler's life by mistake, died in hospital. At first, he was promoted by Hitler to General to increase the pension for his family, until fellow patients recalled him crying out in delirium, 'How callous it was of Stauffenberg to place the bomb at my feet, when I was one of the conspirators.'

Had Hitler died, it would have shortened the war by nearly a year, saving ten million lives and preventing Eastern Europe going behind a savage Iron Curtain.

What a terrible slip to move that briefcase.

Ford, de Lorean, Sinclair & their funny cars

With its Model T, the Ford Motor Company changed the world for ever, liberating us from the horse and the railroad. Had stubborn Henry Ford had his way, he would have produced Model Ts for ever, preferably painted black. His son Edsel was a more decent man and he really loved cars, 'Father makes the most popular car in the world. I would like to make the best.' Edsel managed to persuade his father to buy Lincoln and he created the Lincoln Continental. But even with the title of President of Ford, his father gave him little power and he was forced to watch General Motors overtake the family company as the biggest car maker in the world. In 1943, a spent force, Edsel died of cancer.

Ten years later, grandson Henry Ford II realised that Ford needed a mid-level marque to rival G.M's Pontiac, Buick and Oldsmobile. A new car was secretly conceived and designed. Ford turned to famous poet Marianne Moore for names: 'Mongoose Civique', 'Varsity Stroke', 'Resilient Bullet', 'Pastelogram' and 'Utopian Turtletop' were just some of her bizarre offerings. No wonder they reverted to 'Edsel'. There was huge expectation built up by the teaser advertisements, showing out of focus

The Ford Edsel, curiously styled, slow and badly built

details of the car, hidden or wrapped up, with the slogan 'more YOU ideas'.

When, in September 1957, two and a half million eager Americans poured into the Edsel showrooms, they found a rather odd-looking car with an upright radiator, which some compared to a horse-collar or something more salacious. Others quipped, 'It looks like a Merc sucking on a lemon!' The Edsel was found to have only leisurely acceleration, and, much worse, was built and finished very badly. On the *Ed Sullivan Show,* in front of millions of viewers, its door handle actually came off in Frank Sinatra's hand, the type of experience repeated all over America. By bad luck, the country had also now gone into recession, so even established car models suffered 50% sales declines. The result was that instead of selling the planned

A door handle came off in Frank Sinatra's hand.

200,000 Edsels in the first year, Ford only sold 63,000. Next year, even with changes, it was worse, with 45,000, and with real ignominy, the 1960 model was withdrawn after just a month. Poor Edsel would have been mortified by how his name would now stand for stupendous marketing failures.

But there would be others who would let their car enthusiasm create 'Edsels' or banana skins. John de Lorean was a handsome, flashy General Motors executive, who had helped to create Pontiac's hot GTO. To build his dream sports car, he persuaded the Bank of America to lend him millions,

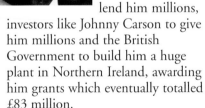

John deLorean

investors like Johnny Carson to give him millions and the British Government to build him a huge plant in Northern Ireland, awarding him grants which eventually totalled £83 million.

The DMC 12 looked exciting, with its stainless steel body and its gull-wing doors. (Remember it in *Back to the Future*?) Its first problem was that it was not, in fact, a very

good car. Even after extensive modifications by Lotus, it was heavy and underpowered. *'It's not a barn burner'* wrote *Road & Track*. In truth, it had the same sluggish acceleration as the Edsel. And, like the Edsel, it was badly built – costing huge amounts per car to correct. Thus it ended up retailing for $25,000, pushing it into the Porsche 911 price bracket, with none of the Porsche's performance and quality.

With the car selling at only half its break-even numbers, the final banana skin was provided by John de Lorean himself, caught trying to import $24 million's worth of cocaine into the US. Acquitted because he was technically 'entrapped' by the FBI, his reputation was finally blown and the company went bankrupt – a shattering

blow for the strife-torn economy of Northern Ireland.

Another automotive banana skin was provided by one of the cleverest men in Britain, Sir Clive Sinclair. A leading member of MENSA, this rather eccentric genius had made a fortune making visionary electronic devices – calculators, watches, pocket TVs and micro computers. He decided to produce an

'ecology-friendly' road vehicle, based on the new legislation that now allowed such electric vehicles to be used without a driving licence – just as long as they did not exceed 15 mph.

Thus was the Sinclair C5 born, a small tricycle with an electric motor and a stylish plastic body, selling for just £399. It seemed a great idea, but it was not just its public launch that was a disaster. (In the middle of winter, the C5's body skated on the snow.) It was found that the C5 also had to be pedalled to start on hills, its heavy batteries only lasted 20 miles and took eight hours to re-charge. Above all, it did not take too long for people to realise how dangerous and how vulnerable

the tiny thing was, invisible and dwarfed by trucks towering about it. After a few weeks and £8.5 million of his money, Clive Sinclair called it a day.

We will probably never see the likes of these automotive banana skins again. Cars are too well-researched, designed and built. More's the pity.

Left: an anniversary meeting of deLorean owners at Belfast's Stormont Castle

Left: Sir Clive Sinclair, prolific creator of inventions. The C5 was one of his few failures.

Charles Lindbergh & the Nazi medal

It was a golden cross with four small swastikas, on a red ribbon. Charles Lindbergh showed it to his wife, Anne, who glanced at it casually and then remarked, both enigmatically and prophetically, 'The Albatross.'

It is hard for us now to cast our minds back and appreciate just how famous Charles Lindbergh was.

In 1927, Lindbergh, a heroic pilot and the only man whose life had been saved four times by parachute, determined to be the first to fly non-stop from New York to Paris. Needing 400 gallons of petrol for the 3,600 mile flight, he decided to fly alone. On the side of the huge extra fuel tank blocking his forward vision was painted SPIRIT OF ST LOUIS. The media took to this brave, shy, good looking 'Kid Flyer', also calling him the 'Human Meteor' or the 'Flying Fool'.

At 7.54 on the morning of May 30 1927, the two-ton flying fuel tank staggered into the air. After hours desperately trying to stay awake, he spotted fishing boats. 'WHICH WAY IRELAND?' he shouted, circling. No answer. But soon the coast of Dingle Bay appeared out of the mist. At 10.39 at night, after 33 hours 39 minutes, he rolled to a stop at Paris, Le Bourget, thunderstruck by the 150,000 people flooding onto the airfield. Overnight he was the most popular man in the world.

France went mad for Lindbergh, led by Prime Minister Raymond Poincaré. Then it was King Albert of the Belgians, before landing at Croydon to be greeted by an ecstatic, cheering crowd of 150,000 normally reticent British. George V and Queen Mary presented him with the Air Force Cross, Britain's highest peacetime honour; the House of Commons rose in spontaneous applause. But America was desperate for his return, and even sent a cruiser to collect him. '*Lucky Lindy*' was the first of 200 songs churned out by 'Tin Pan Alley,' and the '*Lindy Hop*' dance was

Lindbergh circles above the Irish fishing boats. By Roger Middlebrook

already the rage as he arrived, accompanied by four destroyers, two airships and 40 aircraft. President Calvin Coolidge was one of a crowd of 250,000 people waiting in Washington, presenting him with the first Distinguished Flying Cross, with the prophetic words 'He has brought unsullied fame home.' The Post Office issued the first stamp in honour of a man still living. Five million New Yorkers gave him an ecstatic ticker-tape parade, while millions of American wrote letters to him and sent him cables and gifts. The grateful city of St Louis greeted him with half a million of its citizens, the first of 82 cities he flew to, all with the same ceaseless adulation. It was like combining Princess Diana, The Beatles, The Pope and about ten others into the fame of a tall, handsome, shy boy from Detroit.

The picture of 'The American Dream' seemed complete when Lindbergh fell for Anne Morrow, the beautiful daughter of a distinguished Ambassador and Senator. Married in May 1927, she obtained a pilot's licence and went off with him all over the world as co-pilot and navigator – 'The First Couple of the Skies.' Popularity only grew with the happy domestic news of the arrival of Charles Junior, 'Baby Lindy' or 'The Eaglet.'

Then any chance that their fame would dissipate was eliminated by a dreadful event. The 'Lindbergh baby' was kidnapped. The world watched, with horrified fascination, the desperate search, the ransom drama and the trial of the suspected murderer. In spite of immense public sympathy, it was a gruelling, publicity-filled period, which made the Lindberghs leave for England and Europe. There, he made several visits to Germany where he plainly admired her technical aviation skills. So, at an American Embassy dinner on October

Goering presents Lindbergh with 'the Albatross', while a worried Anne (left) looks on.

18 1938, the Ambassador and his guests were not unduly surprised when Reichsmarschall Hermann Goering presented Lindbergh, 'By order of the Führer,' with the *Verdienstkreuz Deutscher Adler*, the Service Cross of the German Eagle, for his services to the

world's aviation and his 1927 flight. Apart from Anne's cryptic 'Albatross', he probably thought no more about it.

But just two weeks later came *Kristallnacht* – the burning of synagogues, the wrecking of Jewish shops, the arrests and street attacks, the first public pogrom against the Jews in Germany. This opened the world's eyes to the true nature of the Nazis. Suddenly the medal indeed looked like an albatross.

What is more, Lindbergh then became America's symbol of neutrality, now publicly equated with being defeatist or pro-Nazi. He led the 'American First' movement, to the growing fury of President Franklin D. Roosevelt, with whom he had quarrelled in the past and who now said, 'I am convinced Lindbergh is a Nazi.' Having resigned his US Army Colonel's commission, he was then constantly lambasted for stubbornly not giving back the Nazi medal, pilloried as 'The Knight of the German Eagle.' With Poland and Western Europe over-run and the Battle of Britain raging in the skies above his old home in England, his popularity slumped further, especially when he made speeches accusing the British, and the 'American Jews,' of dragging America into a war. 'The Lone Eagle' was transformed from 'Public

'I am convinced Lindbergh is a Nazi.'

Hero No 1' into 'Public Enemy No 1'. Columnist Walter Winchell sneered, '*His halo has become his noose.*' Even his wife's sister admitted that he had gone, 'from Jesus to Judas!'

The treacherous Japanese attack on Pearl Harbor saw Lindbergh close down 'America First' and try to rejoin the colours. Roosevelt spitefully blocked it and even used his power to stop any commercial war-effort appointments until, at last, Henry Ford stepped in.

Lindbergh hurled himself in to his work at Ford, and found himself improving aircraft like the P-47 Thunderbolt. In the Far East, he vitally extended the range of the P-38 Lightning. He even secretly flew 50 combat missions and downed a Japanese plane. When Roosevelt died, he was somewhat rehabilitated and joined a technical mission to Europe. There, he saw with horror the real results of aviation under the Nazis, in the appalling conditions in the tunnels of Camp Dora where thousands of prisoners had perished building the V1 and V2 rockets.

For the rest of his life, he was unrepentant about his neutrality attitudes. But we can be sure that he regretted accepting that dreadfully symbolic medal from Goering and then, foolishly, keeping it.

Hoover & the airline promotion

What was the most disastrous marketing promotion in British commercial history? Many people would agree that it was Hoover's Free Travel Offer.

In 1907, James Murray Spangler sought to solve his asthma attacks by rigging up a crude contraption of a soap box, broom handle, pillow case and an electric motor. He showed it to his friend, Susan Hoover, and her husband took over the patent and made Spangler a partner. W. H. 'Boss' Hoover then advertised a free 10-day trial, and 'Hoovers' took off, with many such offers boosting their sales over the years. For a century, the vacuum cleaner and the name 'Hoover' were synonymous.

The Hoover Company was bought by the US Maytag Co in 1989. In early 1992, the stock control people at Maytag-UK realised that they had an excessive amount of vacuum cleaners and washing machines gathering dust in the warehouses. Once again, a promotion was needed to shift the backlog of stock and turn around a £10 million deficit. So someone had the bright idea of offering two free flights, initially to European destinations, for every £100 spent on Hoover products. They expected good sales, but only a reasonable take-up of the flights offer, because there was a mass of small print to be worked through which would deter many people. And, in any case, the company hoped that sales staff would be able to sell profitable extras that would help defray the cost of the promotion.

But this soon seemed to anyone even vaguely thinking of buying a new appliance to be an offer too good to refuse. In fact, it *was* literally too good to be true, as two return airfares (in the era before Ryanair and Easyjet) would have cost much more than £100, dwarfing the profit margin from any appliance sale. The maths did not add up.

Needless to say, sales of vacuum cleaners took off like a rocket, and the Scottish plant was not only working flat out, but had to take on extra workers. At first, the company thought this was such good news that it launched a second promotion, this time offering free flights to the USA. The strapline for the promotion was: 'Two return seats: Unbelievable.' The TV ads for this offer even reminded those customers who were entitled to the European tickets to send in

It was literally too good to be true

their vouchers and claim their flights.

Soon, of course, the company was unable to cope with the flood of applications and stories started to appear in the press. But all this publicity only attracted more attention to the offer and made it more popular, even though there were ever more disgruntled customers who had bought Hoover products and were failing to get their flights. Some of them took matters into their own hands. One was so angry that he even kidnapped a Hoover delivery van.

Eventually questions were asked in Parliament, and the Hoover Holiday Pressure Group was formed, which went on to attract a total of 8,000 members. With the help of the pressure group, hundreds of customers began taking legal action, and the company soon found itself fighting legal battles in small claims courts all over the country. These cases continued for six years after the promotion ended.

The end results were that 220,000 people did eventually fly, though Hoover had to charter planes to clear the backlog. The Board was fired. The company lost tens of millions, and Maytag eventually sold the UK operation to Candy, the Italian appliance manufacturer. The only people who did well out of it were electrical retailers, who

Dyson, the technology that Hoover tried to use

added millions to their profits during the sales boom.

This was not to be the decade's only banana skin for Hoover. James Dyson, the British inventor, spent 15 years developing his revolutionary idea of using cyclonic separation to create a vacuum cleaner that wouldn't lose suction as it picked up dirt. He struggled and failed to get manufacturers, including Hoover, interested in his revolutionary 'bagless' cleaner, eventually launching the bright pink 'G-Force' cleaner in 1983 through catalogue sales in Japan. This helped to fund the setting up of his own manufacturing company (the selling price was £2000 and Dysons started to sell really well). Then Hoover made another fatal slip. It copied Dyson's patented technology – and not even very well. The Hoover Vortex emitted 200 times more dust into the air than the Dyson DC04. James Dyson offered to settle the case for £1 million, but Hoover fought on and lost. It had to pay over £4 million, funding Dyson's expansion. Dyson now outsells many of the companies that rejected his idea, and his is not only one of the most popular brands in the United Kingdom, but in 2005 Dyson cleaners became the market leaders on Hoover's home turf, the United States. Dust can slip up anyone.

China & its gender crisis

For many cultural, social and economic reasons, it still remains true that all over the world most couples would prefer their first baby to be a boy, while after that, they have little preference. Up until now, this has not caused problems, but modern science threatens to create a dangerous imbalance. A shocking foretaste of the potential crisis has now come from a country where the momentous legal decision was made to allow only one child – China.

With 1.3 billion people already, few would deny that China has a population problem. Such vast numbers mean that food and water shortages will always be a threat, and increasing wealth will mean growing use of the world's resources. The high price of oil is a reminder.

During the 1960s China experienced a 'baby boom', and at 7.5 children per mother, it dwarfed America's famous baby boom a decade earlier with only 3.7 babies per mother. Thoroughly alarmed, in 1980, the Chinese Government decided on a radical idea – no couple was to be allowed more than one child.

However, and especially in the countryside, a critical factor intervened – the traditional Chinese desire to have a boy both to work the land and to look after the parents in old age. On top of that, China is also a Confucian patriarchal society – where the male inherits the wealth. Popular discontent and resistance grew towards the draconian new law. So today there is a compromise 'one and a half child policy.' If the first baby is a male, the parents must not have more. But if it is female, they can try for a second child.

This has not worked. The authorities under-estimated the desire for boy children, which was so

Males needed to work the land

overwhelming that, over the past two decades, a huge imbalance has emerged.

On average, 116 boys are now born to 100 girls. In some places, like Hainan Island, it has even reached 135 boys. The core reason is modern science, in the form of ultrasound scanning. Even though it is illegal, Chinese parents are bribing doctors and technicians to tell them secretly if the foetus is male or female. The girl embryos are often secretly aborted. Even if they are allowed to be born, they are likely to die as infants. One paediatrician sadly revealed the attitude, 'If a baby boy gets sick, his parents will sell everything they own to save his life. With a girl, they do not have the same positive feelings and they may just stop the treatment and take the baby home to die.' Female babies are also dumped at huge 'orphanages', where they are not expected to survive.

The real crisis is that the Chinese authorities, in their dash to stabilise the population, have managed to do the opposite, because there are now no less than forty million men who have no chance of finding a wife or even a girlfriend. They are called *guang guan* or 'bare branches'. Such young men are already more prone to ordinary crime, but much more serious is the wave of kidnapping of thousands of young women to be sold as wives, or into prostitution. It is also feared that the millions of 'bare branches' may begin to live in crime-ridden bachelor ghettoes in the big cities, served by massive brothel areas.

The Chinese are now trying to stop a problem that may only get worse. New allowances are being offered for families with two girls. One hopes it is not all too little, too late. Wars and invasions have been fought over women, and China has her own bloody history to recall. The Nien Rebellion in 1852 in Shandong was partly caused by an excess of 100,000 men – the result of female infanticide, coupled with famine. It took the Qing dynasty sixteen years to overthrow the six million rebels, and it would be worse today.

So that is China's problem. But the alarming lesson is that this dangerous imbalance could easily be repeated elsewhere in Asia, and even in Europe and the Americas, where families are shrinking and ultra-sound and abortion are freely available.

A world with too few women and too many men is a very poor prospect

China's dangerous imbalance could be repeated all over the world.

'New Labour' & old sleaze

Sleaze, once a Tory word, was key in propelling Tony Blair to power. In 1997, he managed to portray John Major's government as decadent, venal and only out for big business. 'Sleaze has become the hallmark of the dying days of this administration', he intoned. Blair then promised to be 'whiter than white, adding to the hyperbole, 'tough on sleaze, tough on the causes of sleaze.' The phrases tripped lightly off the tongue and helped this charming young man to convince a trusting 'Middle England' to let him into Number Ten. But they were to prove utterly empty and meaningless phrases.

Almost at once, a very public embarrassment was provided by the redoubtable Bernie Eccleston, 'King of Formula One', who had given £1 million to the Labour Party. Blair exempted motor racing from an agreed Europe-wide ban on tobacco advertising. His excuses  set the scene for the next nine years.

'I hope people know me well enough, and realise the kind of person I am, to realise I would never do anything improper. I never have. I think most people who have dealt with me think I am a pretty straight sort of guy, and I am.'

Nowadays, we would fall about laughing, but in the euphoria of the 'New Labour Project', people gave him the benefit of the doubt. We have long since realised that Tony Blair is a long way short of 'a straight sort of guy.' First he had planned all along on a *coup d'état* against the old Labour Party, with its dependence on trade unions and its loyal members. As one of his inner circle later admitted, 'We captured a entire party with a tiny army of believers.' This 'party within a party' was backed by the efforts of spin doctors like Peter Mandelson and Alistair Campbell that have seen no equal. Small wonder that 'dodgy dossiers' were produced to take us into the Iraq war (page 238).

It is not just Old Labour figures like John Prescott who were squirming in the knowledge that, for the purpose of electoral gain, they had been outsmarted and that New Labour had hijacked a great party that once stood for something. Gordon Brown also knew it

'We captured an entire party with a tiny army of believers.'

only too well, and had his own reason to distrust a Prime Minister – who had apparently agreed to step aside earlier.

As for sleaze, Tony Blair and his 'New Labour' friends have given it new meaning. Blair allies like David Blunkett and Peter Mandelson (twice) have been forced to resign after scandals. Railtrack and Rover mendaciously destroyed, postal voting tainted, Royal Flight aircraft used for electoral trips and holidays and Cherie Blair involved with curious flat purchases and highly paid speaking engagements thought to abuse the role of a Prime Minister's wife.

Then came Tessa Jowell's 'separation' from her husband, David Mills, to distance herself from alleged £350,000 Italian bribes and offshore hedge funds – not very Labour to say the least.

However, the final nail in the coffin of Blair's image of 'straight guy' integrity was the 'loans for peerages' scandal. Faced by a financial crisis in 2005, Blair turned to his ace fundraiser, Lord Levy, whose first claim to fame was as manager of 'Alvin Stardust.' But this smooth, persuasive man came to political notice when he raised £12 million for Labour's 1997 landslide victory, although eyebrows were raised when he was elected to the peerage. Levy was asked to use his

Lord Levy

magic again, but now the ideas was to *lend* money to the party because *loans* did not have to be declared. The other parties did it, but it cut right across Tony Blair's 'whiter than white' stance. 'We were going to cheat on our own rules. It was an absolutely extraordinary thing to do,' said one outraged MP.

At Levy's £4 million hacienda-style home, millionaires were invited to dinner or lunch ('Tony might come in from playing tennis'). Most ended up lending money, £14 million in all. And most were put forward for peerages. It was only after one of them, Dr Chai Patel, health guru and owner of the Priory, became furious when barred from his peerage by the Appointments Commission, that he spilled the beans to the *Sunday Times*.

One of those who read the story was Jack Dromey, the Labour Party Chief Treasurer, who was appalled that he knew nothing of this private Number 10 system. Furious, he went public on *Channel 4 News*. All hell broke loose. Chai Patel himself was typical of the rich men who now wished they could run for cover. 'I am not ashamed of having donated money to the Labour Party, but I have been driven to distraction by the cynicism associated with it. I never thought it would come to this.'

In surveys, the public now thought Labour was sleazier than Major's government, but even the loans for peerages row that engulfed Blair was less serious than a new revelation – that Des Smith, a headmaster and advisor to the Specialist Schools and Academies Trust had been arrested. To an undercover *Sunday Times* reporter he had allegedly revealed that 'if you invested in five City Academies (one of Blair's favourites schemes) – you would be certain of a peerage.' To offer an honour for cash is directly and criminally in breach of the 1925 Honours (Prevention of Abuses) Act bought in after the scandal of Lloyd George's blatant selling of honours.

Sadly, Blair will now be compared not with the staunchly upright Margaret Thatcher (whom he most admired) but with Lloyd George, or even worse with Harold Wilson and his 'Lavender List' of honours. As several newspapers have pointed out, both Wilson and Blair were political wizards who delivered electoral victory. But both were shallow men, who *thought that making a good speech was the same as action.'* And both were proved to be not quite 'straight.'

Winston Churchill & Gallipoli

C hurchill was recently voted 'the greatest Briton.' However, his reputation was once tainted, perhaps unfairly, as the 'Butcher of Gallipoli.'

Gallipoli is a narrow, hilly promontory, which forms the western shore of the Dardanelles, the narrow straits leading from the Aegean Sea up to Istanbul. Historically, the straits have been of great strategic importance, guarding the Greek colony turned great city that was successively Byzantium, Constantinople and Istanbul. The siege of ancient Troy (page 217) probably took place due to quarrels over the passage of Greek ships through the Dardanelles up into the Black Sea.

By 1915, the Great War had already congealed into bloody trench warfare in France and Belgium. Winston Churchill *(right)*, then First Lord of the Admiralty, and as always, a man of brilliant and original mind, conceived and initiated an astonishingly bold plan to break the stalemate of the fighting. The Allies would seize and seal the Dardanelles, sail up and engage the Turkish fleet in

*'It is the
biggest
coup he
has ever
played
for.'*

the Sea of Marmara and persuade Constantinople to surrender. If Turkey were knocked out of the war, the result might be to encourage Bulgaria to withdraw support from the Central Powers (Germany and Austria-Hungary), to reduce Turkish pressure on Egypt and the Suez Canal, and release Russian armies fighting the Turks on the Caucasian front. Then Britain and her allies could concentrate on the battle against the Central Powers on the Western Front, and quickly bring the war to a decisive conclusion.

Only 41, the restless and mercurial Churchill had enjoyed a career packed with drama. As a soldier, he had galloped in one of the last cavalry charges; as a journalist he had escaped from a South African prison camp; as a politician he had changed sides from Conservative to Liberal; as a Minister he had played a controversial role in 'the siege of Sidney Street;' and in the miners' strike at Tonypandy; and as First Lord of the Admiralty he had switched the Royal Navy from coal to oil, and secretly obtained the oil in Mesopotamia to do so.

For six months of the Great War, Churchill had chafed at the bit, waiting for his Navy to have a decisive role. Now, in

*An Australian
soldier carries a
wounded comrade.
(Imperial War
Museum)*

January 1915, came a plea from Grand Duke Nicholas of Russia for a 'demonstration.' Churchill led a small group of amateur strategists to conceive Gallipoli, including First Sea Lord Fisher, Secretary of State for War Lord Kitchener and David Lloyd-George.

'It is the biggest coup he has ever played for' said a colleague, and at first Churchill tried to rush the Straits with ships. 'Well, you won't do it with ships alone' said the Third Sea Lord. 'Oh, yes we will!' growled Churchill. But he was wrong, and his miscalculation would cost the Allies dear.

Gallipoli was defended by the 85,000 men of Turkey's Fifth Army, its best, under the effective control of the German General Otto Liman von Sanders. Any naval attack would have to get past his hidden artillery and mobile guns, and crucially, the mines easily laid in the narrow straits. On March 18, the fleet, including 18 battleships, tried to neutralise, with their guns, the Turkish artillery so that the minesweepers could clear a passage. Suddenly, the rickety old French battleship *Bouvet*, whose Captain had begged, with tears, to take part, blew up and sank in 45 seconds. This disaster was quickly followed by that of HMS *Irresistible* and HMS *Ocean*, while several smaller ships were damaged. The little

Turkish minelayer, *Nusret,* had done her work well during the night, and the flags of 'General Recall' were hoisted. It had been a humiliating episode. Churchill, convinced, wrongly, that the Turks were short of shells, but rightly that they were out of mines, signalled to try to rush the narrows the next day. But the Admiral in charge lost his nerve, and it was decided that the Army must be used.

However, the Army fared no better than the Navy. Once again, there was to be courage, muddle, hesitation and weak leadership. The Australians and New Zealanders, who had volunteered in their thousands to fight for Britain, had the bad luck to come up against the Turkish 19th Division, commanded by the unknown Colonel Mustapha Kemal (later Turkey's legendary President). He was hit in the chest by a bullet, but was (literally) saved by his silver cigarette case. He told his staff to ignore his bleeding, and rushed his troops decisively to the high ground first, thus dominating the beaches. The untried Australians, in some cases commanded by poor officers, were then lacerated by Turkish sniping and shrapnel fire and began to 'straggle' dispiritedly back to the beaches. Requests to be re-embarked were luckily (or unluckily) refused. The ANZAC troops stayed on to display huge courage.

Things were even worse at the Helles landing. The old freighter SS *River Clyde* was beached, and men were meant to reach the shore across a makeshift bridge of lighters. As they emerged from the ship's side ports, the Royal Munster Fusiliers were cut down steadily by Turkish machine-guns, or drowned, weighed down with equipment; only 21 of the first 200 made it to the beach. The Dublin Fusiliers, on towed boats, were 'like rats in a trap' and shot to pieces. A pilot was horrified to see the surf red with blood for 50 yards. Only one young officer survived the landing, and of

Troops from the beached SS River Clyde *run into murderous Turkish machine-gun fire. From a painting by C. Dickson (Courtesy of the Council, National Army Museum)*

1,000 Dubliners only eleven would survive the campaign. The two Irish regiments had so few men left that they were amalgamated. The Lancashire Fusiliers suffered 600 casualties out of 1,000. Thirteen Victorian Crosses were awarded, but bravery was not enough.

In spite of fresh landings at Suvla, nowhere came the planned breakthrough. The campaign became exactly the same as the Western Front – static, murderous trench warfare, because once again the projectile dominated the battlefield (page 134). This was the first miscalculation. The second was, from Churchill downwards, to underestimate fatally the Turks, who displayed tenacity, bravery, skill, high morale and excellent leadership. Indeed 'Johnnie Turk' became a British nickname of respect. The Russians might sneer at Turkey as the 'Sick Man of Europe', but Turkey had hardly built the Ottoman Empire by her soldiers being vacillating weaklings.

Eventually, after a blazing summer involving suffering, destruction and disease (including the death, by mosquito bite, of the poet Rupert Brooke), the Allies evacuated in the freezing winter – the only success of the whole campaign, which had cost both sides hundreds of thousands of casualties. Although fewer than those of the British, and even the Irish, the losses among the volunteer Australian and New Zealand contingent, still commemorated each 25 April on ANZAC Day, produced a sense of grievance that did much to begin to sever ties with 'the old country' during the 20th century, and to set these two young nations on the road to independence and their own national identity.

Among the political casualties was Churchill, who resigned and went to fight as a battalion commander on the Western Front. Bowed and beaten, in many ways his great banana skin was not his fault. With stronger, more decisive Generals and Admirals he might well have pulled it off. We can only be grateful that he survived the setback to lead Britain in the next Great War.

Those heroes that shed their blood and lost their lives, you are now lying in the soil of a friendly country. Therefore, rest in peace. There is no difference between the Johnnies and the Mehmets to us where they lie side by side, now in this country of ours. You, the mothers who sent their sons from far away countries, wipe away your tears; your sons are now lying in our bosom, and are in peace. After having lost their lives on this land, they have become our sons as well.

eccentricity, addiction & obsession

'Every form of addiction is bad, no matter whether the narcotic be alcohol or morphine or idealism.'
Carl Gustav Jung

'You're not drunk if you can lie on the floor without holding on.'
Dean Martin

Michael Jackson & his journey into Neverland

Never has a musical career started so successfully at such a young age. At the age of five, Michael Jackson was already the lead singer of early boy band The Jackson Five, formed in 1964. The band was a sensation, and its first four singles, including *'I want you back'* went straight to number 1 in the USA. Under the Motown label, it released fourteen albums; only a taste of the youngest band member's future solo success.

Perhaps most famous is Michael's 1982 album *Thriller*, a perfect paradigm of all the promise and genius of his early career. It sold 50 million worldwide, the largest-selling album of all time, and produced seven hit singles. He won a record-breaking eight Grammy Awards in one night, and his subsequent albums *Bad* and *Dangerous* cemented his place as one the icons of pop music. However, Michael's problems were never in the recording studio or on stage. Rather, they were to manifest themselves in a self-destructive spiral of bizarre personal behaviour.

As his career progressed, Michael Jackson began to exhibit the peculiar traits that would earn him the memorable title 'Whacko Jacko'. The most obvious of these were the disturbing changes that have occurred to his face. Jackson's skin colour has altered radically over the years, from his original dark black skin through a range of increasingly pale, and now ghostly, shades. The shape has also changed, with his cheekbones re-formed, and with widely observed work on his nose. This was a disaster that led to the famous 'third nostril' – a growing hole in the side of Michael's nose.

As well as his appearance, his personal life has increasingly troubled the public. Though he has three children, two from his marriage with Debbie Rowe (his second wife after his short-lived union with Elvis Presley's daughter, Lisa Marie) and one from a surrogate, he rarely allows them out in public. When he does, they are forced to wear masks or veils (an attempt to disguise their identity, ensuring that they are the most recognisable children on the planet). Furthermore, he was universally accused of putting his youngest in danger when the world watched, horrified, as he dangled Prince Michael II from the balcony of a Berlin hotel in 2002.

But none of these eccentricities would be as serious or as damaging as the accusations that have comprehensively marred Jackson's public image. In 1993 he was accused of having molested 13-year old Jordie Chandler. Despite the seriousness of the charges, the case never actually reached the courts. Vehemently denying that he abused Jordie, he reached an agreement with the boy's parents, paying them a rumoured $20 million. But many now felt that his actions had gone several steps too far. People heatedly debated whether or not Jackson's lack of a conventional childhood had fomented in him such a dangerous fascination with children.

It is far from the end of the controversy. Michael continued to have children to stay at his Neverland ranch, a property which contains a zoo and amusement park, swimming pools, gardens, a basketball court and an internal electric train. The details of these 'sleepovers' were revealed in Martin Bashir's in-depth 2003 Granada

documentary about Jackson, Neverland, and the children who have stayed there. Branded by some as a deceitful and intrusive piece of journalism, it brought to light (in Michael's own words) his strange treatment of the young. He admitted to allowing children to share his bed, but denied there was any sexual motivation. 'We go to sleep, I put the fireplace on. I give them hot milk, you know, we have cookies. It's very charming. It's very sweet. It's what the whole world should do.' The footage horrified the parents of one of Neverland's guests, Gavin Arvizo, who was immediately whisked home.

More accusations have been levelled at Jackson. Two youths came forward and claimed that he abused them within the confines of Neverland. He faced seven counts of lewd acts on a child under the age of 14, and two counts of plying a child with alcohol in order to seduce him, but was found not guilty. However, his conduct over recent years has surely ensured that his star will never shine as brightly again. His last two albums, *Blood on the Dance Floor* and *Invincible,* have been, by his standards, failures. He still retains a base of loyal fans, but now cuts an infinitely less popular figure than the good looking young black man who took pop music by storm all those years ago.

The gate at Neverland, strangely topped with the British Royal Coat of Arms

the kitchen table. The idea of claiming on the insurance on four cars gradually emerged, and after abandoning one mechanic's idea of simply crushing the cars, they decided to keep the engines and running gear and remove the bodies, so they could one day be rebuilt. His two helpers eventually demanded £100,000 for their help. The trio reluctantly carried out this act of sacrilege over three nights, and put the surviving parts into a container locked up in Greenford. They then waited several weeks to make 'the discovery.'

Brocket claimed £4 million from General Accident, who rejected the claim, buying time. However, all this effort proved unnecessary, because Brocket's bank, feeling guilty that it had encouraged him to invest so heavily in classic cars, now offered a £15 million loan interest free over ten years. So, Charles Brocket withdrew the insurance claim, and as he had not actually received any money, thought that no harm had been done. The cars could even be rebuilt. Wrong. Firstly, they had not allowed for Isa's unstable attitude. Secondly, a curiosity of English law is that 'conspiracy to defraud' is regarded as much worse than actual fraud, and indeed attracts a sentence of 12 years worse than attempted murder (in fact

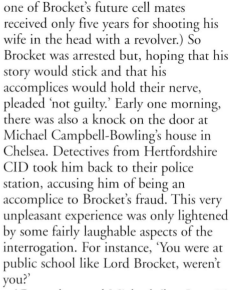

one of Brocket's future cell mates received only five years for shooting his wife in the head with a revolver.) So Brocket was arrested but, hoping that his story would stick and that his accomplices would hold their nerve, pleaded 'not guilty.' Early one morning, there was also a knock on the door at Michael Campbell-Bowling's house in Chelsea. Detectives from Hertfordshire CID took him back to their police station, accusing him of being an accomplice to Brocket's fraud. This very unpleasant experience was only lightened by some fairly laughable aspects of the interrogation. For instance, 'You were at public school like Lord Brocket, weren't you?'

'Correct', agreed Michael, 'but I am 20 years older than him, so I would have left Westminster before he was born, let alone before he went to Eton.'

'Well', sneered the Sergeant, 'you were an officer in the armed forces like Lord Brocket, weren't you?'

'Correct', continued Michael patiently, 'but as I have said, I am 20 years older, so I would have left the RAF, before he was in kindergarten, let alone before he went into the cavalry.' The attempt to establish guilt through some obscure class bonding was failing.

'But it is true to say that you are an

insurance broker?'

'Correct, but I am only licensed to handle life and pensions, so if you are implying that I insure motor cars you will find that you are wrong'.

This rather dim level of interrogation continued for hours, and, as evening drew on, Michael's lawyer said, 'perhaps we could go now and continue tomorrow'.

'No', snarled the woman police Sergeant (perhaps miffed at Michael's remark that 'the police were more Clousot than Poirot'), 'Let him spend a night in the cells and see how the other half live!'

So began a twelve-month nightmare. The Crown Prosecution Service, without any evidence, had plainly picked on Michael thinking he was a good friend of Brocket's and that Brocket might crack – if only to help his mate. But Brocket himself was trapped. He was still pleading innocent, so could scarcely now say that Michael was not part of a scam he claimed was non-existent. Michael's life was wrecked, his wife and daughters badly affected, his job stalled and it cost him a huge amount to defend himself. At seven magistrates hearings, the mechanics, who had turned Queen's Evidence and admitted their role, kept repeating that Michael had nothing to do with the project, as did Brocket's

solicitor, but, summing up the general attitude, Counsel for the Prosecution stated 'Mr Campbell-Bowling's mistake was to be a friend of Lord Brocket's.' It was only when the case reached a proper Crown Court that the judge ordered Michael to leave the dock 'without a stain on his character', because 'there was no shred of evidence against him', and awarded all costs against the CPS. In reality, he received only a fraction of his real losses. It was, of course, much worse for Charles Brocket. He effectively lost Brocket Hall, his beloved cars and his liberty, being jailed for 5 years. Brocket Hall was luckily kept in trust and will eventually go back to his children. Three of the cars have been rebuilt as, in a way, has Charles, who has since become something of a media personality, catapulted to general fame by his stint in the jungle in 'I'm a celebrity, get me out of here' with such luminaries as the well-endowed Jordan.

As he ruefully commented about his car obsession later to Michael Campbell-Bowling, 'The galling thing is that when one looks back, one sees how irrelevant such material things as cars are!'

Just as with Jonathan Aitken (page 94), one does, however, wonder how much similar effort the authorities would have made with less high-profile suspects.

Charles Brocket's book 'Call me Charlie' was a bestseller.

Holland & Tulipomania

It really was 'the flower that made men mad.'

The theft of plants and trees from suburban gardens is probably viewed as a modern crime. Yet such misdemeanours go back a long way. Indeed, a theft 400 years ago of a collection of bulbs created a banana skin for a whole nation. And the Netherlands, only just free of the Spanish yoke, could ill afford the turmoil of 'tulipomania'.

Of all ornamental plants, tulips have most captured the imagination. Natives of steppes and stony hills across a broad belt from the Aegean to Afghanistan and Central Asia, they began to trickle into Europe from the mid-16th century via diplomatic links between the Turkish Sultan, Suleiman the Magnificent, and the Holy Roman Empire. In particular, Charles de l'Ecluse (better known to botanists as Carolus Clusius) spread tulips through Europe and promoted many of the spring bulbs we plant today. Born in France, he travelled and studied widely in Europe and in 1593 came to Leiden to establish a new physic garden, bringing with him both years of scholarship and a prized collection of tulip bulbs from Vienna. Clusius was well known for championing tulips, and produced an early classification – but his greatest influence was inadvertent. Someone sneaked into his garden and stole his tulips. Soon they were out, 'distributed in the trade'. Breeders set to work on a natural variation, and soon a range of garden forms were available, some rare and most highly prized.

From the early 1600s, tulips became more and more fashionable in Holland. Painters extolled their virtues and prices of the bulbs rose, especially those of the more extravagantly marked parrot tulips, with their intricate white or yellow 'breaks', or feathery patterns caused by viral infections, then a complete mystery even to scientists. Tulips rapidly became status symbols reflecting the new wealth derived from the Dutch East Indies trade. Propagation was slow, but buyers could rely upon small daughter bulbs or offsets, which yielded faithful replicas of a carefully bred and selected parent bulb, to recoup their investment. As tulip expert Anna Pavord notes, these 'were the equivalent of the interest earned on the capital invested in the bulb.' Tulips were sold by the weight of the bulb, rather like truffles, and by 1634 they were changing hands for 5000 guilders each, literally the price of a substantial town house in Amsterdam. For Holland, the banana skin of 'tulipomania' had arrived.

The craze went far beyond those with a fondness for plants and gardens. People from all walks of life, not just the conspicuously wealthy, speculated wildly on the bulbs, properties were mortgaged, individuals bankrupted and livelihoods lost. And pure greed rapidly overtook sensible investment or even social aspiration and status. One story from this surreal interlude of Dutch history (when, after all, much of Europe was being ravaged by the Thirty Years War), captures the hysteria. A sailor found what he took to be a spare onion sitting on a dockside warehouse counter and took it off to embellish his breakfast. By the time the merchant who owned the bulb, a fantastically rare '*Semper augustus*' tulip, arrived to reclaim his missing property, the sailor was digesting his breakfast, contentedly seated on a coil of rope. The poor man was jailed for his innocent botanical mistake!

But it was not so surprising. In 1635, a single bulb was sold for 4 tons of wheat, 8 tons of rye, 1 bed, 4 oxen, 8 pigs, 12 sheep, 1 suit of clothes, 2 casks of wine, 4 tons of beer, 2 tons of butter, 1,000 pounds of cheese and one silver cup. It really was 'the flower that made men mad.'

Like all such investment pyramids, 'tulipomania' had to end in tears, and early in 1637 the bottom dropped out of the ridiculously distorted market as professional speculators began to offload tulips. The government tried to step in to call a halt, but was unable to control the wave of legal recrimination by aggrieved punters with 'negative equity.' The bizarre crisis substantially dented the Dutch economy at home and abroad, and allowed rivals such as England to move into lucrative overseas markets, an excuse for repeated, futile and expensive naval conflict between the two countries in the 1650s–70s.

All in all, the banana skin of 'tulipomania' had done great harm to The Netherlands. But in this case, there is a silver lining. The tulip has turned out to be the basis of a huge, successful worldwide flower industry.

Tulips were changing hands for the price of a large house.

The Greeks & the plane-spotters

Lesley Coppin thought she was on a delayed honeymoon. A 53-year-old grandmother and pizza restaurant manager from Suffolk, she had reluctantly agreed with her new taxi driver husband Paul's request that they could meet up with 'a couple of his plane-spotting friends' for their first few days in Greece. But she had been rather surprised to find nine of his middle-aged and nerdish pals waiting at the airport for their Easyjet flight, all bent on 'some quality spotting' – a bizarre hobby of collecting the serial numbers on civilian and military aircraft, for which they organised trips all over the world.

Uninterested in aircraft numbers, Lesley stayed in the minibus doing crossword puzzles while Paul and his friends wandered round Greek airbases noting the numbers on rather antiquated aircraft. So, outside Kalamata Airbase, she was amazed to look up and find herself surrounded by jeeps of armed police. Taken to the local police station,

Lesley Coppin, distraught at her unexpected ordeal

Paul confidently produced his letter of permission from a Greek Air Force General, but it seemed to have no effect and they were all put in the cells for spying. Soon the charges were increased from *'simple'* to *'distinguished espionage'*, meriting jail sentences from 3 to 20 years, and in national emergency, death. Quite who they were meant to be spying for was not made clear, but the inference seemed to be Turkey.

Four days later, on 16 November 2001, it became really hard for Lesley when she was suddenly transferred to the Korydallos women's prison in Athens. Not only was she separated from her husband and his friends, but her cellmates were now 18 murderers, thieves and prostitutes, the food was appalling and the lavatory a hole in the floor. Subject to asthma attacks and very depressed, she began to lose weight rapidly.

Meanwhile, in Britain, initial public incredulity and amusement had changed to outrage and fury. On 19 November, when a judge had again postponed any decision on charges, Britain's Minister of Europe, Peter Hain, raised the matter with Greek Foreign Minister, George Papandreou in Brussels. Two days later, Prime Minister Tony Blair protested to Greek Prime Minister Costas Simitis. But all seemed powerless to intervene as the furore escalated. Ross Benson of the

Daily Mail on 5 December described the heart-rending visit of Paul's mother, Jean Butt, to a bedraggled and emaciated Lesley, who clung to her like a weeping child, 'Please don't leave me, Please. Please'.

The already Eurosceptic British media were up in arms. The *Daily Mail* delivered 10,000 protest letters and coupons to the Greek Embassy. 'DONER BUY GREEK' thundered the *Sunday Sport* with typical inaccuracy (as Doner happens to be Turkish), continuing with farcical Jingoism, *'These poor Brits with their albeit sad hobby are the victims of Greek ignorance and misunderstanding. If these hairy blighters want to pick on innocent Brits, it's time for them to learn the British Lion's bite is worse even than its roar'.*

Finally, after six weeks in jail, members of the group were shocked to receive, variously, three year and twelve month sentences, but were granted bail of £9,000 each and allowed to leave the country. Lesley, particularly, rose to the occasion, lobbying politicians and working on the legal case. Next year, on 24 April 2002, they returned for trial in Greece. In spite of the fact that they could show that all the 'secret information' about Greek obsolescent military aircraft could freely be found on the internet and in aviation magazines and books, to the world's stupefaction, they were again found guilty. It was not until November that an appeal court acquitted them, by which time their legal costs had reached £25,000 each.

For the Greeks, it was a real and embarrassing banana skin, because after their initial puzzlement and suspicions about grown men taking down numbers as a hobby, they could have quickly dropped the case. Most sensible people would have agreed with Lesley's son, Steven, 'They are a bunch of anoraks with a strange hobby, but it's not something they should be jailed for.'

With their vital 2004 Olympics looming, the Greeks probably let the plane-spotters go only just in time. After all, if you cannot appreciate the harmless hobby of plane-spotting, you are unlikely to understand why thousands of young adults would train for years and for no money in order to run in skimpy clothing round a track. Highly suspicious, but not as plainly dangerous as the bomb-throwing abilities of shot-putters, let alone the threat of limpet mines posed by high divers. It was a miracle that their Olympics were not closed down by the Greeks themselves.

The Greeks could not understand grown men taking down aircraft numbers as a hobby.

'Bestie' & 'Gazza' & their wasted genius

Stormont, the magnificent Palladian edifice that looks out across Belfast, has seen many dramas. Most of them, appropriately for Northern Ireland's parliament building, have been political. But, in November 2005, a different parade took place. A funeral. Belfast's own local football hero had come home to rest.

George Best was one of the greatest football players the world has ever seen. In 1961, Manchester United scout, Bob Bishop, cabled his manager Matt Busby 'I THINK I'VE FOUND A GENIUS'. Indeed he had. When Best first played for United against West Bromwich in 1964, he was dubbed the 'Fifth Beatle'. Apart from his amazing skills on the pitch, George was also intelligent and with film star looks; a dimpled chin, a ready smile and piercing blue eyes. He became football's first superstar, and a magnet for women. 'Pulling girls had become a sport for me'. Indeed, it is claimed that he pulled no less than seven Miss Worlds.

'I think I've found a genius.'

But there was a fatal flaw. George was addicted to drink. He simply could not stop, and alcoholism, sadly, would be his great downfall. In 1968, he scored his greatest triumph during the European cup against Benfica, for which he was named 'European Footballer of the Year'. The night of this triumph, he was so drunk that he could remember little of the game and nothing of the celebrations. For six years, he was also Manchester United's top scorer. However in 1969, Matt Busby retired and one of Best's key emotional anchors was gone. The drinking continued – sometimes morosely, sometimes cheerfully. Once, a worried hotel waiter, delivering champagne, asked, 'Mr Best, where did it all go wrong?' There was £20,000 in cash on the bed, together with the reigning Miss World!

But Tommy Docherty, his new manager, became steadily more exasperated, and was to say; 'If only George had been able to pass nightclubs the way he passed the ball'. In 1972, Best's top-flight career was over at the tragically young age of 26. He retired to second-class football, speech making, womanising and drink.

In 2002, he was given a new liver, to the dismay of many liver disease sufferers and of the medical profession, who feared he would abuse it as badly as the old one. Their fears were well founded. His tempestuous and doomed life ended in a coma in hospital three years later.

There have been many players briefly called the new George Best, and Paul Gascoigne was one of them. Sadly, the label stuck in more ways than one. A brilliant young prodigy, who became really famous when he cried into his England shirt, he was dubbed 'daft as a brush' for his madcap antics. But 'Gazza', too, succumbed to drink, 'his refuelling problems'. He was shocked when he was dropped by Glen Hoddle from the 1998 England Squad, after the coach had seen newspaper parties of Gazza carousing the night away with DJs Chris Evans and Danny Baker. In 2005, he was fired as manager from lowly Kettering Town, 'for being drunk 37 out of 39 days'.

Best and Gascoigne are merely the most dramatic examples of British footballers taking British way beyond any sensible limit.

How many more geniuses are to be wrecked off the pitch? Whatever happened to the concept of serious athletes being 'in training' – not touching cigarettes or booze? The bottle can start a slippery slide.

Gazza crying into his shirt, his worst and most famous moment

Adolf Hitler & the lure of the East

Millions of men waited in the darkness before dawn on 22 June 1941, facing east. Ever since Adolf Hitler unleashed them in his massive, brutal and ill-fated invasion on his nominal ally, Russia, an obvious question has been asked, 'Why did he do it?' With Britain unbeaten, he knew that he should not expose himself to fighting on two fronts and, in any event, he had the awful warning of the 1812 destruction of Napoleon's *Grande Armée*.' The answer must surely be because this was a war against the two types of people he most feared and loathed, the Communists and the Jews. To destroy Communism, he must destroy Soviet Russia. To get his hands on the Jews, he had to invade the East, where three-quarters of his intended eleven million victims lived.

He had cynically bought time with his 1939 Non-Aggression Pact with Stalin, which was, within days, followed by his (and Stalin's) attack on Poland and months later the West – except for Britain, behind her Channel and saved by her Spitfires and Hurricanes. But now it was time to return to Hitler's true and ultimate purpose, his treacherous attack and attempted annihilation of his enemy in the Kremlin.

Hitler with his Generals. How confident were they?

Hitler was confident. 'Smash in the door and the whole rotten structure will all come down!' Many in Germany and abroad agreed. In 1937, in a fit of paranoia, Stalin had amazingly destroyed his own officer corps. 37,000 had been executed or dismissed, including 60% of his Generals. Those who remained were either inexperienced, or worse, terrified of showing any initiative. Russia's pathetic performance against tiny Finland in 1940 only confirmed the world's low opinion of the Soviet military.

However, if *'the whole structure'* did not, indeed, collapse very quickly, Hitler was likely to be proved overconfident.

His army appeared huge, three million strong, but some were weak and unenthusiastic allies like the Romanians, Hungarians and Italians. The Germans were also attacking on a huge front, 1,200 miles, but with only the same number of tanks and aircraft that had invaded France. Germany's production had actually been in the doldrums, long overtaken by Britain and dwarfed by Russia. It had far too few motor vehicles and was constantly short of fuel and other key materials. So, apart from its flashy and spectacular armoured spearheads, the German army had to march hundreds of miles on foot, or ride – with 600,000 horses. The Luftwaffe was short of aircraft and had lost many of its best pilots in the Battle of Britain. Above all, with Hitler confident that he could win in weeks, no provision at all had been made to fight in Russia's famously cruel winter.

However, when the Germans did attack, all seemed to go to plan. In spite of all the obvious signs and warnings, the Soviets seemed paralysed; 2,000 aircraft destroyed in days, and whole armies surrounded. One General later wrote, *'When I heard the first bombs, I knew we would be indulging in an old Russian manoeuvre – running with suitcases across broken ground!'* Stalin at first appeared to suffer a nervous breakdown, waiting fearfully in his dacha to be arrested and executed for his naivety and lack of preparation.

But in spite of his initial stunning successes, Hitler's concept of a pitiless *Rassenkampf,* or 'race war', was to spell his doom. His maniacal hatred of both Communists and Jews drove him to order that the honourable rules of war 'need not apply on the Eastern Front.' This swiftly transformed a population that had welcomed the Germans as liberators from Stalin's oppression into fanatical resisters. The crazy order to shoot all political officers attached to the Soviet army, the notorious 'Commissar Order', made resistance stiffen at once, as did the rumours filtering out that two million Russian prisoners were being starved to death. The appalling behaviour of Himmler's *Einsatzgruppen (below)* as they methodically killed tens

DONOUGH O'BRIEN

of thousands of Jewish men, women and children, as 'partisans', together with the starvation of Russian civilians, created a huge guerrilla movement behind the long German lines. (The Germans were to lose 325,000 men killed in Russia by *partisan action alone,* amazingly more than Britain's total losses in six years of World War II.)

The effect of Hitler's treacherous and murderous attack was that the Russians rallied behind Stalin and his 'Patriotic War'. New commanders were appointed, like Zhukov, Koniev and Rokossovsky – who had to be plucked from the gulag where he had been imprisoned. Massive new factories, safe in Russia's interior, began to turn out thousands of tanks,

Walled up in her own castle

would work better, so she began to murder those of high birth. Now, at last, the authorities began to worry about her misdeeds; the rumours could not be kept from her family and other nobles, and even reached the ears of the Holy Roman Emperor. He ordered her cousin, Count Thurzo, Palatine Prince of Transylvania, to investigate Elizabeth's activities and finally raided her castle lair. There, his horrified men found corpses littering the place. At her trial, a witness produced an inventory of 650 murders, made out in the Countess's own careful handwriting. The court sentenced Elizabeth to be walled up in a cell in her own castle at Czej, where she died four years later.

This was not to be the last time that villains were brought to book only because they moved on from attacking the vulnerable, the poor, drifters, gays and prostitutes, and then unwisely turned to the well-born and connected to be their victims. John Gacy, Ted Bundy, Fred West and the Yorkshire Ripper all largely slipped up in the same way.

Shaka the Zulu & his mother

Everything that the ferocious Zulu ruler Shaka did in his spectacular and bloody reign was influenced by his mother. It was a baleful influence which would doom many in Africa, and then doom Shaka himself.

Shaka was born in 1787, the illegitimate son of chief Senzangakona and a young girl called Nandi from the nearby Langeni tribe. The union having broken many tribal rules, the boy was cruelly called '*Shaka*', literally an unwanted intestinal beetle. Mother and son were both thrown out of Senzangakona's family when Shaka, aged just six, could not prevent a dog killing one of his father's sheep. When Nandi tried to return to her own tribe at a time of famine, the unwelcoming Langeni banished both her and Shaka into destitution – for which the tribe would later pay dearly. Shaka's burning resentment and his anger on behalf of his mother grew and grew.

Befriended by another tribe, Shaka grew up strong and fearless and was soon invited to join the army of King Dingiswayo. There, he changed forever the way the Zulus were to fight. He melted down the ineffective throwing assegais into fearsome stabbing spears called *iXwas* (the noise of the spears being withdrawn), he re-designed his shields to hook an enemy's shield to expose the body and trained his men to run 50 miles a day barefoot.

Soon it was time to try out his new methods. One afternoon, the Buthelezi tribe faced Shaka for the traditional *giya*, by convention a bloodless confrontation of display and abuse. Shaka and his warriors killed all of them in moments. Soon in command of an army of 50,000, with well-drilled, ruthless discipline, Shaka perfected the battlefield tactics which would rule Africa for fifty years, the *Impondo Zankhomo,* with the 'head of the buffalo' supported by the 'loins', with encircling 'horns'. The *infecane* or 'crushing' of the other tribes of Africa probably resulted in an appalling two million deaths in a decade.

Shaka brought his beloved mother, Nandi, to Bulawayo, 'the place of killing', where she was set up in a magnificent kraal. Shaka now ruled a huge area of Africa, threatened by no-one, not even the British with whom he was friendly because one of them had saved his life. But in 1827 disaster struck. His beloved mother died. Something extraordinary then happened. Shaka became literally demented with grief, killing nearly 7,000 of his own followers for 'not showing enough respect' for his mother. On pain of death, for months he even forbade the conceiving of children, the drinking of milk and the planting of crops, nearly causing starvation.

His obsessive, erratic behaviour went too far. When his army was away, his half brothers Dingane and Mhlangana assassinated him and buried him in an ignominious unmarked grave.

Shaka's driving force in life had been his obsessive love for his mother. The same love condemned him to an early death at the height of his power.

Caligula & the password

The people of Rome first saw him standing proudly in a chariot next to his hero-father Germanicus in a triumphant parade. The mascot of the Roman army, he was a pretty boy of four in a tiny soldier's uniform, complete with little boots, 'caligae.' A few years later, Romans would know the nickname 'Caligula' for much less pleasant reasons.

Sadly, Germanicus did not enjoy his popularity for long. He died mysteriously of poison two years later. His wife Agrippina foolishly pointed the public finger of suspicion at his jealous brother, the Emperor Tiberius. She and Caligula's older brothers paid for this rash talk with their lives. So, with most of his family cruelly destroyed, it was already hardly surprising that Caligula would turn out more than a little strange.

For six years, Caligula went to live with his uncle on the debauched island of Capri, seemingly fitting in only too well as he started incestuous affairs with both his sisters. He also forged an alliance with Macro, Commander of the Praetorian Guard, with whose wife he also slept – with Macro's consent.

As Tiberius neared death, he predicted to Caligula, 'You will kill my grandson Gemellus and another will kill you'. Within a year Gemellus, joint-Emperor in name, was dead, and Caligula became supreme ruler.

There was a brief honeymoon period with the Romans seduced by elaborate circuses and bloody spectacles, but which nearly bankrupted the Empire. The strain suddenly made the still-popular Caligula ill – a complete physical and mental collapse.

High-ranking Romans offered to sacrifice themselves, and all traffic and noise was silenced. When he recovered from his breakdown, Caligula's true madness emerged. 'I wasn't really ill, I

Caligula, when young and handsome

was being reborn a God'. He proceeded to insist that the promised sacrifices or suicides did happen. When hecklers interrupted his Games, they had their tongues cut out and were killed by the animals in the arena.

The beautiful boy had become tall, ugly, balding but hairy. He did not let people look down on him from above. Even to mention 'goats' could lead to death. He turned on Macro, cynically charging him with prostituting his wife! Both were forced to kill themselves. With Macro gone, all restraint went. Caligula slept with anyone he wanted, even brides on their wedding day – he created a brothel in his palace. He extracted money on pain of death. He appointed his horse 'Incitatus' as Consul, and he forced Senators to run beside his chariot like slaves. To fulfil a prophecy, he built a three-mile bridge across the Bay of Naples. And all the while he murdered and tortured. His most bizarre behaviour was at Boulogne where he made his army attack the sea with arrows, swords and lances to 'punish his fellow God Neptune', later collecting up seashells as booty.

The tale of Caligula's barbarities fills volumes, yet strangely, it was a chance and frivolous banana skin that brought him to his horrible and well-deserved end.

It had been the custom since the days of the Republic for the Captain of the Guards to ask the Senate, or later, the 'Imperator', for the day's password. Caligula enjoyed giving the silliest, most mocking and lascivious passwords like 'Priapus' and 'Venus'. Then he went too far. He had frequently and cruelly mocked the Captain of the Praetorian Guards, Cassius Chaerea, because of his effeminate voice. Here was a secret Republican, longing for the old ideals. 'Buttocks' was the word Caligula demanded as the password. Years of misery had scored Chaerea's heart with the pages of injustice, and he had endured it – but humiliation he would not suffer. He and two other conspirators, called the Tiger and the Wolf, prepared a trap for the mad emperor. Walking back through the Circus Maximus after a particularly vicious entertainment, Caligula found himself cut off from his German guards. Chaerea, the Tiger and the Wolf encircled him. He screamed out to Jupiter, the God over whom he claimed precedence, before they stabbed him – thirty times. His atrocious reign, even more destructive and barbarous than that of Nero or Commodus, had lasted just three years and eleven months.

The Duke of Buckingham & his carriage drive

The second Duke of Buckingham must rate as one of the most foolish and wasteful of English eccentrics. The mansion he had inherited is one of the grandest and most beautiful in Britain. Resembling the finest of Palladian palazzos, Stowe House is 500 yards long and with 400 rooms.

In the seventeenth century, it was no less than the centre of political and social Britain. Started in 1677 by Sir Richard Temple, it was steadily expanded by his son Viscount Cobham and his heir Richard Grenville, Earl Temple.

Architects included Vanbrugh (soon to create Blenheim Palace), William Kent, Gibbs and Robert Adams. The greatest gardener of the age, 'Capability' Brown, created the lovely valleys and the lakes reflecting the house and its many temples.

The result was, in the opinion of one expert, 'the largest and most completely realised private neo-classical building in the world'. Everything was

The Duke's Royal Patron, George IV

Stowe's magnificent South Front

done on a grand scale by the Temple-Grenville family, now Dukes of Buckingham.

The great house echoed to the talk of many great men: the Earl of Chatham (Pitt the Elder), Sir Robert Walpole, William Pitt 'the Younger', Alexander Pope, Disraeli and Sir Robert Peel, the creator of Britain's police. The house and its families produced four Prime Ministers in just fifty years.

But a century and a half of amazing expenditure was not to last. The second

Duke was to wreck everything. His greatest folly was to attempt to buy all the land on each side of the road the entire way from Stowe to Chandos Square in London, so that he could refer to the 60 miles as his 'carriage drive'. He ran out of money after about a mile. As *The Times* wrote acidly: '*He has thrown*

away his high position for the baubles of a pauper and the tinsels of a fool.' Another newspaper described him as the '*greatest debtor in the world.*'

It was the visit in 1845 of Queen Victoria which sealed the financial fate of Stowe. The bailiffs were already in residence during the Queen's visit, which was costing £1,000 a day. They refused to move out, but they sportingly agreed to wear the Duke's livery and to pretend to be his servants!

Finally, hundreds of paintings and artefacts together with 40,000 acres had to be sold in a month-long 'Sale of the Century' in 1848, helping, incidentally, to launch Christie's as an auction house.

In 1921, for the paltry sum of £50,000, the magnificent building and 450 acres were bought for a new school, Stowe. And as you approach it, you can still drive for a mile on the Duke's eccentric folly, his carriage drive.

'Bix', 'Fats' & the bottle that kills

'L'Absinthe' by Degas

Since man first learned to brew and distill, alcohol has created its own epidemics. Britain was nearly ruined by gin. Reeling from the 'South Sea Bubble scandal (page 223), the country was by 1750 drinking millions of gallons of cheap gin. It may well have provided much-needed tax for the Government and even created a vital market for England's struggling barley farmers, but it created appalling social havoc, as Hogarth so cruelly depicted in his terrifying picture, *'Gin Lane.'*

Vodka has always ravaged Russia. Centuries of despair and deprivation have forced her people to drown their sorrows in alcohol. The Soviet Army even suffered deaths from its soldiers drinking the anti-freeze from their military vehicles.

France, too, has had to worry. On every bar wall there is still a notice about *L'ivresse publique* or public drunkenness. During her *belle époque,* absinthe became the rage and the favourite tipple for artists. 'The Green Fairy,' with its hallucinogenic wormwood, was to kill off some of the greatest talents of France.

The fast-growing, rip-roaring New World was not to escape addiction to drink. The saloon forms the backdrop for nearly every 'Western'. In reality, the strong 'gut-rot' whiskey they drank would have made most cowboys incapable of standing, let alone shooting anyone with any precision.

So great were the perceived dangers of alcohol to family and working life in the United States, that a powerful temperance movement was able to push through the Volstead Act in 1919, the well meaning and noble experiment of prohibition. This was to prove one of the greatest banana skins in history. Overnight, respectable bars were replaced by many more thousands of 'speakeasies.' Everyone drank illegally and the control of the illicit distribution of booze created America's organised crime as we now know it. It made millionaires out of thugs like Al Capone and the streets echoed to the gunfire between the rival gangs.

The 'Jazz Age' of the 'Roaring Twenties', with its bob-haired, short-skirted 'flappers' and their hip flasks was dominated by illegal drink. Jazz itself was played in speakeasies and nightclubs, with the most famous of all, Duke Ellington's Cotton Club, a Harlem beer distribution front

Bix's battered cornet

Fats Waller

for the English-born hoodlum 'Owney' Madden, catering for the 'mink set' of New York.

Sadly, at a time when theoretically you could not drink, many of the jazz age greats were to be carried off by booze. 'Bix' Beiderbecke's lyrical, bell-like notes were described by 'Mezz' Mezzrow in 1924. 'Despite the whiskey fumes that blew out of his battered cornet, I had never heard a tone like he got before or since.' Just a few years later, that tone was silenced. Bix died of drink at 29.

Thomas 'Fats' Waller, the bubbly, wisecracking piano and vocal genius and the creator of '*Ain't Misbehaving,*' certainly misbehaved with drink all his life. '*I always love my gine,' (sic)* he quipped in '*That's what I love about you.*'

Indeed he did, and once finished every bottle of gin in the house of an English Countess in New York. 'Fats' died one night in a Pullman car. He was only 39, just ten years older than Bix.

America finally saw sense in 1933 and Prohibition was repealed. The Depression was to finished off America's orgy of drinking. Nobody could afford it any more.

Today in Britain people can afford it and 'binge-drinking' has arrived on a massive scale. Many towns are reduced to chaotic shambles every weekend by thousands of drunken young people, while the Government is further relaxing the licensing hours.

That will probably be yet another banana skin.

Sex, Drugs & Rock 'n' Roll

If drink was often the downfall for jazz musicians in the first half of the 20th century, a new danger engulfed their successors in the second half – drugs. It is not for nothing that 'Sex, drugs and rock 'n' roll' is now part of our culture.

A startling survey of premature deaths among rock singers reveals that they die on average at 36, when most of us die at 76. Only a few, including Bill Haley, succumbed to drink, but a

horrifying number were to die of drug overdoses. Meteoric success appears to offer no protection. Indeed, some of the greatest icons were felled by addiction. Elvis, 'the King', may have over-dosed on May-wee

Langston's peanut butter and banana sandwiches, but it was far more likely that it was the 14 drugs found in his bloodstream that killed him.

The roll call of fallen stars is sad and terrifying. Janis Joplin *(below)*, Jimi

Hendrix *(left)*, Keith Moon, Sid Vicious – the list goes on. Hardly a group did not lose members – the Carpenters, the Pretenders, Deep Purple, Free, U2, Blood Sweat & Tears, the Grateful Dead, The Byrds, Uriah Heap, Sha Na Na, the Rolling Stones,

and many others.

What is even more depressing is that nearly as many rock singers have committed suicide as have overdosed – Kurt Cobain, Brian Jones *(right)* and perhaps Michael Hutchence are only the most famous. How many of these died under drug influence? And how many have been affected by the nihilistic, suicidal lyrics that that

encourage such self-destruction? Elton John *(left)*, who sweetly sang '*Candle in the Wind*' for Princess Diana, also sang some rather more sinister lyrics, '*Think I'll buy a forty five / Give 'em all a surprise / Think I'm gonna kill myself / Cause a little suicide.*' The Healing Faith were among others with the same message, '*I put a bullet in the chamber / Put the barrel in my mouth / Six to me I'm gonna make it / One in six I'll snuff it out.*'

Small wonder that suicides among young people have tripled since 1950. Teenagers have even been found dead

under AC/DC posters proclaiming, '*Shoot to thrill*', or with Pink Floyd's '*Goodbye Cruel World*' and '*Waiting for the Worms*' playing by their bodies.

We can also wonder about the presence of drugs in the huge number of car crashes that have taken out rock stars in their twenties, and the strange number of early, fatal heart attacks among those in their thirties and forties.

Why have drugs felled so many? Is it greedy management forcing stars to work to exhaustion unless drugged up ('Here, take this. It will get you through the night'), or is it that danger is so much part of the rock 'n' roll mix? Far more likely, when you have it all, what else is there?

Idi Amin & his sense of humour

In 1973 Idi Amin, the dictator of Uganda, wrote to Edward Heath, Prime Minister of Great Britain, and offered him bananas 'to help Britain's starving population.' He would have signed himself '*His Excellency President for Life Field Marshal Al Hadji Doctor Idi Amin, VC, DSO, MC, Lord of All the Beasts of the Earth and Fishes of the Sea, and Conqueror of the British Empire in Africa in General and Uganda in Particular*'. The banana joke was perhaps a quip too far.

Idi Amin's career is a chapter of banana skins, first by others and then himself. He started as a cook in Britain's

King's African Rifles, but at 6ft 4 inches and twenty stone, became a boxing champion of Uganda and a Sergeant Major and was then commissioned. The banana skin of the British was that they thought of him as 'jolly' and a 'bit stupid' and ignored stories of his brutality. When independence came in 1962, Amin was steadily promoted, so that in 1966 as Army Chief of Staff, he was able to use his troops to help Prime Minister Milton Obote to overthrow the King – the Kabaka. Five years later, Idi Amin did the same to an overconfident Obote and thus became President.

The mask of lighthearted, childish humour fell quickly away. His 'Public Safety Unit' killer squads began to hunt down Obote supporters in the Adoli and Langi tribes, killing 3,000 army officers and 10,000 civilians. The Nile Mansions Hotel in Kampala became a feared torture and execution centre, and rank and status were no protection. He murdered the Archbishop of Uganda, the head of the University, the Governor of the Bank and many of his own Ministers. Some he killed personally, and their heads were, incredibly, kept in his refrigerator.

He was plainly paranoid and completely unbalanced. For example, he asked the Israelis for 24 Phantoms 'to bomb Tanzania', and the Queen for a plane, some Highland soldiers and a pair of brogue shoes to attend the Commonwealth Games.

His own first banana skin came in 1972 when he suddenly threw out the 70,000 Asians who ran 85 per cent of Uganda's business. He gave their shops and factories to his officers, who, of course, had not the slightest idea what to do with them once they had looted the shelves.

Soon Kampala was a ghost town, and staple products like sugar and butter virtually disappeared.

When an Israeli airliner was hijacked to Entebbe airport in 1976, Amin was openly supporting the hijackers before they were rescued by Israeli commandos. This did not help his international image. Meanwhile, every year, tens of thousands of his citizens were being maimed, tortured and murdered by this mad tyrant, who was now suspected of being affected by neurosyphilis.

In 1978, in spite of the fact that he had recently married a go-go dancer from his 'Suicide Mechanised Unit Jazz Band', he offered to marry Julius Nyerere, the leader of Tanzania, and then invaded his country with 3,000 troops. It was his last banana skin. Enough was enough. Tanzania counter-attacked and Idi Amin escaped to Libya whence, after molesting Gadaffi's daughter, he finally ended up in exile in Saudi Arabia where he died in 2003.

He had hardly been an object lesson on how to dismantle colonialism calmly and successfully.

He asked the queen for a plane, Highland soldiers and a pair of brogues.

David Koresh & Waco

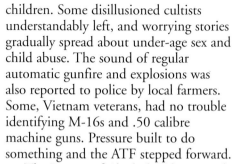

At first, nobody seemed to think it peculiar that a religious community near Waco seemed to be armed to the teeth, with assault rifles, heavy machine guns and grenades. After all, Waco reflected the attitudes of Texas, the 'Lone Star State', in which more people die by guns than traffic accidents; where there are more gun dealers than obstetricians; and, in 1991, where 16,500 residents owned machine guns.

The Branch Davidians were members of a religious cult who thought they were chosen to be among 144,000 virtuous souls who would be borne away to Heaven. Unluckily for them, the cult in Waco had fallen under the control of a goodlooking, guitar-playing young man called Vernon Howell. Changing his name to David Koresh, he had ousted all rivals and dominated his flock with apocalyptic religious speeches sometimes lasting fifteen hours, with discipline enforced by his 'Mighty Men'.

As with many cults, followers came from all over the world and had turned over their money. However, unlike most cults, they had also turned over their women to Koresh, who ran the compound as a one-man harem called the 'House of David', fathering several

David Koresh

children. Some disillusioned cultists understandably left, and worrying stories gradually spread about under-age sex and child abuse. The sound of regular automatic gunfire and explosions was also reported to police by local farmers. Some, Vietnam veterans, had no trouble identifying M-16s and .50 calibre machine guns. Pressure built to do something and the ATF stepped forward.

The Bureau of Alcohol, Tobacco and Firearms is the direct descendant of Eliot Ness and the 'Untouchables', once called revenuers, prohibition agents or Treasury men. It was the ATF who decided to intervene because of the allegedly huge stockpile of weapons, and mounting public anxiety about how they might be used. In spite of careful training and personal courage, they were probably not the right people for the job.

Early one Sunday morning, a convoy of ATF vehicles approached the compound, dark-clothed agents leaping out and confidently heading forward in armed squads. Koresh peered out of the door. 'Federal Agents, with a search warrant – COME OUT! But a hail of gunfire engulfed the agents. Using heavy weapons, the cultists even fired *through* the walls. The surprised ATF agents began dropping. Heavily armed themselves, they had actually been outgunned. No less than ten thousand rounds were fired. Firing died down and a truce was called which was to last 51 days, while the whole world looked on. Four agents were dead, sixteen wounded. Casualties among the cultists were never exactly established, although Koresh himself was wounded.

Meanwhile a hailstorm of criticism fell on the ATF. Were they really equipped for such a raid? Had they gone ahead after the cultists had been tipped off? Why had they not just snatched Koresh on one of his frequent trips into Waco? Was their show of force part of a turf war to keep up their budgets?

The siege went on for weeks with 'Ranch Apocalypse' surrounded by a cordon of 500 heavily armed men and women, the media and thousands of tourists. Patient negotiating experts tried to reason with Koresh, who constantly broke his word and delayed. 'God told me to wait'.

On the fifty first morning, the Government lost patience, and the second half of the tragedy played itself out. With permission from President Clinton and Attorney General Janet Reno, and because of fears that Koresh was attempting to orchestrate a mass suicide killing including the children, an FBI assault was mounted. Surely, using tanks and heavy armoured vehicles would do the trick? Greeted with bullets, the vehicles tried to break up the buildings and shoot CS gas into them. It should have been quick, but the FBI took six long hours, and then cultists were seen setting fires. Suddenly the buildings were ablaze, with explosions of ammunition and chemicals adding to the holocaust. The world watched helplessly and in minutes it was all over. Of 94 people, only eight survived. The cult had indeed achieved its Apocalypse.

Now the recriminations extended further than the FBI and the ATF, and Janet Reno took the rap for the double disaster. 'I approved the plan and I'm responsible for it. The buck stops with me.' President Clinton took a little time before supporting her.

There are many who have since sided with the cult, feeling that the Government was not just incompetent but out of control. Unfortunately, one such supporter was Timothy McVeigh, who decided to wreak revenge on the second anniversary of Waco by blowing up a Federal Building in Oklahoma, killing 168 innocent workers and many children. Before 9/11, this was America's worst terrorist tragedy.

Waco led to the home-grown terrorism at Oklahoma.

Eliza Lynch & her mad dictator

Among all the 'Wild Geese', who have left Ireland to escape poverty and oppression and to seek their fortunes abroad, none was to prove as destructive as Eliza Lynch.

Eliza arrived in Paris in 1849 soon after the Irish Famine, and was married off to a French army officer at just 15. After three boring years in Algiers, she returned to Paris alone and was soon successfully selling her statuesque body to rich and influential men. She decided to attract a foreign 'sugar daddy', and into her salon one night came a rather ugly, short man with brown teeth and a cigar. Enter Francisco Lopez, the millionaire son of the President of Paraguay. They become lovers that very night, and soon Eliza agreed to go back with him to what she was blithely told was a 'paradise' in Latin America.

Arriving with crates of Parisian gowns, china, furniture and even a piano, Eliza was shocked to find a hot, humid and run-down capital, Asunción, whose aristocratic women plainly regarded her as the 'Irish whore'. But soon she bore him six children and they built a 'palace', the first two-storey building in Paraguay. When his father died, Lopez became Emperor and demanded that his mistress be accorded the courtesies due to a wife. All this was rather petty and provincial. He could then have settled down to be a normal corrupt, incompetent Latin American dictator. But Eliza provided the banana skin, because she now filled the strange mind of Francisco Lopez with grandiose ideas of military glory and of how they could become Emperor and Empress of the whole of South America. The now hugely fat megalomaniac proceeded to attack his larger and more powerful neighbours, Argentina, Uruguay and Brazil. In a series of suicidal, disastrous and bloody wars, he not only wrecked the progress of much of South America, but also virtually managed to destroy his own country, in the process reducing its population from 1,337,000 to 221,000, of whom only 28,000 adult males survived – a feat unmatched by Hitler, Stalin or Genghis Khan. Eliza tried to help by recruiting 'Amazon' regiments of women with lances, leading them into battle on a white horse. Even more in character, she took great pleasure in confiscating the jewels of her rivals 'for the cause' and promptly shipping them to Paris for her future private plans.

Eliza's rather sexy and improbable monument in Asunción

When his mother revealed that Lopez was illegitimate and had no right to be President at all, he cracked, ordering the population of Asunción into the jungle like Pol Pot in Cambodia a century later. He also demanded to be recognised as a Saint and simply shot the 23 bishops who disagreed. Worse, he even ordered the national treasure of gold to be thrown off a cliff and then all killed the witnesses.

He even flogged his mother in public, who only rescued from death by a sudden attack by Brazilian soldiers who chased the waddling, gargantuan dictator around and finally killed him.

Eliza escaped and went back to Paris, where she lived, naturally enough, in considerable comfort. For an emigrant girl from Cork she had been able to do an amazing amount of damage.

Jim Morrison & his extreme exposure

Jim Morrison, enduring rock icon, poet, lyricist and lead singer with the legendary 60s rock band, *The Doors*, was a man of enormous ability and innate intelligence, but driven by drink, drugs and self-obsession to expose himself on stage – a moment of stupidity that led inexorably to the dimming of his career. His impetuous, self-destructive nature also led to an early death.

James Douglas Morrison was born in Florida on 8 December 1943, the son of a US Admiral. After school and college, he attended UCLA where he received an MA in Fine Arts; and at this point apparently broke off contact with his family, later falsely claiming his parents and siblings were 'dead'. Already writing songs, in 1965 he met eclectic keyboard virtuoso Ray Manzarek. Teaming up

with drummer John Denslow and guitarist Robby Krieger, they served a hard apprenticeship in the clubs of LA with their fusion of rock, blues and jazz.

Morrison took the band's name, *The Doors*, from an evocative phrase, The *Doors of Perception*, borrowed from William Blake via Aldous Huxley. Frequently stoned and ingesting frightening doses of LSD, it was not for nothing that they were later dubbed the 'Kings of Acid Rock'.

Signed in 1966 to the prestigious progressive rock label Elektra, the band released its first album, *The Doors*, in February 1967, which contained its biggest hit single, *Light my Fire*. This album was a smash, and was soon followed up by the equally successful *Strange Days*. *Waiting for the Sun* in 1968

Bugatti, Ferrari & Offy

'I make cars to go, others can make them to stop!'

Nowadays we are entirely used to motor racing being a technological battleground. For twenty years teams have been locked in a scientific and electronics struggle to gain superiority. Every few years the rules have been changed to slow down the cars, or to eliminate some advantage created by one of the teams.

It was not always so. Some of the greatest names in motor racing history were able to adopt a disdainful attitude to innovation. The great Ettore Bugatti refused to put four wheel brakes on  his earlier cars, with brakes on only the rear wheels. Confidently, he asserted, 'I make cars to go, others can make them to stop!' Only when race losses mounted could he be persuaded otherwise.

Another automotive legend, Enzo Ferrari, was always really an engine man. As his cars began to be beaten either by Vanwall and Mercedes, an unhappy member of his design team complained, 'Disc brakes came from England, fuel injection from Germany and neither have yet reached Maranello.'

So Ferrari battled on with lovely red cars with outmoded Weber carburettors and fade-prone, finned drum brakes. Worse was to come. John Cooper suddenly produced a little car with an underpowered Coventry Climax engine behind the driver. But this innovation cut weight and drag, and improved acceleration, braking and cornering. It was immediately competitive – especially when British engine power improved. In 1958, Stirling Moss won the Argentinian Grand Prix in the little car. It was the writing on the wall. Cooper was soon joined by Colin Chapman and his superb designs for Lotus. BRM followed. World Champions included Jack Brabham, Graham Hill and Jimmy Clark. Enzo Ferrari was contemptuous of what he called the British *garagistas*, who 'did not even build their own engines'. But they kept the great Ferrari out of Grand Prix contention until after Enzo's death.

An amazingly similar story emerged the other side of the Atlantic. Carl Fisher had laid out the Indianapolis circuit in 1909 and had come up with the inspired decision to have just one race a year – the 'Indy 500', but with the richest purse in the world. By the end of the 1950s, design had stagnated and the cars had become over-sized dirt track racers – identical, big front-engined 'roadsters', all powered by venerable 4-cylinder, 4.7 litre Offenhauser (Offy) engines, as they had been since 1949!

However, suddenly in 1961, a small mid-engined 'funny car' arrived. It was once again a Cooper, driven by Jack Brabham and with an engine of just 2.5 litres. Indy veterans laughed. A.J.Foyt decribed the Cooper as a 'bunch of tubes held together by chicken wire' and loudly boasted that he would never drive one. (Never?) But the Cooper came a respectable ninth, and next year Jimmy Clark's Lotus was second.

By 1965, the mid-engine revolution was complete, with Britain's Jim Clark winning with Foyt second (in guess what?). In 1966 Graham Hill became the first 'rookie' to win for almost forty years.

Soon something else amazing emerged at Indianapolis. By the 1970s, five out of six of the engines used were from overseas, and all three of the car types were made in southern England. It is as if all the European Grand Prix cars and all their engines were made in Indiana. Britain had created a dominant expertise in motor racing which it has never lost – and an industry worth £3 billion a year.

'A bunch of tubes held together by chicken wire'

Jack Brabham's Cooper, about to blow apart the cosy world of the 'Indy' roadsters

Index

4/8/1x

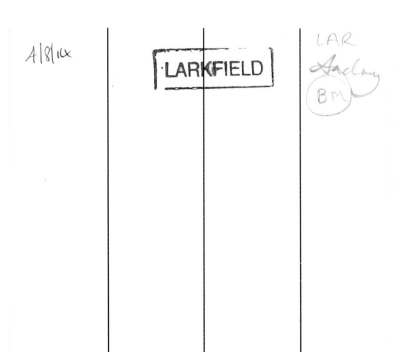

Please return on or before the latest date above.
You can renew online at *www.kent.gov.uk/libs*
or by telephone 08458 247 200

AF/LP
01/14

CUSTOMER SERVICE EXCELLENCE

Libraries & Archives

00884\DTP\RN\07.07   LIB 7

DIAMOND
IN THE DESERT